TRANSLATING HEIDEGGER

Despite Martin Heidegger's influence on twentieth-century philosophy, understanding his way of thinking is difficult if one relies solely on English translations of his work. Since Gilbert Ryle misjudged his work in a 1929 review of *Sein und Zeit*, Heidegger's philosophy has remained an enigma to many scholars who cannot read the original German texts. Miles Groth addresses this important issue in his illuminating work.

The main cause of misunderstanding Heidegger, says Groth, is that translators have not achieved clarity about Heidegger's fundamental words, an understanding of which is crucial to gaining access to his thought, including Heidegger's seminal interest in the philosophical implications of translation. A basic theme of his translation theory is that key words from the ancient Greek tradition were mistranslated, first into Latin and then into modern European languages, so that early and classic Greek thinking has been obscured for two millennia and Western philosophy has lost sight of its authentic roots.

Groth examines the history of the first English translations of Heidegger's works and reveals the elements of Heidegger's philosophy of translation, showing it at work in Heidegger's radical translation of *Parmenides, Fragment VI*. The volume concludes with a complete research bibliography of English translations of Heidegger.

This unique study makes an original contribution to Heidegger scholarship as well as the philosophy of language.

MILES GROTH is chair of the psychology department, associate professor of psychology, and director of the honors program at Wagner College, in New York City. He is also an existential psychoanalyst and the author of *Preparatory Thinking in Heidegger's Teaching* and *The Voice That Thinks: Heidegger Studies*.

New Studies in Phenomenology and Hermeneutics

Kenneth Maly, General Editor

New Studies in Phenomenology and Hermeneutics aims to open up new approaches to classical issues in phenomenology and hermeneutics. Thus its intentions are the following: to further the work of Edmund Husserl, Maurice Merleau-Ponty, and Martin Heidegger – as well as that of Paul Ricoeur, Hans-Georg Gadamer, and Emmanuel Levinas; to enhance phenomenological thinking today by means of insightful interpretations of texts in phenomenology as they inform current issues in philosophical study; to inquire into the role of interpretation in phenomenological thinking; to take seriously Husserl's term *phenomenology* as "a science which is intended to supply the basic instrument for a rigorously scientific philosophy and, in its consequent application, to make possible a methodical reform of all the sciences"; to take up Heidegger's claim that "what is own to phenomenology, as a philosophical 'direction,' does not rest in being *real*. Higher than reality stands *possibility*. Understanding phenomenology consists solely in grasping it as possibility"; to practise *phenomenology* as "underway," as "the *praxis* of the self-showing of the matter for thinking," as "entering into the movement of enactment-thinking."

The commitment of this book series is also to provide English translations of significant works from other languages. In summary, **New Studies in Phenomenology and Hermeneutics** intends to provide a forum for a full and fresh thinking and rethinking of the way of phenomenology and interpretive phenomenology, that is, hermeneutics.

For a list of books published in the series, see page 315.

TRANSLATING HEIDEGGER

MILES GROTH

UNIVERSITY OF TORONTO PRESS
Toronto Buffalo London

© University of Toronto Press 2017
Toronto Buffalo London
www.utppublishing.com

First published in 2004 in hardcover by Humanity Books,
an imprint of Prometheus Books

ISBN 978-1-4875-2252-0 (paper)

Library and Archives Canada Cataloguing in Publication

Groth, Miles, author
Translating Heidegger / Miles Groth.

(New studies in phenomenology and hermeneutics)
Previously published: Amherst, N.Y.: Humanity Books, 2004.
Includes bibliographical references and index.
ISBN 978-1-4875-2252-0 (softcover)

1. Heidegger, Martin, 1889–1976. 2. Philosophy – Translating. I. Title.
II. Series: New studies in phenomenology and hermeneutics (Toronto, Ont.)

B3279.H49G743 2017   193   C2017-903416-2

University of Toronto Press acknowledges the financial assistance to its publishing program of the Canada Council for the Arts and the Ontario Arts Council, an agency of the Government of Ontario.

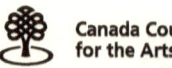 

CONTENTS

Preface   7

Acknowledgments   13

Part One: Early Translations of Fundamental Words   15

    Introduction   17

    Chapter One
        Mistranslations in the Early Critical Literature (1929-1949)   29

    Chapter Two
        The First Heidegger in English   95

Part Two: Hermeneutics and Philosophy of Translation   113

    Chapter Three
        Elements of a Theory of Translation   115

Chapter Four
Paratactic Method: 165
Translating Parmenides, Fragment VI
Conclusion 195

Epilogue 197

Bibliography *199*

Part I: Works by Heidegger Cited in the Text 199

Part II: Other Sources 203

A Research Bibliography of Heidegger in English Translation *223*

Index of Proper Names *305*

General Index *311*

PREFACE

What follows is a contribution to the history of philosophy. As part of the story of Heidegger's appearance in English, it may serve scholars of his life and thought, but as an account of Heidegger's philosophy of translation, it should not even be possible, since by his own admission, there is no such thing as Heidegger's philosophy.[1] All the same, it cannot be denied that there is a coherent, if not systematic, teaching about the nature of translation in Heidegger's published writings.

This study is part of an ongoing meditation on Heidegger's fundamental words, which are our unique source of access to his way of thinking. At this point, therefore, a few preliminaries about my renderings of the early Heidegger's fundamental words are in order. Of course, providing a full philosophical defense and rationale for these translations is precisely one of the burdens of the study itself. I base my renderings on a familiarity with the choices made by other translators beginning in the late 1940s and a dissatisfaction with many of their choices, which often do not make philosophical sense when one considers the synergy of usage among the fundamental words themselves: *Seiende, Sein, Dasein, Existenz.*

I translate *das Seiende* with 'be-ing'. The German word is a substantive of the present participle *seiend* (being) of the verb *sein* ([to] be). I hyphenate the English word to highlight the root 'be' (*sei-*) and to make plain (as Levinas said in 1949) that, for Heidegger, *sein* is a transitive verb.[2] The word 'be-ing' denotes the active ongoing manifesting of an effective actuality, in contrast to what is not to be found at all. It does not mean a static, finished entity or a totality of such entities, as some translators have had it when translating *Seiende* with 'being,' 'beings', 'entity', 'entities', or 'that-which-is'. *Das Seiende* is Heidegger's term for any and all ways of manifesting of anything whatsoever. There are many kinds of manifesting, including the kind peculiar to the "human being" [*Mensch*]: *Dasein*, which I translate with 'existence' (see below). On rare occasions, Heidegger uses the phrase *seienden Menschen* (actual human beings).

In my opinion, *Seiende* is the pivotal term in Heidegger's way of thinking beginning with *Sein und Zeit* (1927), and finding a way of translating it that is philosophically coherent with renderings of the early Heidegger's other three basic words is crucial for providing access to his thought. Even as late as *Der Begriff der Zeit* (1924), the word might still be understood to refer to entities in the traditional sense, as formed and fixed (e.g., created) entities, but by the time of the publication of *Sein und Zeit*, it is clear that the word works for Heidegger to indicate the temporal quality, that is, the ongoing, changing becoming, of whatever comes about.[3]

Only with the meaning of *Seiende* in focus can the sense of *Sein*, which I render with the rather awkward formation 'be[-ing]', become intelligible. *Sein* is a substantive of the infinitive *sein*. In its longstanding orthography, *sein* is a contraction for *seien*, the root *sei-* and the suffix *-en*, which are combined to form the German verb. The second 'e' has long since dropped out of the formation, although it is still visible and audible in most German verbs. In a sense, it is restored in *Seiende*, a fact that surely did not escape Heidegger's attention. In my rendering, the word is written and read as 'be[-ing]', but pronounced /be/, in order to emphasize the root *sei-* , which, as already emphasized, has an active sense in Heidegger's way of thinking. Be[-ing] is that which is common to the possibility of any kind of be-ing that emerges; in other words, that "of which" any sort of be-ing has its possibility. Just how be-ing and be[-ing] are related is, of course, one of Heidegger's central questions; namely, the question of the "ontological difference." Their difference and the relation between the two is the meaning of be[-ing].

In order to sound at all, be[-ing] requires the human kind of be-ing, *Dasein*, which I render with the word 'existence'.[4] As we will see, be[-ing] may be construed as speaking in the grammatical middle voice, which is lacking in modern languages. I would suggest that in his analysis of be[-ing], Heidegger tries to recover the middle voice in German, and we are implicitly prompted to do the same with English.

The habit of translating *Sein* as 'Being' (capitalized) introduces the tendency to see be[-ing] as something like a privileged or highest kind of entity. This was favored by early translators who thought Heidegger was writing about God when he used the word *Sein* in *Sein und Zeit* and later works. Translating *Sein* with 'being' (not capitalized) allows for easy confusion between Heidegger's usages of *Sein* and *Seiende*, which is so often also translated with 'being' in the same text.

Existence is the name for the unique status of the human kind of be-ing (*Seiende*) that distinguishes it from every other way or kind of be-ing; for example, that of a rock, a tree, God. When Heidegger hyphenates the word (*Da-sein*), which he encouraged English translators to do, it may be best translated with "being there" (as some translators have done) in order to stress the temporal and situational singularity (*da*) of existence in every instance. Rendering *Da-sein* with "there being," like translating it with "being there," is literal but awkward. It works philosophically much like "being there" as a translation of *Da-sein*.

Translating *Dasein* with the word 'existence' has been avoided, I think, because of the problem of what then to do with the word *Existenz*, which figures prominently in the early Heidegger. I render *Existenz* with 'life' in the sense of a way of life, an orientation in the world, and a way of comportment, such as is seen, for example, in a philosophical, scientific, aesthetic, or contemplative way of life. *Existenz* refers to what a biography recounts, not the physiological viability of the human sort of be-ing. By the time of *Sein und Zeit*, Heidegger had abandoned the word *Leben* (which is usually translated with 'life') and talk of "human life" as understood by the *Gesieswissenschaften* (human sciences) in order to distance himself from Dilthey's *Lebensphilosophie*. I am keenly aware of the tendency to see a reference to Dilthey in rendering *Existenz* with the word 'life', but this must be avoided. Finally, *Existenz* is marked, above all, by its temporal feature. Sometimes Heidegger spells the word *Ek-sistenz* and uses forms of the latinate verb *existieren*. His purpose is to highlight the ecstatic or temporal nature of any way of life.

Now I invoke the readers' patience to make their way through what follows, where in a review of early translation decisions and a discussion of Heidegger's philosophy of translation, I flesh out and defend philosophically what I have merely sketched here about my renderings of Heidegger's fundamental words.

NOTES

1. Martin Heidegger, "Einige Hinweise auf Hauptgeschichtspunkte für das theologische Gespräch über 'Das Problem eines nichtobjectivierenden Denkens und Sprechens in der heutigen Theologie.'" *Heidegger Gesamtausgabe* (Frankfurt: Klostermann, 1975-) [hereafter GA, followed by the volume number and page], 9: 69. This is the text of a letter, written on March 11, 1964, to American philosophers meeting at Drew University, in Madison, New Jersey All translations of Heidegger's texts throughout this volume are my own unless otherwise noted.

2. Quoted in Jean Wahl, *A Short History of Existentialism* (New York: Philosophical Library, 1949), p. 51.

3. Heidegger reserves the word *Seiendheit*, which I give as 'be-ingness', for this feature of manifestation as some sort of effective actuality or be-ing. The phrase *Seiende im Ganzen* is an expression that means both "be-ing as a whole" (when Heidegger is pointing to the totality of any and all ways of be-ing), and to "being at all"(when he is pointing to the possibility of there be-ing something rather than no-thing at all).

4. Be[-ing] and utterance (*Sagen*) may be compared to two tones which need each other to produce an interval, hence harmony, or musical meaning. The voice of be[-ing] is silent without utterance, which mediates between

be[-ing] and existence. On the other hand, existence would not speak, were it not for be[-ing]. Be[-ing] may also be understood as the ground bass of a melody (language).

ACKNOWLEDGMENTS

I want to thank John van Buren and Joan Stambaugh, who read earlier versions of the manuscript, for their comments, and to Thomas Sheehan for his confidence in my work. I am indebted to Graeme Nicholson and Hugh Silverman, who helped the text on its way to publication, and to Bruce Stutz, who patiently reviewed the manuscript. Finally, I am proud to acknowledge the long influence and personal support and friendship of William J. Richardson, S.J., and the late André Schuwer, O.P., whom I thank for their example and guidance.

PART ONE

EARLY TRANSLATIONS OF FUNDAMENTAL WORDS

INTRODUCTION

With few exceptions, mainstream academic philosophers have not fully appreciated the overarching importance of Martin Heidegger's thought for twentieth-century philosophy.[1] One reason for this is the near inaccessibility of his thought in even the best of the available English translations of his works. More's the pity, since Heidegger has so much to offer. For example, as early as the 1920s, Heidegger's critique of technology was prescient. His influence on clinical psychology is only now really coming into its own, as more psychotherapists acknowledge the inappropriateness of the medical model for understanding human suffering.[2] Before Heidegger, no academic philosopher of his competence had turned to analyzing literary texts. For better or for worse, he is the wellspring of deconstructionism.

Heidegger's writings about returning to the land and the poetic nature of human existence influenced one nonpolitical inner tendency of the 1960s counterculture.[3] His still not well understood discussions of the essence of language remain as provocative as anything produced by twentieth-century linguists or philosophers of language, including the later Wittgenstein. Above all, Heidegger diagnosed the spiritual vacuum at the heart of modernity and recognized the impending reunion of the Eastern and Western spiritual traditions. His influence on Japanese philosophy in the twentieth century is greater than that of any other European philosopher.[4]

Heidegger brought Husserl's phenomenology to life and breathed fresh vitality into the study of the Greek philosophers and the history of philosophy. He saw the place of the experience of art as central in existence and understood that authenticity is a fundamental human challenge. His interest in literature and the arts ranged from the poets Hölderlin, Rilke, Trakl, Stefan George, and Paul Celan, to the painter Cézanne and the sculptor Eduardo Chillida.[5] Perhaps his greatest challenge was directed to the prosaic teaching of digest philosophy carried on by world-weary academics.

What are the grounding ideas of Heidegger's thought? The plain fact is that the translations of his texts and the secondary literature on those texts have failed to make Heidegger's thought directly and fully accessible to English-reading scholars. This is a bold statement, but it is the reason for the present study. My purpose is not to abuse Heidegger's translators and commentators, but rather to explain why the reception of Heidegger continues to range from bemused bewilderment to downright hostility. I am convinced that Heidegger's thought deserves an honest hearing, and I would like to see it made available to the widest possible audience. Readers may do what they wish with what they have heard. I only urge an experience of thinking along with Heidegger, which is what he undertakes, for example, with the pre-Socratics, Plato, Aristotle, Leibniz, Kant, Hegel, Schelling, and Nietzsche.

At the present time, reaching Heidegger's thought in English translations of his works remains difficult. Since Gilbert Ryle got it wrong in 1929 in his review of *Sein und Zeit*, Heidegger's thought has remained an enigma to most scholars who cannot read the original German texts. The cause of this, in my opinion, is that in seventy years, translators have not achieved clarity about his fundamental words (*Grundworte*).[6] Illuminating Heidegger's fundamental words uncovers his philosophical roots. This would have been obvious to

Heidegger, since he recognized that in his own time (as since the time of the early Greek thinkers) obliviousness about the meaning of the fundamental words of Greek thought reigned.

A major theme of Heidegger's thought is translation. For Heidegger, translation (*Übersetzung*)[7] is perhaps the crucial matter both for the Western philosophical tradition and for our philosophical way of life (*Existenz*). In 1942, he wrote: "Tell me what you think about translating and I'll tell you who you are."[8] Heidegger believes that the fundamental words of the tradition, which originate with the early Greek thinkers, have been mistranslated, first into Latin and, subsequently, into the modern European languages, and that, as a result, the thought of the pre-Socratics and the classic Greek philosophers has remained in obscurity for two millennia.[9] In "Hegel und die Griechen," Heidegger lists what he takes to be the fundamental words of the Greek thinkers: ἀλήθεια (basic to all Greek thinkers), ἕν (Parmenides), λόγος (Heraclitus), ἰδέα (Plato), and ἐνέργεια (Aristotle). The (mis)translations of these and other key words of early Greek thinking, he says, have determined the course of Western philosophy.[10] Thus, the early Latin translations of Greek words by Cicero and Sextus Empiricus, and by those who later preserved and passed along the Greek texts to the Middle Ages, were critical events in the history of philosophy. The later translations of Aristotle's texts into medieval Latin by William of Moerbecke and others (translations on which Thomas Aquinas and many great medieval philosophers relied) profoundly affected the evolution of Christian philosophy and theology, and in turn, the beginning of the modern period with Descartes, whose Latin texts are steeped in the language of Scholasticism.

Much of Heidegger's work returns thoughtfully to the sources of Western philosophy in the pre-Socratics, in order to recover in their fundamental words an original experience of thinking. He attempts this by way of radical translations of those words into German and, in the process, effects a fresh experience of the German language as well.

In *The Anatomy of Disillusion*, William Macomber neatly summarizes what, for Heidegger, is at stake in translation:

The loss of its living roots is the fate of the Western tradition. It reflects the transition from speaking out of one's own experience to speaking from hearsay.... Language becomes instrumental. Henceforth, Heidegger thinks, philosophy is really in search of language.[11]

On the fate of Greek words translated into Latin, there is, for example, the translation of αλήθεια as *veritas*:

> The Greek word [ἀλήθεια] loses its negative character and becomes positive and underived, paralleling the new conception of knowledge. What we *call* truth Heidegger now regards as not simply a question of etymology or semantics; it reflects the basic intuition which the word expresses, either negative or positive and underived. (p. 154)

For Heidegger, thinking leaves traces (*Spuren*) of itself in written and spoken words (*Worte*). This accounts for the importance of *single words* in his understanding of the relation between translation and thinking.[12] Heidegger uses the image of the tracks left behind by a living thing to characterize the traces of thinking left in words and suggests that an author's thought can be reached only by following these tracks or traces back to their source.

In a letter written in March 1922, Rilke anticipates Heidegger's view that single words bear the weight of meaning in the interpretation of a text. Summarizing Rilke's position on the status of single words in one kind of text, a poem, George Steiner writes that "each word in a poem is semantically unique, that it establishes its own completeness of contextual range and tonality."[13] I think Heidegger would agree that this also applies to the words of a philosophical text which give utterance to thought.

The literature on Heidegger's philosophy of translation is fairly spare. However, three important essays on the topic of "Heidegger and Translation" are included in John Sallis's important anthology, *Reading Heidegger: Commemorations*.[14] Parvis Emad, in "Thinking More Deeply into the Question of Translation: Essential Translation and the Unfolding of Language," clarifies the relation between what has come down to us of be[-ing] and how language speaks (p. 334), but he does not address how the "words of thinking" (p. 336), which are fundamental to Western philosophy, are related to thinking itself. In his treatment of "essential translation," Emad cites several of Heidegger's texts from the early 1940s that I will mention below, but omits reference to those places where Heidegger talks about the relation between language, thinking, and translation. Emad's essay is among the few that discuss Heidegger's view of translation in any detail, however.[15]

In "Ontology of Language and Ontology of Translation in Heidegger," Elaine Escoubas also sees translation as a key to Heidegger's understanding of the relation between the thinking of be[-ing] and language. According to Escoubas, for Heidegger, "'translation' becomes the *name* for the history of philosophy." The issue of translation thus refers us to "the *unthought* of the history of ontology and the very mode of this history. Hence 'translation' and 'thinking' coincide." In short, the history of philosophy is the history of a series of translations.[16]

Finally, in "Mimesis and Translation," Samuel Ijsseling underscores Heidegger's view that the translation of the fundamental words of Greek thinking into Latin was a step down for thinking. By contrast, Heidegger himself maintains that any translation always amounts to a "step up (*versetzen*),"[17] because it enables the advance of thinking.

Then there is John Macquarrie's essay, "Heidegger's Language and the Problems of Translation," in which the co-translator of the first translation of *Sein und Zeit* discusses his seven-year-long work on the project.[18] While Macquarrie does not mention Heidegger's views on translation, he makes several important observations about the reputed "difficulty" of Heidegger's language. Unlike many commentators who have decried its vagueness and obscurity, Macquarrie asserts that "Heidegger's language is a complex and formidable structure, but there is nothing woolly about it" (p. 51). Safely respectable within the British analytic tradition, he does not share the derision for Heidegger's work that so many of his colleagues have felt. He explains that Heidegger's so-called archaisms "are probably not just an affectation on his part, but are a way of suggesting to us his intention, in *Sein und Zeit*, of going back to the original sources of philosophizing" (p. 53). Macquarrie even goes so far as to dare to say that "[o]n the whole, Heidegger's new words do not occasion too much difficulty for the translator" (p. 52), adding that "an English translation can show, with reasonable fidelity, most of what is happening in Heidegger's German" (p. 56). He concludes that

> much of the criticism of Heidegger's language, which has been made from time to time, has been quite unjustified. When *carefully studied*, his language is seen to be an impressive and consistent structure.... *Sein und Zeit* is not the morass of verbal mystification that it is sometimes said to be. On the contrary, it is a work of quite extraordinary power and originality expressed in *a language which is never lacking in precision, though it may be complex* [emphasis added]. Heidegger is neither a pedant nor an obscurantist, but a careful and penetrating thinker whose work deserves to be studied with the greatest respect. (p. 56)[19]

While there are, then, a few commentaries on aspects of Heidegger's view of translation, none has presented his philosophy of translation as such. My aim in what follows is to elucidate the elements of Heidegger's philosophy of translation, a topic which is closely related to his question about the nature of thinking and philosophizing, and language. It will become clear, I think, that at the heart of Heidegger's way of thinking lies the question of translation.

I will not attempt a study of all of the English translations of Heidegger's texts, some of which are very fine indeed. Instead, I will begin by looking at the earliest translations and the critical literature that preceded them. This will demonstrate how Heidegger's thought was initially distanced from the English-speaking reader and will suggest the extent to which those early influences still affect the work of translating Heidegger's thought.

How an author's texts have been rendered in another language will determine whether or not those who read him in translation will have access to his thought, although to understand the meaning of the words used to translate his thought does not guarantee that we

Introduction

23

will grasp his thought. As we will see later on, Heidegger views interlingual translation as a secondary sort of translation, the primary form of which occurs when thought is brought over into utterance. The latter form of translation, which one might call proto-translation, is effected by an author when he writes. Writing, that activity so mistrusted by Socrates, places the author one step removed from his own thought. The reader of a written text therefore begins his quest for an author's thought already at some remove from it. Interlingual translation, which we might call deutero-translation, only further distances us from an author's thought.

As a justification for this work, before trying to bring together the elements of Heidegger's philosophy of translation, I will review the many mistranslations of Heidegger's fundamental words in the critical literature that preceded the publication, in 1949, of the first translations of four of Heidegger's texts. The fate of Heidegger's fundamental words in the hands of his earliest translators parallels what Heidegger saw had happened to the fundamental Greek words of the Western philosophical tradition.

Just as ἀλήθεια, ἕν, λόγος, ἰδέα, and ἐνέργεια are the fundamental words of Greek thinking, *Sein, Seiende, Dasein, Existenz, Nichts,* and *Ereignis* are the fundamental words of Heidegger's thought.[20] It is from these words that we take our bearings and find our way to Heidegger's thought when reading him in German. We must somehow be able to do the same when reading Heidegger in English translations and this will depend on whether we have an adequate starting point in thoughtful translations of his fundamental words.

We should not forget, however, that as Heidegger's thought moves on, his fundamental words change. We notice, for example, that a word drops out of Heidegger's German vocabulary and is replaced by another word. When that happens, we must find another word in English. Thus, for example, when in the later Heidegger, *Sein* is replaced by *Grund* (and later on *Grund* is replaced with *Sprache*, and *Sprache* is replaced with *Denken*), we see that *Grund* is a translation of *Sein*, not a definition of the word *Sein*, and so on in the series. In turn, when we replace 'be[-ing] with 'foundation' (then 'foundation' with 'language', and 'language' with 'thinking') in the later Heidegger, we are translating 'be[-ing]', not *Sein*. Translation, then, is philosophical activity, not merely a process of lexical exchange.

I do not propose *definitive* renderings of Heidegger's words, in particular his fundamental words, but only renderings that best provide access to his thought at steps along its way. To do so would be to provide definitions of German words, not indications of a way of thinking. At any given moment, one's thought is a plenum that can never be fully fathomed. Heidegger's thought is such a whole, and the question about whether it has been grasped cannot be answered by anyone, including Heidegger himself, who believed that a thinker never achieves full apprehension of his own thought. Others may help a thinker uncover the depths of his thought by bringing to expression what he left unsaid. They may contribute to the revelation of his thought, but their effort always remains an approximation and full revelation can be approached only asymptotically.

Nor are there *correct* renderings of Heidegger's fundamental words, but only more evocative renderings, those which illuminate Heidegger's thought by giving expression to some of its elements. Nonetheless, I think it is possible to settle on best renderings of Heidegger's fundamental words *at a certain time in the development of his thought*. A case in point is the trio *Sein*, *Seiende*, and *Dasein*, which are central to the early Heidegger of *Sein und Zeit*. I will take a close look at these words, as well as *Existenz*, in an attempt to see how early critics and supporters alike obscured several important ideas in the early Heidegger, including the ontological difference, the meaning of *Sein* (be[-ing]), the status of *Seiende* (be-ing), and the relation between existence (*Dasein*) and a given way of life (*Existenz*), both of which are contrasted with the fact of living (*Leben*). I maintain that faulty translations of the five fundamental words just named continue to obscure our understanding of basic elements of Heidegger's early thought, as they have from the start, when Heidegger's thought was first discussed by Gilbert Ryle in his review of *Sein und Zeit* in 1929.

I suggest that the stage was set early on for important misunderstandings of Heidegger's thought, even before the first English translations of four of his texts were published in 1949. In other words, these misunderstandings were already at work in the first published translations and continue to have an effect. Happily, we have now reached a time when *original* English versions of Heidegger's texts are possible. They will be based on adequate translations of Heidegger's thought. But in order to be freed of the influences of the early mistranslations, we must understand how they originated and continue to affect the work of translating Heidegger's thought.[21]

NOTES

1. Richard Rorty, *Essays on Heidegger and Others* (Cambridge: Cambridge University Press, 1991).

2. Recent publications of the founders of the British school of existential analysis, Emmy van Deurzen-Smith, Ernesto Spinelli, Simon du Plock, and others, appear in issues of the *Journal of the Society for Existential Analysis*. The record of Heidegger's work on *Daseinsanalytik* with Medard Boss from 1959 to 1971 has been published in Martin Heideger, *Zollikoner Seminare. Protokolle—Gespräche—Briefe*, ed. Medard Boss (Frankfurt: Klostermann, 1987).

3. Martin Heidegger, "Schöpferische Landschaft: Warum bleiben wir in der Provinz?," GA 13: 9-13. The title of Heidegger's meditation is simply, "Why Do I Live in the Country?"

4. The influence of East Asian thought on Heidegger from early on has recently become clearer. See *Heidegger and Asian Thought*, ed. Graham Parkes (Honolulu: University of Hawaii Press, 1987); Parkes's article, "Heidegger and Japanese Thought: How Much Did He Know and When Did He Know It?," in *Heidegger: Critical Assessments*, ed. Christopher Macann, 4 vols. (London: Routledge, 1992), 4: 377-406; and Reinhard May, *Heidegger's Hidden Sources: East Asian Influences on His Work* (London: Routledge, 1996). In the late 1940s, Heidegger even worked on a translation of the *Tao te Ching* with Paul Shih-yi Hsiao. See Parkes, *Heidegger and Asian Thought*, pp. 93-103.

5. Gilbert Ryle, review of *Sein und Zeit*, by Martin Heidegger, *Mind* 29 (1929): 355-70.

6. The word *Grundwort* also means "etymological root."

7. The German verb *übersetzen* evidently comes from the longstanding

medieval practice of placing (*setzen*) the words of the translating language in smaller hand (or, later, type) above (*über*) the original text. This was still a common practice in the early part of the century in school editions of the Greek and Latin classics where an English translation was printed in smaller type above the original text.

8. "Sage mir, was du vom Übersetzen hältst, und ich sage dir, wer du bist." Martin Heidegger, *Hölderlins Hymne "Der Ister,"* GA 53:67. See in this connection Robert Bernasconi, "'I Will Tell You Who You Are': Heidegger on Greco-German Destiny and *Amerikanismus*," in *From Phenomenology to Thought, Errancy, and Desire: Essays in Honor of William J. Richardson, S.J.*, ed. Babette Babich (Dordrecht: Kluwer, 1995), pp. 301-13, for a discussion of Heidegger's statement and his attitude toward the "Americanization" of scholarly work, including translation (pp. 304-305, 312, n. 2).

9. George Seidel, in *Martin Heidegger and the Pre-Socratics: An Introduction to His Thought* (Lincoln: University of Nebraska Press, 1964), recognized early on the importance for Heidegger of the translation of Greek words into Latin and formulated the core of Heidegger's philosophy of translation, that *authentic translation translates thinking, not words* (pp. 33, 83, 126-28, 152). Stephen Erickson also notes the importance for Heidegger of the Latin translation of Greek words, which is a typical point of entry for Heidegger into the discussion about translation. Stephen Erickson, *Language and Being: An Analytic Phenomenology* (New Haven, Conn.: Yale University Press, 1970), pp. 7-8.

10. GA 9: 435-44. Heidegger's lecture course, *Die Grundbegriffe der antiken Philosophie* (1926), GA 22 is a general introduction to the Greek thinkers. Many courses are extended efforts at translating the fundamental words of Greek philosophical activity. See, for example, a manuscript written in the fall of 1922 that outlines Heidegger's then current and future research. "Phänomenologische Interpretationen zu Aristoteles (Anzeige der hermeneutischen Situation)," *Dilthey-Jahrbuch für Philosophie und Geschichte der Gesisteswissenschaften* 6 (1989): 235-69. The text is a veritable glossary of Aristotelian words and Heidegger's translations of them. On Heidegger's estimation of the uniqueness of the Greek language, see *Was ist das—die Philosophie?* (Pfullingen: Neske, 1956), where Heidegger translates the word Φιλοσοφία as the "strebende Suchen for the σοΦόν, nach dem ῍Εν Πάντα, nach dem Seienden im Sein" (pp. 50-52). The essays "Aletheia (Heraklit, Fragment 16),""Logos (Heraklit, Fragment 50)," and "Moira (Parmenides, Fragment VIII, 34-31)," which are devoted to the translation of single words, were published as Volume III of the first publication of his *Vorträge und*

Aufsätze (Pfullingen: Neske, 1954). An entire course given in 1931 is devoted to several paragraphs from Aristotle's *Metaphysics* (GA 33). His paper, "Vom Wesen und Begriff der Φύσις. Aristoteles *Physik* B,1," which was based on a seminar on the same topic, is a translation of a short passage from the *Physics* (9: 239-301). The lecture course, "Einführung in die Metaphysik," from the summer semester of 1935, contains important studies of fundamental words of Greek philosophy (GA 40, pp. 56-79). Finally, the second part of the lecture course from 1951-52, *Was heißt Denken?* (Tübingen: Niemeyer, 1954), is a meticulous translation of Fragment VI of Parmenides, which I will examine in depth later on in chapter 4. On the question of Latin rendering of Greek words, see Franco Chiereghin, "Der griechische Anfang Europas und die Frage der Romanitas. Der Weg Heideggers zu einem anderen Anfang," in *Europa und die Philosophie* (Frankfurt: Klostermann, 1993), ed. Hans-Helmuth Gander (Frankfurt: Klostermann, 1993), pp. 197-223, and Andrew Benjamin, *Translation and the Nature of Philosophy: A New Theory of Words* (London: Routledge, 1989), p. 15.

11. William Macomber, *The Anatomy of Disillusion: Martin Heidegger's Notion of Truth* (Evanston, Ill.: Northwestern University Press, 1967), pp. 153-54.

12. "Der Spruch des Anaximander," GA 5: 369.

13. George Steiner, *After Babel: Aspects of Language and Translation* (Oxford: Oxford University Press, 1992), p. 253.

14. *Reading Heidegger: Commemorations*, ed. John Sallis (Bloomington: Indiana University Press, 1992).

15. Emad, who is an important translator of Heidegger in English, contrasts Heidegger's hermeneutics with that of Gadamer and Derrida. Emad, "Thinking More Deeply into the Question of Translation: Essential Translation and the Unfolding of Language," in *Reading Heidegger*, ed. Sallis, p. 339, n. 7. His essay was reprinted in Macann, *Heidegger: Critical Assessments*, 3: 58-78.

16. Elaine Escoubas, "Ontology of Language and Ontology of Translation in Heidegger," in *Reading Heidegger: Commemorations*, ed. Sallis, p. 341. Escoubas also discusses the double meaning of translating, as both a *carrying over* from one language to another and as *transition* to a different way of thinking. She contrasts Heidegger's view with the three traditional notions of translation he identifies—*Übertragung* (transcription), *Umschreibung* (paraphrase), and *Umdeutung* (reinterpretation)—and concludes that translation is "a mode according to which *truth* is thought and unfolded in the course of the history of being" (p. 342). She attributes the following con-

clusions about language to Heidegger: "(1) A language is not a language unless it is *exposed* to another language (exposed to translation); and (2) a language comprises something untranslatable, some idiom, for a language that is entirely translatable would not be a language but a code of behavior" (p. 343). Finally, Escoubas summarizes Heidegger's view of original translation as he practices it in the Parmenides course: (1) "A language is always in the course of translation; it is itself and in itself a process of translation. 'To translate' is . . . *to produce a language*"—(2) "A language is a monologue with itself. . . ."—(3) "An *idiom* is not a language. An idiom exceeds language . . . [it] can pervade and run through several languages" (pp. 344-45), for example, Greek and German. "Translation, in all its Heideggerian forms, goes back to another τόπος; the τόπος of the unthought (*Ungedachte*). The *unthought* is . . . what calls for and forth thought" (p. 347). See chapter 4, below, for an illustration of Heidegger translating.

17. "Vom Wesen und Begriff der Φύσις. Aristoteles, Physik B,1," GA 9: 245. See Frank Schalow, "Language and the Etymological Turn of Thought," *Graduate Faculty Philosophy Journal* 18, no. 1 (1995): 187-203, for another recent discussion of the relation between language and thinking in Heidegger.

18. Macann, *Heidegger: Critical Assessments*, 3: 50-57. See p. 50.

19. See also Macquarrie's excellent recent overview of Heidegger's thought in *Heidegger and Christianity* (New York: Continuum, 1994), which includes Heidegger's previously untranslated letter to David Edwards, the director of Student Christian Movement (SCM) Press, which first published the Macquarrie/Robinson translation of *Sein und Zeit* (pp. 111-12).

20. In a sense, *Existenz* is the pivotal word in understanding where many translations of Heidegger's thought have gone astray, but, as we will see, an understanding of the word in Heidegger's usage depends upon fathoming the meaning of the word *Seiende*, which in turn depends on the meaning of *Sein*.

21. The word *Dasein* is emblematic of the problem of Heidegger in translation. In a display of word mysticism (which Heidegger deplored), the word still remains untranslated after fifty years. Doing so gives the impression that access to Heidegger's thought is reserved only for those who can read German. The practice is nothing more than cabalistic snobbery. More important, not translating *Dasein* is evidence for the deep trouble commentators have had in knowing what to do with the closely related words *Existenz* and *Leben*.

CHAPTER ONE

MISTRANSLATIONS IN THE EARLY CRITICAL LITERATURE
(1929–1949)

I turn now to a review of the earliest translations of Heidegger's fundamental words. Fairly little literature on Heidegger in English existed prior to the appearance, in 1949, of *Existence and Being*, the first Heidegger to appear in English. The book consists of four essays preceded by an extensive introduction by the editor, Werner Brock, one of Heidegger's former pupils.[1] I will consider only the sources that focus on the fundamental words in Heidegger's early thought.

In this section, I have opted for a chronological review of the secondary literature, rather than a general summary of how Heidegger's fundamental words were rendered early on, since a chronological review reveals not only the fate of those words but also the changing appreciation of Heidegger's thought during the period under consideration.

GILBERT RYLE REVIEWS *SEIN UND ZEIT*

It is not an overstatement, I think, to say that Gilbert Ryle's review, in 1929, of *Sein und Zeit* set the tone for how Heidegger has been received by English-speaking readers.² The prestige of the journal *Mind*, in which his review article appeared, guaranteed that Ryle's opinion would be taken quite seriously. The review has been cited as Ryle's first important contribution to philosophy.³ Because of his later renown among English-speaking philosophers, Ryle's review influenced translators and those who authorized, edited, and published Heidegger's work in English translation.

A number of articles of varying degrees of scholarliness, representing diverse points of view and written for very different readerships, were published beginning the year after Ryle's review. Several books appeared that included sections on Heidegger. Most of what scholars knew about Heidegger when *EB* was published was gleaned from these sources. By 1949, the academic world had spawned only two doctoral dissertations on Heidegger. One compared Heidegger with Alfred North Whitehead on the theme of time, while the other was a comparative study of Heidegger and Jaspers on conscience.⁴

Having used the words 'existence' and 'existential' in their conventional, metaphysical sense (i.e., in contrast with essence and essential) in the preface to his discussion of *Sein und Zeit*, Ryle makes the fateful translation of *Sein* as 'Being' (p. 363). There was no reason to capitalize the word other than Ryle's tendency to capitalize what he considered to be important words in the text, such as 'Life', 'Thought', 'Intentionality', 'Concern', 'Conception', 'Opinion', 'Belief', 'Metaphysic', 'Care', 'Meaning', 'Categories', 'Mind-Matter', 'Experience', 'Phenomenology', 'Ontology', 'Subject-Object', 'Consciousness', 'Hermeneutic', and 'Reality'. He does not italicize the German words he cites. Thus begins the tradition of capitalizing 'Being' as a translation for *Sein*.

Ryle tells us that, for Heidegger, Being is "timeless 'substance'" (p. 368) and existing means "existing in the world of time and space" (p. 363). Ryle thus entirely misunderstands Heidegger's analysis of *in* in §§ 28–38 of *Sein und Zeit*. He introduces *Dasein*, which he refers to parenthetically as the "title Heidegger appropriates for an 'I' who thinks and in particular is asking questions, using the methods, and appreciating the answers that I am now doing" (pp. 364–65). Later on, *Dasein* is characterized as "our conscious being" (p. 369) and Heidegger's analysis of *Dasein* is referred to as a "phenomenological analysis of the root workings of the human soul" (p. 370). Ryle does not translate the term. Why not? Why does he not explain that, and how Kant, Fichte, and Hegel, for example, used the term and then say how Heidegger's usage differs? Why does he not translate *Dasein* as 'existence', as Hegel's British translators had done in the *Science of Logic*? With few exceptions, the term in Heidegger's texts has remained untranslated ever since. As we will see, this has had much to do with what to do with the word *Existenz*.

In the context of discussing the meaning of *Dasein*, Ryle speaks about "my being" and "a being-myself" (p. 365), but soon after writes that "'Dasein's' being is 'being-in-the-world'," without giving the German words (*Seiende* and *In-der-Welt-sein*) that the words 'being' and 'being-in-the-world' translate. The use of the word 'being' (uncapitalized) in reference to *Dasein* is not glossed, so the reader is likely to think of 'being' and 'Being' as synonyms. The verb *besorgen* is translated with 'being-about', which is said to be "the primitive mode of 'Dasein's' being" (p. 365). Ryle writes about "the essence of [*Dasein*'s] being" (p. 365) and its "attitudes or ways of 'being-an-I'" (p. 366), without making it clear whether he is quoting and translating or paraphrasing and merely characterizing Heidegger's words. At the climax of his discussion, he writes variously about "a 'Dasein'" and "the Dasein," and asks the question: "What is it to *be* an I ('Dasein')?" (p. 366). He replies: "The answer rings at first strangely. 'Dasein ist Sorge.' What I am is Concern or Care (Cura)," which is said to be "the absolutely primitive Being that an 'I' as such has" (p. 366). But what is the difference between 'Being' and 'being', which had been introduced earlier? The fundamental distinction Heidegger makes in *Sein und Zeit*, the "ontological difference," is entirely overlooked.

Ryle thinks that many dangers lurk in the murk of Heidegger's "Hermeneutic of Being *via* the Hermeneutic of 'Being an I' ('Dasein')" (p. 368), not the least of which is the danger that Heidegger has smuggled in an "anthropologistic Metaphysic (smelling a little oddly both of [William] James and of St. Augustine)" (p. 370). Having confounded an understanding of *Sein* with knowledge of *Sein*, Ryle lumps Husserl and Heidegger together and criticizes the "Husserl-Heidegger treatment of Meaning" (p. 370). In that way, his review of *Sein und Zeit* eases back into a commentary on Ryle's problems with phenomenology, with which the review had begun.

Ryle admits to having "fallen short of understanding" *Sein und Zeit*. This is undoubtedly true. The point, however, is that Ryle's mistaken assessment of what Heidegger is doing in *Sein und Zeit* is based on his misunderstanding of Heidegger's fundamental words. He does not see that *Dasein* is Heidegger's word for existence, that singular way of be-ing (*Seiende*) that human beings embody. He does not see that be[-ing][5] is what makes any kind of be-ing, including existence, possible. Finally, Ryle does not see that, in each case, a concrete way of life (*Existenz*) is the outstanding feature of existence. As a result, he does not know what to do with the word *Dasein* and simply leaves it untranslated. His mistranslation of *Sein* and *Seiende* are, by his own admission, based on having "fallen short of understanding" the philosophical importance of the ontological difference in Heidegger's thought.

Forty years later, Ryle published a postscript to his review, which was being reprinted ("Martin Heidegger: *Sein und Zeit*, Afterword").[6] The review is a document of some importance to my thesis.[7] Once again, the context of Ryle's comments is phenomenology, and he now admits that, in 1929, his interest in Heidegger's book "was adjectival upon my anterior interest in the very un-Cartesian Logical Objectivisms of Bolzano, Meinong and the earlier Husserl" (p. 13). He explains how he came to review Heidegger's book. Ryle admits that he

> felt uncordial towards the 'transcendental Egology' [of Husserl] into which Phenomenology promised to sweep everything. Nor were intuitions of essence the sorts of accomplishments of which any Anglo-Saxon could boast with a straight face. However, as I had already done some fairly industrious work on and around Husserl's new '-logy', I volunteered to review his pupil's *Sein und Zeit*, in the mistaken expectation that it would help me, as it certainly did force me, to consolidate, for my own benefit and problematically for the benefit of others, what I knew and thought about the origins of Husserlian Phenomenology. (pp. 13-14)

Ryle concludes that, in 1929, he had seen Heidegger chiefly as an apostate from phenomenology. In 1969, however, he has still not decided how to place Heidegger. He continues:

> Not having read *Sein und Zeit* for forty years, I am not in the state, and am anyhow not the proper person, to review my review of it. *A priori* I should expect a lot of its emphases to be askew; its silences about Kierkegaard and, I fancy, also about Hegel to be damaging lacunae; and *a lot of its readings of Heidegger's German to be distortions* [emphasis added]. Its larger injustices and justices, if any, would be for someone else to assess, if it were worth the trouble. (p. 14)

It is certainly worth our trouble. There is not much more to the postscript than I have given. I have quoted it at length to provide a context for the phrase I have highlighted. If the review's "readings of Heidegger's German" were, as Ryle admits, "distortions," they were momentous distortions. As we will see, these "distortions" were repeated by English interpreters and translators of Heidegger for many years.

NEOSCHOLASTIC APPROPRIATION

The article "Modern German Existentialism" by Alfred Delp, S.J., who taught at St. Ignatius College, The Netherlands, was the first notice of Heidegger by the neoscholastics.[8] Delp first translates the *Sein* in *Sein und Zeit* as "reality," but, referring to the text itself, says that *Sein* means "Being," which in turn means "being in the world." A few sentences later, we read the following:

> This implies that being or reality is only discovered in the concrete individual and that this concrete being is always close to the world. ... Existence is close to the world by reason of its reality-nature, which is to be in the world. This being in the world is a quality of existence. Heidegger calls such existential qualities *Existentialien* (existentials). (p. 64)

In these passages, the words 'existence', 'being,' and 'reality' are used without clarification of Heidegger's usage. The distinction between *Sein* and *Seiende*, both of which are translated with 'being', is lost, and it is not clear whether Delp translates *Dasein* or *Existenz* with 'existence'. The reader might easily and wrongly assume that *Sein und Zeit* is a philosophical anthropology that focuses on the theme of Man and time. Delp also makes Heidegger over into a theologian *manqué* who thinks of man as the modern world's god, what Rosa Obermeyer Mayreder, in 1933, had called *Der letzte Gott*.[9]

The penchant for imitating Heidegger's hyphenated formulations is already in play in Delp's article and continues through much of the secondary literature.

NOTES OF A STUDENT

Marjorie Glicksman's "Note on the Philosophy of Heidegger" is based on her reading of Heidegger's published works and class notes from two courses and a seminar she attended in 1931–32 while a student at the University of Freiburg.[10] As a young student, Professor Glicksman was evidently confounded by Heidegger's lectures, which she caricatures. The tone of her article is sardonic and acidic throughout. Citing Carnap's critique of "Was ist Metaphysik?," which appeared in 1932 in the periodical *Erkenntnis*, she mockingly quotes the propositions "nothing nothings"[11] and "world worlds"[12] (p. 100), without giving the original German. Her trek through "the impossible jungle of Heideggerian vocabulary" (p. 95) leads her to conclude that "Heidegger's philosophy is unique only in its rampant misuse of language..." (p. 94). What was, for Heidegger, an attempt to make German evoke thinking in powerful ways was perceived by Glicksman as a lapse of good usage. In her discussion of the course "Vom Wesen der Wahrheit," the terms 'existence' and 'being' are introduced (p. 95) without reference to the German words they render. Quoting from notes taken during the other course she attended, "Der Anfang der abendländischen Philosophie," she translates *Seiende* variously as "that which is," "existents," "something," and "being" (in the phrase "being as a whole [*das Seiende im ganzen*]"). Here the careless and "rampant misuse of language" is Glicksman's own.

Glicksman writes that Heidegger sees "being" as what is "here-at-hand, ready for use" (p. 98). She is not clear that what is *vorhanden* is only one way of be-ing (*Seiende*). Nor does she apprehend Heidegger's distinction between any sort of be-ing and the be[-ing] that makes them possible. Citing *Sein und Zeit*,[13] Glicksman correctly translates *Dasein* as 'Existence', but equates "insistence," which (again quoting from "Der Anfang der abendländischen Philosophie") is "a special mode of existence," with *Verfallen*. She says that Heidegger's "definition" of "*Dasein* (personal existence)" is "*Sorge* (care)," where care is: "*Das Sich-Vorweg-Schon-Sein-In (der Welt) als Sein-bei (innerweltlich begegnendem Seienden)*."[14] The verdict follows after little deliberation:

> Paraphrased, this gnarled definiens states the platitude that human nature participates through anticipation in the future and through memory in the past; and at the same time is bound by indissoluble ties to the insistent cares of the present. (p. 102)

So much for the analyses of existence and temporality in *Sein und Zeit*! Glicksman's interpretation is both glib and incorrect. In the years to come, Glicksman's outlook was tempered somewhat, but by then the impact of her earlier pronouncements had taken its toll among quite a few readers of the secondary literature on Existentialism.

Marjorie (Glicksman) Grene's *Dreadful Freedom*, which appeared in 1948, purported to be a general introduction to Existentialism.[15] In it, Grene repents in part for her earlier, hard-hitting critique of Heidegger. In the "Preface to the 1959 Edition" of the book, which was published as *Introduction to Existentialism*, she makes the following confession: "I had not, when I first wrote this book, faced up to Heidegger's ontology. I could follow his argument on Being, I said then, only in the sense in which one might follow Alice down the rabbit hole. That was lazy" (p. v). Her lapse, however, was responsible, in part, for the partial misrepresentation of Heidegger's thought to a public that was just becoming aware of him. But even in 1959, as in 1938 and 1947, when she published her first articles on

Heidegger, his thought remains for Grene "an abominable wonderland, and an ugly and almost empty wasteland it is" (p. vi).

The tone of Grene's opinion of Heidegger continues to be deprecating. She says that Heidegger's statement "Das Nichts nichtet"[16] (which she presents out of context and without reference, and translates with "Nothing nothings") is "obviously nonsense" (p. 52). When the neologism *nichtet* is rendered with "nihilates," it makes perfectly good sense. *Dasein* is translated with "human existence" (p. 54), a tautologous formulation. Quoting a passage from *Sein und Zeit*, Grene writes: "If one can render Heidegger's *weird language*: 'The call of conscience has the character of calling existence to its properest capacity of being itself, and that in the manner of calling it up to its properest guiltiness' [emphasis added]" (p. 65, n. 9).[17] In fact, Heidegger does not say that conscience calls out to one like the "voice of conscience" or the superego, but rather that existence calls on itself to exist. He terms this characteristic of existence *Gewissen* (conscience). Heidegger adds that the challenge of existence to itself takes place as an appeal to its indebtedness (*Schuld*) to that very existence, which is always its very own, singular and unique.

Heidegger's language is not "weird," as Grene says, although his thought is challenging. In the dialectic between thought and words, thought is given expression. Once the transition to his way of thinking is accomplished, one's own language finds words to express the thought that has been revealed. This process is at the heart of Heidegger's philosophy and practice of translation.[18] Chapter 4 of Grene's *Dreadful Freedom* is peppered with observations on Heidegger's "politics." Against this background, Grene reviews the fundamental words of *Sein und Zeit*. *Dasein* is correctly translated with 'existence', *Mitdasein* is given as 'existing-with', but *Seiende* translates as 'existent' (e.g., p. 72).

HEIDEGGER AND THE THEOLOGIANS

"The Contributions of *Existenz-philosophie*," by Julius S. Bixler, a professor of theology at Harvard Divinity School, was a full-scale attempt to recruit Heidegger as a theologian.[19] Following the trend emerging from Europe at that time, Existentialism, Bixler suggests that Heidegger's key word is *Existenz*. *Existenz*, says Bixler, is "a name for certain similarities in the thought of otherwise diverse philosophers" (p. 36).

> In Heidegger's hands *Phänomenologie* [Husserl] by becoming *Existenz* has turned from the logical to the more imaginative and emotional side of experience. *Existenz* is thus a poetic and philosophical attempt to describe the subjective experiences of religion. . . . (p. 35)

Bixler uses the word *Existenz* both as a shortened version of the name *Existenzphilosophie* and as a basic word in Heidegger's vocabulary. He is on the mark when he says that the notion of "*Existenz* is an attempt to put into words the essentially indescribable experience which we call personal life, with special reference to its sensitive, suffering, and decision-making moments" (p. 37). Although his characterization of *Dasein* is mistaken, what Bixler says about the meaning of the word *Existenz* in Kierkegaard applies to Heidegger's usage as well:

> What does the word *Existenz* mean for Kierkegaard? We must observe that it is a word arbitrarily chosen which has to be explained since it does not have the meaning that attaches to our English word 'existence'. . . . It is not *Dasein*. . . . It is not *Sein*—this is too broad a term, covering existence [sic] of all sorts. It is not *Leben*, for this is shared by men with animals and plants. *Existenz* is peculiarly human. . . . (pp. 38-39)

I have quoted Bixler's review at length to set the stage for his interpretation of Heidegger's usage of the word *Existenz*. "Human beings have *Existenz* and this, he agrees with Kierkegaard, means historical existence in time, with the unfolding of possibilities which time implies, but they also have *Dasein*, and in this fact of 'placedness' here and now Heidegger finds a significance which Kierkegaard did not" (p. 50). Unfortunately, Bixler fails to see the unique sense of existence

(*Dasein*) in Heidegger's thought, which, following the Western metaphysical tradition, Bixler attributes to things in general. He rightly echoes Heidegger, however, in saying that only human beings *existiert*.

Bixler introduces a great deal of confusion, however, in this synopsis of Heidegger's thought: "[Heidegger] points out five different kinds of existence: man has *Dasein*, or *Existenz* as a special type of *Dasein*, animals have *Leben*, material things have *Vorhandensein*, useful things *Zuhandensein*, and for abstractions such as number and space we must use the word *Bestehen*" (p. 52). The word that appears to confound him in all this is *Existenz*.

Near the end of the discussion, Bixler reveals what he takes to be the source of Heidegger's "wayward style." He notices something important, but his conclusions are wrong: "In his admiration for the Greeks *Heidegger tries to use German as the Greeks used their language*, employing many words to bring out differing shades of meaning. He carries the method so far, however, that the distinctions become too complicated for either the common man or the trained student to follow [emphasis added]" (p. 56). It is true that Heidegger meditates on fundamental German words in order to invoke the thought to which they point, a practice he had acquired in his meditations on the fundamental words of Greek thought. Bixler is wrong, however, to see this as mere word play.

Finally, he gives the question of the sense of *Sein* short shrift, saying only that Heidegger "treats being as a set of practical relationships."

EARLY SUPPORT

"An Approach to Heidegger's Ontology," by Walter H. Cerf, was published in the first volume of *Philosophy and Phenomenological Research*. It was the first essay in English that supported Heidegger.[20] The words 'Being' and 'beingness' are given as equivalent, however, both translating *Sein*, which Cerf glosses with εἶναι. The word 'being' translates *Seiendes*, which he glosses with ὄν (p. 182, n. 2). In fact,

Heidegger reserves the term *Seiendheit* for 'beingness', which refers to the general characteristic of any and all sorts of be-ing, not to the source of their possibility, be[-ing]. According to Cerf, Heidegger wants to establish "a genuine concept of man" through an "existential analysis" of the "beingness of man" (pp. 183-84), which, he says, is "called 'existence' (Dasein)" (p. 184). To his credit, Cerf easily translates *Dasein* with 'existence', which, he explains, is a formal structure that can be characterized as "to be in order to be" (p. 184). Cerf's account of Heidegger's *analytique*[21] of existence as "to be in order to be" is also on target, but Cerf does not see that Heidegger questions the meaning of this "to be." He is therefore puzzled by the "status" of what Heidegger calls the "understanding of [the] beingness" (p. 190) of existence. Heidegger is not concerned with the "understanding of 'Seiendheit'," however, but with the "understanding of 'Sein'." As already noted, Cerf has fallen afoul of a mistaken identification of *Sein*, that which makes possible any kind of be-ing (*Seiende*), and *Seiendheit*, the general characteristic of any kind of actual be-ing. As a result, he fails to see the place of the ontological difference in Heidegger's thought.

A DIALOGUE ON THE "PHILOSOPHY OF EXISTENCE"

A series of three related pieces appeared in the 1940/41 volume of the journal *Philosophy and Phenomenological Research*: Julius Kraft's "The Philosophy of Existence," followed by a "Discussion Concerning Kraft's 'Philosophy of Existence'," by Fritz Kaufmann, and a note "In Reply to Kaufmann's Critical Remarks about My 'Philosophy of Existence'."[22] Kraft's analysis of *Dasein* in "The Philosophy of Existence" is based on *Sein und Zeit*, although in a footnote he also refers to Heidegger's 1929 inaugural address, "Was ist Metaphysik?," but without telling the reader that he is no longer treating *Sein und Zeit* (p. 355, n. 4). As Kraft hacks his way through the pages of *Sein und Zeit*, *Seiende* is rendered 'things'. The phrase "being of things" (p. 348) is probably a translation of *Sein des Seiendes*. The word *Dasein* is rendered 'being-there' (p. 350) and *da* alone is given as 'there' (p. 354). "Existence" (which presumably translates *Existenz*) is "the alleged 'substance' of man" (p. 349). According to Kraft, "the 'being-there' possesses 'being-in' as it lodges with the world. That relation of 'lodging' is the 'formal existential expression of the being-there (*des Seins des Daseins*), having the essence-like (*seinshafte*) constitution of being-in-the-world'" (p. 350).

Fritz Kaufmann's discussion of Kraft's paper correctly assesses its tone and perspective. His comments on Kraft's appraisal of Heidegger's language are important. "*Mr. Kraft's depreciation of* [Heidegger's] *language deafens his ear to the wisdom inherent in it* and as it is conjured up by Heidegger in so fascinating a way. It is true that Heidegger's own language is often biased though it is never so clumsy as *Mr. Kraft's uncongenial and careless translations* indicate [emphases added]" (p. 360). To Kaufmann's credit, he points out Kraft's mistranslations, but does not provide adequate alternate renderings of Heidegger's fundamental words. In his discussion, *Dasein* crosses over into English as "human being" and both *Sein* and *Seiende* become 'being' (p. 363). In the end, his attempted rescue of Heidegger the man does not help further our understanding of Heidegger's thought.

Kraft's rejoinder to Kaufmann is unrepenting. His remarks make it clear that even in the early 1940s there were strong feelings for and against Heidegger, the man and his work, that sometimes led to crude misinterpretations of his texts.

AN AMERICAN ACADEMIC IN BERLIN

While an American "exchange professor" in Berlin, William Werkmeister, as he notes in "An Introduction to Heidegger's 'Existential Philosophy'," "had the honor and the great pleasure of being Professor Heidegger's guest at his home in Freiburg. We spent countless hours discussing his philosophy—his central problem, his approach, *and his terminology* [emphasis added]."[23] Given such an auspicious background, Werkmeister would seem to have been in the best position of anyone of his time to translate Heidegger's fundamental words into

English. The problem is that Heidegger did not know English very well. He also took a dim view of Americans. Most important, what Werkmeister may have suggested to Heidegger about translating certain fundamental words into English may not have been clear to Heidegger.[24] Werkmeister's discussion centers on *Sein und Zeit*.[25] We become doubtful about Werkmeister's reliability as a spokesman for Heidegger, when he translates Heidegger's basic work *Sein und Zeit* as "beingness and time." He notes that, with Heidegger, a "step beyond Husserl is taken, however, when Heidegger considers not only the individual *modes* of being but *being as such* or 'being-ness'—not *Seinsweisen* but *das Sein als solches*" (p. 82). What happens to Heidegger's word *Seiendheit*, however, when *das Sein als solches* is rendered 'being-ness' and "being as such?" Werkmeister does not see that beingness is the general feature of any kind of be-ing, but is not equivalent to the be[-ing] of be-ing of whatever sort. He claims that "Heidegger's use of such words as *Was-sein, So-sein, Dass-sein, Da-sein, Wahr-sein, Gestimmt-sein, Seiendes,* and *Sein make it almost impossible to discuss his philosophy in English* [emphasis added]" (p. 84). Given the author's presumed personal intimacy with Heidegger, this pronouncement must have been discouraging to the readers of *Philosophy and Phenomenological Research*. Werkmeister adds that Heidegger's "handling of basic words is unique and often contrary to established usage even in German. Moreover, there is more than a suspicion that some of Heidegger's questions, or at least the manner in which he puts them, arise out of peculiarities of the German language rather than out of factual situations; and that his arguments often are linguistic rather than material" (p. 84). But if this were so and Heidegger's distinctions merely linguistic peculiarities of the German language, his entire *analytique* of existence in *Sein und Zeit* would be undermined.[26] Werkmeister repeats his concern that Heidegger's "problem" must appear "in an entirely new light" in English translation, "because it is rooted in, or grows out of, [the German?] language rather than the actual content of experience" (p. 85). From this we would have to conclude that Heidegger's philosophy is accessible only in German and that it could have been written only in German. But then, why even try to translate Heidegger into English?

For Werkmeister, *Seiende* becomes 'beings' or 'things' or "that which is already in itself," which corresponds, rather, to what is *vorhanden*. As we have already seen, *Sein* becomes 'beingness'. *Dass-sein* is rendered "question of existence," and *Da-sein* is variously "being there," "being-there," and "being-thereness." Werkmeister's presumed authoritativeness based on his personal contact with Heidegger may have lent greater credence to his discussion than it deserved. His frequent appearance later on as a reviewer of early translations of Heidegger's texts attests to his reputation, but Werkmeister's translations of Heidegger's fundamental words fail to provide access to Heidegger's thought.

AN EARLY STUDENT

Helene Weiss has figured prominently in the editing and publication of Heidegger's lecture courses for the Klostermann *Gesamtausgabe*. Her transcripts of Heidegger's lectures and other first-hand sources have been compared with Heidegger's typescripts and handwritten texts in the preparation of editions of several of his early lecture courses. Her article, "The Greek Conceptions of Time and Being in the Light of Heidegger's Philosophy," may therefore have special merit because of her closeness to Heidegger as his student and the recognition accorded her by the editors of the *Gesamtausgabe* as a source of what Heidegger said.[27] Weiss renders *Dasein* with "human existence," which is redundant, since for Heidegger, only human beings exist. As a result, like many other commentators, Weiss is thrown about what to do with *Existenz*, which is translated "existentially," rather than ontologically. She does not mention the key word *Seiende* in her article.

In connection with the word *Seiende*, it is important to recall that, in rendering a passage from Plato's *Sophist* at the beginning of *Sein und Zeit*,[28] Heidegger translates the word in the guiding question with *seiend*, the unadorned present participle of the verb *sein* ([to] be). In Heidegger's translation, the word functions as an adjective. When *seiend* is made over into the noun *Seiende* and used in the pages of *Sein und Zeit*, the word means what manifests itself in its occurring as an effective actuality. The question remains, however: How is the occurring of anything possible? What is the sense of occurring? That, of course, is the question of *Sein* (be[-ing]) and, later, the question of the sense of *Ereignis* (event). Heidegger argues that an examination of the beingness (*Seiendheit*) or general qualities of any sort of be-ing does not go far enough. Instead, one must understand its be[-ing], that is, the source of its possibility as a sort of be-ing. As Heidegger indicates at the opening of *Sein und Zeit* and repeats so often, this question (and not the question about the be-ingness of any sort of be-ing) has not been taken seriously, not even by the early Greeks, who founded philosophy and the metaphysical view of *Seiende* as present things.

KARL LÖWITH

Karl Löwith's article, "M. Heidegger and F. Rosenzweig or Temporality and Eternity," in *Philosophy and Phenomenological Research* examines the "striking similarity" between the "philosophical starting point" of Heidegger's thought and that of Franz Rosenzweig (1886-1929).[29] In 1928, Löwith was a lecturer at Marburg University, where Heidegger headed the philosophy department. Their correspondence from those years contains a number of revealing personal statements from Heidegger.[30] Löwith's analysis in "M. Heidegger and F. Rosenzweig" is perceptive in a way that no other commentator in English had been up to that time. He speaks of Heidegger's thinking as "grammatical thinking, . . . the peculiarity of which stamps the words of everyday speech, denoting a quality of time ('alltäglich'—everyday; 'jeweils'—at the time being; 'zunächst'—first of all, and 'zumeist'—mostly; now and then; to be present at; 'schon immer'—already and always; 'im voraus'—beforehand; 'um-zu'—in order to, etc.) into philosophical terms" (p. 57). This is an important insight about Heidegger's thought which, unfortunately, Löwith does not develop in the article. It points to the temporal quality of language and raises questions about the relation of linguistic tense and the temporality of existence.

Löwith correctly translates *Dasein* with 'existence' (p. 58), while also characterizing it as "deaf-blind selfhood" or "some pure 'existence' in man" (p. 60). In spite of his apparent familiarity with Heidegger's thought, Löwith still gives Dasein an "existential" reading. He also fails to understand the relation between an instance of human be-ing (*Mensch*) and existence (*Dasein*) as such. Löwith's difficulty with English may be responsible in part for his mistranslations of Heidegger's fundamental words.[31] The word *Seiende* is rendered 'being', but so also is *Sein*; for example, in the sentence "Being [*Seiendes*] as being-in-the-world concerned with its being [*Sein*] itself is ontologically a circular structure" (p. 60).[32]

Löwith explains that, for Heidegger, since existence is always "a peculiar and proper one" (p. 62), the world is an "Existenzial," one among several "Existenzialen." He thus betrays a fundamental misunderstanding of Heidegger's notion of world in *Sein und Zeit*. He claims that the world is "a being of the same ontological kind as I myself," adding that (1) the world is "a mode of being of the existence, [2] the existence of man and that of the world is an 'undivided phenomenon,' [and 3] the world's being there and being discovered is bound up with the being of existence" (pp. 62–63). Here Löwith's own use of the words 'existence' and 'being' is confused with Heidegger's, for whom existence is the singular feature of human be-ing.[33] He explains what he takes to be Heidegger's "characterization of the world as an 'Existenzial'," noting that it is based, first, on "the distinction between the things existing in the world (*innerweltliche Seiendes*) and the being (*Sein*) of 'worldishness' (*Weltlichkeit*) itself" (p. 63). In two nearby sentences, the participial and gerundive senses of *Seiende*, which is translated as 'thing', are confused.

In the following passage, Löwith mistranslates *Sein* as 'existence': "The 'outline of a proper existence toward death' leaves no doubt about it that being toward death as the most intimate and genuine potentiality of our existence represents the key to the discovery of the finite truth of existence" (p. 65).[34] No reader could make sense of what Löwith has Heidegger say here. The words 'existence' and 'being', like the word 'existential', seem to be used carelessly by Heidegger. In fact, much of what Löwith has Heidegger say is Löwith. The problem, here as elsewhere among the early commentators, is a misunderstanding of Heidegger's thought, which is translated by his fundamental words. Löwith's concluding comments make it clear that he saw Heidegger as a "godless theologian" (p. 69) and had read *Sein und Zeit* from an theological perspective. It was to Löwith, of course, that Heidegger had written in 1921: "I am no philosopher. I do not even presume to do something comparable; it is not at all my intention. . . . I am a 'Christian theo*logian*'."[35] The comment may be understood as having been directed at someone whose deepest concern (theology) was well known to Heidegger and with whom he may have wanted to express an affinity, but I do not think the statement can be taken literally.[36]

GERMAN NEOSCHOLASTICISM

"The German Neoscholastic Approach to Heidegger" reviews the secondary literature written between 1929 and 1944 by a number of neoscholastic philosophers, among whom Heidegger had been given "a sympathetic if critical response" (p. 144).[37] Collins bases his discussion primarily on Alfred Delp's *Tragische Existenz: Zur Philosophie Martin Heideggers*[38] but also cites the work of Delp, Bernhard Jansen, and Christof Ertel on Heidegger's historical "sources" in Kant, Luther, and Kierkegaard.[39] He notes that Heidegger's basic concepts have been dealt with in works by Caspar Nink and Adolf Dyroff.[40] Collins adds that the neoscholastics have made "contributions to the clearer understanding of Heidegger's *rather obscure and difficult turns of phrase* as well as to a doctrinal evaluation in the light of the great philosophical tradition [emphasis added]"; in other words, efforts have been made to accommodate Heidegger's ideas to those of Thomism. In fact, Collins's use of the terms 'being', 'essence', and 'existence' are Thomistic. The usage is made to overlap with Heidegger's, but without being distinguished from it.

According to Collins, for Heidegger, *Seiende* means "that which is" (which Collins also translates with 'existent') and "is the ontic thing mistakenly assigned by ancient philosophy as the object of metaphysics, that order of being where the real distinction between essence and existence obtains." *Sein*, he says, means "being itself." Without introducing the word *Dasein*, Collins comments on Heidegger's *analytique* of existence:

> Only in the being of man is the tension between essence and existence removed in favor of a pure existential being which is the proper object of first philosophy. By the problem of ontological being is meant the study of human existence as leading to a fundamental ontology or general metaphysics, rather than to an empirical anthropology. (p. 144)

While trying to show that Heidegger's work in *Sein und Zeit* is not anthropology, Collins mistakenly identifies fundamental ontology with *metaphysica generalis*. He later translates both *Sein* and *Seiende* with 'being' and adds the qualifiers ontic and ontological to distinguish two kinds of being. He assumes that the distinction between what is ontic and what is ontological is evident, when in fact, for Heidegger, the problem is to make the distinction clear for the first time. He does not see that, for Heidegger, God "is" in the same way that plants, animals and angels are, although God is the *summum ens*. All are therefore ontic entities, but only human beings "exist." The expressions "unique and self-possessed existent," "existence" (as "*ens ab alio* [being of another]"), "existence in the world," "human being," "exister" (attributable to Kierkegaard), "human nature" (as "being-in-the-world"), and "concrete self" (pp. 145-46) seem to refer to *Dasein*, but Collins is not explicit about this. His essay exemplifies the ambivalent relation between Heidegger and the neoscholastics (and with theology and theologians in general) that marked the first period of response to his writings. It may be that Heidegger's critics among the neoscholastics hoped that he would one day admit that he was not only a Catholic theo*logian*, but a Catholic philosopher as well. In the following years, the idea that Heidegger is a neoscholastic who has committed doctrinal errors is often explored.

ANOTHER STUDENT IN FREIBURG

In his article, "Man's Fall in M. Heidegger's Philosophy," in the *Journal of Religion*, Ernest Hans Freund notes that he studied with Heidegger at the University of Freiburg, where he was awarded a doctorate.[41] He acknowledges that he is "indebted to Lester J. Smart, M.A., for help in translating quotations from Heidegger" (p. 181, n. 2). I suspect that such reliance might have been required by other early authors of articles on Heidegger, who were also just beginning to write in English and whose first language was German. As I have already suggested in the case of Karl Löwith, this may account, in part, for some of the problems translating Heidegger's fundamental words in the period I am reviewing. Freund's translation of *Sein* with 'beingness', for which Heidegger reserves the term *Seiendheit*, illustrates his misunderstanding of the ontological difference and the meaning of the term *Seiende* in Heidegger.

Freund rightly translates *Dasein* with 'existence', but also with 'human existence', which is redundant (p. 181).[42] On the same page, he apparently also translates *Existenz* with 'existence', which seems to be convertible with "way of life" (p. 181) in his text. If this is the case, Freund was among the few who saw the distinction between *Dasein* and *Existenz* in Heidegger's usage. On the other hand, the word 'man' and the expression "human existence" are used interchangeably, which shows how little Freund appreciated the difference between the ontological notion of *Dasein* and the anthropological concept human being.

A PROTESTANT THEOLOGIAN

Paul Tillich's well-known article "Existential Philosophy" appeared in the *Journal of the History of Ideas* while he was teaching at Union Theological Seminary in New York.[43] In 1944, Tillich was an important Protestant theologian. The article reached an even wider audience when it was reprinted in 1959 as a chapter of his book *Theology of Culture*.[44] In his article, Tillich equates 'Being' with 'Reality' (p. 44) and capitalizes both terms throughout. He refers the reader to Werner Brock and Herbert Marcuse[45] for a history of existentialist philosophy, which, he claims, is to be traced back to Dilthey's "philosophy of life" (p. 46). He says that "*Dasein*, a word which has received a pregnant meaning in Heidegger's *Sein und Zeit*, adds the concrete element of 'being in a special place,' being *da* or 'there'" (p. 47) to the notion of existence. But *Dasein* is also translated with the expression "Existential Being" and with the word 'self-relatedness', while *Existenz* is translated with 'existence', understood in the sense it had already taken on in popular discussions of existentialism. By the time Tillich wrote this essay, the use of the words 'existence' and 'existential' was widespread in the scholarly and popular literature.

Tillich explains that *Existenz* comes from the traditional distinction between "essence" and "existence": "In that distinction, 'essence' signifies the What, the τί ἐστιν or *quid est* of a thing; 'existence' signifies the That, the ὅτι ἐστιν or *quod est*" (p. 47). Heidegger might have stopped Tillich here and asked: But what about the ἐστιν, the *est*, the 'is' in those definitions of *essentia* and *existentia*? And how had the question of the distinction come to be raised at all? Was it raised in terms of the one or the other? For Tillich the be[-ing] of *essentia* and *existentia* remains unclarified, yet the very distinction itself depends upon an understanding of be[-ing], which is invoked by the little word 'is'. As we have seen, the term *Existenz*, as Heidegger uses it, means *a kind of life which each of us, at any moment, is leading*. As such, it is the distinguishing feature in each case of existence (*Dasein*). I may move from one kind of life to another—for example, from my philosophical life as a scholar and teacher to my fatherly life as a parent—but I am always leading a certain kind of life.

Well into his history of "existential philosophy," Tillich finally focuses on Heidegger. He now renders *Dasein* with "finite Existence" (p. 58). Tillich surveys *Kant und das Problem der Metaphysik*. Quoting a sentence from the text, Tillich translates *Seiende* with both 'being' and 'Being', which here refer, respectively, to a particular entity and to the greatest entity of them all, God.[46] In doing so, he reveals his position squarely in the midst of the Western metaphysical tradition, which Heidegger had set out to "bring down" or dismantle, in order to reveal its underlying foundation and supporting ground. Here, as in the neoscholastic theological literature on Heidegger, "Being" is tacitly assumed to be the God of traditional Christian philosophy.

HEIDEGGER AMONG THE EXISTENTIALISTS

Ralph Harper's "Two Existential Interpretations" is a brief discussion of Kierkegaard, Heidegger, and Pierre Rousselot, a French Jesuit who was killed in action, in 1915, in World War I.[47] Harper cites Heidegger's fundamental interest in and attempt to understand "what we mean when we use the word 'being'" (p. 393). Considering Kierkegaard and Heidegger together, Harper follows the lead already established by Tillich and others. Both are said to distinguish between "actual existence" (where 'existence' means "actuality") and "personal existence" (where 'existence' means "personality") (p. 393). Harper's article is a morass of confusing terminological imprecisions. From the context of his citations, it can be determined that he renders *Dasein* with 'person', both *Sein* and *Seiende* are given as 'being', and *Existenz* becomes 'existence' (p. 394). In a few sentences, Harper throws quite a lot of dust into the reader's eyes. Perhaps the most important problem of Harper's reading is his use of the term 'existential', which he employs in the prevailing "Existentialist" sense of what is of great moment for an individual. By contrast, Heidegger's use of *Existenz* refers to the singular feature of existence, that it is always manifested as a determinate, qualitatively unique kind of life. As we know, in *Sein und Zeit*, Heidegger uses the term *Existenzial* to name one of the "categories" of existence, while reserving the ontic word *existenziell* for what is of great importance (existentially significant) to the person. The words *Existenzial* and *existenziell* have been confused by Harper and many interpreters of Heidegger at that time and since.

HANNAH ARENDT

The occasion for Hannah Arendt's article "What Is Existenz Philosophy?" is recounted by William Barrett's informal history of, among other things, the *Partisan Review*.[48] Arendt's text is an article on the cultural movement by that time known as Existentialism. She traces the current usage of the word *Existenz* to "the later Schelling" (p. 37).[49]

> The term 'Existenz' indicates, first, nothing more than the being of man, independent of all qualities and capacities that can be psychologically investigated. Thus far, what Heidegger once rightly remarked about 'life-philosophy', that the name was about as meaningful as the botany of plants, also holds for Existenz philosophy. Except that there is no accident that the word 'Being' is replaced by the word 'Existenz'. In this terminological change one of the fundamental problems of modern philosophy is, in fact, concealed. (p. 34)

The section of the article devoted to Heidegger is entitled "The Self as All or Nothing: Heidegger." Heidegger's work, Arendt writes, "led to a far-reaching alteration of the traditional terminology" (p. 46), but the "*revolutionary . . . terminological appearance* <of Heidegger's writing> has very much interfered with the correct estimate of his thought" (p. 46). Unfortunately, Arendt does not do much to help us gain clarity about Heidegger's language. *Existenz* remains untranslated; *Dasein* is given as both "human reality" and "the Being of Man." On the *analytique* of "human reality" or "the Being of Man," she writes: "Heidegger maintains that he has found a being, in whom essence and existence are immediately identical, and this is Man. His essence is his existence. 'The substance of Man is not mind . . . but Existenz'" (p. 47). No reference is given to the opening paraphrase. In any case, nowhere does Heidegger say that man's existence and his essence are identical. He does say that the essence of man "is in [*liegt in*]" the kind of life he leads, his *Existenz*.

The all-important context of Heidegger's use of the classic metaphysical category term *Substanz* in the passage Arendt quotes is omitted.[50] Heidegger encloses the term in quotation marks, to indicate that he is not using the term in the conventional way. In this passage, as elsewhere, much depends on translating *Dasein* with 'existence' and *Existenz* as "way of life."

Arendt continues: "Man as the identity of Existenz and essence appeared to give a new key to the question concerning Being in general. One need only recall that for traditional metaphysics God was the being in whom essence and existence coincided . . ." (p. 47). Here she is close to saying, as Collins had, that Heidegger makes man into God, "the Master of Being" and the author and "ground for all this world's Being" (pp. 47-48), by discovering that, as in the case of God (on the scholastic account), so in man (on the Existentialist account), "essence" and "existence" coincide. But Heidegger says nothing of the kind.

The essential error in Arendt's interpretation is perhaps found in this formulation: "The Being of Man Heidegger calls Existenz or *Dasein*." As already indicated, nowhere does Heidegger equate *Existenz* and *Dasein*. Nor does he "through establishing this terminology <of calling the Being of Man *Existenz* or *Dasein*>" thereby avoid "using the expression 'Man' [Mensch]" (p. 48), as Arendt suggests. He uses the expression *Mensch*, but distinguishes this anthropological term from the ontological term *Dasein*. Like so many early interpreters, Arendt mistakenly believes that Heidegger is developing a philosophical anthropology. At that time, readers would have been mightily confused by Arendt's usage of the words 'Man' (translating both *Man* and *Mensch*) and *Existenz*.

We can now better understand Arendt's insistence on not translating the word *Existenz* in the essay. If she had, she could not have retained its "Existentialist" meaning elsewhere in the article where she discusses her former teacher and friend, Karl Jaspers. Instead the unique meaning it had come to have for Heidegger is sacrificed. Once again the critical difficulty seems to be how to render the word *Existenz* in discussions of the early Heidegger. Another confusion Arendt introduces is connected with an isolated quotation on philosophizing that she offers: " . . . philosophical questioning must be existentially seized as a possibility inherent in the Being of existing human reality" (p. 48).[51] Heidegger's point is that only with the individual human being (something ontic), do existence, the existential *analytique*, and the question about the meaning of be[-ing] (all ontological concerns) arise at all, and that philosophizing is the basic "possibility" of existence.

Arendt translates *existenziell* with 'existential' (in the sense Kierkegaard and Jaspers gave the term), because she misses the distinction between the *existenziell* (what is of vital importance to someone or, in the then current "Existentialist" terminology, what is of "existential" significance) and the *existenzial* (relating to the "categories" of *Dasein*). Although it was not clear to Arendt and most commentators, the meaning of *Existenz* for Heidegger has nothing in common with Jaspers's term *Existenzphilosophie* but the grapheme.

The difficulties I have pointed out explain why, in the passage quoted above, Arendt translates Heidegger's "*Seinsmöglichkeit des je existierenden Daseins*" with "the exceptional existential possibility of human reality," which should read: "a possibility of the be[-ing] of every extant existence." The addition of the word 'exceptional' to modify 'existential' conflates the "Existential" and the "ek-sistential" dimensions.[52] Arendt is then forced to translate "*existierenden Dasein*" as "existing human reality," a move that once again forces the reader back into the metaphysical usage of 'exist' and its participle 'existing'. As a result, however, the word *existierenden* loses the special sense Heidegger gives it; namely, as applying only to the human kind of be-ing—existence.

The problem of understanding the difference between the *existenziell* and the *existenzial* is also seen in Arendt's discussion, later in her essay, of what she calls "the existential [Heidegger's *existenzial*]," "the existentiel [Heidegger's *existenziell*]," and "existentiality [Heidegger's *Existentialität*]" (p. 49). By that time, Arendt is using the term 'existential' for Heidegger's *Existenzial*, which, she maintains, is a "structure's of Man's Existenz" (p. 49). In fact, the existentials are the structures of *Dasein* (existence). Her word 'existentiel' means "existing in an explicit sense" (p. 49).

Like Marjorie Glicksman in her later years, Hannah Arendt's estimation of Heidegger moderated as time passed.[53]

POPULAR PHILOSOPHY

In his article, "Rationalism and the Philosophy of Despair," in the *Sewanee Review*, David Baumgardt claims to report several of Heidegger's leading questions: "How does and must *being* appear to man, who struggles along with it in time? Why is being at all and why does being exist instead of its definite negation, mere thinking" (p. 232)?[54] In fact, Heidegger asks quite different questions: What is the meaning of be[-ing]? What is the relation of temporality and be[-ing]? Echoing Leibniz, he asks: Why is there anything, rather than nothing at all? Nowhere does Heidegger contrast be[-ing] and thinking as opposites. Baumgardt translates *Sein* with 'being', but his use of the words 'being' and 'exist' in the second question just quoted produces a formulation that does not make sense either grammatically or conceptually, yet the reader is expected to assume that something of Heidegger's thinking is being expressed here. In many of the early and later translations of Heidegger, similarly incomprehensible formulations are offered, which the reader assumes must make sense, if only she is astute enough to understand them. In fact, these formulations usually mask the translators' misapprehensions of Heidegger's thinking, which is inaccessible to them because of a lack of clarity about the sense (*Sinn*) of Heidegger's fundamental words. For example, Baumgardt writes that

> we find, according to Heidegger, that being can realize itself, so to speak, only by a constant reduction of the nothing to nothing. As we read in Heidegger's brief essay "What Is Metaphysics?"—a lecture given at Freiburg University in 1929—the existence of all existing things realizes itself solely by a permanent annihilation of the nihil. (pp. 232-33)[55]

These sentences surely do not make any sense. What can a "reduction of the nothing to nothing" mean? Baumgardt is evidently translating *das Nichts* with "the nothing." Presumably basing himself on Heidegger's discussion of the no-thing in the lecture cited and in its "Postscript" (1943), Baumgardt construes existence in the traditional sense, which is derived from the medieval distinction between *essentia* and *existentia*. In fact, Heidegger's discussion in the texts referred to turns on the relation between be[-ing] and the no-thing, not on the relation between existence (*Dasein*) and the no-thing. Heidegger's concern in the lecture is our understanding of the sense of be[-ing].

Another confusing formulation is offered when, purporting to represent Heidegger, Baumgardt says that "death is an integrant mood of existence, belonging to being as soon as being is." In this sentence, although *Dasein* is translated correctly as 'existence', the words 'being' and 'existence' are used interchangeably (p. 233). In this passage, the word 'being' is a cipher, and talk of "being as soon as being is" merely raises a great deal of dust. The reader of the interdisciplinary journal in which Baumgardt published his article must have turned the page with incomprehension and even some amusement, his impression of Heidegger's thought having been marred.

Later, Baumgardt explains that

> anxiety [the integrant mood of existence] manifests itself, first, in the sorrow over, the care for, the daily needs of life, the trouble taken in order to subsist—that is, in Heidegger's *expressive but eccentric language, full of untranslatable etymological allusions*: 'das Be-Sorgen des Zu-Handenen, des Zeugs in der Welt' [emphasis added]. (p. 233)

To his credit, Baumgardt is one of the few commentators to risk translating *Sorge* with 'sorrow', which captures an important sense of the fundamental structure of existence. He is mistaken, however, when he treats anxiety (which translates *Angst*) and sorrow as psychological phenomena, claiming that 'anxiety' and 'sorrow' are two names for the "main trait" (translating *Grundbefindlichkeit*) of existence. His wish to make Heidegger's terminology work as an ethical discourse leads to incomprehensible formulations, which then force him to assert that Heidegger is untranslatable. At one point, Baumgardt fabricates a sentence fragment out of elements of one of Heidegger's sentences. Presumably quoting Heidegger in the second sentence, he writes:

Confronted with the nothing, we realize that we can never be perfectly at home in being. We realize "die Unheimlichkeit des in die Existenz Geworfene-Seins,"[56] the homelessness, the terror of an outcast, thrown into the world and lost in a reality foreign to him. (p. 233)

Heidegger had written the following question: "Was soll aber das Dasein aus der Unheimlichkeit seines geworfenen Seins aus berichten?"[57] Baumgardt has substituted *Existenz* for *Dasein* because he misses the distinction between the unique kind of be-ing of human beings (existence [*Dasein*]) and the essential feature of that kind of be-ing (a determinate way of life [*Existenz*]). Has he "heard" the meaning in English of the German (his native language) word *Dasein* and "translated" it with another word Heidegger uses in certain passages of *Sein und Zeit*? In any case, he reinforces the traditional metaphysical account of *Existenz* which was alive and well in Jaspers's German Existentialism. Once again, part of the problem may have been that English was Baumgardt's second language, after German.

TEMPORALITY

Philip Merlan, in his paper "Time Consciousness in Husserl and Heidegger," sets out to "interpret Heidegger by Husserl" (p. 24).[58] Concerning *Angst*, Merlan paraphrases Heidegger on how the mortality of existence is experienced under the impact of anxiety: "My existence is no longer something included between two points, something extending between two Nothings" (p. 39). In the place Merlan cites, however, Heidegger, in fact, says: "The 'between' in relation to birth and death is already in the be[-ing] of existence. Nor is it the case, on the other hand, that existence 'is' actually within a point of time and in addition 'surrounded' by the nonactual of its birth and death."[59] Heidegger does not speak of existence being tensed between two "Nothings," as Merlan suggests, but rather as stretched between what are "nonactual [*Nichtwirklich*]" moments, his birth and the end of his life at death.

There are a number of problems with Merlan's essay that are directly related to his efforts to translate Heidegger. Consider the following paragraph:

> No more and Not yet: the true meaning of those expressions reveals itself when we consider being-unto-death [*Sein zum Tode*] in anxiety.... Not yet and No more reveal themselves ... as constituting my temporality. I have never been; I *am* having been.[60] And never shall be: I *am* shalling be—though *the language must be raped* [emphasis added] to express that being as a whole I always *am* futurical (p. 40).[61]

Merlan suggests that Heidegger "rapes" language, but Heidegger has done no such thing. On the other hand, it is evident that his translators often have.

In the passage Merlan cites from *Sein und Zeit* that refers to the temporality of the past, the key term is *Gewesen-sein*. A legitimate translation of this term depends upon realizing that, in German, the auxiliary verb with the verb *sein* is also *sein*, not *haben*. Grammatically, be-ing permeates the verb "[to] be (*sein*)" in the German perfect tense, compared to the German preterite, which does not take an auxiliary. By contrast, in English, *having* permeates the verb "[to] be" in the past tense. Moreover, the past participle of *sein*, *gewesen*, resonates with the verb *wesen*, which means "to come to pass." Thus, *Ich bin gewesen* means "I am come to pass." By contrast, the future tense in German is a combination of a form of *werden* ("[to] become") and the infinitive *sein*. Thus *Ich werde sein* means "I come to be." With these details of German grammar in mind, the temporality of the past (which is expressed in German by the perfect tense) can be formulated, as Heidegger does, as *Gewesen-sein*, which might translate as "being come to pass." That is needlessly jarring, however, and ultimately meaningless ("We call authentic being come to pass repetition"). But consider that, as an adjective, *gewesen* means "formerly" or "once," as in "once upon a time." Since the sense of the past participle of *sein* is retained in the meaning of *gewesen* (meaning "formerly"), we may more legitimately render *Gewesen-sein* as "being formerly" or "being once." An authentic translation of Heidegger's sentence would run: "We call authentic being-once revival."

With respect to the next passages cited, which refer to the temporality of the future, the formulation provided by Merlan is hopeless: "I *am* shalling be." Merlan's construction does not reveal anything about Heidegger's conception of temporality. The *werden sein* of the German future tense translates as "come to be." But, if we consider that *werden* also means "going to be" (as in "When I grow up, I am *going to be* a fireman"), the temporality of the future can be understood as "coming to be." There is no need for "am shalling be," which attempts a literal, word-for-word exchange between German and English terms. Heidegger's formulation is designed to capture the imminence of the ex-sistential or forward-reaching future. In his analysis of temporality, Heidegger restores to the three dimensions of time their dynamic interpenetration and ex-sistential (that is, forward-reaching) liveliness as imminent (future), anticipatory (present), and engendering (past). All three temporalities have something of the oncoming about them.

Finally, Merlan proposes the following formulation of Heidegger's view of the finiteness of existence: "I am my own foundation,—which precisely means that I can never master the fundament on which I rest" (p. 44). Here he appeals to "Heidegger's *untranslatable* words: Grundsein besagt . . . des eigensten Seins von Grund auf nie mächtig sein [emphasis added]" (p. 44, n. 109). Merlan's translation of *Grundsein* works quite well here.[62]

HEIDEGGER AND EXISTENTIALISM

In December 1947 and January 1948, Eric Unger published a series of two articles entitled "Existentialism" in the *Nineteenth Century and After*.[63] Unger combines psychological and Existentialist readings of Heidegger in his essays. It is interesting to note Unger's impression that, to the best of his knowledge, no synopsis of Heidegger's philosophy "is available to the English reader" (p. 279). That being the case, we would suppose that the average educated reader's level of familiarity with the secondary literature on Heidegger in English was meager. In fact, up to that time, apart from a journalistic piece by

Stefan Schimanski,[64] the only substantive discussion of Heidegger's thought in a British publication was, of course, Ryle's review of *Sein und Zeit*, which had been published eighteen years earlier. What Unger provided his nonspecialist readers may have been the first serious treatment of Heidegger's thought then available in the United Kingdom.

Unger first offers the following disclaimer:

> Before trying to convey a general impression, however vague, of this complicated system of thought, we must ask the reader's indulgence regarding an inevitable *difficulty and harshness of expression*. The unwieldiness of German philosophical language is well known; but *Heidegger's work is written in a style and terminology whose strangeness is quite extraordinary even by German standards*. This is not entirely due to the *stylistic eccentricities* of the author, but may be explained, in part at least, by the unusual object of his inquiry and the unusual way of his approach. Since the strange perspective in which he sees things cannot simply be replaced by the natural and familiar one without missing the point of what he has to say, *we can hardly avoid imitating in English some of the liberties he takes with his own language* [emphases added]. (p. 279, n. 1)

Unger gives the impression that Heidegger's language is awkward and odd, and above all difficult. Before examining what the "liberties" attributed to Heidegger amount to, let us consider the impact of Unger's comments on those who were reading about Heidegger for the first time. What Unger takes to be "stylistic eccentricities" are, in fact, explorations of the infolded meanings of related fundamental words used to express Heidegger's thought. The purported "strangeness" of his language is the effect it has of forcing the reader to give pause to what is being said, to listen closely to the words uttered, and to search for the thought to which they give expression. From the start, however, these characteristics of Heidegger's language were construed by commentators and translators working in English as deliberate efforts at mystification, aberrant verbal formulations, or the result of limitations of Heidegger's ability to express himself.

In "Human Life, Personality, and Time" (p. 279), the first section of his first essay, Unger considers the notions of *Dasein, Existenz*, and *Leben* in the context of Heidegger's philosophy. The "technical term" "human life," which translates *Dasein*, is "used to indicate as a *single coherent entity* the collection of data which, from the normal point of view, would be looked upon as all the separate real things or events that make up a human life" (p. 279). With this concept of human life, Unger claims, Heidegger "abolishes the *independence* and autonomy of the two factors [of the life of a person]—that of the human person on the one hand, and that of the social and natural environment on the other—and makes them the two *features* of the sole independent and basic entity: Human Life or Dasein" (p. 280). "Human life" (or "the Human Life") is glossed with "the-man-in-the-world-in-time" (pp. 280–81), and any possibility of understanding Heidegger's notion of existence is foreclosed by Unger's translation of *Dasein* as "human life," a translation decision that is, in turn, based on his tendency to see Heidegger's *analytique* of existence as a continuation of Dilthey's *Lebensphilosophie*, which it is not.[65]

Matters are further complicated when Unger discusses the difference between "being, in the way in which Selfhood is, and being, in the way in which all other things are. The first is called *Existence*, the second *Reality* (literally being like a *res* or thing)" (p. 282). Here Unger cites *Sein und Zeit* to confirm his reading, commenting that "although Heidegger, in making the word 'existence' [translating *Existenz*] a technical term, deprives it of part of its normal meaning (in which 'to exist' is simply an equivalent of 'to be'), it should be observed that he does not intend it to signify anything less 'real' than reality" (p. 282). What promised to be an illuminating interpretation of the meaning of existence founders on Unger's mistranslations of *Existenz* as 'existence' and *Dasein* as "human life."

Heidegger does not contrast reality with existence, as Unger suggests. Instead, he contrasts the kind of be-ing of whatever can be said to *be* in some way with the kind of be-ing of existence, *who* (i.e., as a self, "the who of existence") properly speaking never *is* in a fixed, static way; that is to say, who, as existing, is always surpassing himself. The entire ontological problematic is exposed in this distinction, but

Unger does not see it. Existing and essence (in the senses just distinguished) are both real; that is, reality comprises both what *is* and existence. For Heidegger, the reality of the world is never an issue.⁶⁶

Unger cites the often quoted sentence from *Sein und Zeit*, "Das 'Wesen' des Daseins liegt in seiner Existenz,"⁶⁷ explaining that it means that "the qualities which Human Life may have are determined by its kind of being" (p. 282). Here, as above, *Sein* is rendered with 'being'. Unger misses Heidegger's point, that the so-called essence or nature of existence is its always occurring as a certain kind of life (*Existenz*). Existence never *has* a nature. Unger then considers the meaning of "reality" in contrast to "existence." "Reality," he says, refers to

> the class of all entities of which it *cannot* be said that they are 'concerned with their own being' and which are normally called inanimate things, objects, events, etc. He [Heidegger] characterizes their mode of being by the word '*Vorhandensein*', which means being simply there, being to be found, being real—a meaning that is usually regarded as the only one of the verb 'to be'. (p. 283)

In this passage, it becomes plain that Unger's earlier use of the word 'reality' renders the German *Seiende*.

That same year, Stefan Schimanski published a brief article in the British magazine the *Listener*, "Martin Heidegger and Existentialism."⁶⁸ I will discuss it later along with his report "On Meeting a Philosopher," when considering Schimanski's "Foreword" to *Existence and Being*.

A CRITICAL VIEW OF HEIDEGGER

Günther [Stern] Anders's essay "On the Pseudo-Concreteness of Heidegger's Philosophy" is a serious all-out attack on Heidegger.⁶⁹ Even so, his characterizations of some of Heidegger's ideas are helpful; for example, his discussion of *Dasein*: "The 'Dasein'—the topic of Heidegger's philosophy, is 'hiesig [local]', belongs to τούτῳ τῷ κόσμῳ [the order of things], but it is not 'nature', much less 'life' in its biological sense" (p. 337). *Dasein*, he explains, "designates the specific *modum existendi* of man, the 'being there'; *not* the *fact* of his existence. *Being untranslatable* the German term will be adopted throughout this article [emphasis added]" (p. 337, n. 1). Perhaps for Anders, whose first language was German, the term was untranslatable. Understood in the context of Heidegger's thought as a whole, however, it is appropriately rendered with existence, as I have argued. Anders says that "it was one of Heidegger's tasks to answer the question": "What, however, was the meaning of 'ὄν'" in Husserl's notion of objects as (be-ings)? "Somehow," says Anders, "he [Husserl] meant his objects as ὄντα, to speak with Plato's Parmenides" (p. 339), but Heidegger's question, for Anders, is about the meaning of be-ings. This is not so; in fact, Heidegger thinks the decisive question is about the meaning of the be[-ing] of the various ways of be-ing. Anders eventually comes to the conclusion that *Dasein* is the "strange phenomenon of an εἶναι [(to) be] without an identifiable ὄν [be-ing]."

"The 'Dasein'," he explains, "is defined by Heidegger as '*Sorge*'." He goes on to say that "'*Sorge*' meaning 'being after *something*' ('Aussein auf etwas') . . . represents to a certain degree the common denominator of Husserl's and Heidegger's philosophies" (p. 339), since, for Husserl, *Sorge* refers to intentionality, the "tendency" of the "intentional act" toward its "object," while, for Heidegger, *Sorge* is the meaning of 'Dasein', "the 'being there' . . . of existence" (p. 237). This is a curious and novel comparison of the two philosophers. Anders adds that the word *Sorge*, which "combines the connotations of 'cura,' 'worrying,' 'caring for . . . ,' and 'taking care of,' would best be translated by 'interest,' if understood in its broadest meaning although the word, unfortunately, lacks the gloomy nuance of the German original. Thus we will keep Heidegger's word again" (p. 339, n. 5). It is to his credit that along with Baumgardt, Anders is among the few commentators who translate *Sorge* with 'sorrow', in the sense of *thoughtfulness about things,* which is perhaps the best rendering of *Sorge*, the basic structure (*Struktur*) of existence.[70] The "gloomy nuance" Anders senses here derives from a psychological (ontic) reading of Heidegger.[71] By way of clarification, Anders explains, that compared to the "*modum existendi* of man" (p. 337), we find the very different *Vorhandensein*, "the naked 'esse' of objects of Nature . . . *res existentes*" (p. 339, n. 4). The *modum existendi* is "the way *one is in the world* . . . in all those acts of everyday life which . . . at best are casually touched upon by this or that science." And this is the province that [Heidegger] called '*Dasein*' (p. 341).

In a note, Anders explains why he also leaves *Sein* untranslated:

> In Heidegger's ontology the distinction between [*sic*]⁷² (be) and (being), 'Sein' and 'Seiendem', is of capital importance; while the English language disposes but of the one participle 'being', we will have to keep this German term, too, at least where the substantivation of the verb 'to be' is in question. (p. 341, n. 8)

Anders is quite right in stressing the "capital importance" in Heidegger's thought of the distinction between be-ing and be[-ing], but he is unable to make sense of it. He says that *Dasein* is "a sort of 'to be in the world'" (p. 342), an expression that does not make grammatical sense in English. On the other hand, to say that to be there (*Da-sein*) is to be in a world (*In-der-Welt-sein*) makes Heidegger's meaning plain. In saying that "'Dasein' . . . finds its actuality as 'Sorge' and 'Besorgnis [apprehensiveness]', i.e. in a thousand dealings with the world" (p. 342), Anders suggests that existence comes into its own by doing certain things and feeling certain ways. Heidegger's *analytique* of existence, however, is not about how we human beings feel, but about what we can be.

Anders continues: "Our 'Sein', as distinguished from things just 'being', is 'in der Welt sein' or 'Sorge', our acts are aiming at 'world'" (p. 312).⁷³ Unfortunately, this sentence, which attempts to convey Heidegger's characterization of existence and the ontological difference, is not intelligible. Since *Dasein* and *Welt*, existence and world, are indistinguishable, existence cannot "aim" at the world. To exist is to already be in a world. Anders complicates understanding further by saying that, for Heidegger, "any other type of 'Sein' than <that of Dasein> is, what it is, only *sub species* Dasein, only 'for' 'the Dasein'" (p. 342).⁷⁴

Anders also confuses *Seiende* (be-ing) and *Sein* (the be[-ing] which makes any be-ing possible). In another passage where he attempts to explicate the meaning of *Dasein*, Anders reveals the limits of his understanding of Heidegger's thought:

> Since, however, 'Dasein' is not just a sort of 'to be', but a 'being there', a 'being present'; since it says 'here I am' or 'I am there'; since it is living in the light of this 'I am' and not only 'exists about' (*herum existiert*) obscurely and unmentioned, the factor which formerly was called 'Bewußtsein', now becomes the *specificum* of this *modum existendi*; in a traditional and, we admit, still insufficient way we could put it: consciousness is embedded by him into being. (p. 342)

In this passage, it is not clear what "embedded by him into being" means, mostly because the meaning of the word 'being' is unclear. Moreover, the notion of consciousness is entirely absent from Heidegger's account of existence, since it implies a view of the human being as already estranged from the world and in need of making contact with it by means of acts of consciousness. For Heidegger, consciousness is not presupposed. It must be explained by our ontological status. Anders speaks of "the light of this 'I am'" in the way Descartes speaks of the *ego sum*; that is, as the conscious subject, alienated from objects with which it must somehow (re-)establish contact. Unable to escape the Cartesian frame of reference, Anders suggests that Heidegger is developing a theory of consciousness, which is not the case.

Anders implies that Heidegger does not define *Dasein* (which he does), and that he resorts to deliberately ambiguous language in order to avoid deciding just what *Dasein* means. The *analytique* of existence takes up nearly the whole of *Sein und Zeit*, but that does not mean we do not know what the word *Dasein* means from the outset.

Then comes what is perhaps the most peculiar element of Anders's discussion of *Dasein*. He says that "never does [Heidegger] formulate the question of how 'Dasein' becomes 'Daseiende' (<how> εἶναι [to be] becomes ὄντα [be-ings])," a question, Anders suggests, that Heidegger avoids "like all questions that border on biology." But Heidegger's question is about how *Sein* and *Seiende* differ; that is, about the ontological difference between [to be] and [kinds of being], not about how be[-ing] becomes be-ing. Anders reveals his distance from Heidegger's thought when he says "the fact that the word ['Dasein'] simultaneously contains those different meanings, one blending into the other, is an extraordinary chance for *making obscure statements, of which chance Heidegger never fails to take advantage* [emphasis added]." Somewhat later, he adds: "Now, the *deliberate vagueness* of the term 'Dasein' and Heidegger's failure to give it a definite hypostasis, allows him to call both himself and history 'Dasein.' To put it clumsily, either is made out of the same ontological [stuff] [emphasis added]" (p. 358). Here again, Anders betrays his basic misunderstanding of the sense of Heidegger's fundamental ontology.

Finally, Anders comes to Heidegger's term *Nichten*. "There's no such intransitive word as 'Nichten', only the transitive one 'vernichten'. What Heidegger means is: to become nothing, to vanish" (p. 344, n. 10). Anders does not cite Heidegger here, but presumably he is referring to passages from *Was ist Metaphysik?* As it happens, the word *Nichten* was in current German usage when Heidegger gave his address in 1929. The noun *Nichten* means "nihilating," while the verb *vernichten* means "to annihilate." When he uses the noun *Nichten*, Heidegger does not mean "to become nothing, to vanish." Perhaps Anders means to say something about the verb *nichten*. In that case, it is true that Heidegger devised a neologism, the verb *nichten*, which means "to nihilate," but not "to become nothing, to vanish." The verb *nichten* is used as a transitive verb in Heidegger's vocabulary.[75] Later in the essay, *Vernichtung* is translated with 'annihilation' (p. 366) and *Nichtung* becomes 'nihilation' (p. 367), all of which further reflects Anders's confusion about Heidegger's usage.

Existenz is translated with "existence," which, says Anders, is the product of the "self-transformation" (p. 353) of *Dasein*. He suggests that "the concept of 'Existence' is . . . the intensive wholeness of 'Dasein'" (p. 363), but adds that "Heidegger's 'existence' commits *lifelong suicide*, a pitiful death which, nonetheless, since it lasts as long as life itself, offers certain undeniable advantages" (p. 355). Anders's anthropological reading of Heidegger is no clearer than in this part of his exposition.

ITALIAN EXISTENTIALISM

Nicola Abbagnano's "Outline of a Philosophy of Existence" was written in Italian and then translated expressly for *Philosophy and Phenomenological Research*.[76] Since the Italian text has not been published, it is impossible to know how Heidegger's German was taken over by Abbagnano and then translated once again into English.[77] I have the impression, however, that Abbagnano was not well served in the translation. At the very least, it is certain he did not have an opportunity to work with the text after it had been translated.

Abbagnano's name was well-known in Europe in connection with his "positive Existentialism," which was an alternative to the "negative Existentialism" of Jaspers and Heidegger. What he has to say about Heidegger's "philosophy of existence" was probably looked at with considerable interest by American readers who were by nature more optimistic than Europeans at that time. Since the opening sections of the essay are about Existentialism in general, Abbagnano's use of terms there may not reflect his reading of Heidegger. Section 8 of the essay is devoted to "The Existentialism of Heidegger," where, unfortunately, Abbagnano gives only a very general impression of Heidegger's thought, which as an "existential philosophy," is said to emphasize "nothingness": "For Heidegger existence is defined by its fundamental impossibility not to be nothingness." It "is an emergence or a detachment from nothingness, but the detachment is fictitious because nothingness binds existence to itself since the latter is impossibilitated to identify itself with beingness and to *be* beingness" (p. 208). Anyone reading this sentence must have shaken her head in bewilderment. Just how much of the confusion is Abbagnano's misunderstanding of Heidegger and how much is to be attributed to mistranslation of Abbagnano's text must remain undecided until the Italian text is made available. At the very least, the reader is left with an overwhelming sense of obscurity and incomprehensibility about Heidegger's so-called existential philosophy.

CATHOLIC PHILOSOPHY

There is little new in the essay on "Existentialism" by Frederick Copleston, published in the inaugural issue of the journal *Philosophy*, that is not found in his article "The Tragedy of Man," which was written a year earlier (1947).[78] Heidegger's fundamental words are not clearly distinguished in Copleston's translations, and he mentions only *Sein und Zeit*, from which he quotes without citing specific passages. Copleston begins his essay by saying that Heidegger "sets out in *Sein und Zeit* to construct an ontology, to investigate the problem of being." In an interesting aside, he notes that Heidegger had written to Jean Wahl that "his philosophy was not *Existenzphilosophie* . . . and that his philosophy should not be confused with that of Karl Jaspers . . ." (p. 20). This is an important clarification, one which, up to that point, no other commentator had made. All the same, Copleston does not see that *Dasein* (which he does not translate) is not equivalent with 'Man', as he says it is (p. 21). He suggests that Heidegger's "view of the world is obviously strongly reminiscent of Fichte's conception of the world of objects as the field for the self-realization of the ego, the field of the ego's moral activity" (p. 25). This is a provocative observation, given Fichte's use of the word *Daseyn* in his *Die Anweizung zum seligen Leben* (1806), where *Seyn* refers to God and *Daseyn* refers to Christ.[79]

GERMAN EXISTENTIALISM ONCE AGAIN

Writing in the *Hibbert Journal,* Frank McEachran[80] associates Heidegger and Jaspers, "two German professors of great genius" who have worked out "a definite *Existenzphilosophie* which derives its motif from Kierkegaard and its structure, so to speak, from Husserl" (p. 233). He writes that "the existentialism of Karl Jaspers is identical in structure with that of Heidegger" (p. 235). This important mistake was made for many years by commentators and readers. McEachran claims that Heidegger uses three words which mean "existence," "and *none of them is easy to translate into English* [emphasis added]":

(1) *Existenz*, which means "*real* existence, the sort of existence which Kierkegaard thought might come into being as a result of the 'leap'," is "something that is which *ex-sistet, stands out*, in being"; (2) *Dasein*, which means "*mere* existence," is something that "reflects the transitory experience of day to day life"; and (3) *Vorhandensein*, which means "tenuous existence," is a way of being "led by non-conscious beings which have no hope, not merely of *Existenz* but even of *Dasein*" (p. 234). He adds that "in *Dasein* the self comes into contact with other selves and achieves, albeit only in embryo (*Entwurf*, i.e. sketched out), a relationship with the whole of existence" (p. 234). For Heidegger, says McEachran, "transcendence" is "the development from *Dasein* to *Existenz*" (p. 234). This is an important distortion of Heidegger's thought; moreover, the distinctions made among "real existence," "mere existence," and "tenuous existence" are not Heidegger's. They are McEachran's own characterizations and do not serve to clarify what Heidegger had written. Like most commentators, McEachran's understanding of existence is based on the scholastic distinction between *essentia* and *existentia*.

LÖWITH ONCE AGAIN

Two essays by Karl Löwith may be treated together: (A) an article published in *Social Research*, and (B) a short paper which was read, in 1949, at Argentina's First National Congress of Philosophy, held in Mendoza.[81] The author, who was then on the faculty of Hartford Theological Seminary, translated a frequently quoted text that is close to Heidegger's thought: "Man's nature or essence is nothing but 'existence'" (A, p. 350).[82] But he continues: "This *Da-sein* which is thrust upon itself and into the world, and, at the same time, transcends itself and the world, Heidegger calls 'existence'" (B, p. 391). Like so many others, Löwith mistakenly equates *Dasein* with *Existenz*.

Sein is rendered with 'Being' or 'to-be' (A, p. 350), and *Seiende* is given as 'being', for example, in the following sentence: "Man is in his real being an ontological being . . . capable of transcending every other concrete being toward Being as such" (A, p. 351). In this passage, the usage of the word 'being' lacks precision, so that the sense of 'being' (first occurrence) seems to be distinguishable from 'Being'; in its second occurrence, however, 'being' seems to translate *Seiende*. When Löwith summarizes his understanding of the meaning of *Dasein*, he comes close to seeing the distinction between *Dasein* and *Existenz*: "This kind of Being or rather to-be, which is peculiar to human *Da-sein*—that is, responsibility *to* one's own being, without, however, being responsible *for* being-there—Heidegger calls existence. It is man's way or manner of being-there" (A, p. 351). In the end, however, Löwith's formulation is confusing, since for Heidegger, nothing else exists except man. Löwith explains that existence is "ecstatic" because it is radically "exposed," and hence vulnerable (A, p. 353). If Löwith is speaking about existence in this passage, he rightly highlights its exposure and ontological vulnerability, which are features of existence not often stressed by commentators.

HEIDEGGER AND THOMISM

The year before *EB* was published, the *Thomist* published a two-part, monograph-length article by Vincent Edward Smith entitled "Existentialism and Existence."[83] "Heidegger, the metaphysician" (p. 146) is discussed in part 3 of the first installment of Smith's essay. Here *Sein* is translated wih 'being' and *Seiende* becomes 'beings' (p. 161). According to Smith, *Dasein* or "the *Dasein*" means "human reality" or "being there," but also "has the wider meaning of *existence* as opposed to *essence* in German" (p. 162, n. 66). Here Smith inappropriately introduces the scholastic distinction between *essentia* and *existentia* into Heidegger's text. He says that the *da* in the word *Dasein* points to the fact that "the world is always 'there' with the *Dasein*, never thought away" (p. 162). "But," Smith adds, "Heidegger, it will be seen, describes man in terms of existence, and hence man and *Dasein* become equivalent." Smith's logic is imperfect, however, since characterizing something X (for example, human beings) in terms of Y (for example, existence) does not make X equivalent to Y. In conformity with "the convention of [Heidegger's] critics" (p. 162, n. 66),

Smith leaves the word *Dasein* untranslated. Smith's rationale for not translating the word *Dasein* is still given by translators, if any explanation is offered, and readers unfamiliar with German remain mystified. In this chapter, I am attempting to show that the "convention" was established long before the first translations of Heidegger's works were published.

Smith tells us that Gabriel Marcel "remarked that philosophers of the future will be reading [Alphonse de Waelhens's book *La Philosophie de Martin Heidegger*],[84] rather than Heidegger, to see what Heidegger said" (p. 162, n. 67). I have the impression that this had already begun to happen by the mid-1940s. By now, more recent substitutes for de Waelhens's book still do duty for reading Heidegger. Quoting a passage from *Sein und Zeit*, Smith makes his most significant mistranslation, rendering *Seiende* with 'existence' (p. 163). He thus has Heidegger say: "Dasein is existence, to which as being-in-the-world existence is for itself" (p. 163). In fact, Heidegger writes: "Dasein ist Seiendes, dem es als In-der-Welt-sein um es selbst geht."[85] This is a very expressive passage, which makes many demands on the translator, but Smith has brought Heidegger's thought to grief with the crucial mistranslation of *Seiende*, and once again we have a misunderstanding of Heidegger's thought, although it is not the result of his "difficult" language. Like many authors writing on Heidegger at this time, the author presents Heidegger's terminology in isolated fragments. Landing here and there in Heidegger's text, Smith tries to make bits and pieces belong to a whole, but the result is incoherence. The second installment of Smith's essay is mostly polemical. Smith's articles were the last to appear that made significant mention of Heidegger in its pages before *EB* was published.[86]

CHAPTERS IN BOOKS

Several books published between 1931 and 1949 discuss Heidegger's fundamental words. I will review these next. Heidegger's philosophy is mentioned for the first time in a book-length study in William Tudor Jones's *Contemporary Thought in Germany*.[87] This first introduction to English-speaking readers of the thought of Martin Heidegger does Heidegger a serious disservice. In a few paragraphs, Jones mistranslates most of Heidegger's fundamental words. No page references are given when he quotes from *Sein und Zeit*. Jones says that Heidegger "has created a terminology of his own, and even when he has not done so he has given the ordinary terminology certain meanings which it has never had before." He says that "probably no two readers will understand the book in a similar way." This would surely have happened if readers had had at their disposal only what Jones presents. I will quote at length from his text to show just how badly Jones misrepresented Heidegger.

> Man is *Dasein (Da-sein)*, i.e. he is a *being here and now*. As such a *being* he is *in-the-world*, or, as the author continually points out, he is a being in the World of *Existence*. *Existence* means all that is known to exist. Thus Existence includes more than man and less than the *All* of things. This *Existence* has a *horizon*, and beyond it is the *Seiende* (the being: not necessarily a person) that has brought *Existence* into being. This *Seiende*, in its turn, must have its *Sein* (or its being). Man, then, who is *Da-sein* is related to *Existence*, to *Seiende*, and to the *Sein* of the *Seiende*. Man, further, has something of all these in his nature. In other words, his nature is *cosmic*. But he is not aware of what his nature consists of in any ready-made kind of manner. The reason for this is that he has *fallen*. He has come down from the *Sein* of the *Seienden* to *Existence*, and finally to *Dasein*.... [Man's] main object is to find his way back to his cosmic home—a home beyond his *Dasein*, beyond *Existence*, in the *Sein* of the *Seienden*.... According to Heidegger, what is in man must be in the *Sein* of the *Seienden*. This is all that can be said according to the author. Throughout the book there is not a word concerning what is either in or at the back of this *Sein* of the *Seienden*. This *Sein* of the *Seienden* is the further continuation of *Existence*, and it presents something of its meaning to man, just as *Existence* presents something of its meaning to *Dasein* (Man). (p. 118)

The hopeless confusion of this undergraduate-level essay is followed by a discussion of 'anxiety', 'death', and 'courage' (p. 119). Jones comments on the part played by these elements in Heidegger's "existential idealism":

The author <of *Sein und Zeit*> pleads that this story of man demands placing in this light. When it is thus placed sorrow will turn into joy; interest without waning will be found connected with all things right up from the things nearest to our hands to the ever greater questioning of what constantly reveals itself beyond the horizon of *Existence*, where the *Sein* of the *Seienden* is. (p. 120)

If one can make any sense out of what he says here, Jones seems to be picturing something like a medieval metaphysical hierarchy that leads from *Sein* ("being") down to *Dasein* ("a being here and now"), with intermediate levels of *Seiende* ("a being") and *Existenz* ("Existence"). He mistakenly attributes such an ontology to Heidegger. Most readers must have turned away from this "introduction to Heidegger" feeling utterly bewildered.

HEIDEGGER'S FIRST EDITOR

Several years later, Werner Brock published *An Introduction to Contemporary German Philosophy*.[88] It is a book of special importance, given Brock's role as the editor of *EB*, the first volume of Heidegger's writings translated into English. Brock's *Introduction* is based on a course of lectures he gave at Bedford College, London, where he had relocated during World War II. Brock makes a distinction between *"Existenz"* and "Life," without clarifying the difference between *Existenz* and *Dasein*. He notes that *Dasein* has the "usual sense" of "existence" and translates the word with "human existence" (p. 115ff.). Unfortunately, this leaves the reader with the impression that there are other kinds of existence, but for Heidegger, of course, existence is the singular feature of the human way of be-ing. "*Being and Time*," Brock writes, "is the title of the work in which Heidegger, by a phenomenological analysis of human existence ... endeavors to open a new approach to the philosophical problem of Being [*Sein*]" (p. 109). The practice begun by Ryle is also adopted by Brock, who also capitalizes 'Being' in translating *Sein* (p. 116). In Brock's case, the reason for doing so seems to be based on the convention of capitalizing the highest being (the Judaeo-Christian God) in order to distinguish it from all lesser beings.

WILLIAM BARRETT

More than a decade passed before the appearance of William Barrett's *What Is Existentialism?*[89] It was well worth the wait, however, since in Barrett, Heidegger finally had his first authentic voice in English. In 1964, Barrett reissued the text unchanged, but with the addition of a part of equal length called "Heidegger: The Silent Power of the Possible."[90] Barrett, who was a fine teacher of philosophy as well as an accomplished writer, must be considered among those who popularized existentialism, yet *What Is Existentialism?* does not sacrifice depth for ease of formulation. Two of Barrett's later full-length books also include important discussions of Heidegger.[91]

In 1978, looking back on *What Is Existentialism?*, Barrett wrote that Heidegger's German "was simple and well within my ken."[92] On the other hand, in 1947, he had said that "Heidegger develops *a language of Gothic heaviness, lumbering under its weight of jargon and coinage*, but in his use of it he often attains an extraordinary degree of expressiveness [emphasis added]" (pp. 10–11). It is difficult to know how to square what seem to be two very different reactions to Heidegger's language. It is likely that Barrett always found Heidegger's language both simple and expressive, as he says, but, like the rest of us, struggled a very long time to understand Heidegger's thought.

Barrett's monograph (1947) begins with "An Imaginary Conversation" between Alfred North Whitehead and Heidegger on "concreteness." *Dasein* is translated variously as "human existence" (p. 14), "existence" (p. 14), "human reality" (p. 17), and "conscious existence" (p. 47). Following some remarks on the historical background of existentialism in Kierkegaard, in section 2, "Existentialism Seeks Its System," Barrett systematically discusses Heidegger's philosophy. He assigns himself the "job of straightforward exposition, which may serve to make accessible to the English reader the main outlines of Heidegger's thought": "The whole structure of Heidegger's thought seems to nestle so closely in the bosom of the German language that *all his writing might be alleged as evidence for an inescapable identification of thought and language* [emphasis added]" (p. 24).

This is a provocative suggestion that Heidegger himself discusses but rejects, as we will see in the next chapter. Barrett predicts that "probably these *difficulties of language* banish to a remote future, if we shall ever see it at all, the time when Heidegger's writing, in any considerable bulk, will be available in English translation" (p. 25). Although a great deal of Heidegger's writing is now available in English, one can argue that, in a basic sense, Heidegger's thought still remains untranslated in English.

Barrett concentrates on

> *Being and Time* (1927), which besides being by far the best of Heidegger's books, setting a standard to which he never came near again, is also the most comprehensive, containing all the themes that he was to elaborate or modulate (not always fortunately, alas) in his subsequent writings. By reason of its completeness, we may take it as being something of a Bible of non-religious Existentialism—or if this seems a bit paradoxical, anyway a very convenient textbook. (p. 25)

Sein is translated with both "Being" and "to be" (p. 26). Referring to "human be-ing," Barrett writes that "to be means to be *in* the world and *with* others" (p. 28). This confuses the sense of be[-ing] as such and the be-ing of *Dasein*. Barrett notes that Heidegger "resolutely avoids the use of the words 'man', 'human', 'human being', which might carry traditional connotations of a definite human nature" (p. 26), and instead uses the word *Dasein*, which, he explains, is "a common German philosophical term to designate *existence,* which in [Heidegger's] use is also meant to preserve its literal meaning of 'being-there' (*Sein-Da*). Man, for Heidegger, is Mr. Being There" (p. 26). Few of Barrett's readers seem to have paid attention to this simple clarification about the meaning of *Dasein*, choosing instead to retain the German word untranslated, because, as I have suggested, they did not know what to do with the word *Existenz*.

Barrett describes "the One," "this subject of everyday existence," as an "existent who is in the world and with others—through the clues of language" (p. 28). Evidently, in this passage, Barrett renders *Seiende* with 'existent'. This is unfortunate, since he then confuses beings of all sorts with the uniquely human kind of be-ing, existence. Barrett comes close to correctly reflecting Heidegger's use of *Sein* in a sentence about *das Selbst*, the 'self': "the self that cries <out> is not something that already exists, but something that *is to be*—i.e., is projected as future" (p. 36).

ITALIAN EXISTENTIALISM ONCE MORE

Existentialism: Disintegration of Man's Soul is E. M. Cocks's translation of Guido de Ruggiero's Italian text.[93] Unhappily, Rayner Heppenstall, whose preface to this work includes a lexicon of Heidegger's fundamental words, has revised Cocks's translations of the words, which are also used in Ruggiero's treatment of Kierkegaard and Jaspers. Heppenstall's interpretation of *Dasein* and *Existenz* in Heidegger are, in fact, based on Jaspers's usage of the terms. As a result, in Heppenstall's preface we are therefore three times removed from what Heidegger actually may have thought.

In his preface, Heppenstall makes a keen observation about *Sorge*: "It may be borne in mind that there is an English word etymologically related to 'Sorge' and to some extent still contained in it, and that is the word 'sorrow'" (p. 19). He says that *Dasein* means "mere existence for human beings"; that "it is 'Dasein' which in the philosophy of existence is opposed to 'Existenz' as its fleeting, rudimentary, fallen . . . objective underpinning." He adds that "the important thing is to remember that 'Existenz' is not 'mere existence', that 'mere existence' is, for human beings, 'Dasein' and for inanimate things, 'Vorhandensein'" (p. 17). Assuming he is legitimately translated by Heppenstall, Ruggiero also appears to be operating with the traditional distinction between *existentia* and *essentia* (where Being is identified with *essentia* and *Dasein* is identified with *existentia*), which sees existence as adding nothing to something's essence (hence the sense of "mere existence"), and therefore misreads Heidegger's discussion of *Existenz*.

In Cocks's translation, Ruggiero's discussion of Heidegger claims to begin with Heidegger's own words, yet much of what Ruggiero presents is paraphrase. As already indicated, we cannot determine from the preface which words are being translated by the terms in Ruggiero's text. We have already been introduced to the terms 'existent', 'nothingness', 'anguish', 'being', 'not-being', 'human existence', and 'the null' when the following sentence appears:

> To explain how something emerges out of nothing, Heidegger distinguishes, in idea, existence true and proper from 'being', being here and now, the *Dasein*. Existence is . . . something complex which embraces the positive and the negative, the 'that' and the 'what', being and Being or essence. The *Dasein* is only the fleeting, momentary existence, the immediate presence, the given that is not explained or justified, swaddled as it is by the nothing. (p. 32)

From that point on, *Dasein* is not translated, following the decision of Cocks/Heppenstall to "*keep on plugging in the German words themselves* [emphasis added]" (p. 17). The comment reveals a view of translation that misses its fundamental philosophical nature, which is central to Heidegger's own view of the matter, as we will see in chapter 3.[94]

SARTRE, JASPERS, AND HEIDEGGER

Ralph Harper's *Existentialism: A Theory of Man* treats Heidegger in company with Sartre, and Jaspers as a representative of *Existenzphilosophie*.[95] *Dasein* is rendered with "being-there" or "merely existing . . . in our unreflective, vaguely conscious states, when we are not thinking of anything in particular" (p. 30). As "being-there," "we are aware of ourselves as being not all there, just there" (p. 30). Harper is describing a psychological state, not an ontological structure. The adjective *seiend*, quoted from the prefatory page of *Sein und Zeit*, is translated 'being' (p. 68), but in Harper's text this "being" is not distinguished from what translates the words *Sein* and *Seiende*. Harper can therefore say that

> to be one's own consciousness, with all its content and activity, is what Heidegger means by *Dasein*. Man *is* just *there* (present,

awake). *Dasein* signifies mere existence, the brute fact of being, and consciousness, something being opposite to the self within itself. *Das Dasein ist Seiendes, dem es in seinem Sein um dieses selbst geht* (man's being is distinguished by the fact that he is concerned about himself). (pp. 74-75)

Other early commentators on Heidegger make the same mistakes in translating this sentence.[96] In Harper's transformation, even though the verb's subject is 'being', it reads as though the subject of the verb is 'man', betraying his confusion between the ontic psychological subject and the ontological structure of existence.

Harper mistranslates two more key passages from *Sein und Zeit*. Writing about the "human being," Harper has Heidegger say that "its essence consists in the fact that it has its being as its own to be" (p. 75).[97] He continues: "The essence (Wesen) of this being lies in its being-for. The essence (Was-sein) (*essentia*) of this being must be conceived from its being (*existentia*)" (p. 77).[98] Throughout the text, *Existenz* is rendered with 'existence' (for example, p. 75), and *Dasein* is translated variously as "man's being" or "being-there." In all of these passages, the difference between existence (*Dasein*) and a kind of life (*Existenz*), as well as that between the human way of be-ing (*Seiende*) and the be[-ing] that makes it possible, is entirely missed.

While for the early Heidegger, the focus is on *Dasein*, the site of the relation of be[-ing] and the human kind of be-ing (*Seiende*), the later Heidegger is more concerned with the relation of thinking and be[-ing]. In part, the shift is a result of the inadequacies of the philosophical language he had inherited. Heidegger's abandonment of the vocabulary of *Sein und Zeit* attests to this.

A GATHERING OF FRENCH EXISTENTIALISTS

Jean Wahl's *A Short History of Existentialism* appeared around the same time as *EB*.[99] It is based on a lecture given at a meeting in Paris, in October 1945, of the *Club Maintenant*.[100] Following the text of Wahl's lecture is a transcript of the discussion that ensued. Among

Mistranslations in the Early Critical Literature (1929-1949) 77

the participants in the discussion were Nikolai Berdayev, Maurice de Gandillac, Georges Gurvitch, Alexandre Koyré, Emmanuel Levinas, and Gabriel Marcel.

Wahl's brief *histoire* is an important contribution to the story of how Heidegger fared in French, as well as in France following World War Two. However, the reader faces the problem of understanding what Wahl has taken over into French from Heidegger's German and what has, in turn, been rendered into English by Forest Williams and Stanley Moran, Wahl's translators. In the end, the results do not help make Heidegger's thought more accessible to the English-speaking reader. In many cases, it is not clear which of Heidegger's fundamental words are being translated, since Wahl does not cite sources.

Wahl summaries the distinctions Heidegger makes among various kinds of "things [*choses*]," termed 'beings' (*Seiende*) of one sort or another.

> To be sure, there are other forms of Being [*formes d'être*] for Heidegger <than "the being of man [*l'être de l'homme*]>: there is what he calls 'the being of things seen,' or scenes [*l'être des choses vues, du spectacles*]; there is the being of tools and instruments [*l'être des outils et des instruments*]; there is the being of mathematical forms [*l'être des formes mathématiques*]; <and, finally,> there is the being of animals [*l'être des animaux*] . . . (p. 11).

Unfortunately, it is difficult to distinguish between various "*formes*" of be[-ing] (*Sein*) and be[-ing] as such (capitalized by the translators), since Wahl renders both words ('be[-ing]' and 'be-ing') with *être*. To further complicate matters, the words 'being' and 'existent' are used interchangeably. It is to Wahl's credit, however, that he made an observation that no one else had up to that point in discussions of Heidegger published in English. Thus, in spite of the many imperfections and confusions of the essay, Wahl's observation set his brief history apart from nearly everything in English that had appeared up to that time. Wahl ends his sentence about the different "forms of Being" with this clause: "but only man truly exists [*existe*]" (p. 11). Anticipating the passage from Heidegger's "Introduction" to *What Is Metaphysics?* (which did not appear until the following year), he writes: "Animals live [*vit*], mathematical things subsist [*subsiste*], implements remain at our disposal [*reste à notre disposition*], and scenes manifest themselves [*se manifestent*]; but none of these things exists [*aucune de ces choses n'existe*]" (p. 11). Wahl thus made it possible for the French to have an understanding of Heidegger's use of the verb *existieren* from the start, since French lends itself to a usage that makes clear this basic point in Heidegger's *analytique* of existence.[101]

Wahl continues: "Why we are flung [*jeté*] into the world, we do not know ... we are existence [*existence*] without essence [*essence*]" (p. 13). He adds: "There can be no essence of an existent individual, of man [*d'un individu existant, de l'homme, il ne peut y avoir d'essence*]" (p. 14). In Wahl's text, the term *existence* ('existence', in the English version) translates *Dasein*, while *existents* ('existents', in the English translation) renders *Seiende* (p. 14). Unfortunately, here Wahl's usage and that of the English translators obscure the difference between existence and every other sort of be-ing. The word *être* is rendered with both 'being' or 'Being' (p. 14), which introduces confusion, since Wahl also translates *Seiende* with *existents*. Moreover, sometimes 'being' (translating *Seiende*) is pluralized by Wahl as 'beings'; for example, when he writes that we humans are "beings-in-the-world" (p. 20).[102]

The discussion that followed Wahl's lecture includes the comments of a number of the most important figures in modern French Continental philosophy. Their names may therefore be added to the list of those whose comments on Heidegger were available in English before the appearance of *EB*. Alexandre Koyré claims that "when Heidegger speaks of *Dasein*, it is of Man [*de l'homme*] that he is speaking, and he says so himself in his little tract on truth. There is the essential fact."[103] At this point, the translators gloss *Dasein* with both 'Being-there' and 'being-in-the-world' (p. 40). Koyré had already referred to "the mode of existence of man," which implies that there must be other modes of "existing." Unfortunately, he misses the essential observation that Wahl had made in his lecture, to the effect that, for Heidegger, only the human being exists. Koyré concludes that "the Heideggerian *Dasein* is neither a 'nature' nor an 'essence'," although it "possesses an essential structure [*structure*]" (p. 43), which, one may assume, he understands as *Sorge*. Unfortunately, he uses the term "existent being" for the human kind of be-ing (p. 41).

Gabriel Marcel comments on what he sees as "the *profound ambiguity of Heideggerian terminology* [emphasis added]." He concludes that, for example, "*Sein zum Tode* can not be translated into French" (p. 45). Directing his comment to Koyré, who had written an introduction to Henri Corbin's translation of *Was ist Metaphysik?* in 1931, he asks: "You have said: être vers la mort (to be towards death), which was a correct translation—but what does it mean?" (p. 45). Marcel's question about *Sein zum Tode* might also be directed to English and American translators of Heidegger.

The few comments about Heidegger by Emmanuel Levinas are essential and constitute *one of the most helpful introductions to Heidegger's thinking in English at the time of the publication of EB*. Levinas makes more sense of Heidegger's fundamental words than any other commentator, even though the translators of Wahl's book have obscured some of the light Levinas was able to shed. At the outset, he observes that "the only existentialist is Heidegger himself, who rejects the term" (p. 48). On the fundamental distinction in Heidegger's thinking between *Sein* (be[-ing] = *être*) and *Seiende* (being = *étant*), and on the nature of *Dasein* (existence = *l'existant*), Levinas in his lucid, lyrical way says the following:

> I think that the new philosophical "twist" originated by Heidegger consists in distinguishing between *Being* [*être*] and *being* [*étant*],[104] and in giving to *Being* the relation, the movement, the efficacy which until then resided in the existent [*existant*]. Existentialism is to experience and think existence—the verb "to be" [*l'être-verbe*][105]—as event, an event which neither produces that which exists, nor is the action of what exists upon another object. It is the pure fact of existing [*fait d'exister*] which is event. The fact of existing, until then pure and reticent and tranquil; the fact which, in the Aristotelian notion of the act, remained quite serene and equal to itself among all the adventures that befall a being [*étant*]; the fact which was transcendent to all *being* [*étant*], but which was not itself the event of transcending; this fact appears in existentialism as the adventure itself, containing History itself.

When Heidegger says "being-in-the-world" and "being-for-death" and "being-with-others," what he adds that is new to our millenary knowledge of our mortality, our social nature, and our presence in the world,[106] is that these prepositions—"in [*dans*]," "for [*pour*]," and "with [*avec*]"—are in the root of the verb "to be" [*être*] (as "ex" is in the root of the word "to exist" [*de 'exister'*]); that these phrases are not created by us as existents placed in determinate conditions; that they are not even mathematically contained, as in Husserl, in our nature [*nature*] or our essence as existents [*notre essence d'existants*]; that they are neither contingent nor necessary attributes of our substance [*substance*]; and finally, that they *are* articulations of the event of *being* [*être*], heretofore considered to be tranquil, simple, equal to itself. One may say that existentialism consists in feeling and thinking that the verb "to be" is transitive [*que le verbe être est transitif*] . . .

Thus, in existential philosophy there are no longer any linking verbs [*copules*]. The copulas express the very event of being [*être*].

I think that a certain use of the verb "to be"—which does not mean that I give to Being a purely verbal signification—corresponding to this notion of transitiveness, is more characteristic of this philosophy than the evocation of ecstasies [*exstases*], anxiety [*souci*], or death, which are in themselves as Nietzschean or Christian as they are existentialist. (pp. 50–51)

In this elegant passage, Levinas summarizes the major theme of Heidegger's *analytique*, points to the profound stimulus of his thinking in Aristotle, and emphasizes his concentrated efforts to illuminate the language of be[-ing].[107] In particular, in his discussion of the verb "be," Levinas sees the close connection between Heidegger's fundamental ontology and language.

Finally, in the last of the secondary literature in English that appeared before *EB* was published, there was a suitable, albeit brief, introduction to the sense of Heidegger's fundamental words in renderings that still have the potential of making his thought accessible to the English-speaking reader. I now turn to the book that ostensibly first introduced the English-speaking audience to Heidegger's thought.

NOTES

1. Martin Heidegger, *Existence and Being* (Chicago: Regnery, 1949) [= *EB*].

2. Gilbert Ryle, review of *Sein und Zeit*, by Martin Heidegger, *Mind* 29 (1929): 355-70.

3. See, for example, J. O. Urmson's sketch of Ryle in *The Encyclopedia of Philosophy*, ed. Paul Edwards, 8 vols. (New York: Macmillan, 1967), 7: 271.

4. Charles H. Malik, *The Metaphysics of Time in the Philosophies of A. N. Whitehead and M. Heidegger* (Harvard University, 1937); and A. B. Downing, *A Study of the Conception of Conscience in the Philosophies of Martin Heidegger and Karl Jaspers* (University of Manchester, 1947).

5. A peculiarity of English is that when the infinitive is named, it is preceded by the particle 'to'. This does not happen in German (or Greek). In German syntax, the infinitive is sometimes preceded by *zu* (to), but *zu* is not part of the infinitive. The bare infinitive or base form of "to be" in German is *sein*, which is composed of the root '*sei-*' and the suffix '*-en*', the 'e' of which has been absorbed in combination with the root to produce its final form *sein* (*sei[e]n*). In English, the bare infinitive of the verb "to be" is 'be', without the particle 'to'. Hence, my rendering of *Sein* with be[-ing], which sounds as /be/ but is read as including the suffix.

6. Gilbert Ryle, "Martin Heidegger: *Sein und Zeit*, Afterword," *Journal of the British Society for Phenomenology* 1, no. 3 (1969): 13-14 (with excerpts from a letter by Edmund Husserl to G. Daws Hicks, March 15, 1930).

7. The importance of the review is indicated by Wolfe Mays's decision to reprint it, in 1969, in the inaugural issue of the only British journal devoted to phenomenology.

8. Alfred Delp, "Modern German Existentialism," the *Modern Schoolman* 14 (1936): 62-66.

9. Rosa Obermeyer Mayreder, *Der letzte Gott* (Stuttgart: Cotta, 1933). Also in the air was another novel of the same name by Claude Farrère, originally published in French as *Le Dernier Dieu* (Paris: Flammarion, 1926), which had been translated into German in 1928. In the late 1930s, Heidegger wrote a series of brief reflections which were published eventually, in 1989, as *Beiträge zur Philosophie (Vom Ereignis)*, GA 65. One of the sections of the book is entitled "Der letzte Gott" (pp. 405-17).

10. Marjorie Glicksman, "A Note on the Philosophy of Heidegger," *Journal of Philosophy* 35 (1938): 93-104. It is noteworthy that two of the most important early introductions to Heidegger in English were written by novices. Both Ryle and Glicksman were only in their late 20s when they wrote their pieces on Heidegger.

11. Heidegger actually wrote a sentence that runs "Das Nichts selbst nichtet" (*Was ist Metaphysik*, GA 9: 114), which means: "No-thing nihilates of its own." Yanked from their context, the words Glicksman gives as Heidegger's own are indeed meaningless. But what she quotes is not what Heidegger wrote, and *nichten* does not mean "to nothing."

12. The expression "Welt weltet . . ." is from "Die Ursprung des Kunstwerkes" (1935–36), GA 5: 30. In the context of Heidegger's discussion of world in that text, the verb *welten* means "make human." "Welt weltet" translates as "the world makes for things human" or "the world makes for existence." A literal exchange of dictionary entries produces the redundant nonsense Professor Glicksman offers up. Closer attention to Heidegger's thought in the lecture she had heard in Freiburg in 1935 might have led her to consider the following. *Welt* is immediately cognate with our English word *world*, since both derive from the same Indogermanic root *w-ro-*, man, which is also the source of the Latin noun *vir* (man). The root itself is a derivative of yet another Indogermanic root, *wei-*, which means vital force (*vis*). Thus the words *Welt* and *world* speak about life (*wei-*), in particular, human life (*w-ro-*). It should be no surprise, then, that the first entry for 'world' in the *Oxford English Dictionary* is "human existence." This, the basic sense of 'world' is preserved in the great opening line of Andrew Marvell's poem "To His Coy Mistress": "Had we but world enough and time. . . ." *Welten* and existence (*Dasein*) are therefore coextensive. *Welten* means to exist, to be human; conversely, existing is worlding. In short, there is a world only where there is (*es gibt*) existence (*Dasein*). All of this makes Heidegger's earlier characterization of the meaning of existence in *Sein und Zeit* even more transparent: to exist is to be in a world [*In-der-Welt-Sein*].

13. GA 2: 56–57, 71–72, 156.

14. Citing GA 2, p. 256. Heidegger's phrase as printed is "Sich-vorweg-schon-sein-in-(der-Welt-) als Sein-bei (innerweltlich begegnendem Seienden)."

15. Marjorie Grene, *Dreadful Freedom* (Chicago: Chicago University Press, 1948), reprinted without any change except the addition of a new preface as *Introduction to Existentialism* (Chicago: Chicago University Press, 1959). Page references to the body of the text remain the same in both editions. Substantial parts of the book had been published in a series of articles in *Kenyon Review*: 9, no. 1 (1947): 48–69 ("Kierkegaard: The Philosophy"); 9, no. 2 (1947):167–85 (L'Homme Est Une Passion Inutile: Sartre and Heidegger"); and 9, no. 3 (1947): 382–99 ("Two More Existentialists: Karl Jaspers and Gabriel Marcel").

16. Once again, Heidegger did not write the sentence "Das Nichts nichtet" in *Was ist Metaphysik?* There are two places in that text where those words begin a sentence: "Das Nichts selbst nichtet" and "Das Nichts nichtet unausgesetzt, ohne daß wir mit dem Wissen, darin wir uns alltäglich bewegen, um dieses Geschehen eigentlich wissen" (GA 9: 114, 116)—"Nothing nihilates of its own" and "No-thing nihilates without fail, but without our really knowing about this event, in the sense of the kind of knowing that helps us get by on a day to day basis."

17. GA 2: 358. "Der Gewissensruf hat den Charakter des *Anrufs* des Daseins auf sein eigenstes Selbstseinkönnen und das in der Weise des *Aufrufs* zum eigensten Schuldigsein."—"The summoning of conscience has the character of a challenge by existence to its very own being able to be, and <is one> that <occurs> in the manner of an *appeal* to its very own being indebted." Words enclosed between <> have been interpolated to make Heidegger's meaning clearer.

18. It is notable that the Japanese, whose language has such a different structure than German, have been able to make the transition to Heidegger's thought more readily than English-speaking readers. On Heidegger's reception in Japan, see *Heidegger and Asian Thought*, ed. Graham Parkes (Honolulu: University of Hawaii Press, 1987); Parkes's article, "Heidegger and Japanese Thought: How Much Did He Know and When Did He Know It?" in *Heidegger: Critical Assessments*, ed. Christopher Macann, 4 vols. (London: Routledge, 1992), 4: 377-406; and Reinhard May, *Heidegger's Hidden Sources: East Asian Influences on His Work* (London: Routledge, 1996).

19. Julius S. Bixler, "The Contribution of *Existenz-Philosophie*," *Harvard Theological Review* 33 (1940): 35-63.

20. Walter Cerf, "An Approach to Heidegger's Ontology," *Philosophy and Phenomenological Research* 1 (1940/41): 177-90.

21. On the analogy of translating *Kritik* with 'critique', I translate *Analytik* with 'analytique'.

22. Julius Kraft, "The Philosophy of Existence," *Philosophy and Phenomenological Research* 1 (1940/41): 339-58; Fritz Kaufmann, "Discussion Concerning Kraft's 'Philosophy of Existence'," in ibid., pp. 359-64; and Julius Kraft, "In Reply to Kaufmann's Critical Remarks about My 'Philosophy of Existence'," in ibid., pp. 364-65. During the years preceding the translation of *Sein und Zeit*, in 1962, *Philosophy and Phenomenological Research* published fifteen papers on Heidegger. The journal is therefore responsible in great part for setting the tone of how Heidegger was received by English-speaking and especially American readers.

23. William H. Werkmeister, "An Introduction to Heidegger's 'Existential Philosophy'," *Philosophy and Phenomenological Research* 2 (1941/42): 79-87. See p. 79 for the quotation.

24. Heidegger's work with French translators was another matter, since his French was evidently quite good, but he was faced with problems regarding the translations of his texts into English, since he had to rely on what others told him about them. See Heidegger's letter to John Macquarrie on the first translation of *Sein und Zeit*, in Macquarrie's *Heidegger and Christianity* (London: SCM Press, 1994), pp. 111-12. The German text is included.

25. Werkmeister reviewed many of the first translations of Heidegger's in *The Personalist:An Introduction to Metaphysics*, in 1960; *Essays in Metaphysics: Identity and Difference*, in 1961; *Kant and the Problem of Metaphysics*, in 1962; *Being and Time*, in 1963; and *Discourse on Thinking*, in 1966. He was also the author of several papers on Heidegger published in the 1970s. Werkmeister's reviews and reflections on Heidegger have been published as *Martin Heidegger on the Way*, ed. Richard T. Hull (Amsterdam: Rodopi, 1996).

26. On this question, see John Macquarrie's essay, "Heidegger's Language and the Problems of Translation," in *Heidegger: Critical Assessments*, ed. Macann, 3: 50-57. Macquarrie, who spent seven years working with Edward Robinson on the first English translation of *Sein und Zeit* (p. 50), frames the question in this way: "Could there be anything but a German-speaking Heidegger?" He is not as sure about this as many of the commentators I have cited seem to have been. Macquarrie is "content with pointing out the problem." In general, he is not among those who consider Heidegger's language to be difficult and obscure. He concludes that

> much of the criticism of Heidegger's language, which has been made from time to time, has been quite unjustified. When carefully studied, his language is seen to be an impressive and consistent structure.... *Sein und Zeit* is not the morass of verbal mystification that it is sometimes said to be. On the contrary, it is a work of quite extraordinary power and originality, expressed in a language which is never lacking in precision, though it may be complex. (p. 56)

27. Helene Weiss, "The Greek Conceptions of Time and Being in the Light of Heidegger's Philosophy," *Philosophy and Phenomenological*

Research 2 (1941/42): 173-87. As an orientation to Heidegger's thinking, the article is still an essential source. Now available for more than fifty years, it is not cited often, however.

28. Weiss notes that the Eleatic stranger, who utters the guiding question of Plato's dialogue, is "the representative of true philosophy in its highest rank text" (p. 176). The text of *Sophist* 244a serves as the epigraph of *Sein und Zeit* (GA 2: 1).

29. Karl Löwith, "M. Heidegger and F. Rosenzweig or Temporality and Eternity," *Philosophy and Phenomenological Research* 3 (1942/43): 53-77. When he wrote the article, Löwith was associated with the Hartford Seminary Foundation, which ten years later accepted Johannes Hanselmann's dissertation, *Martin Heidegger's Fundamental Ontology and Its Theological Implications*. Hanselmann's doctoral paper was among the first dissertations on Heidegger in English. Löwith's influence in promoting Heidegger as a theologian was considerable.

30. See Löwith's *My Life in Germany before and after 1933: A Report* (London: Athlone, 1994).

31. No translator of his article is given.

32. The passage is from *Sein und Zeit* (GA 2: 204): "Seiendes, dem es als In-der-Welt-sein um sein Sein selbst geht, hat eine ontologische Zirkelstruktur." The sense of the sentence is this: "Existence is <that sort of> be-ing to which it belongs, as <it does> to *be* in a world, to be at stake for itself."

33. Löwith refers the reader to GA 2, §§ 12 and 28.

34. Here Löwith quotes from GA 2: 346: "Der existenziale Entwurf eines eigentlichen Seins zum Tode muß daher die Momente eines solchen Seins herausstellen, die es als Verstehen des Todes im Sinne des nichtflüchtigen und nichtverdeckenden Seins zu der gekennzeichneten Möglichkeit konstituieren."

35. Quoted in John van Buren, *The Young Heidegger: Rumor of the Hidden King* (Bloomington: Indiana University Press, 1994), p. 154. Heidegger emphasizes the root of the word 'theologian', thus presenting himself as a student of the god, not a church dogmatist or practitioner of the science of god. Moreover, the words are presented in quotation marks, indicating the need for interpreting them. It seems to me that Heidegger identifies himself in this way to Löwith primarily to distance himself from academic philosophy (metaphysics).

36. It is interesting to compare this article with what Löwith said forty years later in Heidelberg on the occasion of Heidegger's eightieth birthday. See "The Nature of Man and the World of Nature: For Heidegger's 80th

Birthday," *Southern Journal of Philosophy* 8, no. 4 (1970): 37-46, which includes excerpts of letters from Heidegger to Löwith during the years 1919-1925, including the letter containing the sentence "I am a Christian theo*logian*."

37. James Collins, "The German Neoscholastic Approach to Heidegger," *Modern Schoolman* 21 (1944): 143-52. Collins mentions, among others, Karl Rahner and Edith Stein. James Collins, who was then at the Catholic University of America, was among the first to write about existentialism as a movement or school in contemporary philosophy, in *The Existentialists: A Critical Study* (Chicago: Regnery, 1952), especially pp. 168-210.

38. Alfred Delp, *Tragische Existenz: Zur Philosophie Martin Heideggers* (Freiburg: Herder, 1935). Delp's paper from 1936, which is reviewed above, may be assumed to reflect his views in this book.

39. He refers to Ertel's "Von der Phänomenologie und jüngeren Lebensphilosophie zur Existentialphilosophie M. Heideggers," *Philosophisches Jahrbuch der Görresgesellschaft* 51 (1938): 1-28.

40. Caspar Nink, S.J., "Grundbegriffe der Philosophie Martin Heideggers," *Philosophisches Jahrbuch des Görresgesellschaft* 45, no. 2 (1932): 129-58; and Adolf Dyroff, "Glossen über Sein und Zeit, in *Philosophia Perennis*, ed. Fritz von Rintelen, 2 vols. (Regensburg: Habbel, 1930), 2: 773-96.

41. E. Hans Freund, "Man's Fall in M. Heidegger's Philosophy," *Journal of Religion* 24 (1944): 180-87.

42. Heidegger's sentence "Und weil Dasein wesenhaft je seine Möglichkeit ist, *kann* dieses Seiende in seinem Sein sich selbst 'wählen', gewinnen, es kann sich verlieren, bzw. nie und nur 'scheinbar' gewinnen" (GA : 57) is rendered by Freund/Smart: "Human existence can choose the true nature of itself; it can also lose itself or only seemingly achieve itself" (p. 181). Here is an especially egregious example of just how poorly Heidegger was first rendered into English early on.

43. Paul Tillich, "Existential Philosophy," *Journal of the History of Ideas* 5 (1944): 44-70.

44. Paul Tillich, *Theology of Culture* (New York: Oxford University Press, 1959), pp. 76-111.

45. Werner Brock, *An Introduction to Contemporary German Philosophy* (Cambridge: Cambridge University Press, 1935); and Herbert Marcuse, *Reason and Revolution* (New York: Oxford University Press, 1941). Brock was Heidegger's assistant at the University of Freiburg from 1931-33. In 1934, he fled Nazi Germany and moved to Cambridge University on a research fellowship. Brock who, of course, was the editor of the first trans-

lations of Heidegger in English, returned to the University of Freiburg in 1951 and taught there until 1969. He died in Emmendingen, Germany, in 1974.

46. Part of a sentence is translated:". . . wie muß das endliche Seiende, das wir Mensch nennen, seinem innersten Wesen nach sein, damit es überhaupt offen sein kann zu Seiendem, das es nicht selbst ist, das sich daher von sich aus muß zeigen können?" (GA 3: 43). Tillich: "How must that finite being we call man be equipped in order to be aware of a kind of Being which is not the same as he himself?" (p. 60). I translate:". . . how must that finite kind of be-ing, which we call man, be in its innermost nature, so that it can be open in general to a kind of be-ing that it itself is not, <but> which must <itself> be able to appear out of itself on its own?"

47. Ralph Harper, "Two Existential Interpretations," *Philosophy and Phenomenological Research* 5 (1944/45): 392-97. Harper's book, *Existentialism: A Theory of Man*, appeared in 1944.

48. Hannah Arendt, "What Is Existenz Philosophy?" *Partisan Review* 13 (1946): 34-56 (esp. pp. 46-51). See William Barrett, *The Truants: Adventure among the Intellectuals* (Garden City, N.Y.: Anchor Books, 1982), p. 102. Barrett reports that Arendt wrote the present article in German and asked Barrett to translate it for her. He adds that Arendt insisted on retaining the German word *Existenz* in the title in opposition to his recommendation to translate it. Arendt, whose first language was German, admitted that she gave all of the texts she wrote in English to various editors for "Englishing." See, for example, Mary McCarthy's "Editor's Postface" to Hannah Arendt, *The Life of the Mind*, 2 vols. (New York: Harcourt Brace Jovanovich, 1978), 2: 243.

49. "Hegel was for us the last ancient philosopher. . . . With Schelling modern philosophy [of the individual] begins" (p. 39).

50. Quoting GA 2: 157: "Allein die '*Substanz*' des Menschen ist nicht der Geist als die Synthese von Seele und Leib, sondern die *Existenz*." In the passage preceding this sentence, Heidegger makes reference to the well-known distinction between *Essenz* and *Existenz*, but in order to say that it and the concepts based on the distinction must be "interpreted existentially [*existential interpretiert*]." Moreover, in this context, it is one thing to say that "*die 'Substanz' des Menschen ist . . . die Existenz*" and quite another thing to say that "*Das 'Wesen' des Daseins liegt in seiner Existenz*" (GA 2, p. 56). Arendt's explanation of Heidegger's meaning in §25 ("The Approach to the Existential [*existentialen*] Question of the 'Who' of Existence") must be understood in the context of what he had already explained in §9 ("The Theme of the *Analytique* of Existence").

51. Arendt is quoting part of a sentence from GA 2: 18. Here is the context of the passage:

Die existentiale Analytik ihrerseits aber ist letzlich existentiell, d.h. ontisch verwurzelt. Nur wenn das philosophisch-forschende Fragen selbst als Seinsmöglichkeit des je existierenden Daseins existentiell ergriffen ist, besteht die Möglichkeit einer Erschließung der Existentialität der Existenz und damit die Möglichkeit der Inangriffnahme einer zureichend fundierten ontologischen Problematik überhaupt. Damit ist aber auch der ontische Vorrang der Seinsfrage deutlich geworden.

[But for its own part the ex-sistential *analytique* is ultimately *existential*, that is, *ontic*. Only if philosophically inquisitive questioning is itself grasped existentially as a possibility of the be[-ing] of every extant existence is a disclosure of the ek-sistentiality of life possible and therewith the possibility in general of getting hold of an adequately grounded ontological problematic. And with that the ontical priority of the question of be[-ing] has become clear.]

52. Rendering *existenzial* with 'ek-sistential' reminds us of Heidegger's discussion of the ecstatic or temporal nature of existence.

53. See Hannah Arendt, "Martin Heidegger ist achtzig Jahre alt," *Merkur* 10 (1969): 893-902, translated by Albert Hofstadter as "Martin Heidegger at Eighty," *New York Review of Books* 17 (October 1971): 50-54. On aspects of the personal relationship between Heidegger and Arendt, see Elzbieta Etinger's journalistic and sensationalistic account, *Hannah Arendt: Martin Heidegger* (New Haven, Conn.: Yale University Press, 1995) and Rüdiger Safranski's intellectual biography of Heidegger, *Martin Heidegger: Between Good and Evil* (Cambridge: Harvard University Press, 1998), pp. 136-42, 180, 255, 266-67, 371-87.

54. David Baumgardt, "Rationalism and the Philosophy of Despair: Pre-Nazi German Ethics, 1913-1933," *Sewanee Review* 55 (1947): 223-37.

55. GA 9: 113 ff.

56. Baumgardt cites GA 2: 276 passim.

57. "But what can existence tell about the uncanniness of its outcast be[-ing]?" GA 2: 277.

58. *Philosophy and Phenomenological Research* 8 (1947/48): 23-54.

59. "*Im Sein* des Daseins liegt schon das 'Zwischen' mit Bezug auf

Geburt und Tod. Keineswegs dagegen '*ist*' das Dasein in einem Zeitpunkt wirklich und außerdem noch von dem Nichtwirklichen seiner Geburt und seines Tod 'umgeben'." GA 2: 495.

60. Merlan cites GA 2: 448. "Das eigentliche Gewesen-*sein* nennen wir die *Wiederholung*."

61. Citing GA 2: 436, 449, 509.

62. Merlan cites GA 2: 377. The complete sentence runs: "Grundsein besagt demnach, des eigensten Seins von Grund auf *nie* mächtig sein." — "Thus to be <your own> ground means precisely *never* having power over your very own be[-ing] from the ground up."

63. Eric Unger, "Existentialism," *Nineteenth Century and After* 142 (1947): 278-88, and 143 (1948): 28-37. Quotations in the text are taken from the first article.

64. Stefan Shimanski, "On Meeting a Philosopher," *London Tribune* (September 19, 1947): 10-11, reprinted in *Partisan Review* 15 (1948): 506-509.

65. In *Sein und Zeit*, Heidegger distinguishes between Dilthey's notion of *Leben* (living) and his notion of *Existenz* (a way of life). GA 2, §§ 10 and 43 b.

66. The traditional arguments for and against realism and for and against the idealist position are based on the same metaphysical prejudice. See Heidegger's first (1912) published paper, "The Problem of Reality in Modern Philosophy" (GA 1: 1-15), translated by Phillip Bossert, *Journal of the British Society for Phenomenology* 4 (1973): 64-71. See Jonathan Rée's lucid discussion of the question of the reality of the world in Heidegger's thought in *Heidegger* (New York: Routledge, 1999), pp. 29-30.

67. GA 2: 56. The well-known line appears early in *Sein und Zeit* (§ 9) in the context of Heidegger's discussion of the traditional medieval contrast between *essentia* and *existentia*, but taken out of context, the sentence is misleading as a statement of Heidegger's position. This was the case for Sartre and many other existentialists.

68. Stefan Schimanski, "Martin Heidegger and Existentialism," *Listener* 39 (January 29, 1948): 175-76.

69. Günther [Stern] Anders, "On the Pseudo-Concreteness of Heidegger's Philosophy," *Philosophy and Phenomenological Research* 8 (1947/48): 337-71.

70. James Agee gave voice to the ontological sense of Heidegger's term *Sorge* in "Knoxville: Summer 1915," the prologue to his novel *A Death in the Family* (New York: Avon Books, 1938): "By some chance, here they are,

all on this earth; and who shall ever tell the sorrow of being on this earth ..." (p. 14).

71. Heidegger's choice of the latinate word *Struktur* is deliberate. The word is based on *structum*, the past participle of the verb *struere*, which means to build, dispose, set in order, or arrange. A structure in this sense is something that has been set in order and is disposed in a certain way. The *Destruktion*, or dismantling of what has been ordered or set up in a certain way, specifically the *Destruktion* of the history of ontology (as metaphysics), was to have been the task of the projected second half of *Sein und Zeit*.

72. The infinitive of εἰμί (am) (the first person singular, active indicative) is εἶναι (be).

73. Later in the essay, Anders speaks incomprehensibly of "'Sorge'-acts" (p. 358).

74. Earlier, Anders noted that the "for" in "for a Dasein" "is not identical with the classical 'for' in the 'Genesis' according to which Nature has been created for man" (p. 337, n. 2). Here "for" has the sense of "in the eyes of" man, rather than "for the sake of or use and purposes of" man.

75. In the "Postscript" (1943) to *Was ist Metaphysik?* (GA 9: 303-12) Heidegger makes use of a variety of related terms in his discussion of no-thing (*Nichts*). Some were in common use in German, some have technical resonances in the literature of philosophy, and some are Heidegger's neologisms (marked with an * in what follows). Occasionally, I have provided an English neologism (marked with an ** in what follows) when it has been required. The words and their place of first appearance in the "Postscript" are as follows: the pronoun *nichts* (nothing, nothing at all) (p. 105) and its related noun **das Nichts* (no-thing) (p. 105); the noun **das Nicht* (the not) (p. 108); the verb **nichten* (to nihilate) (p. 114), its related present participle and adjective **nichtend* (nihilating) (p. 114), and the nouns **die Nichtung* (nihilation) (p. 114) and *das Nichten* (nihilating) (p. 115); the noun **das Nichthaft* (the not-like) (p. 108), which is based on an implied neologism, the adjective **nichthaft*; the verb *vernichten* (to annihilate) (p. 113) and the noun *die Vernichtung* (annihilation) (p. 113); two composite nouns *das Nicht-Seiende* (what is not be-ing; i.e. what is other than one kind of be-ing or another) (p. 108) and *das Nichtseiend* (not-be-ing; i.e. what is not be-ing at the time) (p. 119); the nouns **das Nichtige* (the null and void) (p. 106) and *die Nichtigkeit* (nullity) (p. 119), from the adjective *nichtig* (null, invalid, void); the verb *verneinen* (to negate) (p. 109), its past participle *verneint* (negated) (p. 109), the related adjective *verneinend* (negative, negating) (p. 113), which is based

on the present participle of *verneinen,* and five related nouns: *die Verneinung* (negation, in the sense of what is accomplished by placing a negative sign in front of a term in symbolic logic or mathematics) (p. 107), **das Verneint* (the negated, the **negatived) (108), **die Verneintheit* (negativity) (p. 108), **das Zu-verneinend* (what is doing the negating) (p. 116), and *das Verneinen* (negating) (p. 117); the noun **das Verneinbar* (the **negatable), based on a neologism, the adjective *verneinbar* (**negatable) (p. 116); the adverb *nein* (no) used as an interjection (p. 118), and its related noun **das Nein* (the No) (p. 117); and the adverb *kein* (no, none, or not any) (p. 112).

76. Nicola Abbagnano, "Outline of a Philosophy of Existence," *Philosophy and Phenomenological Research* 9 (1948/49): 200-11. The text was translated for Abbagnano by Marian Taylor.

77. See Bruno Maiorca, *Bibliografia degli Scritti di e su Nicola Abbagnano (1923-1973)* (Turin: Giappichelli, 1974), p. 52.

78. Frederick C. Copleston, "The Tragedy of Man," *Listener* 38 (August 7, 1947): 224-25, and "Existentialism," *Philosophy* 1 (1948): 19-37.

79. In this connection, see George J. Seidel's paper "A Key to Heidegger's *Beiträge*," *Gregorianum* 76, no. 2 (1995): 365.

80. Frank McEachran, "The Existential Philosophy (Study of Kierkegaard, Heidegger, Jaspers, and Sartre)," *Hibbert Journal* 46 (1948): 232-38.

81. Karl Löwith, "Heidegger: Problem and Background of Existentialism," *Social Research* 15 (1948): 345-69 (cited as A), and "Background and Problem of Existentialism," *Actas del Primer Congresso Nacional de Filosofía* (Mendoza: Platt, 1949), pp. 390-99 (cited as B). The volume in which Löwith's lecture was published contains a letter from Heidegger to the president of the conference, I. Fernando Cruz. See "Adhesion del Professor Martin Heidegger," pp. 115-16. To my knowledge, until now, this letter has not been included in any of the bibliographies of Heidegger's writings.

82. "Das 'Wesen' des Daseins liegt in seiner Existenz." GA 2: 56.

83. Vincent E. Smith, "Existentialism and Existence," *Thomist* 11 (1948): 141-96 and 297-329, especially chapter 3, pp. 160-71.

84. Alphonse de Waelhens, *La Philosophie de Martin Heidegger* (Louvain: Institut Supérieur de Philosophie, 1942).

85. GA 2: 190: "Existence is such a kind of be-ing that, as worldiness, what is at stake for it is itself." When Heidegger constructs a hyphenated term, he indicates a unity of thought expressed by the individual words which translate it. The mere stringing together of English synonyms for the German words to form a hyphenated construction does not necessarily provide a way into Heidegger's thought. In general, there is no formula for translating

hyphenated words which include -*sein* or *Sein*-. Sometimes Heidegger means the base form 'be'; at other times, he means the English infinitive 'to be'; yet again, he may mean 'the be[-ing]' of any sort of be-ing. The suffix -*sein* often means "-ness"; for example, *Was-sein* may be translated with 'whatness'.

86. In 1948, a translation of a number of essays by José Ortega y Gasset appeared in English. In a footnote to one of them, "In Search of Goethe from Within," Ortega says he believes that he should be given priority for a number of ideas that appear in *Sein und Zeit*, including "the interpretation of truth as *aletheia*." *The Dehumanization of Art and Other Writings on Art and Culture* (Garden City, N.Y.: Doubleday, 1948), p. 136, n. 3. See Heidegger's reflection "Begegnungen mit Ortega y Gasset" (1955), in GA 13: 127-29.

87. W. Tudor Jones, *Contemporary Thought in Germany*, 2 vols. (New York: Knopf, 1930), 2: 116-20, 163.

88. Brock, *An Introduction to Contemporary German Philosophy*, pp. 109-17, 132-33.

89. William Barrett, *What Is Existentialism?* (New York: Partisan Review, 1947) (Partisan Review Series #2). At the time he wrote the monograph, Barrett was also an editor at the *Partisan Review*. Page references are to the 1964 edition. See following note.

90. William Barrett, *What Is Existentialism?* (New York: Grove Press, 1964 [expanded edition]).

91. William Barrett, *Irrational Man: A Study in Existential Philosophy* (New York: Doubleday, 1958) and *The Illusion of Technique: A Search for Meaning in a Technological Civilization* (New York: Doubleday, 1978), both of which are still in print.

92. Barrett, *The Illusion of Technique*, pp. 255-56.

93. Guido de Ruggiero, *Existentialism: Disintegration of Man's Soul*, trans. E. M. Cocks (London: Secker and Warburg, 1946).

94. Jasper Hopkins's essay "What Is a Translation?" provides an excellent summary of the problems facing translators of philosophical works, but he does not see the philosophical nature of translation itself. Saint Anselm, *Anselm of Canterbury*, ed. Jasper Hopkins, 4 vols. (New York: Edward Mellen, 1976), 4: 141-48.

95. Ralph Harper, *Existentialism: A Theory of Man* (Cambridge: Cambridge University Press, 1948).

96. The sentence is from GA 2: 190. In Harper's translation, the sentence is conflated with "Das Seiende, dem es in seinem Sein um dieses selbst geht, verhält sich zu seinem Sein als seiner eigensten Möglichkeit" (GA 2:

57)—"The kind of be-ing that in its be[-ing] is at stake for itself is related to its be[-ing] as to its very own possibility."

97. The whole passage runs: "Und weil die Wesensbestimmung dieses Seienden nicht durch Angabe eines sachhaltigen Was vollzogen werden kann, sein Wesen vielmehr darin liegt, daß *es sein Sein als seiniges zu sein hat*, ist der Titel Dasein als reiner Seinsausdruck zur Bezeichnung dieses Seienden gewählt [emphasis added]" (GA 2: 16-17)—"And since an essential determination of this kind of be-ing cannot be accomplished by a statement of some factual what <about it>, its essence being rather that *it always has to be its own be[-ing]*, the term existence is chosen for the pure expression of the be[-ing] of the indication of this kind of be-ing."

98. "Das 'Wesen' dieses Seienden liegt in seinem Zu-sein. Das Was-sein (essentia) dieses Seienden muß, sofern überhaupt davon gesprochen werden kann, aus seinem Sein (existentia) begriffen werden" (GA 2: 56)—"The 'essence' of this kind of be-ing is in its to-be. Insofar as it can be spoken about at all, the what-ness (essentia) of this kind of be-ing must be grasped from its be[-ing]." In a marginal note to the last sentence, Heidegger wrote: "Aber dieses ist geschichtliches In-der-Welt-sein" (GA 2: 56, n. a)—"But this is historical worldliness."

99. Jean Wahl, *A Short History of Existentialism* (New York: Philosophical Library, 1949), trans. Forrest Williams and Stanley Maron. See also Jean Wahl's Sorbonne course, *Mots, Mythes et Réalité dans la Philosophie de Heidegger* (Paris: Centre de Documentation Universitaire, 1961).

100. The book was first published as *Petite Histoire de L'Existentialisme* (Paris: Editions Club Maintenant, 1947), reprinted as *Esquisse pour une Histoire de l'Existentialisme* (Paris: Arche, 1949).

101. On Heidegger and French, see Henry Corbin's discussion of translation in his "Translator's Preface" to *Qu-est ce que la Métaphysique?* (Paris: Gallimard, 1938), pp. 9-17, for which Heidegger wrote the important "Prologue."

102. Wahl writes: "Si nous entendons par sagesse la communion de nous-mêmes avec les choses, la philosophie serait donc la conaissance de l'être dans le monde, non pas seulement de l'existant en tant qu'il est dirigé vers son avenir, et tel que le définit Kierkegaard, mais de l'existant en tant qu'il est en relation extatique avec le monde" (pp. 41-42). The translators turn "être dans le monde" (Wahl's translation of Heidegger's ontological term *In-der-Welt-sein*) into the plural form "beings-in-the-world." See Wahl, *Petite Histoire de L'Existentialisme*, p. 20.

103. Koyré has in mind Heidegger's *Vom Wesen der Wahrheit* (1930), GA 9: 177-238. The text was not available in a French translation until 1948.

104. The parenthetic gloss of *étant* with "thing or person" is an invention of the translators.

105. Levinas means, literally, "the *be* verb" or "the verb of be[-ing]."

106. Here Levinas's originality presents fresh problems of translation. What he understands by *In-der-Welt-sein* in his phrase "présence au monde" is a fine French rendering of Heidegger's term, but does not help us make it over in English.

107. Given the importance during the 1930s and 1940s of the French reading of Heidegger for the reception of Heidegger in America in the late 1940s, it would be important to take a closer look at the translation decisions of the French translators and those who translated the French commentators into English.

CHAPTER TWO

THE FIRST HEIDEGGER IN ENGLISH

TRANSLATION DECISIONS IN *EXISTENCE AND BEING* (1949)

Some remarks of Fr. Frederick Copleston's during a broadcast of the British Third Programme, which were published in the *Listener* in August 1947, prompted a letter from Stefan Schimanski, a young journalist with the *Manchester Guardian*.[1] In his letter, Schimanski recalls a meeting with Heidegger, in June 1946, that was the basis for his article, "On Meeting a Philosopher," which was published in the *London Tribune*.[2] Schimanski had planned to visit Heidegger the following month, but had to postpone his visit for more than a year.[3] His article in the *Tribune* that recounts his visits was reprinted in 1948 in the "Variety" section of *Partisan Review*.

Schimanski notes that Heidegger was "particularly emphatic to me on this point. 'They,' he told me, referring to certain Germans who had objected to his lecturing again, 'never understood my philosophy. . . .'" Heidegger had recently been banned from teaching at the University of Freiburg because of involvement with National Socialism.

Schimanski then mentions the four texts that were later scheduled to appear in *Existence and Being*[4]: "And when the essays which Heidegger gave me and which have now been translated and taken into production are published, they, I hope, finally dispel that impression." He reports that "the second part of *Time and Being* [sic] has been written." Just why he gets the title wrong here and in a piece he wrote for the *Listener* in 1948 warrants a question. Is this just a mistake or had Heidegger spoken to Schimanski about a work called *Zeit und Sein*? In fact, a lecture entitled "Zeit und Sein" was given many years later, in January 1962, but Schimanski's reference may have been to the concluding part of *Sein und Zeit* (part 1, division 3), which was announced by Heidegger but not included in the published version of *Sein und Zeit*.[5]

Schimanski's letter in the *Listener* concludes with the statement: "I cannot help feeling that Fr. Copleston's remarks would have been more balanced if he had mentioned the lamentable situation in which so distinguished a scholar finds himself in this third year of liberation from spiritual oppression." Copleston's reply to Schimanski's letter was published the following week.[6] Oddly enough, Copleston also refers to *Time and Being*, while in the transcript of his broadcast, which initiated the correspondence, he writes about *Sein und Zeit*.

Schimanski's letter sheds light on the genesis of *EB*. He is credited with having brought the four essays included in it from Heidegger's *Hütte* to London for translation. Evidently the translations were rather hastily completed by R. F. C. Hull, Alan Crick, and Douglas Scott. In his conversations with Schimanski, Heidegger is reported to have said: "I am not concerned with Existence. My book is called *Time and Being* [sic], not 'Existence and Being'. For me the haunting question is and has been, not man's existence, but that of being-in-totality and as such." What had Heidegger actually said? Does the term 'existence' translate *Existenz* or *Dasein*? Schimanski uses the expression "human being" in the context of suggesting that "Heidegger's philosophy begins, in fact, where that of Sartre ends." This is an astonishing statement from someone who was Heidegger's link between Germany, from which he was in exile, and the United Kingdom, where his first English translations were about to be printed by Vision Press in

London. Like most commentators, Schimanski had confused existence (*Dasein*), a particular kind of life (*Existenz*), and living (*Leben*). Unfortunately, matters are not improved when Schimanski says correctly in the next sentence that "by existence Heidegger means man's determination to 'stand out into the truth of being'," since we are not certain whether he is translating *Existenz* or *Dasein*.

At one point in the discussions between the two men that Schimanski recounts in his article in the *Tribune,* Heidegger is reported to have said that "God is absent from the world." Schimanksi paraphrases Heidegger: "But absence, as he stated with emphasis, does not mean nonexistence. It means not being present." It is not known what Heidegger actually said then, but, in 1949, in his "Introduction" to *What Is Metaphysics?* he claimed that, like things, God "is"—but does not exist. Only the human kind of be-ing exists. Schimanski adds: "To Heidegger, <the possibility of a God and the possibility of man's dignity> reside in being as such. Being is above the human and above the divine. The truth of its being—that is the meaning of being—prepares for the acceptance of God. . . ."[7] Unfortunately, in his attempt to clarify the sense of God's absence from the world, Schimanski confuses the meaning of *Sein* and *Seiende*. When he writes about the truth of "its being," he has turned be[-ing] into something that "is be-ing" in some sense. In doing so, Heidegger's efforts to elucidate the meaning of be[-ing] as such are laid waste.

Schimanski's article concludes with a discussion of Heidegger's language. He believes that if Heidegger's "task and destiny" had had a more favorable outcome and that "if his message had been transmitted less cryptically, perhaps all these misrepresentations would never have arisen. It has been said that it requires a new language to decipher his thought." In the very next sentence, however, he adds: "But Heidegger can also be crystal clear." He is certainly correct here. In fact, apart from an occasional lapse in precision of expression, which can be found in every writer, Heidegger's prose is directly accessible. Any of his texts can be translated clearly into English. Yet, from the beginning, commentators have charged that Heidegger's language is difficult. As I have been arguing, I believe this is a cover for the difficulty his readers (if they have read Heidegger's texts) and translators have had with his thought, most notably the traces of it found in the words *Sein, Seiende, Dasein*, and *Existenz*.

The essays included in *Existence and Being* were written between 1929 and 1943. The two Hölderlin studies were translated by Douglas Scott and the so-called "metaphysical" essays were co-translated by R. F. C. Hull and Alan Crick.[8] The volume was edited by Werner Brock who provided extensive introductory material. In several of the notes to *What Is Metaphysics?* (nn. 15, 26, 31), the translators admit to relying on the French translation by Henry Corbin (1931) and Alexandre Koyré's introduction to the French translation. Brock's contribution to their translation decisions is not known. While Brock's usage in his lengthy introduction and overview of *Sein und Zeit* is consistent with Hull et al., it is not always consistent with his own earlier usage in *An Introduction to Contemporary German Philosophy* (1935). In several instances in *EB*, he retreats from what were legitimate translations of Heidegger's fundamental words made fifteen years earlier.[9]

In a note to his "Brief Outline of the Career of M. Heidegger" at the beginning of *EB*, Brock makes a very perspicuous observation about Heidegger's language:

> *His employment of a new philosophic language arose probably first in connection with his intense study of Greek* and medieval philosophy, and with his endeavor to find an adequate terminology for the new problems he was analyzing; this tendency seems to have been strengthened by *his belief in the wisdom embodied in language*. It seems to me essentially to resemble the treatment of words by the modern German poets Stefan George and Rainer Maria Rilke who, likewise, felt incapable of expressing their visions and thought with the help of the traditional and generally accepted language. (p. 8, note, emphases added)

Brock indirectly suggests that some of Heidegger's fundamental words are translations of Greek words. For example, Brock says that "On the Essence of Truth" "contains a number of most elucidating notions," which include those of "truth (ἀλήθεια) as an 'uncovering' and of 'ex-sistence' as an 'ex-position' into an 'uncovering' as well as of 'being' (τὸ ὄν, *ens*), 'being as such' (τὸ ὄν ᾗ ὄν), 'being in the whole' (καθόλου), 'essence' (οὐσία, *essentia*, *substantia*) and 'Being' (τὸ εἶναι, οὐσία, τὸ ὄντως ὄν)" (p. 128). Regrettably, this list of "notions," which Brock says are "mostly introduced in passing" in the essay, are not clarified for the reader.

Giving excellent advice about reading Heidegger, Brock modestly hopes only that his "Account of 'Being and Time'" "may assist the reader with a sufficient knowledge of German to find his way better through the text of the original and also in order to make a philosophic discussion of Heidegger's problems possible, while 'Being and Time' is not available in an English translation" (p. 32, note). All the same, Brock does not elucidate the essential direction of Heidegger's thought. The synopsis of *Sein und Zeit* and the four essays founders on the mistranslation of Heidegger's four early fundamental words—*Sein*, *Seiende*, *Dasein*, and *Existenz*—as well as a number of other basic words that embody traces of his way of thinking.

Commenting on the "categories" of existence (*Existenzialia*), Brock explains: "The characteristics of 'Dasein' are not 'qualities,' but possible ways of 'Being.' Therefore the term 'Da-sein' is to express not its 'essence,' but its 'Being'; it means 'Being there'" (p. 15). In translating both *Seiende* and *Sein* with 'Being', however, Brock shows that he does not see the difference between "possible ways" of be-ing (*Seiende*) (first occurrence of 'Being' in the passage cited) and the be[-ing] (*Sein*) that makes any such ways of be-ing possible (second occurrence of the word 'Being' in the passage). The translation of *Da-sein* with 'Being-there' (third occurrence of 'Being'), which appears to include the sense of the second sense of 'Being' in the passage cited, only further confuses matters. Brock notes that "the term 'Existence [*Existenz*]' is applied exclusively to [*Da-sein*]" (p. 15). Just what the relation between the two words might be is not made clear, yet knowing this is essential to understanding the meaning of existence in Heidegger's philosophy. And what is the meaning of 'Being' (by that time regularly capitalized), which is invoked to explain how *Da-sein* "is"? Brock replies: "According to Heidegger, the concept of 'Being' is the most universal one.... At the same time it is obscure and indefinable; 'Being' cannot be comprehended as anything that is

(Seiendes).... 'Being' is not something like a being.... Yet 'Being' seems somehow an evident concept" (p. 12). Brock claims that his statements about 'Being' are "strictly based on 'Being and Time,' pp. 2-4" (p. 15, note). Given his work alongside Heidegger in Freiburg during the years after the publication of *Sein und Zeit*, who should have doubted Brock's authoritativeness as a spokesman for Heidegger?

The word *Seiende* is rendered with 'being', "what there is" (p. 12), and 'beings', so that unintelligible expressions such as the following occur: "one kind of beings" (p. 44) and "the beings in the whole" (p. 48). Brock also misses the meaning of the key expression *Seiende im Ganzen*, which has the double meaning of "be-ing as a whole" and "be-ing at all." This is a not sufficiently appreciated subtlety of Heidegger's discussion of be-ing, particularly when he is talking about the relation between *Sein* and *Nichts*.[10]

Further confusions in Brock's handling of the word 'existence' occur in Brock's text. First, the word *vorhanden* is given as "'existent' in the usual sense of the word; literally: before one's hand, at hand, present," so that "beings" that are *vorhanden* are "here by nature." By contrast, beings that are *zuhanden*, which are "made by men," are "close at hand, in readiness, at one's disposal" (p. 14). Beings of each sort are said to have "special 'qualities'" (p. 15). In addition to his limited sense of what, for Heidegger, is *zuhanden*, Brock does not see the distinction between what is present in the world (*vorhanden*) and what is immediately on hand (*zuhanden*) for use in one's current life situation. Second, attempting to discern what Heidegger means by 'existence', Brock (p. 16) compares Heidegger to Kierkegaard and renders *existenzial* with 'existentialistic' and *existenziell* with 'existential'. He rightly notes that Kierkegaard's edifying writings are on 'existential' themes, while Heidegger's "interest in 'Existence' is essentially different from either Kierkegaard or Jaspers" (p. 17). Brock is also correct when he says that Heidegger carries out his investigations "with a philosophic insight into and grasp of the 'ontological' structure of Dasein" (p. 18), but when he claims that "existence" is "the fundamental characteristic of 'Dasein'" (p. 17), it appears that he has retreated from his earlier rendering of *Dasein* as 'existence'. Like others before him and since, this is evidently because he does not know what to do with the word *Existenz*. As we have seen often enough, this is one of the classic problems in working with the key words of the early Heidegger.

Related difficulties arise about how to handle what is expressed by the word 'ex-sistence' (pp. 48, 128). Brock suggests that "ek-sistence" refers to "transcendence," which is described as "an 'ex-position' into 'discovering' [referring to ἀλήθεια] of beings, one of which is man" (p. 131; see also p. 145). Heidegger's hyphenation of the word highlights the temporal nature of *Existenz* and underscores the ecstatic (*da*) feature of *Da-sein*. In one sentence of Brock's essay, *Existenz* becomes "'existence'" (in scare quotes), *Seiendes* is rendered variously with 'actual' (also in scare quotes), "what is," and 'existent', and *Da-sein* when hyphenated by Heidegger is left untranslated but when not hyphenated by Heidegger is "'being'" (in scare quotes) (p. 307). This creates hopeless confusion, which the notes do not alleviate.[11]

As already noted, the translations of Heidegger's fundamental words in Brock's introductory material, which is intended to enhance the reading of the essays that follow it, frequently vary from those given in the translators' notes, so that the editor and the translators work at cross purposes. For example, Scott translates *Dasein* with 'existence' (p. 274), but *das Dasein des Menschen* is given as "human existence" (p. 281); *Seiende* is rendered "what is existent" (p. 275) or "the existent" (p. 281) and *Seiende im Ganzen* is "the totality of all that exists" (p. 288); and *Sein* becomes 'being' (p. 287). By contrast, we are told, Hull and Crick translate *Seiende* with both 'what-is' (p. 293) and "'existent'" (in scare quotes) (p. 307), and "*Seiendes* or *das Seiende*" is rendered with "'what is' or, on occasion, by 'actuality'," because the "literal meaning" of the words "is 'that which is'" and "in ordinary parlance we speak of it as "existence" or "being" in general (τὸ ὄν), or again, specifically, as "*a* being," "an existent," "an entity" (*ens*). For Heidegger, they add, the German equivalents of "existence" and "being" are used in a special sense" (p. 364, n. 5). We soon learn, however, that they do not clarify what that "special sense" is. In both of the "metaphysical" essays, the word *Seiende* is sometimes translated as 'actuality' (pp. 307, 333).

The words *Dasein* and *Existenz* pose special problems for Hull and Crick. In translating "Vom Wesen der Wahrheit," they must contend with Heidegger's use of the word *Existenz* (now spelled *Ek-sistenz*). At one point (p. 307), they render *Ek-sistenz* with 'ex-sistence' and leave 'ek-sistent' unchanged,[12] while the unhyphenated form of the word *Existenz* is given as 'existence'. Heidegger's use of both spellings in the same paragraph is not for the sake of variety. When he hyphenates the word, he emphasizes the temporal feature of existence (*Dasein*). Translation of the word *existenziell* is dealt with by giving the circumlocution "'existentially' speaking," rather than reckoning with it as a current German used to refer to important events in one's life, in particular, the "limit situations" Jaspers had written about. Soon after in the translation, the word *Dasein* (unhyphenated) is given as "'being'" (in scare quotes). The translators fail to note when Heidegger is using the word *Existenz* in its special sense in *Sein und Zeit* and when he is challenging the traditional usage (occurrences in scare quotes). This is the translators' crucial note about the word *Dasein*:

> It is proposed to leave this key-term in German as a *terminus technicus heideggerianus*. . . . *Dasein*, the noun, is thus in ordinary parlance "existence" and like the verb (*da sein*) simply means "to be there" (in the world). In view, however, of Heidegger's special use of the term "ex-sistence," it has been decided, lest confusion arise, not to employ the word "existence" at all for *Da-sein*, and not to translate it by "being," which term is reserved exclusively for *Sein*.[13] M. Corbin's "human reality [*réalité humaine*]" could hardly be improved on as an interpretation, though an alternative might be suggested in "human being," in the sense of the state of "being human" with all that this state, for Heidegger, involves. (p. 366, n. 15)

This will be a standard argument of later translators for leaving *Dasein* in German.

Hull and Crick introduce further problems in the handling of *Existenz* (and *Ek-sistenz*). In one note, they write that *Ek-sistenz* is "the innate capacity of all earthly or human 'existence' (*Da-sein*) to 'stand out from' (L. *exsistere*: to stand forth, come forth, arise, hence *be*) or transcend itself, transport itself out of itself and the whole of

Da-sein into the 'Overt'" (p. 366, n. 14). But Heidegger does not speak of existence "transcending itself." The ecstatic nature of existence is its temporalizing concreteness as a particular kind of life. To further complicate matters, in one place, Hull and Crick translate *Existenz* with 'existence' (p. 316), noting that this usage employs "*Existenz* in the ordinary sense" (p. 368, n. 24). However, the ordinary sense of the word *Existenz*—not the sense given it by existentialism in its varieties on the Continent—is not existence, but a particular way of life, which sometimes becomes a vocation or calling. Had the translators considered the phrase "wissenschaftliche Existenz,"[14] for example, they would have grasped Heidegger's special usage of the word *Existenz* as early as *Sein und Zeit*. Thus far their translation of "Vom Wesen der Wahrheit."

In the translation of "Was ist Metaphysik?" Hull and Crick translate both *Dasein* and *Existenz* with 'existence' (pp. 325, 327). In spite of what they had written in an earlier note (p. 366, n. 15), *Dasein* is also translated with 'being' (p. 334), but when it is hyphenated by Heidegger, they do not translate the word (p. 327). In this text, *Seiende* is rendered with 'entity' or 'what-is' (p. 327), although in one passage *seienden Menschen* becomes 'existents' (p. 336). On two occasions (p. 345), however, they translate *Seiende* with 'being', noting: "Here *Seiendes* has been translated by 'being,' with the proviso that it be understood as 'being' in simple contrast to 'not-being'" (p. 369, n. 32).

INTERLUDE

As I will argue in Part Two, the work of Martin Heidegger may be seen as a lifelong meditation on translation. It is ironic, then, that for many readers the initial exposure to Heidegger's thought, whether in the earliest critical literature or the first published translations, brought them face to face with serious mistranslations of his fundamental words. The problem of translating Heidegger is usually attributed to the difficulty of his language. But as I have been arguing, the source of the problem lies in the difficulty of Heidegger's thought, not his language. It is therefore important to consider the legitimacy of the reputed *difficulty* of his language and to question whether this is an accurate assessment. I am convinced that, while Heidegger's thought is extremely challenging, the language he used to express his thought does not stand in the way of access to it. It is, in fact, accessible by a different approach to translation, which Heidegger himself provides.

We have seen that Heidegger's thought was not well represented by the earliest English translators who were informed by a two-decade-long critical tradition that for the most part set the ground rules for rendering Heidegger's fundamental words. The amount of verbal nonsense that can be found in the early accounts of Heidegger's thought is astonishing. In my opinion, fallout from multiple mistranslations of his key words and terminological confusions found in the first published translations still pollute the atmosphere of Heidegger scholarship. The half-life of these mistranslations will last through many generations of translators.

My argument here is not brought especially for the sake of the Heidegger scholar, who will always begin with the original German text, but for the beginning student and general reader, who must read Heidegger in English translation, whether in connection with his contributions to philosophy, literary criticism, ecology, psychotherapy, or the influence of technology on everyday life. It is also true that a number of legitimate and engaging translations have been made since 1949, but the early attempts, in particular those produced before the mid-80s, still suffer from a lingering ambiguity about the sense of Heidegger's fundamental words *Sein, Seiende, Dasein*, and *Existenz*.

Finally, it should also be plain by now that I have had the same experience reading Heidegger that William Barrett reported: "His German was simple and well within my ken, and so I was easily admitted past that barrier."[15] The real problem is grasping his thought, but that for Heidegger is the heart of the problem of translation.

Critical Notices of Existence and Being

Before turning to Heidegger's philosophy of translation, I will look briefly at the response to the first Heidegger in English and show what the reviewers of the earliest translations made of Heidegger's fundamental words. In general, the reviewers found the texts of *Existence and Being* unsatisfying in many senses. The book was reviewed in eleven places.[16] Some notices are quite brief; others reflect serious preparation and engage in thoughtful interpretation of Heidegger's texts.

"The publication of this book is an event equal in importance to the publication of the first English edition of Kant's *Critique of Pure Reason.*" So writes E. F. F. Hill in his review of *EB*, which appeared in Britain, in the November 1949 issue of *World Review*.[17] "The aim of these [essays], as well as of all Heidegger's work, is the re-awakening of the question: what is meant by Being" (p. 65). Hill notes that in "*Being and Time* the perspective is that of Da-sein, here it is that of Being" (p. 65). The review, which includes eight photographs taken in Todnauberg by Felix Man (pp. 61–64), challenges the then current opinions against Heidegger, for example, Martin Buber's charge of nihilism. A text quoting Heidegger in conversation with the author of the review accompanies the photographs, which are among the best we have of Heidegger at that time. We would have appreciated as clear a view of Heidegger's fundamental words in these pages as we have of his physical appearance.

Like the translators of *EB*, Hill leaves *Da-sein* untranslated and capitalizes 'Being'. Turning to the essays themselves, he states that "because the text has been very carefully translated, the reader is well equipped with the material necessary to understand Heidegger's thought" (p. 60). Hill, who was a clergyman, is very wrong here, for although the translators may have been careful, they were unfamiliar with Heidegger's thought, which is not illuminated by their work. We are told that Heidegger is preparing a new metaphysics (p. 65). Hill's review perpetuates the conventions of not translating *Dasein* and mistranslating *Sein* and *Seiende*.

Curiously enough, Hill does not mention that the April 1949 number of *World Review*, published only five months earlier, contained the very first translations of anything by Heidegger into English.[18] This text and a translation of "Der Feldweg," which was also published in *World Review* three months after Hill's review, were the first published translations of Heidegger.[19]

The *Dublin Review* published a review by J.H. Macmillan,[20] who is fairly certain that "the fabulous strangeness of [Heidegger's] language" will discourage potential readers (p. 124). Macmillan strains against Heidegger's words, echoing the theme of the difficulty of his language that is found in nearly every review. *Dasein* is given as "human being-in-the-world," and 'Being' is capitalized (pp. 125–26).

The most extensive review of the book was by Kurt F. Reinhardt in the *New Scholasticism*.[21] Reinhardt says the book "is a sort of Heidegger Symposium" (p. 351) of translations and interpretations. Although Heidegger's "rugged personal style and vocabulary" pose many problems, he finds that "the work of translation, paraphrase, and interpretation" is "on the whole . . . a job well done," in spite of the text's "many germanicisms" (p. 251). In his summary of Brock's synopsis of *Being and Time*, Reinhardt translates *Seiende* with "anything that *is*" (p. 356) and uses the term "human *Dasein*" (p. 355). Following the convention of *EB*, *Dasein* is not translated.

Reinhardt mentions the translations of certain key words, including *Befindlichkeit*, "the way in which *Dasein* is placed in life and in the world" and *Entfremdung*, the "self-estrangement of *Dasein*" (p. 354). He then becomes almost lyrical about Heidegger, imitating (as many others have) what he takes to be Heidegger's literary style. He uses the term 'existent' (p. 355) without giving the word it renders but implies that the word plays an important role in the translations. Reinhardt closes by retranslating part of a sentence from the "Postscript" to "What Is Metaphysics?": "Without Being there can never be any existent" (p. 357). Here 'existent' translates *Seiende*.[22] His shift from the translation he is reviewing to his own rendition is not acknowledged. The review ends with another quotation: "Being as such, however, is so far above and beyond all things that are, that 'it *is* without any existents' (*es west ohne das Seiende*). Here, it would seem (and Heidegger has confirmed this interpretation), that the horizon opens toward the divine Being" (p. 357).[23] The ongoing attempted appropriation of Heidegger by neoscholasticism is carried forward by Reinhardt.

Writing in the *Journal of Philosophy*,[24] Robert Cumming reviewed *EB* along with *Martin Heidegger's Einfluß auf die Wissenschaften* (1949), a volume of eleven tributes to Heidegger on the occasion of his 60th birthday by, among others, Ludwig Binswanger, Emil Staiger, Wilhelm Szilazi, and Carl-Friedrich von Weizäcker. Cumming rightly laments that different translators were employed for the two pairs of essays and remarks on the near absence of scholarly apparatus by the translator of the essays on Hölderlin. Beginning with these so-called "literary" essays, Cumming suggests that Heidegger interposes himself between the reader and Hölderlin's text without "justifying his techniques of exposition" (p. 103). The result is that Heidegger merely outshouts the poet with his "disturbingly noisy and distracting" and "*perversely labored misuse of language* that gives the impression of his writing against instead of for an audience [emphasis added]" (p. 103). Cumming warns the reader that Heidegger's "philosophy becomes more rather than less intimidatingly *difficult* in translation [emphasis added]" (p. 103). In fact, the difficulty of Heidegger's thought remains unaffected one way or another by the words chosen to translate his thought.

Cumming, however, takes seriously the problems of translation. He quotes from Heidegger's important "Preface" to Henry Corbin's French translation of several of Heidegger's texts. In the "Preface" Heidegger says that any translation is a "défrichement," the reopening or clearing of a territory that is of common interest to readers of both languages.[25] The review is important because it is the first time that the secondary literature in English mentions Heidegger's ideas about translation. No examples from the translations being reviewed are given, however. Cumming concludes that Heidegger and the English reader, like the poet and the philosopher, must forever "dwell near to each other on distant peaks" (p. 106).[26] This is inevitable, he says, because English cannot accommodate the kinds of disruptions of conventional grammatical forms that German welcomes when, for example, it formulates subtle distinctions "by shifting and twisting prefixes and suffixes and by up-rooting etymological roots. The German language tolerates such misuse to an extent impossible in French and English." The suggestiveness of these comments is easily lost, however, among the reviewer's episodes of poking fun at Heidegger's elevation of poetry and thinking. Cumming concludes that "Heidegger's philosophy seems to be untranslatable" (p. 106). That being the case, he refers the reader to Brock's introduction which he says is of such great length because Heidegger believed his work could not be translated into English and would require extensive paraphrasing. It is unclear whether Cumming was in a position to have gotten this information from Brock.

Fr. Frederick C. Copleston begins his review in *Philosophy*[27] by announcing that "Professor Heidegger writes with a more than Heraclitean obscurity." For this reason, he recommends Brock's "careful introduction" (p. 187). When referring to Brock's epigraph to *EB*, Copleston mistakes 'Being' as the translation of *Seiende*. In fact, the epigraph runs together Heidegger's paraphrase of Leibniz's famous question (with which Heidegger ends "Was ist Metaphysik?") and a line from the closing paragraphs of the first version (1943) of his "Postscript" to the lecture.[28]

The reviewers of *EB* did not see the serious limitations of the first English translations of Heidegger and gave their approval to the presumed accessibility of Heidegger's thought provided by the texts.

Given the disappointing history of Heidegger's first appearance in English, I am led to consider his own view of translating. How does Heidegger understand what happens in translating? Is it merely a matter of exchanging words in one language for suitably equivalent words in another language? This question calls for an examination of Heidegger's philosophy of translating which, as I have indicated, is central to his way of thinking. I have discovered that for Heidegger translating was quite different from finding ways of expressing in one's native tongue what has been written in a foreign language. For Heidegger, translating was not at all a matter of words, but of ways of thinking.

The bewildering and sometimes nonsensical sentences that purported to represent Heidegger's thought point to a philosophical problem. The "improvement" of Heidegger translations has to do with gaining access to his thought, not finding the right English words to stand in for his German terms. As I will argue in the next chapter, for Heidegger, philosophizing is translating. Conversely, translation is philosophical activity *par excellence*.

In my opinion, translation is the as yet unacknowledged heart of

Heidegger's thought. In what follows, I attempt to provide evidence for this claim.

NOTES

1. *Listener* 38 (August 14, 1947): 264.
2. "On Meeting a Philosopher," *London Tribune* (September 19, 1947): 10-11.
3. Schimanski visited Heidegger again in October 1947. During his first visit, he did not know that Heidegger had been at his mountain retreat for an extended period of time following a nervous collapse in early 1946, when he was taken to see the psychiatrist Viktor von Gebsattel. He stayed at von Gebsattel's clinic for three weeks before going to the ski lodge in Todnauberg.
4. Martin Heidegger, *Existence and Being* (Chicago: Regency, 1949).
5. GA 2: 53. In a marginal note to one of his copies of *Sein und Zeit* Heidegger glosses the title "Zeit und Sein" with "Die transzendenzhafte Differenz. / Die Überwindung des Horizonts als solchen. / Die Umkehr in die Herkunft / Das Anwesen aus dieser Herkunft."—"The transcendental difference. / Overcoming of the horizon as such. / Turning back to the origin. / Apprésenting in terms of this origin."
6. *Listener* 38 (August 21, 1947): 311.
7. Words enclosed between <> have been interpolated to make Heidegger's meaning clearer.
8. Considering these translations today, one must conclude that anyone who came away from reading the essays claiming to understand Heidegger's thought was either mistaken or dissembling. The honest ones said they could not made any sense of Heidegger's thought. None of the four translators were equipped to translate Heidegger's thought. R. F. C. Hull (1913-1974) is best known as the translator of Carl Jung, although he also translated works by Martin Buber, Georg Misch, and Eugen Herrigel. His contact with Brock was evidently entirely by mail when he and Alan Crick worked on their translations of the "metaphysical" essays. Hull and Crick had known each other before World War II, and during the war worked together decoding intercepted messages from the Germans and interrogating German prisoners for the British government. Their translations of Heidegger's fundamental words are not consistent with Douglas Scott's renderings and, as we have seen, in some cases the translators' renderings vary from Brock's translations in his introduction.

9. As noted earlier, in *An Introduction to Contemporary German Philosophy*, Brock had translated the word *Dasein* with 'existence' or 'human existence', while in *EB*, it is left untranslated. Brock sometimes uses the expression "human 'Dasein'" (p. 13) or "human life" (p. 14). As I have suggested, in 1948, Brock was probably following already established English conventions, even though in 1935 he had known quite well how to translate the word *Dasein*.

10. Martin Heidegger, "What Is Metaphysics?" in *Pathmarks* (Cambridge: Cambridge University Press, 1998), pp. 82–96, and the "Postscript" to the lecture, in *Pathmarks*, pp. 231–38.

11. When a complete edition of Heidegger in English was being planned, the major figures in the project, Glenn Gray and Joan Stambaugh, were instructed by Heidegger to use the hyphenated form of the word 'Dasein' in all English interpretations. The orthography highlights the singularity and specificity, i.e., the facticity, of existence as always being there in a particular way; that is, always as a certain way of life (*Existenz*). Joan Stambaugh, "Translator's Preface" to Martin Heidegger, *Being and Time* (Albany: SUNY Press, 1996), p. xiv.

12. In a note to this word (p. 366, n. 14), Hull and Crick translate *Dasein* with 'existence', which is correct, although in the following note they explain why they will not translate the word. Once again, the problem seems to be what to do about the word *Existenz*.

13. In a later note, where they propose translating *Seiende* with 'being', Hull and Crick write that "Heidegger's *Sein* is always rendered as 'Being' with a capital B" (p. 369, n. 32).

14. GA 9: 105.

15. William Barrett, *The Illusion of Technique: A Search for Meaning in a Technological Civilization* (New York: Doubleday, 1978), pp. 255–56.

16. E. F. F. Hill, "The Philosophy of Martin Heidegger," *World Review* 9 (November 1949): 61–67; an anonymous review in *German Life and Letters* 3 (1949): 316; Ralph Harper, "An Important Philosopher," *Yale Review* 39, no. 4 (June 1950): 758–60; F. H. Heinemann, "Survey of Recent Philosophical and Theological Literature," *Hibbert Journal* 48 (July 1950): 395; Henry W. Steiger, "Heidegger and Existentialism," *Christian Science Monitor* (August 19, 1950, Magazine Section): 8; J. H. Macmillan, "Heidegger," *Dublin Review* 224 (1950): 124–26; Kurt F. Reinhardt, *New Scholasticism* 25 (1951): 351–57; Robert Cumming, *Journal of Philosophy* 48 (1951): 102–106; Ludwig Marcuse, *Personalist* 32 (1951): 202–203; Marvin Farber, *Philosophy and Phenomenological Research* 12 (1951/52): 580–81; and Frederick C. Copleston, *Philosophy* 26 (1952): 187–88. In an earlier number of *Philosophy and Phe-*

nomenological Research, Farber reviewed "What Is Metaphysics?" in the context of his article, "Experience and Transcendence: A Chapter in Recent Phenomenology and Existentialism."

17. Hill's review "The Philosophy of Martin Heidegger" was not indexed anywhere in the United States and is therefore still unknown to most American readers.

18. *World Review* 2 (April 1949): 29-33. No translator is named. The text, "The Meaning of 'Humanism'," is a heavily edited version of Heidegger's letter to Jean Beaufret that was written in the fall of 1946, expanded into the "Letter on 'Humanism,'" and published for the first time in 1947. The letter first appeared in a French translation by Joseph Rovan following Beaufret's article, "Martin Heidegger et le probleme de la verité," *Fontaine Revue Mensuelle de la Poésie et des Lettres Françaises* (November 1947): 786-804. See GA 9: 313-64. There are no notes to "The Meaning of 'Humanism'" to help the reader of *World Review*. Nor are we told how the text was acquired by the editor, Edward Hulton, who says only that the "the position of Professor Heidegger is unique, in so far as this much-discussed contemporary thinker is also the least read, since his works are unobtainable. For that reason alone, our article is of special interest, for here the philosopher addresses himself to an English audience for the first time" (p. 29).

19. "The Field Path," *World Review* 11 (January 1950): 5-6. The translation is quite sensitive, but no one is given credit for it. See GA 13, pp. 87-90.

20. See note 16, above.

21. See note 16, above.

22. In *EB*, the whole sentence runs: "But this too, in its turn, is not a nugatory Nothing, assuming that it belongs to the truth of Being that Being may be without what-is, but what-is can never be without Being" (p. 354). The translators have rendered *Seiende* with "what is." See *EB*, notes 5 and 32, pp. 364 and 369.

23. Where or to whom Heidegger confirmed this reading is not made clear. The quotation is a snippet from the last half of the sentence just quoted from the 1943 "Postscript" to "What Is Metaphysics?: "Allein, auch diese ist als die Seinsverlassenheit widerum nicht ein nichtiges Nicht, wenn anders zur Wahrheit des Seins gehört, daß das Sein wohl west ohne das Seiende, daß niemals aber ein Seiendes ist ohne das Sein." GA 9: 306.

24. See note 16 above.

25. Martin Heidegger, "Prologue de l'Auteur," in *Qu'est-ce que la Métaphysique?* edited and translated by Henry Corbin (Paris: Gallimard, 1938), pp. 7-8. Corbin's translation first appeared in *Bifur* 8 (1931): 9-27, with an

introduction by Alexandre Koyré. The collection includes translations of "Was ist Metaphysik?" "Vom Wesen des Grundes," "Hölderlin und das Wesen der Dichtung," and excerpts from *Sein und Zeit* (§§ 46-53 and 72-76) and *Kant und das Problem der Metaphysik* (§§ 42-45). It is noteworthy that Heidegger chose "Was ist Metaphysik?" and "Hölderlin und das Wesen der Dichtung" for both the first French and English translations of his work.

26. The reference is to Heidegger's quotation from Hölderlin's hymn "Patmos" in the "Postscript" to "What Is Metaphysics?" *EB*, p. 360.

27. See note 16, above.

28. Copleston copies the epigraph as given in German (*EB*, p. vii). "Warum ist überhaupt Seiendes und nicht vielmehr Nichts? / Das Nichts als das Andere zum Seienden ist der Schleier des Seins." In *EB*, the fragments are translated as: "Why is there any Being at all—why not far rather Nothing?" (p. 349) / "Nothing, conceived as the purely "Other" than what-is, is the veil of Being" (p. 360). For Leibniz's original question, "Pourquoi il y a plûtot quelque chose que rien?" see Gottfried Wilhelm Leibniz, *Leibniz: Die philosophischen Schriften*, edited by C.I. Gerhardt, 7 vols. (Berlin: Weidmann, 1875-90), 6: 607, n. 7. For a perceptive discussion of Heidegger's interpretation of Leibniz, see also Renato Cristin, *Heidegger and Leibniz: Reason and the Path* (Dordrecht: Kluwer, 1998).

PART TWO

HERMENEUTICS AND PHILOSOPHY OF TRANSLATION

CHAPTER THREE

ELEMENTS OF A THEORY OF TRANSLATION

"But how are we to hear, without translating, to translate without interpreting?"[1]

BACKGROUND IN HERMENEUTICS, TRANSLATION THEORY, AND PHILOLOGY

Heidegger's view of translation is fundamentally different in most respects from that of both his predecessors and his contemporaries. It may be best understood against the backdrop of traditional theories of translation prevalent during his lifetime, and the tradition of hermeneutics and philology to which he was exposed as a young scholar.

At one level, Heidegger's philosophy of translation takes on its distinctive form around the issue of the relation between translation and hermeneutics. An examination of the literature on hermeneutics shows that, in general, prior to Heidegger's re-envisioning of the meaning of translation, it was viewed as only one element of hermeneutics. By contrast, for Heidegger, translation is at the heart of hermeneutics.[2]

The practice of hermeneutics Heidegger learned about as a student is perhaps best represented by F. D. E. Schleiermacher, whose understanding of the relationship between hermeneutics and translation begins with the seemingly unproblematic view that thinking occurs in words. For example, in his "Academy Addresses" of 1829, he asserts that "there is no thinking without words." Conversely, as he says in the "Compendium" of 1819: "Indeed, a person thinks by means of speaking."[3] The earliest statement of the view that thinking is a kind of speaking is probably in Plato. In the *Theaetetus* 189e, Socrates says that "when the mind is thinking, it is simply talking to itself, asking questions and answering them, and saying yes and no." Again, in the *Sophist* 263e, the Stranger says that "thinking and discourse are the same thing, except that what we call thinking is, precisely, the inward dialogue carried on by the mind with itself without spoken sound."[4] Heidegger's *questioning* of the Platonic notion of thinking, as echoed in nineteenth-century hermeneutics, is one of the starting points of his radically new philosophy of translation.

Heidegger differs from Schleiermacher and the hermeneutic tradition in several ways. As we will see in detail he holds, first, that translation is interpretation *tout court*, not just an element of it, and second, because thinking does not occur in words, the words that comprise a text are only a representation of an author's thought, which is the actual focus of hermeneutic activity. Thus the form thought takes is not linguistic even though Heidegger sometimes somewhat enigmatically refers to thinking as utterance [*Sagen*]. While thinking may be initiated by listening to words by reading, speaking, or writing (each of which has its unique structure), it is not a linguistic process. According to Heidegger, thinking is a response to be[-ing].

Heidegger's view that thinking does not occur in words has been overlooked by both Richard Palmer and Kurt Mueller-Vollmer, whose work on the relation of hermeneutics and philosophy has been very influential.[5] It is an important oversight, especially in Palmer, whose book on hermeneutics was for many scholars also their first introductions to Heidegger's thought. Josef Bleicher shows how Heidegger's hermeneutics differs from that of Wilhelm Dilthey, who attempted to provide objective criteria for a science of historical research in the humanities (*Geisteswissenschaften*).[6] As Bleicher shows, the concluding sections of *Sein und Zeit*, in which Count Paul Yorck von Wartenburg's critique of Dilthey is the focus, show Heidegger's departure from a hermeneutics based on everyday life or living (*Leben*) (Dilthey's starting point) to one based on existence (*Dasein*), which, for Heidegger, is the source of access to everyday life and the distinctive way of life (*Existenz*) each of us embodies at any given moment.[7] What Dilthey saw as an epistemological and historical problem, Heidegger approached as a problem of fundamental ontology; that is to say, the possibility of ontology itself.

Traditional hermeneutics begins with language. Heidegger's departure from the tradition of interpretation theory and hermeneutics is required by his view of language. On several occasions, he makes the by now well-known though ever-provocative statement: "Language speaks."[8] This extraordinary pronouncement illuminates the background of Heidegger's philosophy of translation and helps us understand how he saw the relation between language and thought. For Heidegger, language is not a human performance; rather, language speaks through us. Our relation to language is perhaps least evident in speaking (vocalization), which while seeming to be the source of language, merely provides a vehicle for its articulation. As we will see, the relation of language to thinking is more readily discernible in writing.[9] As a response to be[-ing], thinking is not up to the thinker. Understanding our dependence on both the advent of be[-ing] and the initiative role of language is basic to appreciating how Heidegger construes the relation between language and thought.

In *Sein und Zeit*, Heidegger still believed that words and language are built on the significations (*Bedeutungen*) existence makes accessible (*erschließen*).[10] His later understanding of language departs from this position and depends to a great extent upon his understanding of what happens in translation. In an effort to explain Heidegger's shift in position from seeing language as a "category" of existence to seeing that language speaks, J. L. Mehta notes that "as compared with the writings of the earlier period, in which language is still in some measure an instrument for the expression of universal meanings, Heidegger's later thinking is much more intimately language bound."[11] That is to say, in the later Heidegger, language is no longer thought of as a tool, and human beings are no longer understood as speakers who utilize language. Instead, we are seen as the mouthpiece of language, on which we are dependent for something to say. When Mehta says that, in the later Heidegger, "the project of thinking merges into linguistic composing," he is correct, but this does not imply that thinking and language are the same; rather, as he correctly concludes, they "both together are creative and evocative of genuine novelty, of a new conception of Being, that is, of new Being" (p. 64). Just how language, thinking and be[-ing] are related only becomes clear, however, in Heidegger's philosophy of translation.

The literature on Heidegger and language is extensive, but I will mention only a few essential sources, all of which fall short of an appreciation of Heidegger's philosophy of translation, however, because they share the same Platonic view of the relation between language and thinking.[12] Kockelmans's collection of papers on *Heidegger and Language* is basic and especially valuable because of the inclusion of a translation of Johannes Lohmann's important early (1948) essay "Martin Heideggers 'Ontologische Differenz' und die Sprache" (pp. 303–63), which points out the centrality of an adequate understanding of the words *Sein* and *Seiende* in Heidegger's philosophy of language. Several of Jacques Derrida's important texts belong here as part of the ongoing discussion of Heidegger and language.[13] Then there is perhaps the most influential contemporary work on hermeneutics, Hans-Georg Gadamer's *Wahrheit und Methode* (1960; revised in 1986),[14] which although heavily influenced by Heidegger's philosophy of language still sees translation as a matter of the relation between the reader as subject and the text as object.[15] All of the philosophers mentioned err together in failing to appreciate how Heidegger's philosophy of language focuses on the word. This is crucial, since his notion of the word suggests a fresh solution to one the fundamental problems of translation theory.

As an approach to grasping Heidegger's notion of the word, we may recall a distinction made in literary criticism between literal (*wörtlich*) translation and loose or figurative translation or intralingual paraphrase (*Umschreibung*).[16] Translators of *philosophical* texts need not have bothered themselves with this distinction until recently. If pressed they would probably have observed that they were translating science, which unlike literature claims to attain objectivity, and that scientific knowledge can be formulated in expressions that are timeless and in a certain sense neutral, like the terms and operators of mathematics that easily move unchanged from one natural language to another. An understanding of the content of philosophy as scientific knowledge encourages philosophers to attempt to reduce all epistemologically meaningful propositions to the ciphers of symbolic logic. But unlike such symbols, words are not placeholders in a syntactic system of signification, and expressions of thought are not at all comparable to the information science generates.[17] On the other hand, Heidegger cautions that a philosophical text is not a work of literature and should not be approached as such.[18] Any concern about the literary value of the translation of a work of thinking fails to recognize what translation is supposed to accomplish in the first place; namely, to introduce the reader into the author's way of thinking, not to serve as a means to produce an aesthetic effect.

More specifically, Heidegger's understanding of the word begins with a distinction between terms and words. Literal translation works with terms (lexical units) that have the same ontological status as numbers. It consists in the word-for-word replacement of terms from the translated language with corresponding terms from the translating language. The exchange is easily accomplished by consulting a dictionary, which is literally a "book of terms (*Wörterbuch*)." The process is now carried out instantly by translation programs. By contrast, what Heidegger calls *faithful translation* is concerned with *words*, which are entities of a very specific nature that bear the traces of thinking. Unlike terms, words are not units of exchange. A faithful translation, one which is true to the word, considers one word at a time in an attempt to attain the experience of thinking to which the word points. For Heidegger, words are not primarily related to other words, but to experiences of thinking, and the words that comprise a text are indications of a way of thinking, not the signs of things. They are, alas, all we have by way of access to a way of thinking, but in themselves are nothing remarkable.

While separating himself from the tradition of hermeneutics, Heidegger also distinguishes his method of working with philosophical texts from philology. When Heidegger was a young man, philology was still a discipline distinct from both hermeneutics and philosophy, even though some philosophers had recently distinguished themselves as philologists; for example, Immanuel Bekker, Hermann Diels, John Burnet, and their successors in Germany and at Oxford who had first established powerful versions of the texts of the pre-Socratics, Plato, and Aristotle.

Two well-known English translations of the pre-Socratics may serve as typical examples of the approach to the translation of philosophical texts taken by philosophers who were also philologists. Kathleen Freeman's translation, in 1948, of the fifth edition of Hermann Diels's *Fragmente der Vorsokratiker* (1934; first published in 1903) does not contain any discussion of her approach to translating the early Greek thinkers.[19] Nor do G. S. Kirk, J. E. Raven, and Malcolm Schofield disclose the view of translation informing their influential edition of the pre-Socratics.[20] It may be fairly assumed that these translations were guided by techniques that originated in nineteenth-century philology, the principles of which Heidegger rejects as being inadequate to the task of gaining access to the thought of the classical Greek thinkers.

Nineteenth-century Continental philology attempted to establish the integrity of classical texts by employing methods that aspired to scientific precision. Heidegger rejects both this approach to language and, later, the science of linguistics as ways of reaching the thought of an author through his text, because, in the end, both philology and linguistics are technical pursuits.

At one point, however, Heidegger refers to authentic or thoughtful translation as being "more philological (*philologischer*)" than the procedures of professional philologists.[21] Here he is faithfully translating the word 'philology' as love for the λόγος. Heidegger's real quarrel with classical philology is that it is not radical enough, which means it does not take seriously the meaning of the Greek λόγος, which he relates to the ancient Greek language itself. He explains himself in *Was ist das—die Philosophie?*:

... [ancient] Greek is not merely a language like the European languages with which we are acquainted. The Greek language, and it alone, is λόγος. ... in Greek, what is said (*das Gesagte*) in it is in a remarkable way at the same time that which what is said names. If we hear a Greek word in Greek, we then follow its λέγειν, its immediate displaying (*Darlegen*) [i.e., what it lays out before us]. What it displays is what is being made known (*das Vorliegende*). Through a word heard in Greek, we are immediately in company with the very matter [i.e., what matters] (*die Sache selbst*) that is being made known <to us>, <and> not just presented in a mere word meaning (*Wortbedeutung*).[22]

For philologists, of course, λόγος is language in general, and Greek and Latin, German and English are equally viable vehicles of the expression of thinking. For Heidegger, only Greek is λόγος, so that when ancient Greek words are uttered, they present directly what thinking has heard.[23] Thought is somehow presented in and with the word, not by it.[24] As a result, Heidegger believes that hearing an ancient Greek word *as a Greek would have heard it* puts the listener in contact with Greek thinking. Heidegger then understands thinking as listening to language when language speaks.[25] *Translation is the event that retraces the response to language that we call thinking.* How did Heidegger arrive at this view? I will attempt to answer this question in the following section. Much, it turns out, will depend on Heidegger's understanding of the meaning of *word*.

HEIDEGGER'S PHILOSOPHY OF TRANSLATION

Heidegger's philosophy of translation was worked out slowly over many years. In what follows, I present a chronological account of those texts in which he gradually refined his understanding of the place and meaning of translation in his thought. As the years passed, the meaning of translating changed from (1) reading a text written in one language in the vocabulary of another language (literary translation), to (2) interpreting a text (hermeneutics), to (3) moving from thought to word as a response to be[-ing]. Although he comments fairly often on the meaning of faithful, legitimate, and thoughtful translation, Heidegger did not devote a text to the topic. As a result, we must glean his philosophy of translation from observations and discussions scattered throughout his works.

In *Sein und Zeit*, Heidegger still speaks of hermeneutics, which is described in novel fashion as the phenomenology of existence or fundamental ontology (*Fundamentalontologie*).[26] What Heidegger then termed hermeneutics broadened through the years to a meditation on the relation of language and, as the Stranger in the *Sophist* says, what we call thinking.[27]

However, even before *Sein und Zeit* and the lecture courses that were preparing the way for it had been given, Heidegger was already considering questions about the nature of translation and its relation to philosophizing. In a certain sense, Heidegger's *Habilitationsschrift* on *Die Kategorien- und Bedeutungslehre des Duns Scotus* (1915) may be read not only as a study of medieval philosophical grammar, but also as an early application of Heidegger's principles of translation at work rendering medieval Latin into German.[28]

In the recently published "Phänomenologische Interpretationen zu Aristoteles (Anzeige der hermeneutischen Situation)" from 1922, Heidegger broaches the topic, saying that translations are based on interpretations (*Interpretationen*).[29] Thus, although it is not made explicit until *Sein und Zeit*, a basic element of Heidegger's philosophy of translation is already at work in this text; namely, that every translation (*Übersetzung*) is already an interpretation (*Auslegung*). It is all the more remarkable, then, that the translator of the currently available English version of this crucial text does not distinguish between the terms *Interpretation* and *Auslegung* and renders both with 'interpretation', thus overlooking one of the most important distinctions Heidegger makes in his discussion of the hermeneutic situation, a distinction that will be clarified in *Sein und Zeit*.

The following year, in his lecture course, "Ontologie (Hermeneutik der Faktizität)," Heidegger surveys the history of hermeneutics, including its relation to translation, which, in keeping with the tradition, he says is only a part of hermeneutics. He still sees translation as a transaction that occurs "between" languages (interlingual translation).[30]

Sein und Zeit[31] begins with a translation of a passage from Plato's *Sophist* 244a in which the sense (*Sinn*) of the word ὄν is questioned by the Eleatic Stranger. Heidegger renders the neuter singular (nominative) present participle ὄν with *seiend*. The noun *Seiende*, which is formed from the participle, will come to play a central role in Heidegger's phenomenological ontology as the name for the manifesting of something. What determines whether the translation of ὄν (or any word) is correct? Soon enough Heidegger will not refer to the correctness of a translation, but rather to its honesty or legitimacy, which is decided in terms of whether access to the thought of the author of the text is gained in the translating. The criterion of correctness might be applied to the exchange of terms from the translated language with those from the translating language.

In a discussion of Φαινόμενον and λόγος, the two Greek words on which the word *Phänomenologie* is based, Heidegger writes that translation must be aspire to being legitimate (*rechtmäßig*) (p. 43). This suggests that translation might be dishonest or inappropriate (*unrechtmäßig*), as in the case of the standard translations of Φαινόμενον and λόγος. "Λόγος," he writes, "is 'translated', <and> that always means, interpreted (*ausgelegt*)." For example, the seven German words that have rendered λόγος (*Rede, Vernunft, Urteil, Begriff, Definition, Grund, Verhältnis*) represent as many *interpretatii* (*Interpretationen*) that conceal the fundamental meaning of the Greek word. Before recounting the history of the unfolding of these seven meanings (pp. 45-46), Heidegger offers his own rendering of the word, with a view to the *thought* which the word first announces: uttering (*Reden*) or letting be seen (*Sehenlassen*). As we know, Heidegger's translation of λόγος continues throughout his life.[32]

Heidegger's usage in this section of *Sein und Zeit* distinguishes between *Auslegung* (interpretation) and *Interpretation* (*interpretatio*).[33] As *Interpretation*, translation conceals the thought to which a word gives utterance, but as *Auslegung*, translation dicloses thought. The former term denotes a process whereby the interpreter moves away from an author's thought. However, the fact that a word such as λόγος is subjected to *interpretatio* is not a sign of the word's defectiveness. To the contrary, for Heidegger, the importance of a word is gauged by how many traces of thinking are left behind in it by the series of *interpretatii* to which it has been submitted.

An interpreter can also be an elucidator of thought, the traces of which are contained in words. Heidegger uses the verb *auslegen* to designate the process whereby thought is recovered from a word. An *Auslegung* evokes thinking. According to the Heidegger of *Sein und Zeit*, both processes go on in the interpreter. Like the spokes of a wheel, *Interpretationen* radiate from a fundamental word, providing tangential connections from the word to words in the same natural language or to words in a given translating language. An *Auslegung* moves within the wheel's hub to the source of its turning, a way of thinking.

An illustration of Heidegger's translation of fundamental Greek words is his treatment in *Sein and Zeit* of Aristotle's definition of man as "the living thing λόγον ἔχον."[34] Heidegger says that, like single words he examined earlier, this expression was transformed by an *interpretatio* into the classic Latin definition of man as an *animal rationale* (p. 65). He points out that, in the process of *interpretatio*, one of the words in Aristotle's expression has been lost, and along with it we have lost access to Aristotle's thought about the nature of the human being. The missing word is the verb ἔχον, which names *how* λόγος is related to the living thing called man and tells what both λόγος and human be-ing must be in order to be in such a relation. All of this is lost, thanks to what the *interpretatio* leading into Latin has effected. In this case, the interpretative hub itself has disappeared. According to Heidegger, something equally momentous happened when λόγος was translated with *verbum*.

Several other Greek words are translated in *Sein und Zeit*, including, in Heidegger's view, the fundamental word of Greek philosophy, ἀλήθεια, which he here renders with *Entdecktheit* (uncoveredness) (pp. 44, 292). He adds that "the translation <of ἀλήθεια> by the word 'truth (*Wahrheit*)' . . . obscures (*verdeckt*) the sense <of the word> . . ." (p. 291). This illustrates that an illegitimate or inappropriate translation of a word not only fails to reveal the thought which it is meant to express, but also further distances us from it.

Elements of a Theory of Translation

In the summer semester of 1931, Heidegger gave a course entitled "Interpretationen zur antiken Philosophie/Aristoteles, *Metaphysik* Θ," which was published in 1981 as *Aristoteles,* Metaphysik Θ *1-3: Von Wesen und Wirklichkeit der Kraft*.[35] The text is nothing less than a meticulous, word-by-word translation of the first three chapters of the eighth book of Aristotle's *Metaphysics*. Here Heidegger comments on the inadequacy of the *Interpretationen* of λόγος as *Vernunft* (reason), *Urteil* (judgment), and *Sinn* (sense), all of which "miss (*verfehlen*) <what is> original (*ursprünglich*), properly ancient (*Antike*) and, at the same time, essential (*Wesentliche*) about the word and the concept" (p. 122). His remark applies as well to the other fundamental words of Aristotle's text: δύναμις (*Kraft*, efficacity) and ἐνέργεια (*Wirklichkeit*, actuality).

In his lecture course on the *Theaetetus* and the allegory of the cave in the *Republic*, which was given in 1931-32 under the title "Vom Wesen der Wahrheit,"[36] Heidegger praises Schleiermacher's translation of the *Theaetetus*, but adds that it is necessary to go back to the original text (*Urtext*). He describes his translation as a restorative *Auslegung* of Plato's fundamental words: "For a translation is only the final outcome of an interpretation (*Auslegung*) that has actually been carried out: <in translating,> the text is composed <all> over <again> (*über-gesetzt*) in an independently questioning appreciation (*Verständnis*) <of it>" (p. 130). As we now begin to understand, legitimate translation is first of all a return to an author's (writer or speaker) way of thinking.

Heidegger adds that finding appropriate words in the translating language is a further transformation of the original translation, which led back to the author's way of thinking. This passage seems to be the first explicit reference in Heidegger's texts to the relation between translating and thinking, which will supplant the focus in traditional hermeneutics on the relation between the text of the translated language and the text of the translating language.

Heidegger also adds that while knowledge of ancient Greek is necessary in order to understand what Plato thought, merely having a command of the language, its grammar and vocabulary, is not sufficient for grasping Plato's thought, if one does not also understand the *world* in which the language of Plato's words were uttered. Near the end of the course, a *Leitmotiv* of Heidegger's philosophy of translation appears again, although only parenthetically: "Translation is always interpretation (*Auslegung*)" (p. 311).

In 1935, two other elements of Heidegger's philosophy of translation are made explicit: (1) legitimate translating (*Übersetzen*) begins with an experience of thinking that is the same as the author's; and (2) the translating language may have to be adjusted to accommodate the thought expressed in the translated language. At this point in Heidegger's development of his philosophy of translation, there are remnants of the traditional interest in the differences between translated and translating languages alongside his radical understanding of the meaning of translation as *being carried over to an author's way of thinking*.

Now Heidegger emphasizes the process of translating (*Übersetzen*), rather than its result. In his "interpretation (*Auslegung*) of the thingness (*Dingheit*) of the thing" in "Der Ursprung des Kunstwerkes" (1935-36),[37] he explains that producing *interpretatii* is informed by the metaphysical understanding of the be[-ing] of any kind of be-ing. For all concerned, this was the unhappy result of the ancient

> taking over (*Übernahme*) of Greek words into Roman Latin thinking, <in which> ὑποκείμενον becomes *subiectum*, ὑπόστασις becomes *substantia*, <and> συμβεβηκός becomes *accidens*. By no means is this translation of Greek words into the Latin language the inconsequential transaction (*Vorgang*) that it is taken for even today. On the contrary, behind the seemingly literal and therefore attentive translation is concealed a transition (*Übersetzen*) from Greek experience to another way of thinking (*Denkungsart*). *Roman thinking takes over (übernimmt) the Greek words ὑποκείμενον, ὑπόστασις, and συμβεβηκός without, correspondingly,* <having> *just as original an experience of what they say* <as the Greeks had>, <which is to say> *without* <having used the> *Greek words*. Western thinking begins with this translating <of Greek words into Latin>. (pp. 7-8)

Heidegger believes that he (and we) must replace the metaphysical *interpretatio* with a more original *Auslegung*.

Having reached an author's way of thinking, the translating language must then accommodate itself as best it can to the experience of thinking discovered by listening closely to the words in the translated language. Often enough, a thoughtful translation does not "sound (*lautet*)" right. In fact, as Heidegger admits, thoughtful translating is bound to stretch the capabilities of the translating language.

Another element of Heidegger's philosophy of translation is first hinted at in 1938. Translating moves within the spirit of a language (*Sprachgeist*) or between the spirit of one language and that of another language. The idea of the *Sprachgeist* originates with Jacob Grimm,[38] who first mentions it in his address to the Prussian Academy, "On the Origin of Language" (1851).[39] Grimm is oriented to a view of language that was developed by Herder, for whom language is the power of the mind to form and manipulate extratemporal concepts.[40] According to Herder, language originates in the sense of hearing, the "middle sense" between vision (which is "active") and touch (which is "passive") that unifies the other two senses by representing in sounds what the other two senses receive (pp. 142-43). For Herder, of course, hearing language is still "thinking words" (p. 145). In Grimm's hands, however, the power of language is found in language, not in the mind.

Herder via Grimm is not the only influence here, however. The decisive source of Heidegger's understanding of the *Sprachgeist* may be traced back to Wilhelm von Humboldt's view that each so-called natural language has its own national character, which is fundamentally mental or spiritual in nature. Language, says Humboldt, is "the external manifestation of the minds of people. Their language is their soul, and their soul is their language."[41]

While these are important influences on Heidegger's philosophy of translation, he departs decisively from the German Romantic understanding of language represented by Herder and von Humboldt. His use of the term *Sprachgeist* is therefore potentially misleading.[42] It may be best understood as the presence of thought in a natural language (above all, ancient Greek), where a way of thinking is a response to be[-ing], and translating is the means of arriving at a given way of thinking. At this point in the development of his philosophy of translation, Heidegger understands translating as an event that moves within a language or between the spirit of the translated language and the spirit of the translating language, which must find words for the thinking newly experienced by a reader, speaker, or writer. Translating is clearly not an activity that moves between terms. As *Auslegung*, translation activates a way of thinking. The energy of translating as *Auslegung* is provided by the spirit of the translated language.

In Heidegger's important "Prologue" to the publication, in 1938, of the French translation of his Freiburg inaugural lecture, "Was ist Metaphysik?" Heidegger further develops his philosophy of translation. The "Prologue" is an important text that brings together most of the elements of Heidegger's philosophy of translation.[43]

> In translation (*traduction*), the work of thinking finds itself transposed (*transposé*) into the spirit (*l'esprit*) of another language, and thus inevitably undergoes a transformation (*transformation*). This transformation may be fruitful, for it makes the fundamental position of the question [in this case "What is metaphysics?"] appear in a new light. It thus provides an opportunity for it [the work of thinking] itself to become more perspicuous (*clairvoyant*) and <for thinking> to discern more clearly the limits of the question.
>
> That is why a translation does not simply consist in facilitating communication with the world, but is in itself a reopening (*défrichement*) of a question raised in common <by the speakers of both languages>.

In this text, Heidegger makes it clear that the matter (*Sache*) or what is at stake in translating is thinking, not words. In translating, the reader or listener is transported in the spirit of a language to a way of thinking.

Another element of Heidegger's philosophy of translation introduced in this text is that translation is an unsettling procedure. The image he chooses for this is the breaking open (*défrichement*) of compacted earth. This image is of clearing land or territory that has become overgrown by entangling structures, sedimented and made impenetrable. In translation, as in plowing, what has become hardened over time (a question) is reopened for further cultivation (thinking). The effect of translating is to reopen questions that evoke or call for (*heißt*) thinking. In the process, however, ease of communication may be sacrificed for exposure to the demands of a fresh way of thinking. Thus when expressed in the translating language, a way of thinking may become even more enigmatic than it was before.

"Vom Wesen und Begriff der Φύσις Aristoteles, Physik B,1" (1939) is Heidegger's translation of the Aristotelian text referred to in the title. It is a lexicon of Aristotle's basic words. In the essay, Heidegger explains that his

> "translation" <of Aristotle> is not <merely> a transcription (*Übertragung*) of the Greek words into *the sturdiness typical of our language* [German]. It does not want to *take the place of* (*ersetzen*) the Greek words, but <wants> instead precisely to move up (*versetzen*) *to* them and, in the transposition (*Versetzung*), disappear in them.[44]

In this passage, Heidegger once again calls into question the traditional meaning of translation. Hence the double quotes. As he makes clear, legitimate translation is not about rendering superfluous a text written in a foreign language by making it easily available in another language. Instead, it causes the reader to become immersed in and absorbed by its basic words, and in that way to be in a position to think as the author of those words once thought. Through a transformation of the translator's experience, his thought becomes isomorphic with that of the author. Using an image from music, he is transposed from the key in which he thinks into the key in which Aristotle thought.[45] The translator modulates into the new key and is able to think along with the author. The analogy with music is helpful, but with this proviso. For Heidegger, the verb *versetzen* (transpose) always means to move *up* in register, which accords with his view that an *Auslegung* elevates our understanding to what has been thought. There is no better evidence of Heidegger's humbleness as a reader of Aristotle, or any of the great thinkers who preceded him, from Anaximander to Nietzsche.

Heidegger's work with the pre-Socratics was especially important in the development of his philosophy of translation. For example, in "Nietzsche: Der europäische Nihilismus," where he translates Fragment I of Protagoras,[46] Heidegger says he wants his rendering to be "more suitable (*gemäßer*) to Greek thinking" than the standard translations and repeats the basic theme that all legitimate or faithful translation is "already interpretation (*Auslegung*)" (p. 175).[47] In the second part of the lecture series "Grundbegriffe" (1941),[48] Heidegger discusses the one remaining fragment of Anaximander.[49] He acknowledges that his translation of Anaximander's utterance (*Spruch*) may be open to the charge of "being unscientific (*Unwissenschaftlichkeit*)," but suggests that it may be "more philological (*philologischer*)" than the standard translations, since it is more sensitive to the "inner terms of the essence (*inneren Wesensbedingungen*)" of "historical interpretation" (p. 94). He asserts once again that legitimate translating is "always unavoidably interpretation (*unumgänglich Auslegung*)," adding that in such translating invariably "the utterance moves back into what is strange and alienating (*Befremdliche und Befremende*) and lets it stay there" (pp. 94, 96). The movement described is a return to the language of the original utterance and to the thought expressed by it. Although such movement is unsettling, in the end it is also always enlightening.

Heidegger claims that to really *hear* what is revealed in legitimate translation requires a step that allows us to be "able to listen along the right lines (*in die rechte Richtung hören*)" (p. 102) to the original way of thinking of the author of the text at hand. In Heidegger's usage, hearing does not refer to the functioning of the auditory apparatus. The deaf also translate. As we will see, the paradigm case of such hearing is translating a written text which one is silently reading. For Heidegger, hearing is belonging to (*Gehören*) what language says.

Hölderlins Hymne "Der Ister" contains Heidegger's most sustained discussion thus far published of his view of the essence of translation.[50] He suggests that translating occurs in its purest form in writing, that is, as the writer works from his own thought or from a text which he rewrites in the translating language. Heidegger repeats that translation and interpretation (*Auslegung*) are the same (*Selbe*) (p. 61) and admits that the strangeness of thoughtful translations often earns them the unwarranted judgment of being philologically "wrong (*falsch*)" (p. 74). He also introduces the idea that translation occurs *within* a language as well as *between* languages. At one point, he speaks of "translating within our German language."[51]

Again referring to the *Sprachgeist* in a discussion of how to decide whether a translation is thoughtful, legitimate, or faithful, Heidegger asks:

> But who decides and how does someone determine the rightness (*Richtigkeit*) of a translation? We "obtain" our knowledge of the meanings of the words (*Wortbedeutungen*) of a foreign language from the "dictionary (*Wörterbuch*)." But we easily forget, of course, that without exception the accounts <of words> in a dictionary must be based on an antecedent interpretation of the linguistic connections (*sprachlichen Zusammenhänge*) in terms of which the single words and word usages (*Wortverwendungen*) are understood. In most cases, a dictionary will give us a correct account of the meaning of a word, but even given this exactness, to the extent that we inquire about what is referred to as the realm of the essence (*Wesensbereich*) of the word, [the dictionary] still does not guarantee (*verbürgt*) insight into the truth of what the word means (*bedeutet*) and can mean. A "dictionary [literally, a book of words]" can provide hints for the understanding of a word, but it is never simply and *a priori* the definitive authority. Given its nature and its limits, in every case a dictionary reference is merely a reference to an interpretation of language that is in no way comprehensible (*faßbar*). To be sure, as soon as we consider language as only a medium of exchange <which is> geared to the techniques of business and exchange, a dictionary is "without further ado" "right (*in der Ordnung*)" and definitive. On the other hand, seen from the spirit of a language (*Geist einer Sprache*) in its entirety, every dictionary lacks literal standardization (*Maßstäblichkeit*) and definitiveness.
>
> In truth, of course, this is valid for every translation, because it necessarily has to carry out the passage (*Überschritt*) from the spirit of one language (*Sprachgeist*) to that of another. Above all, [thoughtful translation] is not translation in the sense that a word

from one language can or cannot be made congruent (*gebracht werden*) with a word from another <language>. However, this impossibility should not thereby mistakenly lead <us> to devalue translation, in the sense of <seeing it as> being something that fails to work (*Versagen*). On the contrary, translation can even bring to light connections that in fact lie in the translated language but have not been brought out (*herausgelegt*). We see from this that every <instance of> translating has to be an interpreting (*Auslegen*). At the same time, however, the converse is valid. Every interpretation (*Auslegung*) and everything in its service is <an instance of> translating. For translating does not just move (*bewegt sich*) between two different languages; rather, translating <also> occurs within the same language. An interpretation of Hölderlin's hymns is <such an event of> translating within German. The same holds for an interpretation that takes, for example, Kant's *Kritik der reinen Vernunft* or Hegel's *Phänomenologie des Geistes* as its theme. Knowing that here, too, it is necessarily a question of translating is an acknowledgment that such "works" are essentially in need of translation. However, this need (*Bedürftigkeiti*) is not a deficiency (*Mangel*), but rather an inner prerogative (*Vorzug*) <of interpretation>. In other words, it belongs to the essence of the language of an historical people to spread out like a mountain range across both plains and low-lying areas, and at the same time also to tower upward to rare summits to reach otherwise inaccessible heights. In between are the "middle ranges" and "steppes" <where language extends>. To be sure, interpretation (*Auslegung*) as translating is making intelligible (*Verständlichmachen*), not however in the sense of what such understanding (*Verstand*) usually means. To continue with the image: In <thoughtful> translation, the height of poetic or reflective (*denkerisch*) formulation (*Sprachwerk*) is not diminished and the full range over the plains leveled to what is superficial, but in fact just the opposite <happens>. Translation must move <one> up (*versetzen*) the path on its ascent to the heights. Making intelligible never means approximating poetry or thinking to just any meaning (*Meinen*) and horizon of comprehension (*Verständnis-Horizont*). To make intelligible means to awaken the comprehension <of poetry or thinking> in such a way that the blind stubbornness of customary meaning is broken down and abandoned, so that the truth of a work can reveal itself.

> These incidental remarks on the nature (*Wesen*) of translating should remind us that the difficulty of translation is never merely something technical but has to do instead with the relationship (*Verhältnis*) of man to the nature of words (*Wesen des Wortes*) and the dignity (*Würde*) of language. *Tell me what you think about translating and I will tell you who you are* [emphasis added]. (pp. 74-76)

In the next hour of the course, Heidegger sums up his philosophy of translation:

> Authentic (*Echtes*) translation is always a two-way discussion (*Auseinandersetzung*), and this is the source of its possibilities and limits. It was therefore necessary <last time> to make some incidental remarks, which were meant to touch <not only> on the essence of translating but also <on> what is inherent in the relationship of two languages to each other and therewith <in> the relation (*Bezug*) <of language> to words. Every translation is <an> interpretation, and all interpretation (*Auslegung*) is translating. To the extent that we are called upon to interpret poetic and reflective works in our own language, it becomes evident to be sure, nothing at all to be afraid of!—that, in and of itself alone, every historical language is in need of translation (*übersetzungsbedürftig*). . . .
>
> Translating is never primarily a transporting (Über-*setzen*) and going over (*Hinübergehen*) into the foreign language with the help of one's own (*der eigenen*) <language>. Translating is rather an awakening (*Erweckung*), clarification (*Klärung*), <and> deployment (*Entfaltung*) of one's own language, which is aided by the two-way discussion (*Auseinandersetzung*) with the foreign (*der fremden*) <language>. (pp. 79-80)

In these passages, Heidegger brings together most of the major features of his philosophy of translation.

In 1942-43, Heidegger gave a series of lectures on Parmenides,[52] in which he cautions us that an interpretation is "not yet clear <merely> by listening to the translation. Because the <interpretation> speaks in the words of our language, the danger of misinterpretation is, in fact, even increased" (p. 12). In other words, having brought a way of thinking to expression in the translating language does not guarantee that the translator has understood what these new words say, that is, what he has heard. Often enough, the translation is in need of further interpretation, and that means further translating.

In this course, Heidegger takes a fresh look at thoughtful translation, which he once again stresses is not merely "the transcription (*Übertragung*) of one language into another, <that is,> of a foreign language (*Fremdsprache*) into our mother tongue (*Muttersprache*), or *vice versa*" (p. 17). Taking up a theme introduced in the essay "Der Ursprung des Kunstwerkes," Heidegger notes that so-called literal translating (*wörtliche Übersetzen*) merely patterns (*nachbilden*) one term after another. Oriented to the ethos of the grammar of the proposition, such a technique replaces word forms (nouns, verbs, prepositions) with their counterparts in the translating language. By contrast, in thoughtful translation a word in the text transports (*übersetzt*) the reader to a "realm of experience (*Erfahrungsbereich*)" or "kind of experience (*Erfahrungsart*)" (p. 16) of the way of thinking of the one whose words have been heard with what I would term the mind's ear.[53]

For Heidegger, the "translating word (*übersetzende Wort*)" "receives its content in terms of the entirety (*Ganze*) of that which the thinker thinks" (p. 13), and not merely from the sentence in which the word appears. Thus, legitimate translation proceeds, not sentence by sentence, but rather word by word, using the entirety of the thinker's thought as its context.[54] In chapter 4, I will present an analysis of Heidegger's word-by-word translation practice.

Later on in the course on Parmenides, Heidegger introduces another element of his philosophy of translation. Translating occurs in speaking one's own language and in listening to what someone is saying in conversation. In other words, translating is not at all limited to written texts, since

> we are always constantly translating our own language, our mother tongue, into its own words. Speaking (*Sprechen*) and uttering

(*Sagen*) are in themselves translating, the essence of which is by no means that the translating and translated words belong to different <natural> languages. Original translating is at work in every dialogue (*Gespräch*) and monologue (*Selbstgespräch*). (p. 17)

In short, "all dialogue and every utterance (*Sagen*) is original translating within (*innerhalb*) one's own language" (p. 18). Here we have one of the most remarkable elements of Heidegger's philosophy of translation, since it implies that all use of us by language implicates us in translating, and that translating that begins with a written text is only a special case of what is going on all the time when language speaks.[55] Perhaps this is why Heidegger eventually dropped the use of the term hermeneutics to describe what he was doing, since traditionally hermeneutics refers only to written texts.

In the passage quoted above, Heidegger includes monologue among the instances in which "original translating" occurs. Reflecting or running sentences through one's head, which is what I believe Heidegger has in mind here, is the only kind of "conversation with oneself" that Heidegger recognizes, and differs fundamentally from what Plato and the tradition have considered to be the essence of thinking. Similarly, whenever I speak in conversation with another human being, I am translating. In either case, my way of thinking is being transformed. This is a view worlds apart from the notion that one's thought is something fully formed that is routinely replicated. Heidegger will add that a great thinker welcomes this movement of thought that is running its course in his life.

Somewhat later in the course, Heidegger describes what is going on in a philosophical text.

[A] thinker's discussion (*Abhandlung*) <of his own thinking> occurs in his own individual unique words. It forces us to take these words in such a way that, again and again, it is as if we were hearing them for the first time. Each time <we read a thinker's text>, these first fruits of the <thinker's> words cast us onto another shore. In every case, so-called trans*lating* (*Über*setzen) and paraphrasing (*Umschreiben*) follow only on the transition (Übersetzen) of our entire nature (*Wesen*) to the realm of an already transformed

> (*gewandelten*) truth. Only if we have already been carried along (*übereignet*) by this transition are we in the care (*Sorge*) of the words. Only out of respect for language on these grounds can we for the first time take on (*übernehmen*) the easier and more circumscribed problem of how to translate foreign words. (p. 18)

For Heidegger, a thinker returns time and again to the fundamental words that are the nuclei of his own thought, freshly translating them when writing. In the passage quoted, he also makes it clear that being transported into a way of thinking is in the hands of such words. Thinking is in their care. For Heidegger, the power of the fundamental words lies in their capacity to evoke thought, that is, to move the writer, reader, speaker, or listener to think. Reading a text composed by someone else requires being open to hearing the thinker's words as he heard them.

Although Heidegger disavows literal (*wörtlich*) translation, in the following passage from the text, he uses the phrase "'literal' translation" in a special sense to indicate not the one-to-one mechanical replacement of a term with its dictionary equivalent but rather an experience that is "focused on the word." In the following discussion, the word 'literal' means thoughtful.

> A 'literal (*wörtlich*)' translation must not merely transliterate (*nachbilden*) and thereby 'enrich' the translating language with 'new', unusual, <and> often even unwieldy words, but in considering the <translated> words rather must go beyond the 'translating' words. ... We must hear a word taken as word (*wörtlich*) in such a way that we hearken to (*aufhorschen*) the directives <in it> that point back to the word. With such hearkening (*Horschen*), hearing (*Vernehmen*) hearkens to what the word says. (pp. 21–22)

If only the early translators of Heidegger had known this text![56] The "directives" he refers to in this passage are the traces of thinking that lie within a word that compel the reader to return again and again to the word, which acts like a signal beckoning the reader to attend to (*gehören*) the author's thought. In other words, "hearkening to what the word says" is hearing (*Hören*) a word in such a way that it evokes thinking (*heißt Denken*).⁵⁷ It eventuates in belonging to (*Gehören*) a way of thinking. Heidegger adds that he wants his translations of Parmenides to be both *wörtlich* (in the sense just developed) and faithful or true to the word (*wortgetreu*).

In the following passage from his 1943-44 lecture course on Heraclitus, however, Heidegger seems to briefly revert to the customary usage of the word *wörtlich* (literal), in order to contrast literal translation (in the conventional sense) or transcription with *wortgetreu* translation: "In merely literal (*bloßen wörtlichen*) translation, isolated terms (*den einzelnen Wörtern*) that correspond <to each other> lexically are compared with each other in an almost mechanical way. But mere terms (*bloße Wörter*) are not at all words (*Worte*)."⁵⁸ Here Heidegger introduces a fundamental distinction between terms (*Wörte*) (spoken or written lexical units), and words (*Worte*) that he will make much of in the years to come.

Heidegger explains that in thoughtful (*wortgetreu*) translation

> the terms (*Wörte*) must receive their power to name (*Nennkraft*) and <their> structure (*Gefüge*) from an already prevailing faithfulness (*Treue*) to the <thinker's> unified utterance (*Sagen*), that is, to the entirety of the utterance. But <alas!> every translation is <after all merely> a stopgap measure (*Notbehelf*). If the need (*Not*) is modest, the remedy (*Behelf*) can help (*abhelfen*) the need a little; for example, in the case of a translation of business documents. In that case <, of course,> both parties know what [the document] is about. One may perhaps understand <"about"> it <only> too well!

The situation is quite different in *wortgetreu* translating, where the need, that is, *thinking* is at stake. Turning to the topic of the course, he continues:

> In the case of the translation of Heraclitus' words, <by contrast,> the need is great. Here translating (*Übersetzen*) becomes a transporting (*Übersetzen*) to another shore, which is barely known and lies on the other side of a broad river. This easily leads to roaming about, and most of the time ends in shipwreck. In the realm of translating, translations are either very difficult or less difficult, <but>

they are always difficult.... In the realm of the elevated words of poetry and thinking, translations are always in need of interpretation (*Auslegung*), because they are themselves <already> interpretations. Such translations can then either introduce or complete the <initial> interpretation. (pp. 44-45)

Here Heidegger nicely distinguishes between the translating that occurs from thought to word and the translating that has traditionally been called interpretation, a subspecies of which was translation in the traditional sense of a transaction between two languages.

In the introductory review that opens the next session of the course, Heidegger summarizes his view of the connections between interpretation and translation:

Merely on its own and without the interpretation (*Auslegung*) that belongs to it, every translation is therefore entirely given over to possible misunderstandings. For every translation is already an interpretation. It carries with it all of the unspoken formulations, views, <and> paths stemming from the interpretation.... *At the core of their nature, interpretation and translation are the same.*... All uttering (*Sagen*), talking to (*Reden*) and replying to (*Antwort*) is translating [emphasis added]. (p. 63)[59]

Heidegger returns to the one extant Anaximander fragment in "Der Spruch des Anaximander," where he develops the sense of *Sagen* in relation to his philosophy of translation. The essay concludes *Holzwege* (1950), Heidegger's first major collection of essays.[60]

In his discussion of the Anaximander "utterance" or "saying," we can identify another element of Heidegger's philosophy of translation. In writing, reading, or listening, the thinker's utterance is translated, not an ensemble of words. Here Heidegger characterizes *Sagen* as the form of thought and refers to the thinker's words as a utterance, rather than a text. The course of translation runs from utterance to thinking.

Because the Anaximander fragment is considered to be the oldest text in the Western pre-Socratic corpus, Heidegger is keen to point out that mistranslations of its key words have had extensive repercussions for the trajectory followed by Western philosophy to this day. Focusing on the word χρεών, he asks about the conditions of a thoughtful translation of the fragment, noting that language itself "constrains (*bindet*)" the translator in his attempt to "get at what is said in the utterance (*das Gesprochenes des Spruches*)" in such a way that it "guards (*bewahrt*) the translation against arbitrariness" (p. 328). Only a translator who is guided by the individual words of the utterance is in a position to construe the thinking they express.[61]

In one passage, Heidegger observes that "because it writes while thinking (*als denkende dichtet*), a thoughtful translation . . . necessarily appears to be violent" (p. 329).[62] Here he singles out the situation of the translator engaged in *Auslegung*, that is, as interpreter. The violence of thoughtful translation originates in the foreignness of the thought to which the translator is transported and to which he responds, not in the foreignness of the original language.

Some of Heidegger's translators and commentators have misconstrued his use of the word *dichten* here and elsewhere, assuming he had in mind only the writing of poetry (*Dichtung*). Its sense is broader and more basic, and indicates the effect of language that "thickens [*dichtet*]" or slows down the process of apprésenting (*Anwesen*).[63] Apprésenting or what worlding thus thickened and stabilized has brought to a standstill as an utterance (*Spruch*), whether for poetizing or philosophizing.

Explicitly applying his view of the relation between translating and thinking, Heidegger claims that a translation of the Anaximander fragment will be thoughtful only when the translator reaches Anaximander's thought. "In its capacity as thinking, the conveying (*Übersetzen*) to what in the utterance is a matter of its language is an o'erstepping of the grave." The translator must "cross over to (*über-zu-setzen*) where what has been brought up in the utterance has come from" (p. 339), which is another time and culture. Initiated by the word, the passage that takes place in translating may be visualized as a "ray of hope (*Lichtblick*)," a bridge over (*über*) which the translator is taken (*setzen*) to what has been thought elsewhere and "elsewhen." As such, translating bridges eras and cultures in order to join two experiences of thinking; for example, that of Anaximander and

Heidegger, or Heidegger and an English-speaking translator. In short, translating effects thinking. It is not a matter of the words of a text except insofar as words initiate the passage to another way of thinking.[64] Translating is really not at all about words. The words remain as they were before. Nothing happens to them. Translating takes up someone else's thinking and effects a revival (*Wiederholung*) of it, although it does not produce a replica of it (thought of as content), as the hermeneutic tradition asserted.

In this essay, Heidegger repeats that a faithful translation "in the field of thinking" "sounds strange (*befremdlich klingt*)," and therefore makes "unreasonable demands (*Zumutung*)" on us (p. 367). Translations of thought that is unfamiliar to the translator will be unsettling precisely because the way of thinking to which he has been transported disturbs and challenges his customary way of thinking. Heidegger adds that the words of the pre-Socratic thinkers very likely sounded just as peculiar to their cohorts as they still do to us. This is testimony, not to their obscurity, but their power. The strangeness of the pre-Socratics' words is due to the strangeness of their thought that challenged them and their contemporaries as much as it still challenges us. For Heidegger, the early Greek thinkers did not fully grasp what they had thought.[65] He suggests that the tradition has become used to hearing the pre-Socratics through the way of thinking of *Plato and Aristotle*, who were *the first translators of the pre-Socratics*.

We must also recall, says Heidegger, that thinkers have determined the grammar of verbal expressions. Thinkers are not forced to speak in certain terms because of the restraints of the grammar of their language, as philosophers in the analytic tradition have suggested. After all, the grammar of a language is not just there, ready made, to be used by its speakers. Those who speak a language determine and modify its grammar in order to accommodate their thought. The thought of the pre-Socratics surely reshaped Ancient Greek grammar and the language it structures.[66] To repeat, for Heidegger, language is not a tool that we use. Language uses us, even to change its own form and way of speaking.

In a discussion of a passage from the *Iliad* (p. 344), Heidegger again uses the image of translating as transporting. Commenting on the word ὄντα, he again compares translating to crossing a river, cautioning readers that we will be able to cross over (*über-zu-setzen*) to the thought mediated by a Greek word only "providing that we are taken over (*über-holen*) to the distant shore of the matter (*Sache*) spoken of by the writer." Heidegger uses the phrase *Sache des Denkens* to name what lies at the source of any utterance and suggests that the meaningfulness of an utterance is the extent to which it requires interpretation, that is to say, the clarity it invites by compelling the reader to translate it again and again, not its *prima facie* semantic clarity. Utterances that do not invite translation bring thinking to a stop. An utterly clear formulation, the holy grail of analytic philosophy, would be a dead end. On the other hand, often what appears to be perfectly clear—for example, a tautology such as the principle of identity, A = A—may require the most translation.

Heidegger's ongoing translation of the fragments of Parmenides continues in *Was heißt Denken?* (*What Evokes Thinking?*).[67] Indeed, as Heidegger says in "Moira (Parmenides, Fragment VIII, 34–41),"[68] for him "the dialogue with Parmenides never comes to an end."[69] As Glenn Gray reported, these lectures, given in 1951–52, were Heidegger's swan song, the "last before his retirement from the University [of Freiburg]. They were also the first lectures he was permitted to give there since 1944, when he was . . . forbidden to teach by the French occupying powers."[70]

In this text, Heidegger makes explicit two other elements of his philosophy of translation. (1) Translating a group of words, whether a fragment or complete syntactic unit, begins by displaying the paratactic structure or infrastructure of the utterance,[71] and (2) authentic translation begins with the individual words of a text, not the syntactic ensemble to which they belong. Heidegger's translations are based on the elucidation of single words. He does not see the proposition as the bearer of thought. Instead single words (and eventually *one word*) are the source of access to an author's way of thinking as such and as a whole.

In part 2 of the course, Heidegger presents an extended translation of Parmenides's Fragment VI. It is his most striking published example of what I call *paratactic translation*, one of the aims of which as Heidegger says in the "Letter on 'Humanism'" is the "freeing of language from grammar by a more original (*ursprünglicheres*) articulation of its essence."[72] In chapter 4, I will discuss in greater detail the elements of Heidegger's philosophy of translation just mentioned. There I examine Heidegger's translation practice at work. The following remarks serve as background for that discussion.[73]

During the sixth lecture Heidegger makes several general observations about translating that summarize and amplify what he has said in earlier texts. Not unexpectedly, he repeats that "every translation is already interpretation" (p. 107). He encourages a "confrontation (*Vertrautheit*)" between "customary (*gewöhnlich*)" or "familiar (*geläufig*)" (pp. 105, 107) translations and thoughtful translation, which is drawn "from the freshness of the words (*aus der Frische der Worte*)" (p. 107). Such a confrontation is evident in Heidegger's own translations of the fundamental words of the thinking of the pre-Socratics, Plato,[74] Aristotle,[75] Descartes,[76] Leibniz,[77] Kant,[78] Hegel,[79] Schelling,[80] and Nietzsche.[81]

As we will see in chapter 4, in a thoughtful translation of Parmenides VI, Heidegger's first move is to separate the eight words of the fragment into four parts, separated by colons, in order to reveal the underlying "infrastructure or skeleton (*Gliederung*)" of the utterance. He then meditates on each of the words (*Worte*) individually. Eventually, the results are reassembled to form a German version of the fragment. In fact, he will articulate a number of versions of the fragment during the weeks of the course. The open spaces between the words, says Heidegger, point to what is "unspoken" or "unthought" in the fragment (pp. 42, 62, 71, 72). In other words, the author's thought lies in the silences (the *Sagen*) between the words. Heidegger writes: "If we characterize the word order of [Parmenides's] utterance as paratactic in the widest sense, then this happens only from embarrassment. For the utterance *speaks* there, where there are no words, in the open spaces between them which the colons indicate" (p. 114). Another element of Heidegger's philosophy of translation is made explicit here. A thoughtful translation expresses what has not been thought, that is, what has been left unuttered, by the thinker.

Heidegger notes that standard translations of Parmenides's fragment typically add "connecting words (*Verbindungswörten*)" in order to make a whole out of the fragments. The resulting whole sentence is structured according to the rules of grammar of the translating language. Taken as it is, however, the fragment sounds like the paratactic formations of primitive speech or a child's way of speaking.

> For example, a [German] child says of a dog about to jump at him: 'Wauwau, bös, beißen [Bow-wow! Bad! Bite!]'. [Parmenides's fragment] χρὴ τὸ λέγειν τε νοεῖν τ' ἐὸν ἔμμεναι sounds like that. (p. 112)

Whether working with a fragment or an intact sentence, paratactic arrangement of its elements isolates words from each other and reveals several ways in or points of access (the empty spaces between the words) to the one unified thought that says something in the utterance. It is important to stress that even when the text is syntactically complete, as in Leibniz's *Satz vom Grund* or a sentence from an Aristotelian text, Heidegger method of translating is paratactic. The same practice holds for the translation of words from the poems of Hölderlin or Stefan George.

Pursuing what has been left unuttered (that is, unthought), paratactic translation continues a way of thinking that left off at a certain point. Paratactic translation does not aim to improve upon what had been thought, as Schleiermacher believed. Rather, thoughtful translation effects the continuation of an author's thinking. Of course, in order to know where to pick up a thinker's train of thought at the point where it left off, one must first think along with him up to that point in order to be in a position to go on from there on one's own.

Heidegger repeats that translating is not searching for replacements from one's own language for items in the translated language. In the transition between Lectures X and XI, he writes:

> The whole business of replacement (*Ersatzgeschäft*) comes to nothing. If we hear the utterance (*Sagen*), if we are to be brought into question by it, it is not enough to exchange the Greek words

for the all too well-known words of another language. Instead we ourselves must allow to be said by the Greek words what *they* speak of. We must transpose our listening (*Hören*) to the legendary realm (*Sagebereich*) of the Greek language. (p. 175)

Here Heidegger highlights the root common to the words *Sagen* (utterance as "saying" or commonly known expression) and *Sage* (legend or myth). In fact, the more faithful translation of *Sage* is 'legend', especially given the closeness of the word 'legend' to the German word *legen* and the Greek word λόγος, an intimacy explored in the course that we will discuss in the next chapter.

The legendary realm in question is the realm of Greek λόγος, in which, as we know, "what is said in [Greek] is, in a remarkable way, at the same time what that which is said names."[82] In his earlier course devoted to Parmenides, Heidegger distinguished saying from the utterances of expressing oneself in writing or speaking (*Sprechen*). Utterance is, if you will, the silent voicing of thinking, which is seen especially clearly in the act of writing. Almost as an aside, Heidegger adds the crucial observation that "language comes about in utterance."[83] In other words, in utterance, language comes about *for us*. Utterance is the link between language and thinking.

For Heidegger, translating is devoted to making a thinker's utterance as a whole, that is, his *thought*, "hearable (*hörbar*) for the first time in what it expresses (*spricht*)" (p. 126). Expressing oneself or speaking (*Sprechen*) is the merely the effect of utterance. Such expressions arrive from language, which speaks "through" us, not from the speaker.

The remaining elements of Heidegger's philosophy of translation follow from what he has said up to this point. They are perhaps the most unique features of Heidegger's philosophy of translation: (1) Language translates, not the translator; and (2) language translates the thinker's utterance, not his text.

In *Was heißt Denken?* Heidegger also makes the provocative observation that the practitioners of traditional hermeneutics desire to understand a thinker's utterances "in terms of <the thinker> himself (*aus ihm selbst*)." But, he explains, "[t]his is impossible, since no thinker, as little as any poet, understands himself. How then should someone else even presume to be able to understand a thinker, let alone understand him better <than he himself did>?" (p. 113). This implies that *no thinker fully comprehends his own thought*. Otherwise, we might add, why would he continue to attempt to articulate his thought? A thinker understands himself, but only up to a point. It is not clear to me whether Heidegger would say the same thing about a thinker's (or poet's) utterances.

In general terms, if the goal of traditional hermeneutics is to better understand texts, Heidegger's view of translation as interpretation does not necessarily mark an advancement on the tradition, but if the underlying aim of hermeneutics is to interpret thinking, then Heidegger's philosophy and practice of translating marks a breakthrough in the field and enlarges its possibilities. One might even argue that Heidegger has for the first time seen what hermeneutics can be.

In *Was heißt Denken?* Heidegger also further develops the idea that for those who are used to everyday prose, like poetry, the result of thoughtful translation will often be hard to grasp. A thoughtful translation is "strange (*befremdlich*)" to the ear (p. 127) because it "speaks out" and offends standard usage.[84] It does not make matters easier, but exposes the difficulty of a philosopher's thought.

Referring to the last two words of the fragment, Heidegger clarifies what he understands by a transition to another way of thinking. Here much depends on the polysemic richness of the word *Sprung*.

> Such translating (*Über*setzen) is possible only as a transition (*Übersetzen*) to what speaks from these <Greek> words [ἐὸν and ἔμμεναι]. Such a transition is attained only by a sudden transit-ion (*Sprung*), and indeed through the <sort of> transformation (*Sprung*) that comes of a singular insight (*Blickes*) that catches sight of (*erblickt*) what the words heard in <a classical> Greek <way> utter. (pp. 140-41)

In the concluding hours of the course, Heidegger identifies translation with λόγος, the active bringing any sort of be-ing (*Seiende*) to light. Bringing things to presence is equivalent to thinking what has been left unthought by the author of a text. He also suggests that the

Greek word ἐόν (the present participle 'being') names what is found in the silent spaces between words, "at those junctures between the words (*Wortgefüge*), and thus <there> in what matters for (*ausmacht*) the articulation (*Fugen*) of the words" (p. 141) that comprise sentences, statements, or propositions. Ἐόν is the name for translation as bringing things to light. In chapter 4, we will look closely at how Heidegger applies his philosophy of translation to the words of a fragment of Parmenides's thought.

Heidegger added little more to his philosophy of translation after 1952. "Aus einem Gespräch von der Sprache. Zwischen einem Japaner und einem Fragenden" (1953-54) is a late dialogue on the nature of language that discusses, among other things, the problem of translating Japanese into German.[85] The text implies most of what Heidegger has already said about translation, although in the dialogue he emphasizes the gestural elements of language. As in his other essays on language from this period, the background of the discussion is the problem of translation.

The Scholar's description of translating several Japanese words into German provides a glimpse into Heidegger's own experience of translating: "While translating it often seemed to me that I was wandering back and forth from one voice to another, in such a way, however, that something dawned on me that gave me the sense that the source of the very nature of these fundamentally different languages is the same" (p. 109). Speaking through the Japanese scholar (perhaps modeled on Shin'ichi Hisamatsu),[86] Heidegger's point is that, although different so-called natural languages speak in different voices (the voices of different *Sprachgeiste*), the two voices (*Sagen!*) may find unison in the same thought. The scholar's description of his experience of translating as wandering between *different registers within the same voice* suggests that while two utterances may be spoken differently, what they say is the same.

In "Wissenschaft und Besinnung" (1954),[87] Heidegger again relates translation to a relation between the "spirit (*Geist*)" of the translated and translating languages, elaborating what he had said in 1938 about the role of the *Sprachgeist*. He adds, however, that the transition of the translator into the spirit of the translated language (for example, Parmenides's

Greek) is *initiated by the spirit of that language*.[88] To be in the spirit of a language means to be fully attentive to the words language speaks in giving voice to the thinker's utterance. Heidegger reminds his readers that an unfaithful translation has far-reaching consequences and can effect, "in a single stroke," the "disappearance (*Verschwinden*)" of "what the words (*Worte*) utter" (p. 46), making it impossible to "see" what has been thought. Here Heidegger once again relates words (*Worte*) as distinguished from terms (*Wörte*) to the silent utterance (*Sagen*) of language.

In a series of lectures from 1955–56 published as *Der Satz vom Grund*,[89] Heidegger applies his paratactic method of translation to the *principium rationis* or *principia reddendae rationis sufficientis: Nihil ist sine rationis*.[90] He translates the expression two ways, which reveal two approaches to Leibniz's thought: "*Sein und Grund: das Selbe* (Be[-ing] and foundation: the same <thing>)" and "*Sein: der Ab-Grund* (Be[-ing]: <the> ground-less)" (p. 93).[91]

In the twelfth hour of the course, he makes the important observation that the way translating proceeds depends upon which language is the translated language and which is the translating language, because (as he had already pointed out in "Wissenschaft und Besinnung") *the spirit of the translated language initiates the process of translating*. Each translation situation is therefore unique. For Heidegger, of course, the spirit of ancient Greek was always the most powerful initiator of translating and Greek words embodied more than any other the traces of thinking.

Heidegger also claims that the "translation [of a work of poetry or thinking] . . . is not only an interpretation but <also> a legacy (*Überlieferung*)" (p. 164) that establishes a tradition. Here he makes explicit the historical dimension of translation, which is closely related to the historical nature of a natural language and its *Sprachgeist*.[92] The Latin verb *transdare* ("to hand down," "to pass on," or "to pass along"), which is the root of the English word 'tradition', beautifully captures this aspect of translation. Heidegger goes on to say that the movement to another way of thinking that "an essential (*wesentliche*) translation" transports the translator to a different historical era (*Epoch*), in consequence of which the translator later "responds (*entspricht*) to how a <given> language speaks in <that particular instance of> what has come down <to us> of be[-ing]" (p. 164). For example, an essential translation of Parmenides's thought lets his time speak to us, if only briefly. And so it goes for an essential translation Leibniz's Latin and the so-called rationalist tradition, or Heidegger's German and the post-metaphysical (postmodern) tradition. As historical periods succeed one another, translating earlier texts makes it possible for what has been thought in earlier times to speak to those of us who come later.

Heidegger hoped he had taken some preliminary steps toward letting early Greek thinking reveal itself again or perhaps for the first time in his own thoughtful translations of the pre-Socratics, Plato, and Aristotle, but he also knew they were only small beginner's steps, and in the closing moments of the thirteenth hour of the course he even claims that "what has come down <to us> of be[-ing]" in the tradition of early Greek thinking "has not <yet> been uttered" (p. 187). Like Husserl, in this he saw himself as a perpetual beginner.

There are a few scattered comments on translation in the texts following *Der Satz vom Grund*. For example, in "Der Weg zur Sprache" (1959),[93] when translating a passage from Aristotle's Περὶ ἑρμηνείας, Heidegger makes plain that a translation of Aristotle's words can take place only by way of intimacy with Aristotle's thought (p. 233). Then, in his letter of April 1962 to William J. Richardson,[94] Heidegger writes that a translation "thought up in terms of what matters, expresses <something> for the first time when what constitutes the matter of what matters <for thinking> is brought up against thinking" (p. xiii). In 1966, during an interview with reporters from *Der Spiegel*, Heidegger made the surprising statement that, like poetry, thinking cannot be translated at all, for "as soon as one attempts a literal (*wörtlich*) translation, everything is transformed (*verwandelt*)."[95] For an audience of journalists, he adopts the conventional usage of the word *wörtlich* when he says that a literal translation can make "what the words (*Worte*) <of the original language> say" literally go up in smoke. Finally, in a short note to Albert Borgmann on the occasion of a conference on "Heidegger and Eastern Thought" held in 1969 at the University of Hawaii, he writes that every translation is merely an "expedient."[96] Since the German text is not given, it is difficult to know what Heidegger might have had in mind.

CONCLUSION AND SYNOPSIS

We now have before us the elements of Heidegger's philosophy of translation that slowly emerged between 1915 and 1969. When translation is thoughtful, the translator continues the thought expressed in a thinker's utterance and may even take over at the point where the author's thinking left off. For that reason, thoughtful translating sometimes makes explicit what was only implicit in the author's thought. The focus of thoughtful translation is not propositions, but individual words, which bear the traces of thinking.[97] For Heidegger, translating is an event mediated by language, in which the way of thinking of someone who is reading, listening, or speaking is transformed to the way of thinking of someone who has written or spoken. Sometimes these two are one and the same person, as when a thinker meditates on his own thought.

Just as when we listen to a composer's music we are provided access to the composer's thought, when we read or listen to a thinker's (or poet's) words, we have in them the means of approach to his way of thinking, even if it is our own way of thinking that we are attempting to penetrate. For Heidegger, legitimate (*rechtgemäßig*), authentic (*echt*), faithful (*wortgetreu*), and thoughtful (*denkende*) translating aspires to an authentic experience (*Erfahrung*) of the way of thinking (*Denkungsart*) of someone whose words we read or hear spoken. All such translation is interpretation (*Auslegung*), which moves within the spirit of the translated language (*Sprachgeist*) or between it and the spirit of a different, translating language. Language effects the transformation (*Versetzung*) of the reader (listener or speaker), moving him to another way of thinking. Translating occurs whenever language speaks (*spricht*). Heidegger believes that the translator does not improve upon the understanding a thinker has of himself, since no thinker understands himself in any case, yet it may extend a way of thinking. Most attempts at translation result in *interpretatii* (*Interpretationen*), which obscure access to a thinker's utterance (*Sagen*), rather than in an *Auslegung* that leads back to his way of thinking. In thoughtful translation of philosophical texts, often the translating language must be modified to accommodate the way of thinking revealed. In the end, translation recomposes (*übersetzt*) the original text.

Methodologically, translating a group of words, whether they comprise a fragment or a complete statement, begins by delineating the paratactic structure of the word group. Thoughtful translating meditates on each word of the ensemble, at first without regard to the syntax of the utterance, in order to reveal the traces of thinking it bears. While traditional translation practice aspires to the perfection of a technique, the high point of which so far is the development of computer translation programs, thoughtful translating brings about a transformation of the translator's way of thinking. The painstaking work of word-by-word (*wortgetreu*) translation eventually reveals *one* word that is of central importance for a way of thinking. According to Heidegger, every great thinker meditates on just one word, just as he utters the same thing again and again.[98]

Translating does not require spoken fluency in the translated language as a "second language" to one's own "native language." In the case of ancient Greek and Latin, for example, that would be impossible in any case, since no one any longer speaks these languages. For Heidegger, these examples are decisive, especially for the Greek of the pre-Socratics, Plato, and Aristotle.

While understanding the grammar and vocabulary of the translated and the translating languages is essential, such knowledge is not sufficient for gaining access to another way of thinking. What then is required of the translator? Everything depends upon her willingness to permit herself to be caught up in another way of thinking. In *Was heißt Denken?* which I will examine in detail in the next chapter, we will observe Heidegger doing just that with Parmenides's thinking.

Often the translating language must be modified in order to be capable of expressing a way of thinking. Thoughtful translations are therefore often ungainly, but authentic translating always expands the possibilities of the translating language. To the extent that a translator begins to think in a different key, the work of translating has a disquieting effect on him. He may move freely in and out of the other way of thinking, or he may lose himself in it and give up his freedom as a thinker in his own right. In this sense, thoughtful translating presents one with a risk (*Gefahr*).

At this point one may ask who counts as someone whose way of thinking is worth approaching and even continuing? For Heidegger, it is someone whose utterance draws us back time and again to his thought. A translator's way of expressing such thinking in the translated language will change in the process, not because the translator vacillates in uncertainty, but because in renewing a way of thinking, he continues it and changes it.

NOTES

1. Martin Heidegger, *Was heißt Denken?* (Tübingen: Niemeyer, 1961), p. 108. Now GA 5.

2. Two important studies of Heidegger and hermeneutics are Hubert Dreyfus, "Beyond Hermeneutics: Interpretation in Late Heidegger and Recent Foucault," in *Hermeneutics: Questions and Prospects*, ed. Gary Shapiro and Alan Sica (Amherst: University of Massachusetts Press, 1984), pp. 66-83; and Wayne Owens, "Martin Heidegger on Interpretation," *Phenomenological Inquiry* 18 (1994): 53-72. See also Owens's paper, "The Waymaking Movement of Thinking: Heidegger and George's 'The Word'," *Southern Journal of Philosophy* 26 (1988): 522-37.

3. F. D. E. Schleiermacher, *Hermeneutics: The Handwritten Manuscripts (1805-1833)* (Atlanta: Scholars Press, 1977), pp. 99, 193. Schleiermacher's texts were edited for publication in 1959 by Heinz Kimmerle. For an excellent recent introduction to Schleiermacher, see Ben Vedder, "Schleiermacher," in *A Companion to Continental Philosophy*, ed. Simon Critchley and William R. Schroeder (London: Blackwell, 1998), pp. 417-24.

4. The translations are by F. M. Cornford. Heidegger's 1924-25 course on the *Sophist* ends by introducing this passage from the dialogue (GA 22, pp. 607-609). Oddly enough, in his course on the *Theaetetus* he does not discuss the passage on thinking. "Vom Wesen der Wahrheit: Zu Platons Höhlengleichnis und Theätet" (1931-32), GA 34: 277.

5. Richard Palmer, *Hermeneutics: Interpretation Theory in Schleiermacher, Dilthey, Heidegger, and Gadamer* (Evanston, Ill.: Northwestern University Press, 1969), pp. 124-61; and Kurt Mueller-Vollmer, ed., *The Hermeneutics Reader* (New York: Continuum Press, 1990), pp. 32-35. For the most part, both Palmer and Mueller-Vollmer attempt to fit Heidegger into the tradition of hermeneutics that assumes thinking occurs in words.

6. Josef Bleicher, *Contemporary Hermeneutics: Hermeneutics as Method, Philosophy, and Critique* (London: Routledge, 1980), pp. 98-99.

7. *Sein und Zeit*, §77, GA 2: 525-33. See also Palmer, *Hermeneutics: Interpretation Theory in Schleiermacher, Dilthey, Heidegger, and Gadamer*, pp. 130-32. Theodore Kisiel remarks on the importance of the Dilthey-Yorck correspondence for Heidegger's development in "Why the First Draft of *Being and Time* Was Never Published," *Journal of the British Society for Phenomenology* 20, no. 1 (January 1989): 7-22; and in *The Genesis of Heidegger's* Being and Time (Berkeley: University of California Press, 1993), pp. 321-26.

8. "Die Sprache," GA 12: 10-12; and *Der Satz vom Grund* (Pfullingen: Neske, 1957), p. 161. See Claus-Artur Scheier, "Die Sprache spricht: Heideggers Tautologie," *Zeitschrift für philosophische Forschung* 47, no. 1 (1993): 60-74.

9. On reading, see Heidegger's brief text "Was heißt Lesen?" (GA 13: 111):

> What is reading? What is fundamental and dominant in reading is a coming together (*Sammlung*). What comes together here? What is written, what is uttered in the text (*Schrift*)? Authentic reading is the coming together (*Sammlung*) of what without our knowing it has already taken into account (*in den Anspruch genommen*) our nature (*Wesen*), which we may thereby affirm (*entsprechen*) or deny (*versagen*).
>
> Without authentic reading we are unable to see what is facing us (*das Anblickende*), and behold what is appearing (*Erscheinende*) and coming to light (*Scheinende*).

Sammlung may also be translated with 'composition' or even 'composure', which suggests the effect of reading on the reader's disposition. For Heidegger, reading the printed word is listening with our eyes.

10. *Sein und Zeit*, GA 2: 117. In one of his copies of the seventh edition of the work (that is to say, sometime after 1953), Heidegger corrects himself at the passage in which he expresses this view: "Not so (*Unwahr*). Language

is not built upon (*aufgestockt*), but rather *is* the original nature (*Wesen*) of truth as there (*Da*)" (note c to p. 117).

11. J. L. Mehta, *Martin Heidegger: The Way and the Vision* (Honolulu: University of Hawaii Press, 1976), pp. 63-64.

12. Joseph J. Kockelmans, ed., *Heidegger and Language* (Evanston, Ill.: Northwestern University Press, 1972). For a sampling of the literature on Heidegger and language, see Thomas Munson, "Heidegger's Recent Thought on Language," *Philosophy and Phenomenological Research* 21 (1961): 361-72; William J. Richardson, "Heidegger and the Origin of Language," *International Philosophical Quarterly* 2 (1962): 404-16; Irmgard Bock, *Heideggers Sprachdenken* (Meisenheim am Glein, Germany: Hain, 1966), pp. 29-39, 87-102 (on λόγος, language, and utterance); Luce F. de Visscher, "La Pensée du Langage chez Heidegger," *Revue Philosophique de Louvain* 64 (1966): 224-62; John Sallis, ed., *Heidegger and the Path of Thinking* (Pittsburgh: Duquesne University Press, 1970), in particular Theodore Kisiel's "The Language of the Event: The Event of Language," pp. 86, 98-100; Peter J. McCormick, *Heidegger and the Language of the World: An Argumentative Reading of the Later Heidegger's Meditations on Language* (Ottawa: University of Ottawa Press, 1976), which is a study of *Unterwegs zur Sprache*; *Heidegger and Modern Philosophy: Critical Essays*, ed. Michael Murray (New Haven, Conn.: Yale University Press, 1978); Barbara Warnick, "Logos in Heidegger's Philosophy of Language," *Philosophy Research Archives* 5 (1979): 660-75; *Heidegger and Language: A Collection of Original Papers*, ed. David Wood (Coventry, England: Parousia, 1981); Tony O'Connor, "Heidegger and the Limits of Language," *Man and World* 14 (1981): 3-14; David Michael Levin, "The Embodiment of Thinking: Heidegger's Approach to Language," in *Phenomenology: Dialogues and Bridges*, ed. Ronald Bruzinga (Albany: SUNY Press, 1982), pp. 61-77; Christopher Nwodo, "Language and Reality in Martin Heidegger," *Indian Philosophical Quarterly* 12 (1985): 23-26; Kenneth Maly, "Language and Saying," *Philosophy Today* 30 (1986): 126-36; Michael Heim, "The Finite Framework of Language," *Philosophy Today* 31 (1987): 3-20; Hermann Schweppenhauser, *Studien über die Heideggerische Sprachtheorie* (Munich: Text Kritik, 1988); Robert Mugerauer, *Heidegger's Language and Thinking* (Atlantic Highlands, N.J.: Humanities Press, 1988); Jean-Pierre Cometti, "Heidegger et la Philosophie du Langage," *Revue Internationale de Philosophie* 43 (1989): 52-63; Robert van Roden Allen, "Martin Heidegger and the Place of Language," *Dialogos* 60 (1990): 103-21; Jacques Taminiaux, "'Voix' et 'Phénomene' dan l'Ontologie fondamentale de Heidegger," *Revue Philosophique Francaise* 180, no. 2 (1990): 395-408; Véronique Fóti, *Hei-*

degger and the Poets: Poiesis, Sophia, Techne (Atlantic Highlands, N.J.: Humanities Press, 1991); *Martin Heidegger: Critical Assessments*, ed. Christopher Macann, 3 vols. (London: Routledge, 1992); Françoise Dastur, "Language and *Ereignis*," in *Reading Heidegger: Commemorations*, ed. John Sallis (Bloomington: Indiana University Press, 1992), pp. 355-69; Pol Vandevelde, *Etre et Discours: La Question du Langage dans l'Itineraire de Heidegger (1927-1938)* (Brussels: Academie Royale, 1994); and my paper "On the Fundamental Experience of Voice in Language, with Some Notes on Heidegger," *Philosophy Today* 25 (1981): 139-47, revised version in *The Voice that Thinks* (Greensburg, Pa.: Eadmer Press, 1997), pp. 73-82.

13. Jacques Derrida, *Of Spirit: Heidegger and the Question* (Chicago: University of Chicago Press, 1989), p. 4 passim, and *Margins of Philosophy* (Chicago: University of Chicago Press, 1982), pp. 31-67, 123-34. In a provocative comparative study of Heidegger and Derrida, Herman Rapaport discusses time as translation. *Heidegger and Derrida: Reflections on Time and Language* (Lincoln: University of Nebraska Press, 1989), pp. 27-33, 35. Derrida discusses the hearing (*Hören*) of language as an evocation of thinking. "Heidegger's Ear: Philopolemology (*Geschlecht* IV)," in *Reading Heidegger: Commemorations*, ed. John Sallis (Bloomington: Indiana University Press, 1992), pp. 163-218.

14. The most recent translation of the revised edition of Hans-Georg Gadamer's book is by Joel Weinsheimer and Donald G. Marshall, *Truth and Method* (New York: Continuum, 1994). See especially pp. 384-89, and supplement 2, "To What Extent Does Language Perform Thought?" where Gadamer finally seems to accept Heidegger's pan-translational position: "The translation process fundamentally contains the whole secret of how human beings come to an understanding of the world . . ." (p. 548).

15. As Parvis Emad points out, both Derrida's "deconstructive strategy" and the "fusion of horizons" called for in Gadamer's hermeneutics are examples of a hermeneutics of confrontation between a subject and the text, which is a multiplex object comprised of lexical units of meaning. Emad, "Thinking More Deeply into the Question of Translation: Essential Translation and the Unfolding of Language," in *Reading Heidegger: Commemorations*, ed. Sallis, p. 339, n. 7.

16. Both are contrasted with transcription (*Übertragung*) and reinterpretation (*Umdeutung*), which Heidegger sees as moments of translating within one's own language. As I will show, Heidegger makes a more fundamental distinction between literal (*wörtlich*) translation and faithful (*wortgetreu*) translation, which is true to the word.

17. This view brought Heidegger into radical opposition to his own mentor, Edmund Husserl, for whom philosophy should aspire to be a "rigorous science" in search of the pure data of consciousness. See Edmund Husserl, "Philosophie als strenge Wissenschaft," *Logos* 1 (1910): 289-314. Although the tradition of construing philosophy as science antedated him, Hegel, too, strenuously conceives of philosophy as systematic science. Of course, it was precisely against this trend that Kierkegaard reacted so vigorously, and we now know that Kierkegaard's reaction was decisive for Heidegger and opened up the possibility of an entirely new era in philosophy, the first, Heidegger thought, since the time of the ancient Greeks. See *Die Grundbegriffe der Metaphysik: Welt-Endlichkeit-Einsamkeit*, GA 29/30: 225.

18. At the end of his "Postscript" to "What Is Metaphysics?" (GA 9: 312), Heidegger quotes a line from "Patmos," Hölderlin's poem in which he says that the poet and thinker "live nearby on distant peaks." See the bilingual edition of *Hölderlin: Poems and Fragments* (Ann Arbor: University of Michigan Press, 1967), pp. 463-64.

19. Kathleen Freeman, *Ancilla to the Pre-Socratic Philosophers* (Oxford: Blackwell, 1948). Nor does Freeman say anything about translation in her related study *The Pre-Socratic Philosophers: A Companion to Diels, Fragmente der Vorsokratiker* (Oxford: Oxford University Press, 1953). For the work of other philosopher-philologists of the pre-Socratics, see Charles H. Kahn, *The Art and Thought of Heraclitus: An Edition of the Fragments with Translation and Commentary* (Cambridge: Cambridge University Press, 1979), and G. S. Kirk, *Heraclitus: The Cosmic Fragments* (Cambridge: Cambridge University Press, 1962). None of these discuss their philosophy of translation.

20. G. S. Kirk, J. E. Raven, and Malcolm Schofield, *The Presocratic Philosophers* (Cambridge: Cambridge University Press, 1983).

21. *Grundbegriffe*, GA 51: 94.

22. See the bilingual edition, *What Is Philosophy?* (New York: Twayne, 1958), p. 44 (translation modified).

23. In this connection, it is well known that Heidegger held the highly debatable view that great thinking was expressible only in ancient Greek (and perhaps in German).

24. On the special place of the Greek language (and alphabet) on the formation of the relation between the written word and thought, see Ivan Illich, *In the Vineyard of the Text: A Commentary to Hugh's Didascalicon* (Chicago: University of Chicago Press, 1993), pp. 103, 113. Illich's study of "the impact of alphabetic technique on the interpretation of human action"

(p. 86) helps clarify the history of the notions of reading, author, and text more than most of the deconstructionist literature.

25. Gerald L. Bruns, in *Heidegger's Estrangements: Language, Truth, and Poetry in the Later Writings* (New Haven, Conn.: Yale University Press, 1989), pp. 123-49, reflects on what he terms "Heidegger's uncanny hermeneutics," recognizing that, for Heidegger, thinking is a kind of listening (p. 137, n. 7).

26. GA 2: 18, 50.

27. *Sophist* 263e refers specifically to what we "give the name thinking to (ἐπωνομάσθη[,] διάνοια)."

28. Reprinted in GA 1: 191-412. At the time Heidegger wrote his dissertation and until Martin Grabmann's research demonstrated otherwise, Thomas of Erfurt's *Grammatica Speculativa* was attributed to Duns Scotus.

29. "Phänomenologische Interpretationen zu Aristoteles (Anzeige der hermeneutischen Situation)," *Dilthey-Jahrbuch für Philosophie und Geschichte der Gesisteswissenschaften* (Göttingen) 6 (1989): 252, translated by Michael Baur as "Phenomenological Interpretations with Respect to Aristotle: Indication of the Hermeneutical Situation," in *Man and World* 25, no. 3/4 (1992): 355-93. The text is now known to be an important precursor of *Sein und Zeit*. See Kisiel, *The Genesis of Heidegger's Being and Time*, pp. 248-71; and GA 61, *Phänomenologische Interpretationen zu Aristoteles. Einführung in die phänomenologische Forschung*.

30. GA 63, § 2: 10-14.

31. References are to GA 2 (1987). Franco Volpi has argued that *Sein und Zeit* is an extended exercise in translating the basic words of Aristotle's *Nicomachean Ethics*. "Being and Time: A 'Translation' of the *Nicomachean Ethics*?" in *Reading Heidegger from the Start: Essays in His Earliest Thought*, ed. Theodore Kisiel and John van Buren (Albany: SUNY Press, 1994), pp. 195-211.

32. See GA 55, *Heraklit: 1. Der Anfang des abendländischen Denkens, 2. Logik: Heraklits Lehre zum Logos*, which is based on two courses from 1943 and 1944; "Logos (Heraklit, Fragment 50)," as essay written in 1944, based on the second course, in *Vorträge und Aufsätze*, 3 vols. (Pfullingen: Neske, 1978), 3: 3-25; *Heraklit: Martin Heidegger-Eugen Fink: Seminar 1966/67*, based on a seminar given with Eugen Fink during the winter semester of 1966-67, in *Seminare*, GA 15: 9-263. In 1957, writing about the word *Ereignis*, Heidegger said that the word "can no more be translated than the Greek word λόγος or the Chinese *Tao*." "Der Satz der Identität," in *Identität und Differenz* (Pfullingen, Germany: Neske, 1967), p. 25. For Heidegger, this means that the traces of thinking embodied in the word cannot be exhausted.

33. In general, when Heidegger uses a latinate German word such as *Interpretation*, he takes its Latin source word in its original meaning. The basic meaning of the noun *interpretatio* is "translation," in the conventional senses of transcription (*Übertragung*), paraphrase (*Umschreibung*), and reinterpretation (*Umdeutung*). The origin of the verb *interpretare* suggests that the first translators (*interpres*) negotiated the value (*pretium*) of things (at first, probably items of barter or trade) exchanged between (*inter*) two agents who could not communicate with each other because they did not speak the same natural language. The first interpreters included prophets, who mediated between the present and the future, and hierophants, who mediated between divinities and mortals. For Heidegger, translation mediates between the thought of the author and the thought of the reader, listener, speaker, or writer.

34. *Nicomachean Ethics*, 1102b 15, 1138b 9, 1139a 4.

35. *Aristoteles*, Metaphysik Θ *1-3: Vom Wesen und Wirklichkeit der Kraft*, GA 33 (1981). Translated as *Aristotle's* Metaphysics Θ *1-3: On the Essence and Actuality of Force* (Bloomington: Indiana University Press, 1995). For a discussion of the translation decisions at work in the English version, see my review in *International Philosophical Quarterly* 36, no. 4 (December 1996): 492-93.

36. GA 34.

37. GA 5: 1-74. Earlier on in this text, he uses the term *Dingsein*, "to be a thing" (p. 5).

38. *Deutsche Grammatik*, 2 vols. (Hildesheim, Germany: Olms, 1967 [1819]), 1: vi.

39. "Über den Ursprung der Sprache," in *Kleinere Schriften*, 8 vols. (Hildesheim, Germany: Olms, 1965), 1: 290, trans. Raymond A. Wiley as *On the Origin of Language* (Leiden: Brill, 1984).

40. Johann Gottfried Herder, "On the Origin of Language" (1772), trans. John H. Moran and Alexander Gode, in *On the Origin of Language* (Chicago: University of Chicago Press, 1966), pp. 87-166 (esp. 141-66). See Martin Heidegger, *Vom Wesen der Sprache: Zu Herders Abhandlung "Über den Ursprung der Sprache,"* GA 85, a seminar from the summer of 1939.

41. Wilhelm von Humboldt, *Linguistic Variability and Intellectual Development* (Coral Gables: University of Miami Press, 1971), p. 24.

42. In this connection, see Walter Stohrer, "Heidegger and Jacob Grimm: On Dwelling and the Genesis of Language," *Modern Schoolman* 62 (1984): 43-52.

43. *Qu'est-ce que c'est la Métaphysique?* (Paris: Gallimard, 1938), p. 8. I have worked with the third edition (1951) of Henry Corbin's translation of

Heidegger's German text. The original German text seems to be unavailable. Corbin's translation first appeared in *Bifur* 8 (1931): 9-27, with an introduction by Alexandre Koyré.

44. GA 9: 245. Borrowing usage from the traditional literature on translation, Heidegger uses the word *Übertragung* to refer to the transliteration of a language from one of its historical periods into another, as when, for example, we transliterate the Old English of *Beowulf* into Modern English. Heidegger discusses the *Übertragung* of the Alemannic dialect spoken by Johann Peter Hebel into German. "Sprache und Heimat" (1960), in *Aus der Erfahrung des Denkens*, GA 13: 160. In an important passage in the essay, he glosses *Übertragung* with *Metapher* (metaphor) (p. 179).

45. Heidegger's indirect comparison of a translator with a performer of music is apt. A good musician can easily transpose music while reading the score, but the ability to do so is mostly intuitive, so that many musically illiterate performers (those who cannot read the score) can do it quite well while performing "by ear." While certain techniques claim to make transposing music a more fluent practice, it seems to be given to some capable musicians, but not to others, to be able to execute it well. Heidegger does not say so, but I think the same might apply to translators.

46. The text is from the second trimester of 1940 at the University of Freiburg. *Nietzsche*, 2 vols. (Pfullingen: Neske, 1961), 2: 31-256. The original text of this lecture course was published as *Nietzsche: Der europäische Nihilismus*, GA 48: 175-334. I have discussed the translation of these courses devoted entirely to Nietzsche in "Who Is Heidegger's Nietzsche?" a review article of the two-volume edition of a translation of *Nietzsche* by David Krell, Frank Capuzzi, and Joan Stambaugh, in my book *The Voice That Thinks*, pp. 59-71.

47. See Manfred Frings, "Protagoras Rediscovered: Heidegger's Explication of Protagoras' Fragment," *Journal of Value Inquiry* 8 (1974): 112-23.

48. GA 51. See the translation, Martin Heidegger, *Basic Concepts* (Bloomington: Indiana University Press, 1993), pp. 81-106.

49. Hermann Diels and Walther Kranz, *Die Fragmente der Vorsokratiker*, 2 vols. (Berlin: Weidmann, 1952), 1: chap. 12. See also Kirk, Raven, and Schofield, *The Presocratic Philosophers*, pp. 117-18; and Charles H. Kahn, *Anaximander and the Origins of Greek Cosmology* (New York: Columbia University Press, 1960).

50. GA 53. Translated as *Hölderlin's Hymn "The Ister"* (Bloomington: Indiana University Press, 1996). The text is based on the 1942 course, "Hölderlin's Hymns."

51. A German-speaking commentator is once supposed to have asked for a translation of one of Heidegger's texts into German. The comment was meant as more than mild sarcasm, but it accords perfectly with a basic tenet of Heidegger's philosophy of translation, that we translate our thinking every time we speak or reflect on what we have said or written.

52. GA 54. Translated as Martin Heidegger, *Parmenides* (Bloomington: Indiana University Press, 1992).

53. I have adapted Aristotle's phrase from the *Nichomachean Ethics*, 1144a 30.

54. In other words, thoughtful translation does not use the sentence as its context of significance.

55. As we will, Heidegger believes that language makes use of the speaker or writer, not that we use language.

56. Although the text dates from 1943, it was published only in 1979.

57. See the discussion of the "Grundbegriffe" lectures, GA 51, above.

58. "Der Anfang des abendländischen Denkens," GA 55: 3-181. See p. 44 for the quotation. An anthology of Heidegger's translations of Heraclitus is provided in *Heraclitean Fragments: A Companion Volume to the Heidegger/Fink Seminar on Heraclitus*, ed. John Sallis and Kenneth Maly (University: University of Alabama Press, 1980), pp. 3-15. In 1954, Heidegger wrote an essay entitled "Heraklit," which is based on material from this course. It was published that year in his *Vorträge und Aufsätze* as "Aletheia (Heraklit, Fragment 16)" along with "Logos (Heraklit, Fragment 50)" and "Moira (Parmenides, Fragment VIII, 34-31)." *Vorträge und Aufsätze* (Pfullingen, Germany: Neske, 1954), 3: 53-78.

59. When Heidegger uses the word *Sagen* (utterance) in this and other passages, he does not have in mind a spoken utterance, but rather the *entire* thought that is given expression in a spoken or written utterance. In *Was heißt Denken?* he will claim that uttering as writing is the immediate translation of thinking.

60. "Der Spruch des Anaximander," GA 5: 321-73.

61. It is no accident that the verb *bewahren* is formed on the same root form (*wahr*) as the noun *Wahrheit* (truth). In using *bewahren* here, Heidegger is suggesting that, although truth is not found in words, it is protected or looked after by words.

62. This evocative and readily mistranslated formulation, that translation "writes while thinking," is prescient of what Heidegger will later say about the intimate relation between thinking as *Sagen* and writing.

63. See "Der Ursprung des Kunstwerkes," GA 5: 63. I think Heidegger would also consider a work of art to be a *Spruch* in this sense.

64. See George Seidel, *Heidegger and the Presocratics*, p. 127: "This is the absolutely critical thing that translation represents in the thinking of Heidegger. For in trans-lation we grasp or else we fail to grasp the experience (*Erfahrung*) of another thinker; and we either transfer this experience or else we fail to put it across (*Über-setzen*), not simply into another language, but into another way of thinking." Seidel is among the most perspicuous of Heidegger's interpreters. See his recent article, "A Key to Heidegger's *Beiträge*," *Gregorianum* 76, no. 2 (1995): 363-72. To invoke an image: *utterance (Sagen) is the bridge between one way of thinking and another.*

65. Later Heidegger would make the same assertion about all thinkers.

66. In the next chapter, I cite an example from Heidegger of how Plato's thought brought about a change in Greek grammar.

67. Martin Heidegger, *Was heißt Denken?* (Tübingen: Niemeyer, 1954). Page references are to the second edition (1961). See GA 8.

68. Heidegger, *Vorträge und Aufsätze*, 3: 27-52. The essay was originally meant to be included in part 2 of the course which was published as *Was heißt Denken?* although Heidegger did not present it as part of the course in 1952.

69. Ibid., p. 52. Heidegger explicitly characterizes legitimate translating as "thoughtful (*denkende*) translating" (p. 35).

70. J. Glenn Gray, "Introduction," in *What Is Called Thinking?* (New York: Harper and Row, 1968), p. xvii.

71. See Frank Edler, "Heidegger and Werner Jaeger on the Eve of 1933: A Possible Rapprochement," in *Proceedings: Heidegger Conference* (Durham: University of New Hampshire, 1996), where the author calls attention to the importance of Heidegger's paratactic presentation of a text he intends to translate (p. 241) and refers to Heidegger's call for a new foundation for philology (p. 232). See GA 29/30: 438.

72. GA 9: 314. On the lack of an adequate vocabulary for his way of thinking see also GA 2: 52, GA 9: 314, and GA 20: 203-204.

73. Heidegger applies the paratactic or word-by-word method beginning as early as 1929, in *Vom Wesen des Grundes* (1929), GA 9: 127 passim.

74. On Plato: *Platon:* Sophistes (1924-25), GA 19; *Vom Wesen der Wahrheit: Zu Platons Höhlengleichnis und Theätet* (1931-32), GA 34; and *Platons Lehre von der Wahrheit: Mit einem Brief über den Humanismus* (1940), in *Wegmarken* (1967), GA 9: 203-38.

75. On Aristotle: "Phänomenologische Interpretationen zu Aristoteles (Anzeige der hermeneutischen Situation)" (1922), pp. 235-69; *Phänomenologische Interpretationen zu Aristoteles: Einführung in die phänomenolo-*

gische Forschung (1921-22), GA 61; *Einführung in die phänomenologische Forschung* (1923-24), GA 17: §§ 1-2; *Platon:* Sophistes (1924-25), GA 19: §§ 4-32; *Logik: Die Frage nach der Wahrheit* (1925-26), GA 21: § 13 (a-b); *Die Grundbegriffe der antiken Philosophie* (1926), GA 22: §§ 51-67; *Die Grundbegriffe der Metaphysik: Welt-Endlichkeit-Einsamkeit* (1929-30), GA 29/30: §§ 9, 72; *Aristoteles,* Metaphysik Θ *1-3: Von Wesen und Wirklichkeit der Kraft* (1931), GA 33; and "Vom Wesen und Begriff der Φύσις: Aristoteles *Physik* B,1" (1939), in *Wegmarken* (1967), GA 9: pp. 239-301.

76. On Descartes: *Nietzsche: Der europäische Nihilismus* (1940), GA 48: 198-257.

77. On Leibniz: *Metaphysische Anfangsgründe der Logik im Ausgang der Leibniz* (1928), GA 26, and "Vom Wesen des Grundes" (1929), GA 9: 126-37.

78. On Kant: *Phänomenologische Interpretation von Kants Kritik der reinen Vernunft* (1927-28), GA 25; *Kant und das Problem der Metaphysik* (1929), GA 3; *Die Frage nach dem Ding: Zu Kants Lehre von der transzendentalen Grundsätzen* (1935-36), GA 41; and "Kants These über das Sein" (1961), in *Wegmarken* (1967), GA 9: 445-480.

79. On Hegel: *Hegels Phänomenologie des Geistes* (1930-31), GA 32; "Hegels Begriff der Erfahrung" (1942-43), in *Holzwege* (1950), GA 5: 115-208; *Hegel. 1. Die Negativität: Eine Auseinandersetzung mit Hegel aus dem Ansatz in der Negativität (1938/39, 1941). 2. Erläuterung der "Einleitung" zu Hegels "Phänomenologie des Geistes"* (1942), GA 68; "Die ontotheo-logische Verfassung der Metaphysik" (1957), in *Identität und Differenz* (Pfullingen: Neske, 1957), pp. 35-73; and the "Seminar in Le Thor" (1968) on Hegel's *Differenzschrift*, in *Seminare*, GA 15: 286-325.

80. On Schelling: *Schelling: Vom Wesen der menschlichen Freiheit* (1936), GA 42; and *Die Metaphysik des deutschen Idealismus (Schelling)* (1941), GA 49.

81. On Nietzsche: "Nietzsches Wort 'Gott ist tot'" (1943), in *Holzwege* (1950), GA 5: 209-67; *Nietzsche*, 2 vols. (Pfullingen: Neske, 1961) (and the original texts of the lecture courses from which the contents of these volumes were excerpted, in GA 43, 44, 47, 48, and 50); "Wer ist Nietzsches Zarathustra?" (1953), in *Vorträge und Aufsätze*, 1: 93-118; and *Was heißt Denken?* pp. 1-78.

82. *What Is Philosophy?* p. 44.

83. "Im Sagen west die Sprache," *Was heißt Denken?* p. 171.

84. An example of this is my own translation of Heidegger's word *Sein*

as 'be[-ing]'. Wallace Stevens sees the semantic possibility I have exploited: "Let be be finale of seem." Wallace Stevens, "The Emperor of Ice-Cream" (c. 1923), in *The Collected Poems* (New York: Vintage Books, 1982), p. 64.

85. GA 12: 79-146. For a discussion of thinking and translating in the later Heidegger, see David B. Allison, "The *Différance* of Translation," in *The Textual Sublime: Deconstruction and Its Differences*, ed. Hugh J. Silverman and Gary E. Aylesworth (Albany: SUNY Press, 1990), pp. 184-90. On the idea of translation presented in the dialogue, see R. Thomas Harris, "Is Translation Possible?" *Diogenes* 149 (1990): 110-21. Klaus Opilik discusses the question of translation between German and Japanese and the longstanding interest of the Japanese philosophers in Heidegger in "Destruktion und Übersetzung: Zu den Aufgaben von Philosophiegeschichte nach Martin Heidegger," *Zeitschrift für Philosophische Forschung* 54 (1990): 479-84.

86. Alfred L. Copley, *Heidegger und Hisamatsu und ein Zuhörender* (Kyoto: Bokubi Verlag, 1963), reprinted as "Martin Heidegger—Shinichi Hisamatsu: Die Kunst und das Denken: Protokoll eines Colloquiums am 18 Mai 1958," in *Japan und Heidegger: Gedenkschrift der Stadt Meßkirch zum hundertsten Geburtstag Martin Heideggers*, ed. Hartmut Buchner (Sigmaringen: Thorbecke, 1989), pp. 211-15.

87. Heidegger, *Vorträge und Aufsätze*, 1: 37-62.

88. See "Die Sprache," GA 12: 10-12. Jacques Derrida has elaborated the theme of the spirit of language in Heidegger, in *Of Spirit: Heidegger and the Question*, pp. 1-6.

89. Martin Heidegger, *Der Satz vom Grund* (Neske: Pfullingen, 1957).

90. Renato Cristin points out that this was for Leibniz the "vulgar" form of the principle, the broader formulation of which speaks to "that whereby one can always account for why something has *happened* this way rather than in some other way [emphasis added]." *Heidegger and Leibniz: Reason and the Path* (Dordrecht: Kluwer, 1998), p. 1.

91. See "Vom Wesen des Grundes" (1929), GA 9: 127 and passim, where Heidegger also discusses the principle of ground (*Grund*).

92. See also Heidegger, *Hölderlins Hymne "Der Ister,"* p. 79.

93. Originally titled "Die Sprache," the lecture was published first in *Gestalt und Gedanke* (Munich) 4 (1959): 137-70, and is reprinted with a few changes in *Unterwegs zur Sprache*, GA 12: 227-57.

94. William J. Richardson, *Heidegger: Through Phenomenology to Thought* (The Hague: Nijhoff, 1963), pp. xii-xiii. See also Richardson's comments on Heidegger's understanding of the relation between translation and thinking (pp. 526, 611).

95. "Nur noch ein Gott kann uns retten," in *Antwort: Martin Heidegger im Gespräch*, ed. Günther Neske and Emil Kettering (Pfullingen: Neske, 1988), p. 108. The audiotaped interview with Heidegger, which was conducted on September 23, 1966, was published only on May 31, 1976. Reprinted in GA 16: 652–83.

96. Winfield E. Nagley, "Introduction to the Symposium and Reading of a Letter from Martin Heidegger," *Philosophy East and West* 20 (1970): 221.

97. Heidegger does not avoid all considerations of syntax, but attempts to understand the grammar of a group of words by first focusing on the individual words that comprise the semantic ensemble. By proceeding paratactically, he allows grammar to accommodate thought, rather than trying to fit what is uttered into the structures of an existing grammar. In the next chapter, I will cite the illustration he gives of Plato, who revises Greek grammar to fit his thinking. In rejecting the syntactic ensemble as the basis for translation, Heidegger implicitly challenges the hegemony of propositional logic that Western philosophy inherited from Greek philosophy as formalized in the Aristotelian organon and which serves as the basis for the metaphysical tradition.

98. "Brief über den 'Humanismus'," GA 9: 363.

CHAPTER FOUR

PARATACTIC METHOD

Translating Parmenides, Fragment VI

Heidegger's efforts to translate the Greek thinkers are the source of his philosophy of translation, which I have summarized from a review of his published writings. In his 1951-52 translation of Parmenides's Fragment VI, Heidegger brings to bear a half-century-long conversation with ancient Greek and demonstrates his practice of translating in full stride. Until now, Heidegger's philosophy of translation is part of what has been left unspoken of Heidegger's thought. It will have become clear that in my review of the early critical literature and the first English translations of Heidegger, I have had the principles of Heidegger's philosophy of translation in mind, and in my critique, I have countered the *interpretatii* of his early readers with *Auslegungen* of his fundamental words. In this chapter, I will present an account of Heidegger at work in an *Auslegung* of a fragment of pre-Socratic thought.

Heidegger's translation practice, which is determined by his philosophy of translation, is characterized by a procedure that works paratactically, word by word, rather than syntactically, by way of an analysis of propositions. He has written many pages on the few remaining fragments of the pre-Socratics.[1] His translation of three chapters of Aristotle's *Metaphysics* covers less than a thousand words of Aristotle's text.² The same is true for his reading of Aristotle's *Physics* B 1.³ *Hegels Begriff der Erfahrung*, a translation of the preface to Hegel's *Phänomenologie des Geistes* in which Heidegger works with passages several sentences in length at a time, is an exception to his usual way of working with a text.⁴

At the very least, he would expect any serious translation of a philosophical text to take the form of the kind of paratactic analysis he carries out in *Was heißt Denken?* which is perhaps the best example of Heidegger's translation practice at work. His discussions (*Erläuterungen*) of the poetry of Friedrich Hölderlin, Johann Peter Hebel, Georg Trakl, Rainer Maria Rilke, and Stefan George, which are part of his investigations of the nature of language, are a separate but related series of translations in which he works the same way as he does with philosophical texts.⁵

In this chapter, I will focus on the Parmenides translation which he presented during the second semester of the lecture course "Was heißt Denken?," Heidegger's last series of lectures as a regular professor at the University of Freiburg.⁶ Fragment VI is introduced in the transition (*Stundenübergang*) between Session Five and Session Six of the Spring 1952 semester when Heidegger begins the translation itself. He devotes the last six hours of the course to the task.⁷ The background of the translation is the presiding question: What is it that we call thinking?⁸

Heidegger announces that "we will attempt to listen to the utterance (*Spruch*) from (*aus*) the freshness (*Frische*) of its words" (p. 109:25).⁹ He believes that listening to the words of the text as though for the first time will make it possible for us to translate ourselves to Parmenides's way of thinking. He says that "every interpretation is a conversation (*Gespräch*) with the work and with the utterance" (p. 110:20) that leads to a way of thinking and to the realm of what has been left unsaid. Heidegger wants to show that "the utterance <of Parmenides> speaks (*spricht*) where there are no words, in the open spaces between them" (p. 114:17). The extent of what is unsaid is not determined by the limitations of Parmenides's ability to express himself. Rather, the prevalence of the unspoken in this fragment suggests that, in it, Parmenides gives voice to a thought that had never before occurred to anyone. As in the case of Parmenides VI, any initial giving of a name (*Nennen*) to something necessarily leaves a great deal unspoken (p. 119:12).

Although the text is a fragment of something larger, Heidegger implies that even if we had all of Parmenides's words, we would still find that he had remained silent about a great deal. In this fragment something thought for the first time is given voice for the first time. The silences between Parmenides's words are the effect of his having allotted to a single word the burden of his thought, an effect we see in the other fundamental words of the Western tradition, including the word 'be[-ing]' (*Sein*). The silences surrounding a fundamental word act as a source of protective power that contains and withholds more than the word expresses.[10]

George Steiner has traced Heidegger's conception of the centrality of the single word to Hölderlin, whose

> theory of language is based on the search for the numinous, perhaps sacred *Grund des Wortes*. It is in the individual word that the elemental energies of immediate signification are literally embodied. The hermeneutic recapture of original intent at the sentence-level is illusory because all sentences are context-bound and their analysis involves us in a dilemma of infinite regression. Only the word can be circumscribed and broken open to reveal its organic singularity.... Connectives, the inherent causal bias in idiomatic sentence-structure, create a deceptive surface and facade of logic.[11]

Traditional hermeneutics and linguistic analysis have in common a fetish for the proposition, unlike Hölderlin and Heidegger, for whom the single word is the source of access to thought. For Heidegger, the "organic singularity" of the single word is its uncanny capacity to contain the traces of thinking.

THE TRANSLATION OF PARMENIDES, FRAGMENT VI: χρὴ τὸ λέγειν τε νοεῖν τ' ἐὸν ἔμμεναι.

The Diels-Kranz translation, which Heidegger quotes, runs: "Nötig ist zu sagen und zu denken, daß das Seiende ist" (110:40).[12] Heidegger lets the standard rendering serve at first as a plane of orientation. He notes that we must take special care about what is translated by the relative clause "daß das Seiende ist."[13] According to the standard translation, Parmenides seems to be talking about the various kinds of things there are in the world and how they are related to speaking. Questioning the appropriateness of the word *Seiende* in the standard translation, Heidegger focuses on its concluding word *ist*.

In order to make sense of the Diels-Kranz translation, he says, we must already understand the be[-ing] (*Sein*) of this *ist*, adding that, although there have been many philosophical discussions about be[-ing], the be[-ing] of the *ist* is always overlooked. How, then, can we expect to understand what Parmenides means by *Seiende*, which *ist*? The question about the be[-ing] of the *ist* is initially prominent in the background of the translation, but it will step forward and assume center stage during the discussion of the last two words of Parmenides's text.

Heidegger arranges the Diels-Kranz edition of the Greek text paratactically and gives the corresponding German translation as follows:

χρὴ: τὸ λέγειν τε νοεῖν τ': ἐὸν: ἔμμεναι.

Nötig: das Sagen so Denken auch: Seiendes: sein. (p. 111:5-8, 11)

The addition of the colons breaks up the syntactic unity of the translation. The paratactic structure isolates three single words and a five-word phrase. Heidegger claims that Parmenides's words (like all words) express thinking, but because these words also say for the first time what thinking is, Fragment VI is unique among the texts of Western philosophy. "Parmenides' language is the language of thinking, is this alone" (p. 114:19), and thinking, of course, is precisely what the fragment is about.[14]

Heidegger then undertakes a word-by-word (*wortgetreu*) translation of the fragment. I will recount his exposition, recalling how his philosophy of translation, as outlined in the previous chapter, is at work in it.

I. χρή

The first word of the fragment, the adjective χρή, "sets the tone (*Grundton*) of the utterance" (p. 168:12), so that the legitimacy of the entire translation depends how this word is rendered. Looking for the verbal core of the modifier, Heidegger renders the word with *es brauchet* (it is good for). In translating the Greek word as he does, he "responds to a meaning (*Bedeutung*) of χρή that resonates (*anklingt*) with (*in*) the root (*Grundwort*) <of the word>" (p. 118:31).

When used in reference to an object, the verb *brauchen* means "to have use as" or "be good for." There are two ways a thing may be used. It may be used for a purpose determined by the user, or it may be used in a way that is determined by the nature of the thing itself. Using the thing in the second sense does not first consider the needs of the handler. Heidegger suggests that in using the word χρή, Parmenides has in mind the second sense of "having use as."

Since determining the use of something requires handling it, the word *brauchen* is seen to be related to the Greek word for hand, χιερ, which is a cognate of the word χρή. Picking something up and handling it or taking it in hand in such a manner that the thing is allowed to show its nature and use implies that one does not reach for it with a certain use for it already in mind. Only a nonutilitarian handling of the thing allows it to reveal the "having use as" that is suitable to it. Only in this way do we see what it is "good for." The standard translation of χρή with *es ist nötig* ("it is needful") sees the "having use" from the point of view of the needs of the user. We are reminded that, when guided by what it sees fit to do with what it handles, the hand has effected dramatic and sometimes devastating transformation of the earth.[15]

Understood thoughtfully, that is, with a view to hearing Parmenides's thought as a whole, the first word of the fragment speaks in general of the suitability that things have, not to us, who may employ them for our purposes, but to the earth, which is ultimately the source of all things that may be "good as" something.

Heidegger's examples of such suitability are drawn from Hölderlin, whose "enigmatic (*geheimnisvoll*)" translations of fragments of Pindar he mentions in this context (p. 117:14). Hölderlin mentions the suitability to the earth of the farmer's tool, which makes furrows in it, and the miner's tool, which cuts into its rock.[16] Both examples bespeak the accommodation of human beings by be[-ing], which is the referent of the *es* in the phrase *es brauchet*. In this connection, Heidegger likens the phrase *es brauchet* to the expression *es gibt* and others of similar construction, in which the "*es*" refers to be[-ing] (*Sein*) (p. 116:11ff.). The difficulty and importance of understanding the meaning of this *es* is the ground bass running through Heidegger's exposition.

A translation of a word is thoughtful and fitting when the word and its *Grundwort* are enharmonic.[17] Evidence of the legitimacy of the translation of χρή with *es brauchet* is found in the resonance of the first word of the fragment in its root, which the standard translation misses with its references to necessity and what is needy (*nötig*).

Ultimately, for Parmenides, "having use as" refers to the use of words. Evidence for the appropriateness of Heidegger's translation is therefore found in the root of the word χρή, which means "to use words as they are meant to be used," that is, "to use true speech" or "to speak the truth."[18] Heidegger assumes that Parmenides has this in mind. I would add that the word χρή also has the sense of submitting to something, in this case, undergoing the use to which words are put by language.

Merely referring to a Greek-German dictionary would not have helped Heidegger in translating the word χρή as he has, just as looking up Heidegger's choice of the verb *brauchen* in a German-English dictionary does not provide us with any hints about the connection of "having use as" and the hand. What, then, has guided the translation of the word? Heidegger's view of translation, we have seen, requires that the he allow himself to be transported into Parmenides's way of thinking by carrying out an interpretation (*Auslegung*) of a word that revives it, in this case χρὴ. Ongoing intimacy with the word both allows for and demands further translation of it.[19]

II. τὸ λέγειν τε νοεῖν τε

In keeping with his procedure of treating each word independently, Heidegger next examines each of the five words that comprise the second part of the text arranged paratactically. The standard translation reads *das Sagen so Denken auch*, "the saying, so too, the thinking." Heidegger says that one "misses what matters (*die Sache*)" (that is, what matters for thinking) by translating νοεῖν with *Denken*, since this assumes that there was in the Greek language at the time of Parmenides a word that corresponds to what the German word *Denken* denotes, namely, a cognitive process carried out by something called mind. He notes that there was no such word, since the early Greeks had not conceived of such things as mind or psychological functions.

Parmenides's words "conduct us toward (*hin*) the essence" of what thinking is (*was Denken heißt*) (p. 119:34). He conjectures that the word λέγειν, which closely linked to νοεῖν in paratactic proximity, will help us understand how to render νοεῖν. Heidegger thinks the two words are closely associated because they are inseparable in Parmenides's thought. The mutuality of λέγειν and νοεῖν lies in their being two things that work together, one of which is of use or good for the other; in other words they are an example of what the introductory word of the fragment indicates. One has use of the other in a way that befits it, but without disturbing its nature. But which accommodates which? Heidegger claims that a faithful translation of Parmenides will answer this question.

The word λέγειν does not primarily mean to speak (*sprechen*), that is, to utter or vocalize, as the word λέγειν is often translated. "The meaning of λέγειν is not necessarily gotten from language and its goings on" (p. 121:4). The meaning of λέγειν is utterance (*Sagen*), which, we recall, refers to thinking. In German, the full sense is indicated by the verbs *vorlegen* ("to lay out, present, or put forth"), *dar-*

legen ("to expound or set forth"), and *überlegen* ("to think over"), which means both "to lay" (in the now archaic legal sense of "laying claim to") and "to gather" ("to get the meaning of something"). The Latin verb *legere*, which corresponds to λέγειν, confirms only part of the third sense of λέγειν, in that *legere* means "to gather or collect by going over in great detail and with care" (glean) and, of course, "to read."

Heidegger first works with the meaning of λέγειν as *vorlegen*, "to lay out, display, put forth." The result of putting something forth or proposing it is that it now lies there before us. This *something* is expressed by the Greek word ὑποκείμενον and the Latin word *subiectum*. Saying is a putting forth of this kind: "When we say something about something, we let it be known of (*vorliegen lassen*) as such and such (*das und das*)." Thus one sense of saying is "bringing something to light (*zu-einem-Vorschein-Bringen*) and letting it be known about (*Vorliegenlassen*)" (p. 123:32). Even though we may not know anything about the nature of what has been put forth, we now at least know *of* it. Heidegger thinks that the result of saying as *Vorlegen* is on a par with the self-presentation of things in nature as they are arrayed and spread out before us. At the start, we may know nothing about them, but we cannot deny knowledge that they are there. Thus Heidegger claims that what is said is ontologically equivalent to what is always already there in the world, that is, equivalent to "that which is already evident (*Offenkundige*) to everyone which they accept" (p. 123:3).

Heidegger's further translation of λέγειν as *vorlegen* depends upon the fact that in certain German formulations the verb *liegen* can mean "to be" and the verb *vorliegen* can mean "to be known." Heidegger exploits these usages. His translation also depends upon recalling that the verb *vorlegen*, which consists of the verb *legen* ("to lay") and the preposition/adverb *vor* ("before or in front of"/"already"), means both "to present" and "to make something lie there" before us (p. 122:19). Thus *vorliegen* and *vorlegen* coincide in meaning "to make something lie there" and both express the basic sense of λέγειν.

Even more important for the translation than this coincidence of the meaning of certain senses of *vorliegen* and *vorlegen* is the further consideration that what is made to be (*liegen*) is brought to a standstill and fixed. For Heidegger, *such immobilization of what comes to be is precisely what language accomplishes.* What is brought into its own by language is at the same time brought to a standstill. In this connection, a further feature of what is spread out before us in utterance (which Heidegger thinks Parmenides is the first to see) is its being "something ambiguous (*Zweideutige*)" (p. 123:11) or equivocal. Whatever is fixed (like a microscopic slide preparation) by language is necessarily equivocal but, as we saw earlier, the equivocity is precisely what makes it subject to *Interpretationen*.

Heidegger thus translates τὸ λέγειν with the appositives *das Legen, Vorliegenlassen*: "the setting down, letting be known" (p. 124:11). So far, then, the translation runs: *Es brauchet: das Legen, Vorliegenlassen*—It is good for: the setting down, letting be known.

Heidegger now turns to translating νοεῖν, for which the translation of λέγειν was to provide him with some guidance. He first suggests rendering it with the verb *vernehmen*, "to perceive" (p. 124:17). To translate a word, he says, is "to involve (*einlassen*) ourselves with what matters (*die Sache*) which is named by <the word>" (p. 124:21), and this means to let oneself "get into" what is at stake, namely, the way of thinking the utterance indicates.

Heidegger's goal is to think as Parmenides thought in order to find out just what thinking is for Parmenides, so that he can revive and continue Parmenides's way of thinking about thinking. He believes that if he can begin to think as Parmenides thought, both what is at stake in the word νοεῖν and what thinking is for Parmenides will become clear. We recall once again Heidegger's claim that the fragment is unique in providing us with the opportunity to see the birth of thinking about thought.

Heidegger takes a fresh tack with respect to the word νοεῖν. To perceive (*vernehmen*) means to take something into possession (*aufnehmen*) and thus receive it. Looking at the common root of these words he notes that in its basic sense "to take (*nehmen*)" something is to "take it into consideration (*in Acht nehmen*)" (p. 124:38). Taking into consideration is basic to all other kinds of taking; for example, taking in what the senses organs are sensitive to or taking some material thing into one's possession.[20] Taking into consideration is always an active grasping, unlike the passive reception of stimuli or acceptance of something, a gift, perhaps, for which one may not have done anything at all prior to receiving it, but what is taken into consideration is not in any way modified.[21] It becomes clear that νοεῖν is "of use to" what is spoken of in the first element of the fragment by actively letting what is taken into consideration be what it is, but without transforming it in any way.

In the transition to the next lecture, Heidegger translates the first three words of the fragment taken together. As such, however, the words indicate something new about Parmenides's way of thinking. He renders χρὴ τὸ λέγειν with *Es brauchet das Sagen . . .* (p. 170:1): "It is good for (the) saying. . . ." Heidegger notes that now the word λέγειν means not only "to lay out or set forth (*vorlegen*)," but also "to recount (*erzählen*) and report (*berichten*)" and "set down (*legen*)" (p. 170:2). At first glance, the latter two meanings of λέγειν (*erzählen/berichten* and *legen*) do not seem to have anything to do with each other. But it turns out they are intimately related when we consider that the account given of something becomes fixed when it is set down in writing—and that means set down as though once and for all. More of this anon, but, first, we must see how much more involved the relation is between the *erzählen/berichten* and *legen*.

> What matters for the setting down (*Legen*), and that whereby this <setting down> actually comes to matter at all, lies in the fact that what is to be <doing the> setting down (*das zu-Legende*) already is (*liegt*) and, from that moment on, belongs to what is known of (*vorliegen*) in that way. (p. 171:14)

In other words, what has come to be known of and the word that names it have the same immobilizing power. A further implication of this is that because one must already (*vor*) be there (*liegt*) in order to be in a position to do the setting down (*das zu-Legende*) of what is said, one is, from the start, part of what is to be known of (*vorliegen lassen*).

In the language of the fragment, taking into consideration (νοεῖν) does not change what it appropriates or takes by naming. It merely subscribes (λέγειν) to it as it is. Subscribing to what is known of is equivalent to endorsing what is there, and such endorsement of what is taken into consideration is the fundamental meaning of λέγειν. Perhaps the most important feature of λέγειν is letting be what is taken into consideration and known of. In fact, "letting be" or "leaving alone" is another meaning of *Vorliegenlassen* (p. 171:30).[22]

In one of the most telling passages of *Was heißt Denken?* Heidegger discusses an important aspect of his understanding of language:

> Utterance (*Sagen*) is what language is about. What does language utter? What it has uttered, what it utters, and what it remains silent about is always and at all times what is, can be, has been, and is to come, and all of this most immediately and most fully especially where the words 'is (*ist*)' and 'be (*sein*)' are not given voice at all. For in a real sense, everything that comes to [or up in] language (*zur Sprache kommt*) is essentially what is put into the visible and audible form of what is given voice and which, as such, then becomes silent (*verstummt*) again in what is put into written form (*im Geschreibenen der Schrift*). (pp. 171-72)

Utterance, which is "what language is of [or all about]," *puts things (Sache) into words*, where they remain for safekeeping, as it were. These matters are what has been thought. The transformation from thought to word referred to is exemplified by writing. In written form, words most effectively keep thought in hiding. For Heidegger, language harbors what matters (*die Sache*) for thought. Traces of these things remain in the written words and provide hints of what has "come up in" language, that is, what has been "put into words (*zur Sprache kommt*)." Heidegger's play on the colloquial expression *zur Sprache kommen* is at the source of his interpretation of utterance.

Thus far, Heidegger's translation of the fragment runs: *Es brauchet das Vorliegenlassen so auch* νοεῖν: "It is good for letting be known, so also νοεῖν" (p. 171:21). In the process of translating this part of the fragment, however, the word νοεῖν (which is usually translated "thinking") has "fallen silent," that is, it has returned into Greek, which means it must be translated afresh.

Heidegger notes that ever since thinking has been understood merely as what logic mediates (beginning with the Latin translation of λόγος with *ratio*), λέγειν has been rendered with "to think (*denken*)." But νοεῖν has *also* been rendered with *denken*. How has this happened? Do the words mean the same thing? Heidegger explains that both refer to what is given in advance or beforehand (*im vorhinein*), and in this lies their intimacy. The common reference to what has been given beforehand may eventually provide a clue as to why both words have been rendered with "thinking." They differ fundamentally, however, in the respect that λέγειν lets something known of remain as it is, undisturbed and unmodified, while νοεῖν takes into consideration (*in Acht nimmt*), takes to heart, and keeps in mind what has come to be known of. The juxtaposition of the words in Parmenides's text now makes sense.

Taking things to heart or into consideration (*Acht*) (which clearly refers to the things of thinking or what matters for thought) amounts to a kind of guard duty (*Wacht*) that has oversight for what has come to be known of and taken for true (*in Wahr nimmt*). As suggested earlier, this responsibility falls to words, which guard the things (matters) language has brought up, that is, put into words.[23] Anticipating what is to come, Heidegger adds that keeping in mind (νοεῖν) "is good for" what is brought about (*vollzogen wird*) by λέγειν, which later in the text is understood as a gathering process (*Versammeln*). As we will see, Heidegger will work out the meaning of λέγειν as a "gathering process" and in that way demonstrate the dependency of νοεῖν on λέγειν for Parmendes.

The fundamental meaning of taking to heart (νοεῖν), namely, its relation to λέγειν, is to sense (*wittern*) or having a sense (*Witterung*) for what is already there. Heidegger compares this "having a sense for" to what we mean when we say that animals "sense" what is going on. By contrast, "man's sensing (*Wittern*) goes by another name: divining or having a hunch (*Ahnen*)" (p. 172:36). Heidegger believes that this prescience (*Ahnung*) precedes rational cogitation and that attempts to explain this "sense for things" in cognitive terms will always fall short of their aim.[24]

According to Heidegger, νοεῖν is the name Parmenides gives to "authentic divining (*eigentliche Ahnen*)," which is the manner in which what is essential comes to us (*uns ankommt*) and puts us in mind <of what is essential> in such a way that we thereby keep (*behalten*) it in mind. This divining is not the rudiments of a series of steps <on the way> to knowing. It is the open court (*Halle*) in which all that is knowable (*alles Wißbare*) hides (*verhelt*), that is to say, is concealed (*verbirgt*). (p. 172:4).[25]

At this stage of the translation, νοεῖν is rendered with *in die Acht nehmen*, "take into consideration" (p. 173:9), and we have the following translation of the first two elements of the fragment:

> Es brauchet das Vorliegenlassen so (das) In-die-Acht-nehmen auch . . . (p. 173:11).

> It is good for the letting be known, so too for (the) taking into consideration . . .

The ninth session of the semester continues the discussion of the words λέγειν and νοεῖν. So far, Heidegger has clarified why λέγειν precedes νοεῖν in Parmenides VI. Only what is first known of as it is (λέγειν) can be taken into consideration and taken to heart (νοεῖν), and that means taken seriously.

He now adds that one's *reading* of what is given—"for λέγειν, as *legen* (to set down), is at the same time *legere* (to read), that is, to read (*lesen*)" (p. 125:21)—is to be understood as a gathering (*Versammeln*) of what there is in the world. Heidegger has in mind reading in the conventional sense but considers it in the broader context of λέγειν as a gathering together of what is there in the world. The usage is found in by now only rather formal English phrases such as "I gather that you will be staying on through the end of the week." Such gathering has the sense of picking up on hints and grasping what is going on.

Another part of the second element of the fragment remains to be translated: the particle τε, which appears twice in the second element. Its use following λέγειν and again after νοεῖν is reflexive. The "letting be known" and the "taking into consideration," Heidegger says, "successively and within one another, get into (*gehen ein*) <each

other>, and in a mutual way at that" (p. 126:8). This "getting into each other" is indicated by the particle τε. In accordance with the "taking into consideration" or "taking to heart" of the *second* reflexive τε, the entire second element of the fragment is further translated:

> das Vorliegenlassen so (*nämlich wie dieses*) das In-die-Acht-nehmen auch (*nähmlich wie jenes*). (p. 126:13)

> <as with> the letting be known (that is, as just this), so too the taking into consideration (that is, as in the former).

The revision is such that "from that point on <in the translation>, the entire utterance (*Spruch*) becomes audible for the first time in what it expresses (*spricht*)." Thus, in "the structure (*Gefüge*) of λέγειν and νοεῖν, what is called thinking (*was Denken heißt*) is addressed (*angesagt*) for the first time" (p. 126:18, 21). Its nature has yet to be fully determined. At the close of the ninth lecture, Heidegger therefore asks: "[W]hence for its part is this nature <of thinking> determined?" (p. 129:39). That will be revealed in the translation of the third element of the fragment.

III. ἐόν: ἔμμεναι

We have seen that both λέγειν and νοεῖν refer to the same thing; namely, what takes place before anything is actually done by human beings in the world, including speaking. What takes place before anything is undertaken by us? The answer to this question, which is the common referent of the words λέγειν and νοεῖν, is found in the third element of the fragment, in the single word ἐόν, *Seiende* (be-ing).

The word ἐόν, Heidegger explains, is an early form of the word ὄν (entity) and is among the most important of all ancient Greek words, and the loss of the initial *epsilon* in the later form of the word amounts to the loss of the root (*Grundwort*) of the word: "ἐ, ἐς, ἐστιν, *est*, 'is (*ist*)'" (p. 130:4). The word had lost its root by the time of Plato.[26] In the penultimate lecture of the course, Heidegger looks closely at the word ἐόν together with the concluding element of the fragment, the single word ἔμμεναι, which is an old form of the verb εἶναι, *sein* (be) and is usually rendered with *Sein* (be[-ing]). He inquires about the relation of the first two elements of the fragment to ἐόν and sees that for Parmenides,

> letting be known of (*Vorliegenlassen*) [λέγειν] and attending to (*beachten*) [νοεῖν] any kind of be-ing, ἐόν, happen on their own, which is to say because such living things (*Lebewesen*) as human beings are to be found. (p. 130:36)

In other words, various kinds of be-ing, ἐόν, are known of and attended to because there is the human kind of be-ing. Nothing special is required of us to make this happen. It happens simply because of our nature as a special kind of living be-ing. As Heidegger will explain later in the course, this specialness lies in our being a "mouthpiece" for language.

The referent of the letting be known of and taking to heart spoken of by Parmenides is be-ing of one sort or another, not in the sense of an ὄν (entity), but rather in the sense of an ἐόν (a way of be-ing). The fundamental meaning of ἐόν is revealed by the last word of the fragment, which literally "has the last word" with regard to what Parmenides has to say.

In order to be able to translate ἐόν, it is first necessary to translate ἔμμεναι, which names the fundamental meaning of ἐόν. We see now that "clearly, everything depends" (p. 131:31) upon how these two words are translated. Heidegger starts with the infinitive ἔμμεναι. It is possible to translate ἔμμεναι with the participle ἐόν, but since ἐόν is what we want to understand, such a procedure is untenable. Nevertheless, a preliminary sense of ἐόν is in order to indicate what we want to define.

The word ἐόν has two distinct and specific meanings that are explored by means of a grammatical excursus on the word *Seiende*.[27] Using *Seiende* to show what is going on in the Greek participle ἐόν, Heidegger explains that, like any present participle, the participle *seiend* (on which the noun *Seiende* is formed) can be used both nominally and verbally. For this reason, words such as *seiend* are said to *participate* in two meanings and that is why they are called participles. "[T]heir saying remains based on a kind of thing which is in itself two-fold" (p. 134:1).[28]

Among all participles, ἐόν (which Heidegger glosses with the Latin *ens* [p. 134:9]) has special status. Other participles, he claims, have their dual meaning thanks to the dual meaning of ἐόν, that singular participle "in which all the others are rooted (*verwurzeln*) and together grow out of (*concrescere*), and from which they continually spring" (p. 135:17). The twofold meaning of the participle ἐόν is the fundamental two-fold or double (*Zwiefalt*) to which all other participles refer.[29] This is because we can say with the same word ἐόν both "a be-ing <of some kind> comes about (*west*) in be[-ing] (verbal use), and be[-ing] comes about as <the> be[-ing] of a be-ing <of some kind> (nominal use)" (p. 134:20).

In an illuminating and essential aside Heidegger reminds us that the origin of the participle as a grammatical form is not to be found among the Greek grammarians but in Plato. In the *Sophist* Plato uses the word μετοχή (which was translated later into Latin as *participium*) to describe the nominal/verbal duality in question. According to Plato, in any kind of be-ing there is participation (μέθεξις) in an ἰδέα or εἶδος, which is the "face (*Gesicht*) by means of which, at any given moment, something indicates its appearing (*Aussehen*), *looks at us* (*uns ansebt*), and thus appears as <something> . . . [emphasis added]" (p. 135:4).

An ἰδέα or εἶδος is the glance or look any way of be-ing gives us. The participation (μέθεξις) of any kind of be-ing in such a glance is memorialized in the dual sense of the participle ἐόν (cf. 134.20).[30] Heidegger emphasizes that this duality is lost sight of in the transformation of ἐόν to ὄν. From that point on in the history of philosophy the direction of inquiry about the participation spoken of proceeds from the participle ἐόν to its relation to be[-ing] as εἶναι (a translation of Parmenides's word ἔμμεναι). As a result, it is taken for granted that in the search for its be[-ing] every kind of be-ing is transcended, that is to say, abandoned. In other words, fixed by be[-ing], the given way of be-ing is thought of as having been left behind.[31] The study of the transcendence of ways of be-ing is metaphysics, which is so termed because beginning with Plato and Aristotle the Greeks thought of a way of be-ing as "what is arising of its own (*das von sich her Aufgehende*) (<hence the root of the word 'metaphysics' is>

Φύσις)," having gone "over from one something <the ἰδέα> to another <an ὄν>." Such "going over" was designated in Greek by the prefix μετά- (p. 135:25). As transcended, ways of be-ing which are in fact dynamic, active, and ever-changing, are construed as fixed, stabilized, and unchanging, that is, as entities.

With these considerations in mind, Heidegger returns to his translation of the participle ἐόν and the infinitive ἔμμεναι, which brings the fragment to a close. He reminds us that Parmenides antedates the era of metaphysics and therefore does not know anything about transcendence and the attempts to explain be-ing in terms of be[-ing] that we find in Plato and Aristotle. Heidegger claims that the point of Fragment VI is its exhortation to pay attention to and take seriously the profound *difference* between be-ing and be[-ing], not the dependence of be-ing on be[-ing] that has been the basic theme of metaphysics from the start. He stresses that the fragment has nothing to say about defining be-ing in terms of be[-ing], as later interpreters following in the wake of metaphysics have suggested.

Heidegger thinks that, with the utter difference of be-ing and be[-ing] in mind, we can translate the fragment's concluding elements in a way that is faithful to Parmenides's way of thinking. Adding the remaining two words to what has already been translated, he proposes a fresh translation:

> Brauchet es das Vorliegenlassen und so das In-die-Acht-nehmen auch: Seiendes seiend (p. 136:3)
>
> Letting be known is <a> good <thing to do>, and so also <is> taking into consideration being be-ing.

Note that there is a one-time change in the word order of the first element of the fragment in this version that brings into prominence the word λέγειν and prepares for the exclamatory form Heidegger's translation of the fragment will finally take. Heidegger suggests that the fragment has the quality of a *command* or *exhortation*, presumably to warn against and forestall what happened at the inception of metaphysics.[32] The fragment now reads:

Laß vorliegen und nimm in die Acht ἐόν ἔμμεναι, Seiendes seiend (p. 136:8)

Let be known and take into consideration ἐόν ἔμμεναι, be-ing being!

We recall that, at the outset, the translation of the participle ἐόν was supposed to provide us with guidance about how to translate the concluding infinitive ἔμμεναι, but then matters were reversed, so that in order to be able to translate ἐόν, it was first necessary to translate ἔμμεναι, which names the fundamental meaning of ἐόν. We appear to be caught in a vicious circle of some sort. If matters remain this way we will be at something of an impasse. Is there a way out?

Taking a fresh start, Heidegger refers to the mid-July heat he and his students were enduring. He notes how easily the *is* in the statement "This *is* a hot summer" is produced. The *is* is there without any difficulty; in fact, he adds, it is there all the time, in everything spoken. One must wonder, what is the sense of the word *is*? The word *is* seems to be the most common and familiar of all words to speak and yet it is the most difficult word to *think*. Perhaps some clarification of this paradox will result from looking at the infinitive on which the little word 'is' is based. In understanding the infinitive, we will perhaps better understand the *is* (which, we recall, is the abandoned root of the Greek participle ἐόν). Heidegger suggests that to understand the sense of the infinitive 'be' (*sein*) of the third person singular 'is' is at the same time to understand the sense of ἔμμεναι, the closing word of the fragment.

To understand what *be* means, one need only point to or indicate something. True, in doing so, a kind of be-ing is always also pointed to. What is the difference between the be[-ing] (*Sein*) of, say, a mountain and the be-ing (*Seiende*) of the mountain? Before attempting a response, a confusion must be cleared up. "Strictly speaking, <in such pointing> the indication (*Hinweis*) ends up (*landet*) at the mountain, the house, the tree" or whatever is indicated, not at a way of be-ing (p. 137:24). In other words, we always point to a mountain, not to a way of be-ing "as (*als*) mountain" (p. 137:27). Our interest is in the mountain as a kind of be-ing, not in a way of be-ing as a mountain. Moreover, the way of be-ing of the mountain is what we "let be known of" and "take into consideration" or "keep in mind," as Parmenides says in Fragment VI.

Having been guided by the standard translation in considering the last two elements of the fragment, Heidegger now sounds a familiar theme of his philosophy of translation and reminds us that the mere substitution of German words for Greek words will never "transport (über*setzt*) us to what the Greek <words> utter (*sagt*)" (pp. 137–38). We must therefore reject the terms *Seiende* and *sein* as translations of ἐόν and ἔμμεναι, and proceed as we did with the other parts of the fragment, listening to the Greek words as Parmenides heard them. As it turns out, the preceding analysis, which began with *Seiende* and *Sein*, will not have been without importance for the translation that follows.

Heidegger says that, in order to "bring them [the Greek words] over to this side (*herüberzubringen*)" of "the great river" where German words are to be found, we must, first, "for our part, go over (*hinübergehen*) to the realm of the Greek language of ἐόν and ἔμμεναι, ὄν and εἶναι" and bring them back home. Translating is the name for that crossing over and back. To that end, in the *Stundenübergang* to the concluding lecture of the course, Heidegger repeats his preliminary translation of the final parts of the fragment, which began with a clarification of the double meaning of the participle ἐόν.

The duality of the participle is now formulated as *Seiendes seiend: seiend Seiendes*, "being <a kind of> be-ing: a <kind of> be-ing being" (p. 174:16).

Heidegger notes that in the Greek of Plato and Aristotle the infinitive is sometimes used in place of the participle. He also reminds us that, by the time of Plato and Aristotle, the old participle ἐόν had already been transformed into the word ὄν, τὸ ὄν: *das Seiende seiend* (p. 174:20). Earlier, we recall, Heidegger observed that in dropping the *epsilon*, the root form of the participle was lost. This, he now explains, is why for Plato and Aristotle, that is to say, at the beginning of philosophy as metaphysics, the participle can replace the infinitive. In its old form, ἐόν, the participle, *contained* the infinitive. Plato and Aristotle were well aware that the infinitive is implied in the truncated form of the participle ὄν, although it is no longer visible and its presence had been forgotten. They could therefore easily replace the participle with the infinitive in the verb "be" and in all other verbs that are modeled on the verb "be."

The addition of the article τὸ to ὄν indicates the nominalization of the participle. But the philosophically fateful result of the transformation is that the "distinctive (*ausgezeichnet*) participle" (p. 174:24) has been nominalized like any other participle, and when that happened, its singular and unique nature was rendered invisible once and for all.

> Now when we say "be[-ing]" (*Sein*), it means the "be[-ing] (*Seiende*) of <a> be-ing <of some kind>." When we say "be-ing," it then means "a be-ing with regard to (*hinsichtlich*) be[-ing]." We <thus> continually speak *in terms of (aus)* the duality. (p. 174:27)

The duality that comes into view—*Seiendes seiend: seiend Seiendes* (being <a kind of> be-ing: <a kind of> be-ing being)—allows us to see for the first time not only the particle *seiend* (being), but also what it harbors; namely, the hidden root of the participle, the infinitive *sein* ([to] be), or, to be perfectly correct grammatically, its root form *sei-* (*be-*), which was there in the *epsilon* of the old form of the participle (ἐόν). We are also reminded that be[-ing] (*Sein*) is the nominalized form of be- (*sei-*), the root form of [to] be (*sein*).

For further clarification, Heidegger calls attention to Plato's view that "be-ing and be[-ing] are in different places (*Orte*). Be-ings <of different kinds> and be[-ing] are differently placed (*geortet*)" (pp. 174–75). This separation accounts for why from Plato on the participation of the one (be-ing) in the other (be[-ing]) was thought to be required. In other words, the distance between be[-ing] and be-ing that had been set up then had to be overcome. The transcendence of every kind of be-ing had to take place in order to bridge the gap between it and its be[-ing]. Metaphysics accounts for how this was to happen. But, Heidegger notes, the presumed "*difference (Ver-*

schiedenheit)" (p. 175:4) between be-ing and be[-ing] that Plato postulates rests on the *"distinction (Unterschied)"* (p. 175:6) between the nominal and verbal forms of the participle ἐὸν, *a distinction that Plato himself had introduced* in the *Sophist*. The implication is that Plato modified an element of Greek grammar in order to justify his (the first) metaphysical position and with it the inception of philosophy as metaphysics. From that point on in the history of philosophy (that is, the history of metaphyiscs), a way of be-ing is always implicated in be[-ing], which is no longer considered in and of itself. The meaning of be[-ing] (*Sein*) *as such* is forgotten and replaced from then on by a notion of be[-ing] that is always implicated in a way of be-ing (*Seiende*). Conversely, we become caught up in the habit of always seeing a way of be-ing "with respect to" be[-ing]. Their mutual implication, regardless of whether one starts with a way of be-ing or with be[-ing], is the legacy of metaphysics, from which Heidegger attempts to disenchant us.

As a prelude to the last session of the course, Heidegger offers a further argument against translation as the mere interlingual substitution of terms (*Wörte*), because he believes that what he has accomplished so far in translating Fragment VI is still not entirely faithful to the last two words of the fragment. The "business of replacement (*Ersatzgeschäft*) gets us nowhere" (p. 175:23), he repeats, giving another formulation of the central principle of his philosophy of translating:

> [W]e ourselves must let the Greek words utter (*sagen*) what *they* name (*nennt*).[33] We must move (*versetzen*) our hearing (*Hören*) <up> into the legendary realm (*Sagebereich*) of the Greek language. (p. 175:26)[34]

With this in mind, Heidegger renews his attempt to translate the last two words of the fragment. In the context of the course, the question "Was heißt Denken?" has by now been given a provisional answer. Thinking is letting something be known of as it is by taking it to heart. According to Parmenides, the letting be known of and taking to heart are to be understood with regard to ἐὸν ἔμμεναι.

Having found it unsatisfactory to translate the Greek words ἐὸν and ἔμμεναι into German (or Latin), Heidegger translates the words into Greek! With this move, he does something that seems novel, but we now know that for some time Heidegger had realized that translating also goes on within a language, not only between languages.

> Such translating (*Über*setzen) is possible only as a transition (*Übersetzen*) to what speaks from these <Greek> words [ἐόν and ἔμμεναι]. Such a transition is attained only by a sudden transit-ion (*Sprung*), and indeed through the <sort of> transformation (*Sprung*) that comes of a singular insight (*Blickes*) that catches sight of (*erblickt*) what the words heard in <a classical>Greek <way> utter. (pp. 140-41)

This amounts to hearing the Greek words *in Greek*, that is, in fourth-century Eleatic Greek. The much discussed idea of *Sprung* which appears in this passage and elsewhere in Heidegger[35] may be understood as the shift into another way of thinking that for Heidegger takes place *within a word, not between words*.

Heidegger adds that here "it is a question of a transposition (*Versetzung*) within (*in*) that <very> word which is not just one word among many" (p. 141:8); namely, the word ἐόν. In short, the very thoughtful translation of the word ἐόν effects one's transposition to Parmenides's way of thinking. This is the crucial point in Heidegger's interpretation of the Fragment VI, where Heidegger concludes:

> Ἐόν names that <very thing> (*Jenes*) that speaks in every word of a language, <and> not only in every word, but prior to everything in the structure of every word (*in jedem Wortgefüge*) and, accordingly, in what the articulation (*Fugung*) of language constitutes <but which> precisely does not come <through> in the enunciation (*Verlautbarung*) <of words>. Ἐόν speaks through language (*durchspricht die Sprache*) and holds it to the possibility of saying. (p. 141:10)

We are now at the heart of Heidegger's philosophy of translation and, at the same time, the problematic of language.

By way of clarification, he recalls that we may think *Sein* (be[-

ing]) translates εἶναι (the later form of ἔμμεναι) as *Anwesen* (coming to pass) and *Seiende* (way of be-ing) as *Anwesenden* (what is coming to pass) and considers that just as coming to pass is all-prevailing with respect to anything that is coming to pass, be[-ing] may be thought of as all-prevailing with respect to any way of be-ing. The word ἐόν (which in its orthography still shows its root in εἶναι) names the prevalence of be[-ing] or coming to pass of what is coming to pass of any way of being (*das Anwesen des Anwesenden*). Heidegger's translation of Parmenides VI has revealed that the word ἐόν still gave evidence of this be[-ing] (as εἶναι or *Anwesen*) in the now missing *epsilon*. In the truncated form of the word (ὄν) which was in use in Plato and Aristotle, be[-ing] has disappeared, although it is still there.

Heidegger provides an evocative illustration of the fundamental features (*Grundzüge*) of ἐόν as the *Anwesen von Anwesendem*. The clue is found in the root of *Anwesen*, the verb *wesen*:

> The mountain range spread out before us serves as an example <of the *Anwesen von Anwesenden*>. In saying "come to pass (*anwesen*)" we understand the word 'come about (*wesen*)' verbally, not as a substantive <i.e., as *Wesen*>. Used and writ large in the latter sense of the word, 'coming' names a coming to be <here and now> (*ein Anwesendes*), <which in the case of the mountain range is> a farmstead with its surrounding property. Thus in its own way the mountain range is also <part of the> property. Used verbally, the word *wesen* is <found in> the old German word *wesan*. It is the same word as *währen* (to hold out or endure) and means to remain (*bleiben*). *Wesan* stems from the Sanskrit (altindisch) <word> *vásati*, which means he lives <at> (*wohnt*), he stays <at> (*weilt*). What is inhabited (*das Bewohnte*) is called the household (*Hauswesen*). The verb *wesan* speaks of (*besagt*) <an> enduring staying on (*bleibendes Weilen*). (p. 143.22ff.)[36]

To clarify the meaning of *wesen*, which is the root of *Anwesen*, Heidegger reminds us that the word refers to a pair of Greek words, παρεῖναι (to have arrived at), which in German means "to be *herbei* (in the vicinity)," and ἀπεῖναι (to have gone away from, hence, to be absent from), which in German is indicated with the expression "to be *hinweg* (far off)." Coming to pass (*Anwesen*) must be understood in terms of these contrary movements of arriving on the scene and departing, which are unified in coming to pass.

Thus coming about (*Wesen*) expresses both coming to pass (or being present to) (*Anwesen*) and holding out (*währen*), which is the sense of ἐόν:

> Coming about (*Wesen*) is <coming> over here (*her-bei-*); <it> is the tension (*Streit*) of coming to (*an-wesen*) and going away from (*ab-wesen*). (p. 143:38)

The meaning of εἶναι (and its historically earlier form ἔμμεναι in the Parmenides fragment) that is contained in the word finally begins to yield to Heidegger's efforts to translate the word ἐόν in ancient Greek. He notes that one of the two ways already mentioned in which εἶναι "is said (*gesagt wird*)" (p. 143:33) can be discovered in the παρά of the word παρεῖναι, which we have seen means "to have arrived, i.e. to be *herbei* (nearby), in the vicinity." In the word παρεῖναι, the παρά names "a coming to be that has already arrived (*Her-und schon bei-wesen*)" (p. 144:32). In other words, it names the ongoing arrival of something. Heidegger notes that the already "<arrived> at (*bei*)" aspect of the παρά, which is also included in the sense of εἶναι, "means intimacy (*die Nähe*), in the sense of the <kind of> appearing (*Scheinen*) granted in emergence (*Unverborgenheit*) by the emergence" (p. 144:34) of something. This ongoing arrival, which is expressed by Parmenides in the paratactically adjoined participle and infinitive that conclude Fragment VI, is what it is "good for" thinking to be about; more specifically, letting what arrives be known of as it is, without interfering with it, and taking it to heart.

With the last elements of the fragment now in place, Heidegger's translation of the fragment is complete:

> Es brauchet das Vorliegenlassen so (das) In-die-Acht-nehmen auch: Seiendes seiend. (p. 175)

> It is good letting be known and taking into consideration being being.

NOTES

1. "Moira (Parmenides VIII, 34-41)" (1952), an undelivered portion of *Was heißt Denken?* in Heidegger, *Vorträge und Aufsätze* (Pfullingen, Germany: Neske, 1956) 3: 27-52; *Parmenides* (1942-43), GA 54; "Aletheia (Heraclitus, Fragment B 16)" (1954), in *Vorträge und Aufsätze*, 3: 53-78; *Heraklit. Martin Heidegger-Eugen Fink* (1966-67), GA 15: 9-263; "Logos (Heraclitus, Fragment B 50" (1944), in *Vorträge und Aufsätze*, 3: 3-25; "Der Spruch des Anaximander" (1946), GA 5: 321-73.

2. *Aristoteles*, Metaphysik θ *1-3: Vom Wesen und Wirklichkeit der Kraft*, GA 33.

3. "Vom Wesen und Begriff der Φύσις: Aristoteles *Physik* B,1," in GA 9: 239-301.

4. *Holzwege*, GA 5: 115-208. See Herbert Schneider's "Hegel, Heidegger, and 'Experience'—A Study in Translation," *Journal of the History of Philosophy* 10 (1972): 347-50, which is a reflection on Heidegger's "translation of Hegel's theory of experience" in "Hegels Begriff der Erfahrung" (1942-43). Schneider comes close to understanding Heidegger's notion of translation when he concludes that "translating ideas from one mind into another is even more difficult than translating from one language to another" (p. 350). He still sees languages as collections of terms however.

5. *Erläuterungen zu Hölderlins Dichtung*, GA 4; *Hölderlins Hymnen "Germanien" und "Der Rhein,"* GA 39; *Hölderlins Hymne "Andenken,"* GA 52; *Hölderlins Hymne "Der Ister,"* GA 53; *Unterwegs zur Sprache*, GA 12; and *Aus der Erfahrung des Denkens*, GA 13. See also my translation of Heidegger's Hebel-Prize acceptance speech, "Dank bei der Verleihung des staatlichen Hebelgedenkenpreises," *Delos* 19/20 (summer-winter 1994): 30-34.

6. Heidegger returned as professor emeritus in the late 1950s and again in 1966-67. See William J. Richardson, *Heidegger: Through Phenomenology to Thought* (The Hague: Nijhoff, 1963), p. 671. This is his professional swan song and a masterpiece of translation hermeneutics.

7. For Heidegger, a transition is by no means a mere summary or recapitulation of the preceding lecture. It is a further reflection on the topics of the previous hour. In fact, some of Heidegger's most important insights are found in these transitions. Oddly enough, the first German edition relegates them to the end of the book. This is corrected in the GA edition.

8. The verb *heißen* has several meanings: (1) Used transitively, *heißen* means *to call for*: thus, "What cries out to be thought?" Used intransitively, *heißen* has several meanings: (2) *to be called or termed*: thus, "What is

termed 'thinking'?"; (3) *to go or run*, as in: "The concluding sentence of the text goes (or runs) . . ."; (4) *is*, as in the phrase "das heißt," where it is used with the demonstrative pronoun 'that' to introduce a complementary explanatory statement following a word, phrase, or sentence; for example: "that is (to say)"; and (5) *says or must*, when it is used in impersonal formations which mean roughly "they say . . . ," or "it must. . . . " Finally, (6) *heißt* may mean *calls upon*, as in the sentence, "The teacher calls on every student in class to speak." Heidegger exploits senses 1, 2, and 4.

9. Pages and lines are cited from the second edition of *Was heißt Denken?* (Frankfurt: Niemeyer, 1961). Words enclosed between <> have been interpolated to make Heidegger's meaning clearer. Here *Spruch* has the sense of a familiar, well-known expression. I have also translated *Sagen* with 'utterance'.

10. A fundamental word may be compared to a seed, the hard surface of which protects its dormant content but at the same time makes it difficult for an outside force to penetrate its core, in this case the way of thinking of which the word bears traces. Because of their sturdy husks, fundamental words are vessels of thinking, which they protect.

11. George Steiner, *After Babel: Aspects of Language and Translation* (Oxford: Oxford University Press, 1992), pp. 348-49. Quoting (p. 276) Achille Fang's "On the Difficulty of Translation," Steiner comments on the paratactic structure of Chinese, which makes prose and poetry indistinguishable in that language. It is possible that Heidegger's conversations and experience in the 1940s working with Paul Shih-Yi Hsiao at translating the *Tao te Ching* (which proceeded word by word) may have furthered the refinement of his paratactic method. See "Heidegger and Our Translation of the *Tao te Ching*," in Graham Parkes, *Heidegger and Asian Thought* (Honolulu: University of Hawaii Press, 1987), p. 100, and the other articles in this anthology; Graham Parkes, "Heidegger and Japanese Thought: How Much Did He Know and When Did He Know It?" in *Heidegger: Critical Assessments*, 4 vols., ed. Christopher Macann (London: Routledge, 1992), 4: 377-406; Reinhard May, *Heidegger's Hidden Sources: East Asian Influences on His Work* (1989) (London: Routledge, 1996); and *Japan und Heidegger*, ed. Hartmut Buchner (Sigmaringen, Germany: Thorbecke, 1989).

12. "It is necessary to say and think that <a kind of> be-ing (*Seiende*) is." The two current standard English translations run as follows: "What is there to be said and thought must needs be" (G. S. Kirk, J. E. Raven, and M. Schofield, *The Presocratic Philosophers* [Cambridge: Cambridge University Press, 1983], p. 247), and "One should both say and think that Being Is" (Kath-

leen Freeman, *Ancilla to the Pre-Socratic Philosophers* [Cambridge: Cambridge University Press, 1983], p. 43).

13. The Wieck/Gray English translation renders both *Dasein* and *Existenz* with 'existence', and both *Sein* and *Seiende* with 'being'. See *What Is Called Thinking?* (New York: Harper and Row, 1968), pp. 178-81.

14. The paratactic arrangement is an affront to the supremacy of the logic of the proposition (*Satz*) as the unit of interpretation. It reminds us that Heidegger is searching for a more fundamental logic than propositional logic, what we may call a *logic of the word*.

15. "Die Frage nach der Technik," in Heidegger, *Vorträge und Aufsätze*, 1: 5-36.

16. Heidegger cites "Der Ister" (lines 68-69), "Die Titanen" (lines 64-66), and "Der Rhein" (line 114). See Friedrich Hölderlin, *Poems and Fragments* (Ann Arbor: University of Michigan Press, 1967), pp. 497, 535, 415.

17. In music, a degree of the scale in one key (the home key) and a degree of the scale of another key are enharmonic when they have in common the same chord, so that the tonal center can modulate back and forth between the two keys. In music, the tonality of a chord that names its home key is termed the root of the chord, an allusion that was not lost on Heidegger. Heidegger's image of the resonance of a word with its root may be drawn from music.

18. See Liddell-Scott, *Greek-English Lexicon* (Oxford: Oxford University Press, 1990), p. 2002, col. 1, for χράω: (B) C, III, 2.

19. This has been documented for Heidegger's translations of the fragments of Heraclitus in Sallis and Maly, *Heraclitean Fragments: A Companion Volume to the Heidegger/Fink Seminar on Heraclitus* (University: University of Alabama Press, 1980), pp. 3-15.

20. Heidegger's interpretation of νοεῖν has nothing to do with the psychological process of perception (*Wahrnehmung*) by means of which the brain gives meaning to physiological data (neurochemical events) provided by the sense receptor organs.

21. In *Donner le Temps* (Paris: Galilée, 1991), Jacques Derrida explores the possibility of giving and receiving.

22. According to Parmenides (and Heidegger), this is the basic sense of assertion or proposition. The other meanings of assertion are derivative. See *Metaphysische Anfangsgründe der Logik im Ausgang von Leibniz*, GA 26: 155-60.

23. This is also the sense of *Wahrnehmung*, which is conventionally rendered with "perception." For Heidegger, *Wahrnehmung* is yet another *interpretatio* of νοεῖν.

24. At this point in the English translation (p. 207) several important sentences have been omitted and with them perhaps the most important details of why Heidegger translates νοεῖν as taking to heart and having a sense for things. The passage in question also includes further discussion of the impersonal *es* ("it"), as in the phrases *es brauchet* and *es gibt* ("there is"). On the sense of νοεῖν, he writes:

> For example, <one says that> a candidate sitting for an examination hasn't got a clue about what is going on (*hat keine Ahnung von der Sache*). Here the word *Ahnung* refers to the rudiments required for correct knowing. But the venerable word *ahnen* says something more. Just as <the verb> *äußern* ["to express or utter"] stems from the [preposition] *außern* ["outside of"], [the word *ahnen*] stems from the preposition *an* ["to"]. Originally, the word *ahnen* was used impersonally: *es anet mir* ["<now> it comes to me"] or even reflexively, <as in the phrase> *es anet mich* ["it dawns on me <that . . . >"]: something occurs to me (*kommt mich an*), <or even> overcomes me (*überkommt mich*). (pp. 172-73)

25. The image is puzzling until we realize that Heidegger wants us to realize that what is out in the open is hardest to see, that is, is most hidden from us.

26. We recall that the question about the meaning of ὄν is the impetus for *Sein und Zeit*. The epigraph of the book is a passage from Plato's *Sophist* which asks about the meaning of ὄν (GA 2: 1). It is often overlooked that Heidegger renders ὄν with the present participle *seiend*, not the substantive *Seiende*. In doing so, he points to the primary verbal sense of the Greek word that was once ἐόν.

27. The discussion is reminiscent of the grammatical studies of *Einführung in die Metaphysik*, GA 40: 56-79, a course that was given in 1935 but published only in 1953, the year after "Was heißt Denken?" was given.

28. In German, a participle is termed a *Teilhabe*, that which has a part in something else.

29. Here Heidegger has in mind the *analogia proportionatis* first discussed by Aristotle. See Heidegger's *Aristoteles*, Metaphysik Θ *1-3: Vom Wesen und Wirklichkeit der Kraft*, GA 33: §8.

30. We are clearly light years away from the standard view of theory of ideas in Plato, for whose way of thinking ἰδέα was the guiding word.

31. Christian philosophy takes a further step when it thinks be[-ing] as

creation, which also leaves behind entities as its product and prepares the way for the philosophical notion of causality.

32. For Heidegger, Western philosophy is metaphysics. It follows that Parmenides is not a philosopher, but something else, a thinker, and if Heidegger's interpretation is correct, the first thinker to have thought about the nature of thinking. In terms of what the fragment reveals, philosophy as such is a strictly Western enterprise, since it is determined through and through by the duality of the participle ἐόν. See Martin Heidegger, "Das Ende der Philosophie und die Aufgabe des Denkens," in *Zur Sache des Denkens* (Tübingen: Niemeyer, 1969), pp. 61–80.

33. Heidegger's distinction between *Sagen* (uttering) and *Nennen* (naming) (which in earlier texts was associated with *Sprechen* [speaking or uttering]) is quite different from Frege's distinction between *Sinn* and *Bedeutung*. For Frege and the analytic tradition, the same state of affairs or reality (the referent or "what I have in mind" [*Sinn*]; for example, the planet Venus) may have two or more meanings (indicated by two or more names or "what people call it" [*Bedeutungen*]; for example, "the Morning Star" and "the Evening Star"), which may and often does cause confusion. Heidegger is searching for the common source of both what one has in mind (in Frege's terms, the reality) and what one utters (in Frege's terms, the names or meanings) and finds it in the notion of *Sagen*, which is neither material nor linguistic. Gottlob Frege, "On Sense and Nominatum," in *Language, Truth, and Meaning* (South Bend, Ind.: Notre Dame University Press, 1972), pp. 85–102.

34. As indicated earlier, *versetzen* also means "to transpose," as the term is used in music. To move into the realm of Greek is, for Heidegger, not to take just any step, but it is always a step *up* for thinking. This passage is of interest, too, because in it Heidegger associates uttering with words. Lest any confusion arise at this point, we recall once again that, for Plato and the tradition, thinking is characterized as a conversation with oneself using terms (*Wörte*), while for Heidegger thinking is related to words (*Worte*), which are bearers of the traces of thinking. Utterance is the bridge between thinking and language, which has built the bridge itself.

35. See in particular his *Beiträge zur Philosophie (Vom Ereignis)*, GA 65, especially part 4; and George J. Seidel, "A Key to Heidegger's *Beiträge*," *Gregorianum* 76, no. 2 (1995): 363–72.

36. Just as we can look at only what we see and can listen to only what we hear, only what comes to pass can be ("is"). Colloquially, both *bleiben* and *weilen* can mean "be."

CONCLUSION

Heidegger's encounter with Parmenides, Fragment VI, is a sustained example of his paratactic method of translating. Many questions may be raised about the results, but he is consistent in the application of the principles of translation he developed during the preceding years. He listens with the mind's ear for the traces of thinking in individual words of an utterance with such intensity that they provide him with access to Parmenides's thought as a whole.

An obvious objection to Heidegger's method of translation is that it would appear to bring more to Parmenides than is there. Another related criticism concerns how to verify whether Heidegger has attained Parmenides's way of thinking at all, whether to revive it or extend it. In conclusion, I will briefly address these objections together.

When Heidegger claims to think as Parmenides thought, he does not claim to have effected a psychological transformation, in order to somehow become Parmenides, and think, feel, or judge things as Parmenides did. Heidegger's question "Was heißt Denken?"—"What is called thinking?"—looks to Parmenides's utterance because, he believes, it is the first utterance in the Western tradition in which the nature of thinking is interrogated. Heidegger's goal is to transpose himself into the pre-Socratic's way of thinking in order to hear *the question* about the nature of thinking as if for the first time, just as he believes Parmenides did.[1]

Whether he has been successful in doing so is, in any case, unverifiable, since, as we have seen, Heidegger believes that no thinker fully grasps his own thought. So there is nothing to compare with his effort to think as Parmenides did.

For Heidegger, to say that a translator's way of thinking has infiltrated and contaminated the way of thinking embodied in an utterance he is translating would be tantamount to admitting that translating has not occurred at all since, for him, translating is by definition a transition to *another* way of thinking. This implies leaving one's own way of thinking behind for a time. Each path or way (*Weg*) of thinking (to use one of Heidegger's favorite images) is unique. For Heidegger, a mixture of ways of thinking would seem to be out of the question.

Lacking a criterion of verifiability for the successful recovery, revival, or extension of someone else's thought, we might want to substitute a criterion for the authenticity of a translation that would require only that the work of translating must remain provisional and open to further translation. Heidegger's philosophy of translation emphatically requires and calls for this. Like his translations of the other Greek thinkers, his translations of Parmenides in *Was heißt Denken?* and elsewhere seem to satisfy this requirement inasmuch as, by Heidegger's own admission, "the dialogue with Parmenides never comes to an end."[2] The same would hold for every other experience of translating as well.

NOTES

1. The ambiguity of the word *Denken*, which means both way of thinking (an event) and thought (content) contributes to a potential misunderstanding of Heidegger here.

2. "Moira (Parmenides VIII, 34-41)," *Vorträge und Aufsätze* (Pfullingen, Germany: Neske, 1954) 3:52. See also Heidegger's letter to Jean Beaufret of February 22, 1975, a little more than a year before his death, in which he reasserts the never-ending importance of the "Parmenides-Interpretation." Eryck de Rubercy and Dominique le Buhan, *Douze Questions Posées à Jean Beaufret à Propos de Martin Heidegger* (Paris: Aubier Montaigne, 1983), p. 76.

EPILOGUE

The goal of this study has been to present a faithful account of Heidegger's philosophy of translating and an example of how Heidegger applied it to a unique text in the Western tradition against the background of a review of how early translation decisions have affected our understanding of Heidegger's thought. My underlying project is to find a way of legitimately translating Heidegger into English so that it becomes possible to find access to his way of thinking. During the last ten years, I have used Heidegger's method to translate the *Brief über den 'Humanismus'* and the three texts Heidegger published together in 1949 under the title *Was Ist Metaphysik?* I hope they will eventually see the light of day as evidence of the value of the paratactic method of translating. In the meantime, the translations of Heidegger's early fundamental words I have provided and argued for will have given the reader a sense of my way of working with Heidegger. On the other hand, only the results of concentrated work with a major text can demonstrate how powerful Heidegger's method is. Obviously, I believe that as fresh translations of Heidegger are undertaken, his own approach to translating ought to be followed.[1]

In Heidegger's work we see concentrated reflections on a few words that are waymarkers (*Wegmarken*) of his thought as a whole, lifelines that we must grasp if a way to his thought is to be secured. In translating Heidegger, if we care to take up his thinking where it left off, we must work with his fundamental words as he worked with the fundamental words of the early Greek thinkers. If the purpose of translating is to make a way of thinking accessible, we must take Heidegger at his word.

NOTE

1. Retranslations of Heidegger in English are already under way, including, for example, Richard Taft's *Kant and the Problem of Metaphysics* (Bloomington: Indiana University Press, 1990); Joan Stambaugh's *Being and Time: A Translation of Sein und Zeit* (Albany: SUNY Press, 1996); Richard Polt's *Introduction to Metaaphysics* (New Haven, Conn.: Yale University Press, 2000); and Keith Hoeller's *Elucidations of Hölderlin's Poetry* (Amherst, N.Y.: Humanity Books, 2000).

BIBLIOGRAPHY

The following bibliography is divided into two parts:

I. Works by Heidegger Cited in the Text (Chronological by Order of Composition)

II. Other Sources

PART I:
WORKS BY HEIDEGGER CITED IN THE TEXT

Most items in this part of the bibliography, which are given in chronological order of composition, are keyed to a volume in the *Gesamtausgabe (Collected Edition)* [= GA] of Heidegger's works (Frankfurt: Klosterman, 1975-). The date of first publication is given in brackets following the title.

"Das Realitätsproblem in der modernen Philosophie" [1912]. In *Frühe Schriften*, GA 1 (1978): 1-15.
Die Kategorien- und Bedeutungslehre des Duns Scotus [1916]. In *Frühe Schriften*, GA 1 (1978): 191-412.

Phänomenologische Interpretationen zu Aristoteles. Einführung in die phänomenologische Forschung [1921-22]. GA 61 (1985).
"Phänomenologische Interpretationen zu Aristoteles (Anzeige der hermeneutischen Situation)" [1922]. In *Dilthey-Jahrbuch für Philosophie und Geschichte der Gesisteswissenschaften* 6, 1989, 235-69.
Ontologie (Hermeneutik der Faktizität) [1923]. GA 63 (1988).
Einführung in die phänomenologische Forschung [1923-24]. GA 17 (1994).
Platon: Sophistes [1924-25]. GA 19 (1992).
Logik: Die Frage nach der Wahrheit [1925-26]. GA 21 (1976).
Die Grundbegriffe der antiken Philosophie [1926]. GA 22 (1993).
Sein und Zeit [1927]. GA 2 (1977).
Phänomenologische Interpretation von Kants Kritik der reinen Vernunft [1927-28]. GA 25 (1977).
Metaphysische Anfangsgründe der Logik im Ausgang der Leibniz [1928]. GA 26 (1978).
"Was ist Metaphysik?" [1929]. In GA 9 (1976): 103-22.
Vom Wesen des Grundes [1929]. In GA 9 (1976): 123-75.
Kant und das Problem der Metaphysik [1929]. GA 3 (1991).
Die Grundbegriffe der Metaphysik. Welt—Endlichkeit—Einsamkeit [1929-30]. GA 29/30 (1983).
"Vom Wesen der Wahrheit" [1930]. In GA 9 (1976): 177-202.
Hegels Phänomenologie des Geistes [1930-31]. GA 32 (1980).
Aristoteles, Metaphysik Θ *1-3: Von Wesen und Wirklichkeit der Kraft* [1931]. GA 33 (1981).
Vom Wesen der Wahrheit: Zu Platons Höhlengleichnis und Theätet [1931-32]. GA 34 (1988).
"Schöpferische Landschaft: Warum bleiben wir in der Provinz" [1933]. In GA 13 (1983): 9-13.
Hölderlins Hymnen "Germanien" und "Der Rhein" [1934-35]. GA 39 (1980).
"Der Ursprung des Kunstwerkes" [1935]. In GA 5 (1977): 1-74.
Einführung in die Metaphysik [1935]. GA 40 (1983).
Die Frage nach dem Ding: Zu Kants Lehre von der transzendentalen Grundsätzen [1935-36]. GA 41 (1984).
"Hölderlin und das Wesen der Dichtung" [1936]. In GA 4 (1981): 33-48.
Schelling: Vom Wesen der menschlichen Freiheit [1936]. GA 42 (1988).
Beiträge zur Philosophie (Vom Ereignis) [1936-38]. GA 65 (1989).
Erläuterungen zu Hölderlins Dichtung [1936-68]. GA 4 (1981).

Part I: Works by Heidegger Cited in the Text

Nietzsche [1936-42]. GA 6.1(1996)-6.2(1997). See also GA 43 (1985), 44 (1986), 47 (1989), 48 (1986), and 50 (1991) for the original texts.
"Prologue de l'auteur" [March 10, 1937]. In *Qu'est-ce que c'est la Métaphysique?* 7-8. Paris: Gallimard, 1938.
Hegel: 1. Die Negativität: Eine Auseinandersetzung mit Hegel aus dem Ansatz in der Negativität [1938/39, 1941]. *2. Erläuterung der "Einleitung" zu Hegels "Phänomenologie des Geistes"* [1942]. GA 68 (1993).
"Vom Wesen und Begriff der Φύσις: Aristoteles, Physik B,1" [1939]. In GA 9 (1976): 239-301.
Vom Wesen der Sprache: Zu Herders Abhandlung "Über den Ursprung der Sprache" [1939]. GA 85 (1999).
"Nietzsche: Der europäische Nihilismus" [1940]. In GA 6.2 (1997): 23-229. A substantially revised text of this lecture course was published as *Nietzsche: Der europäische Nihilismus*, GA 48 (1986).
"Platons Lehre von der Wahrheit" [1940]. In GA 9 (1976): 203-38.
Grundbegriffe [1941]. GA 51 (1981).
Die Metaphysik des deutschen Idealismus (Schelling) [1941]. GA 49 (1991).
Hölderlins Hymne "Andenken" [1941-42]. GA 52 (1982).
Hölderlins Hymne "Der Ister" [1942]. GA 53 (1984).
"Hegels Begriff der Erfahrung" [1942-43]. In GA 5 (1977): 115-208.
Parmenides [1942-43]. GA 54 (1982).
"Nietzsches Wort 'Gott ist tot'" [1943]. In GA 5 (1977): 209-67.
"Der Anfang des abendländischen Denkens" [1943]. In GA 55 (1979): 3-181.
"Heimkunft / An die Verwandten" [1943]. In GA 4 (1981): 9-31.
"Nachwort zu 'Was ist Metaphysik?'" [1943]. In GA 9 (1976): 303-12.
Heraklit: 1. Der Anfang des abendländischen Denkens. 2. Logik: Heraklits Lehre zum Logos [1943-44]. GA 55 (1979).
"Logos" [1944]. In GA 7 (2000): 211-34.
"Der Spruch des Anaximander" [1946]. In GA 5 (1977): 321-73.
"Brief über den Humanismus" [1946]. In GA 9 (1976): 313-64.
"Adhesion del Professor Martin Heidegger" [1948]. In *Actas del Primer Congresso Nacional de Filosofía*, edited by I. Fernando Cruz, 115-16. Mendoza: Platt, 1949.
"Einleitung zu 'Was ist Metaphysik?': Der Rückgang in den Grund der Metaphysik" [1949]. In GA 9 (1976): 365-83.
"Die Sprache" [1950]. In GA 12 (1985): 7-30.
"Moira" [1951-52]. In GA 7 (2000): 235-61.
Was heißt Denken? [1951-52]. Tübingen: Niemeyer, 1954.

"Wissenschaft und Besinnung" [1953]. In GA 7 (2000): 37-65.
"Wer ist Nietzsches Zarathustra?" [1953]. In GA 7 (2000): 99-124.
"Die Frage nach der Technik" [1953]. In GA 7 (2000): 5-36.
"Aus einem Gespräch von der Sprache. Zwischen einem Japaner und einem Fragenden" [1953-54]. In GA 12: 79-146.
"Heraklit" [1954]. Published as "Altheia (Heraklit, Fragment 16)." In GA 7 (2000): 263-88.
"Was heißt Lesen?" [1954]. In GA 13: 111.
"Wissenschaft und Besinnung" [1954]. In GA 7 (2000): 37-65.
Was ist das—die Philosophie? [1955]. Pfullingen: Neske, 1956.
Der Satz vom Grund [1955-56]. GA 10 (1997).
"Der Satz der Identität" [1957]. In GA 79 (1995): 115-29.
"Die onto-theo-logische Verfassung der Metaphysik" [1957]. In *Identität und Differenz*, 35-73. Pfullingen: Neske, 1957.
"Dichten und Denken. Zu Stefan Georges Gedicht 'Das Wort'" [1958]. In GA 12 (1985): 205-25.
"Martin Heidegger—Shinichi Hisamatsu: Die Kunst und das Denken: Protokoll eines Colloquiums am 18 Mai 1958" [1958]. In *Japan und Heidegger: Gedenkschrift der Stadt Meßkirch zum hundertsten Geburtstag Martin Heideggers*, edited by Hartmut Buchner, 211-15. Sigmaringen, Germany: Thorbecke, 1989. Originally published in Alfred L. Copley, *Heidegger und Hisamatsu und ein Zuhörender*. Kyoto: Bokubi Verlag, 1963.
"Der Weg zur Sprache" [1959]. In GA 12 (1985): 227-57.
"Dank bei der Verleihung des staatlichen Hebelgedenkenpreises" [1960]. In *Reden und andere Zeugnisse eines Lebensweges*. GA 16 (2000): 565-67.
"Sprache und Heimat" [1960]. In GA 13 (1983): 155-80.
"Kants These über das Sein" [1961]. In GA 9: 445-80.
"Letter to Father Richardson" [1962]. In *Heidegger: Through Phenomenology to Thought*, by William J. Richardson, xii-xiii. The Hague: Nijhoff, 1974.
"Einige Hinweise auf Hauptgeschichtspunkte für das theologische Gespräch über 'Das Problem eines nichtobjectivierenden Denkens und Sprechens in der heutigen Theologie'" [1964]. In GA 9: 68-77.
"Das Ende der Philosophie und die Aufgabe des Denkens" [1964]. In *Zur Sache des Denkens*, 61-80. Tübingen: Niemeyer, 1969.
Die Kunst und der Raum [1964; revised 1969]. In GA 13 (1983): 203-10.
"Nur noch ein Gott kann uns retten" [1966]. In GA 16 (2000): 652-83.
"Heraklit" [1966-67]. In GA 15 (1986): 9-263.

"Seminar in Le Thor" [1968] on Hegel's *Differenzschrift*. In GA 15 (1986): 286-325.
"Brief an Albert Borgmann" [1969]. In GA 61 (2000): 721-22.
Zollikoner Seminare: Protokolle-Gespräche-Briefe [1947-1972], edited by Medard Boss. Frankfurt: Klostermann, 1987.

English Translations Cited

Existence and Being. New York: Philosophical Library, 1949.
"The Meaning of 'Humanism'." *World Review* [New Series] (April 1949): 29-33.
"The Field Path: A Meditation." *World Review* [New Series] (January 1950): 5-6.
What Is Philosophy. New York: Twayne, 1958.
What Is Called Thinking? New York: Harper and Row, 1968.
Kant and the Problem of Metaphysics. Bloomington: Indiana University Press, 1990.
Being and Time: A Translation of Sein und Zeit. Albany: SUNY Press, 1996.
Introduction to Metaphysics. New Haven, Conn.: Yale University Press, 2000.
Elucidations of Hölderlin's Poetry. Amherst, N.Y.: Humanity Books, 2000.

PART II: OTHER SOURCES

Abbagnano, Nicola. "Outline of a Philosophy of Existence." *Philosophy and Phenomenological Research* 9 (1948/49): 200-11.
Adorno, Theodor W. "Parataxis: On Hölderlin's Late Poetry." In *Notes to Literature* III. New York: Columbia University Press, 1992: 109-49.
Agee, James. *A Death in the Family*. New York: Avon Books, 1938.
Allen, E. L. "Existentialism." *Adelphi* 2 (1948): 157-60.
Allen, Robert van Roden. "Martin Heidegger and the Place of Language." *Dialogos* 60 (1990): 103-21.
Allers, Rudolf. "On Darkness, Silence, and the Nought." *Thomist* 9 (1946): 515-72.
Allison, David B. "The *Différance* of Translation." In *The Textual Sublime: Deconstruction and Its Differences*, edited by Hugh J. Silverman and Gary E. Aylesworth, 177-90. Albany: SUNY Press, 1990.
Anders, Gunther (Stern). "On the Pseudo-Concreteness of Heidegger's Philosophy." *Philosophy and Phenomenological Research* 8 (1947/48): 337-71.

Anonymous. "Philosopher of Frustration." *London Times Literary Supplement* (December 21, 1962): 993.
Anonymous. Review of *Existence and Being*, by Martin Heidegger. *German Life and Letters* 3 (1949): 316.
Arendt, Hannah. "What Is Existenz Philosophy?" *Partisan Review* 13 (1946): 34-56.
———. "Martin Heidegger at Eighty." *New York Review of Books* (October 1971): 50-54.
———. *The Life of the Mind*, Vol. 2. New York: Harcourt Brace Jovanovich, 1978.
———. *Love and Saint Augustine* [1929]. Chicago: University of Chicago Press, 1996.
Aristotle. *Nichomachean Ethics*. London: Oxford University Press, 1959.
Ashton, E. B. "Translating Philosophy." *Delos* 6 (1971): 16-29.
Aylesworth, Gary. Translator's Foreword to *Basic Concepts*, by Martin Heidegger, xi-xvii. Bloomington: Indiana University Press, 1993.
Babich, Babette E., ed. *From Phenomenology to Thought, Errancy, and Desire: Essays in Honor of William J. Richardson, S.J.* Dordrecht: Kluwer, 1995.
Ballard, Edward G., and Charles E. Scott, eds. *Martin Heidegger: In Europe and America.* The Hague: Nijhoff, 1973.
Ballard, Michel. *De Cicéron à Benjamin: Traducteurs, Traductions, Reflexions.* Lille: Presses Universitaires de Lille, 1992.
Barnstone, Willis. *The Poetics of Translation.* New Haven, Conn.: Yale University Press, 1993.
Barrett, William. *Irrational Man.* Garden City, N.Y.: Doubleday Books, 1958.
———. *What Is Existentialism?* New York: Grove Press, 1964.
———. *The Illusion of Technique: A Search for Meaning in a Technological Civilization.* New York: Doubleday, 1978.
———. *The Truants: Adventure among the Intellectuals.* Garden City, N.Y.: Anchor Books, 1982.
Barzun, Jacques. "Ça existe: A Note on the New Ism." *American Scholar* 15 (1946): 449-54.
Baumgardt, David. "Rationalism and the Philosophy of Despair: Pre-Nazi German Ethics, 1913-1933." *Sewanee Review* 65 (1947): 223-37.
Beck, Maximillian. "Referat und Kritik von Martin Heidegger: 'Sein und Zeit'." *Philosophische Hefte* 1 (1928): 5-44.
———. "Existentialism." *Philosophy and Phenomenological Research* 5 (1944/45): 126-37.

Benjamin, Andrew. "Translation and the History of Philosophy." *Translation Practice* 2, no. 2 (1988): 242-60.

———. *Translation and the Nature of Philosophy, A New Theory of Words.* London: Routledge, 1989.

Benjamin, Walter. "The Task of the Translator: An Introduction to the Translations of Baudelaire's *Tableaux Parisiens.*" *Illuminations*, edited by Hannah Arendt, 69-82. New York: Schocken, 1976.

Bernasconi, Robert. *The Question of Language in Heidegger's History of Being.* Atlantic Highlands, N.J.: Humanities Press, 1985.

———. "'I Will Tell You Who You Are': Heidegger on Greco-German Destiny and *Amerikanismus.*" In *From Phenomenology to Thought, Errancy, and Desire: Essays in Honor of William J. Richardson, S.J.*, edited by Babette Babich, 301-13. Dordrecht: Kluwer, 1995.

Biemel, Walter. *Martin Heidegger: An Illustrated Study.* New York: Harcourt, 1976.

Bixler, Julius S. "The Contribution of Existenz-Philosophie." *Harvard Theological Review* 33 (1940): 35-63.

Blanchot, Maurice. "Translating." *Sulfur* 26 (1990): 82-86.

Bleicher, Josef. *Contemporary Hermeneutics: Hermeneutics as Method, Philosophy, and Critique.* London: Routledge, 1980.

Bobbio, Norberto. *The Philosophy of Decadentism: A Study in Existentialism.* Oxford: Basil Blackwell, 1948.

Bock, Irmgard. *Heideggers Sprachdenken.* Meisenheim am Glein, Germany: Hain, 1966.

Braig, Carl. *Vom Sein: Abriß der Ontologie.* Freiburg: Herder, 1896.

Brentano, Franz. *Von der mannigfachen Bedeutung des Seienden nach Aristoteles.* Freiburg: Herder, 1862.

Brock, Werner. *An Introduction to Contemporary German Philosophy.* Cambridge: Cambridge University Press, 1935.

Brower, Reuben. *Mirror on Mirror: Translation, Imitation, Parody.* Cambridge: Harvard University Press, 1974.

Bruns, Gerald L. *Heidegger's Estrangements: Language, Truth, and Poetry in the Later Writings.* New Haven, Conn.: Yale University Press, 1989.

Buchner, Hartmut, ed. *Japan und Heidegger.* Sigmaringen, Germany: Thorbecke, 1989.

Buren, John van. *The Young Heidegger: Rumor of the Hidden King.* Bloomington: Indiana University Press, 1994.

Catlin, George. "A Reply to Existentialism." *Proceedings of the Aristotelian Society* 47 (1947): 197-224.

Cerf, Walter. "An Approach to Heidegger's Ontology." *Philosophy and Phenomenological Research* 1 (1940/41): 177-90.

Chiereghin, Franco. "Der griechische Anfang Europas und die Frage der Romanitas: Der Weg Heideggers zu einem anderen Anfang." In *Europa und die Philosophie*, edited by Hans-Helmuth Gander, 197-223. Frankfurt: Klostermann, 1993.

Collins, James. "The German Neoscholastic Approach to Heidegger." *Modern Schoolman* 21 (1944): 143-52.

———. *The Existentialists: A Critical Study*. Chicago: Regnery, 1952.

Cometti, Jean-Pierre. "Heidegger et la Philosophie du Langage." *Revue Internationale de Philosophie* 43 (1989): 52-63.

Copleston, Frederick C. "What Is Existentialism?" *Modern Churchman* 1 (1947): 13-21.

———. "The Tragedy of Man." *Listener* 38 (August 7, 1947): 224-25.

———. "The Philosophy of the Absurd." *Modern Churchman* 3 (1947): 157-64.

———. Reply to letter from Stefan Schimanski. *Listener* 38 (August 21, 1947): 311.

———. "Existentialism." *Philosophy* 1 (1948): 19-37.

———. Review of *Existence and Being*, by Martin Heidegger. *Philosophy* 26 (1952): 187-88.

Copley, Alfred L. *Heidegger und Hisamatsu und ein Zuhörender*. Kyoto: Bokubi Verlag, 1963.

Corbin, Henry. Translator's Preface to *Qu-est ce que la Métaphysique?* 9-17. Paris: Gallimard, 1938.

Cristin, Renato. *Heidegger and Leibniz: Reason and the Path*. Dordrecht: Kluwer, 1998.

Cumming, Robert. Review of *Existence and Being*, by Martin Heidegger. *Journal of Philosophy* 48 (1951):102-106.

Dastur, Françoise. "Language and *Ereignis*." In *Reading Heidegger: Commemorations*, edited by John Sallis, 355-69. Bloomington: Indiana University Press, 1992.

Davidson, Donald. *Inquiries into Truth and Interpretation*. Oxford: Oxford University Press, 1984.

Delp, Alfred. *Tragische Existenz: Zur Philosophie Martin Heideggers*. Freiburg: Herder, 1935.

———. "Modern German Existentialism." *Modern Schoolman* 14 (1936): 62-66.

Derrida, Jacques. "*Ousia* and *Grammē*: Note on a Note from *Being and Time*." In *L'Endurance de la Pensée*, 219-66. Paris: Plon, 1968.

———. *Marges de la Philosophie*. Paris: Editions de Minuit, 1972.

———. *L'Oreille de l'autre. Otobiographies, Transferts, Traductions: Textes et Débats avec Jacques Derrida*. Montreal: V1b Editeur, 1982.

———. "Letter to a Japanese Friend [Toshihiko Izutzu]." In *Derrida and Difference*, edited by David Wood and Robert Bernasconi, 1-5. Evanston, Ill.: Northwestern University Press, 1985.

———. "Les langues et les institutions de la philosophie." *Texte* 4 (1985): 26-39.

———. "Des Tours de Babel." In *Difference in Translation*, edited by Joseph Graham, 165-207. Ithaca, N.Y.: Cornell University Press, 1985.

———. *De l'Esprit*. Paris: Galilée, 1987.

———. *Donner le Temps*. Paris: Galilée, 1991.

———. "Heidegger's Ear: Philopolemology (Geschlecht IV)." In *Reading Heidegger: Commemorations*, edited by John Sallis, 163-218. Bloomington: Indiana University Press, 1992.

Diels, Hermann, and Walther Kranz. *Die Fragmente der Vorsokratiker*. Berlin: Weidmann, 1952.

Downing, A. B. *A Study of the Conception of Conscience in the Philosophies of Martin Heidegger and Karl Jaspers*. Dissertation, University of Manchester, 1947.

Dreyfus, Hubert. "Beyond Hermeneutics: Interpretation in Late Heidegger and Recent Foucault." In *Hermeneutics: Questions and Prospects*, edited by Gary Shapiro and Alan Sica, 66-83. Amherst: University of Massachusetts Press, 1984.

Dyroff, Adolf. "Glossen über *Sein und Zeit*." In *Philosophia Perennis*, edited by Fritz von Rintelen, vol. 2, 773-96. Regensburg, Germany: Habbel, 1930.

Edler, Frank. "Heidegger and Werner Jaeger on the Eve of 1933: A Possible Rapprochement." In *Proceedings: Heidegger Conference*, 213-56. Durham: University of New Hampshire Press, 1996.

Emad, Parvis. "Thinking More Deeply into the Question of Translation: Essential Translation and the Unfolding of Language." In *Reading Heidegger: Commemorations*, edited by John Sallis, 323-40. Bloomington: Indiana University Press, 1992.

———. "Zu Fragen der Interpretation und Entzifferung der Grundlagen der Gesamtausgabe Martin Heideggers." *Heidegger Studies* 9 (1993): 161-71.

Emad, Parvis, and Kenneth Maly. Translators' Foreword to *Hegel's Phenomenology of Spirit*, by Martin Heidegger, viii-xviii. Bloomington: Indiana University Press, 1988.

Erickson, Stephen A. *Language and Being: An Analytic Phenomenology*. New Haven: Yale University Press, 1970.

Ertel, Christof. "Von der Phänomenologie und jüngeren Lebensphilosophie zur Existentialphilosophie M. Heideggers." *Philosophisches Jahrbuch der Görresgesellschaft* 51 (1938): 1-28.

Escoubas, Elaine. "Ontology of Language and Ontology of Translation in Heidegger." In *Reading Heidegger: Commemorations*, edited by John Sallis, 341-47. Bloomington: Indiana University Press, 1992.

Etinger, Elzbieta. *Hannah Arendt: Martin Heidegger*. New Haven, Conn.: Yale University Press, 1995.

Evans, Oliver. "The Rise of Existentialism." *South Atlantic Quarterly* 47 (1948): 156.

Farber, Marvin. "A Review of Recent Phenomenological Literature." *Journal of Philosophy* 27 (1930): 337-49.

———. "Experience and Transcendence: A Chapter in Recent Phenomenology and Existentialism." *Philosophy and Phenomenological Research* 12, no. 1 (September 1951): 1-23.

———. Review of *Existence and Being*, by Martin Heidegger. *Philosophy and Phenomenological Research* 12 (1951/52): 580-81.

Farrère, Claude. *Le Dernier Dieu*. Paris: Flammarion, 1926.

Ferrater Mora, José. "On the Early History of 'Ontology'." *Philosophy and Phenomenological Research* 24 (1963): 36-47.

Fóti, Véronique. *Heidegger and the Poets: Poiesis, Sophia, Techne*. Atlantic Highlands, N.Y.: Humanities Press, 1991.

Foulquié, Paul. *L'Existentialisme*. Paris: Presses Universitaires, 1947.

Frawley, William, ed. *Translation: Literary, Linguistic, and Philosophical Perspectives*. Newark, Del.: University of Delaware Press, 1984.

Freehof, S. B. "Aspects of Existentialism." *Carnegie Magazine* 22 (1949): 292-94.

Freeman, Kathleen. *Ancilla to the Pre-Socratic Philosophers*. Oxford: Blackwell, 1948.

———. *The Pre-Socratic Philosophers: A Companion to Diels, Fragmente der Vorsokratiker*. Oxford: Oxford University Press, 1953.

Frege, Gottlob. "On Sense and Nominatum." In *Language, Truth, and Meaning*, 85-102. South Bend, Ind.: Notre Dame University Press, 1972.

Freund, E. Hans. "Man's Fall in M. Heidegger's Philosophy." *Journal of Religion* 24 (1944): 180-87.

Frings, Manfred. "Protagoras Rediscovered: Heidegger's Explication of Protagoras' Fragment." *Journal of Value Inquiry* 8 (1974): 112-23.

Gadamer, Hans-Georg. *Hegels Dialektik*. Tübingen: Mohr, 1971.
——. *Heideggers Wege*. Tübingen: Mohr, 1983.
——. *Philosophical Apprenticeships*. Cambridge: MIT Press, 1985.
——. *Wahrheit und Methode*. Tübingen: Mohr, 1986. Translated as *Truth and Method*, by Joel Weinsheimer and Donald G. Marshall. New York: Continuum, 1994.
Geiger, Moritz. "An Introduction to Existential Philosophy." *Philosophy and Phenomenological Research* 3 (1942/43): 255-78.
Gentzler, Edwin. *Contemporary Translation Theories*. London: Routledge, 1993.
Georgiades, Niki. "What Is Existentialism?" *World Review* (June 1946): 14-17.
Gibson, A. Boyce. "Existentialism: An Interim Report." *Meanjin Quarterly* 7, no. 1 (1948): 41-52.
Gilson, Étienne. "Existence and Philosophy." *Proceedings of the American Catholic Philosophical Association* 21 (1946): 4-16.
Glicksman, Marjorie. "A Note on the Philosophy of Heidegger." *Journal of Philosophy* 35 (1938): 93-104.
Gray, J. Glenn. Introduction to *What Is Called Thinking?* by Martin Heidegger, xvii-xxvi. New York: Harper and Row, 1968.
Grene, Marjorie. "L'Homme Est Une Passion Inutile: Sartre and Heidegger." *Kenyon Review* 9, no. 2 (1947): 167-85.
——. *Dreadful Freedom*. Chicago: Chicago University Press, 1948. Reprinted as *Introduction to Existentialism*. Chicago: Chicago University Press, 1959.
Grimm, Jacob. "Über den Ursprung der Sprache." In *Kleinere Schriften*, 1: 290. Hildesheim, Germany: Olms, 1965.
——. *Deutsche Grammatik*. Hildesheim, Germany: Olms, 1967.
Groddeck, Georg. *The Book of the It*. New York: Vintage, 1949.
Groth, Miles. "On the Fundamental Experience of Voice in Language, with Some Notes on Heidegger." *Philosophy Today* 25 (1981): 139-47.
——. *Preparatory Thinking in Heidegger's Teaching*. New York: Philosophical Library, 1987.
——. Review of *Illustrations of Being: Drawing upon Heidegger and upon Metaphysics*, by Graeme Nicholson. *Review of Metaphysics* 46, no. 3 (March 1993): 636-38.
——. Review of *Basic Concepts*, by Martin Heidegger. *Review of Metaphysics* 48, no. 2 (December 1994): 406-408.
——. Review of *The Other Heidegger*, by Martin Heidegger. *Review of Metaphysics* 48, no. 3 (March 1995): 651-52.

———. Review of *The Young Heidegger: Rumor of the Hidden King*, by John van Buren. *Review of Metaphysics* 49, no. 2 (December 1995): 445-47.

———. Review of *Basic Questions of Philosophy*, by Martin Heidegger. *Review of Metaphysics* 49, no. 2 (December 1995): 411-13.

———. Review of *Reading Heidegger from the Start*, edited by Theodore Kisiel and John van Buren. *Review of Metaphysics* 50, no. 1 (September 1996): 162-64.

———. Review of *Aristotle:* Metaphysics Θ *1-3: On the Essence and Actuality of Energy*, by Martin Heidegger. *International Philosophical Quarterly* 36, no. 4 (December 1996): 492-93.

———. Review of *Heidegger and Christianity*, by John Macquarrie. *Anglican Theological Review* 28 (1996): 354-56.

———. *The Voice That Thinks: Heidegger Studies*. Greensburg, Pa.: Eadmer Press, 1997.

———. Review of *The Fundamental Concepts of Metaphysics: World—Finitude—Solitude*, by Martin Heidegger. *International Philosophical Quarterly* 37, no. 1 (March 1997): 109-10.

———. Review of *Being and Time*, by Martin Heidegger. *Review of Metaphysics* 51, no. 3 (March 1998): 421-24.

———. Review of *Phenomenological Interpretation of Kant's Critique of Pure Reason*, by Martin Heidegger. *Review of Metaphysics* 52, no. 2 (December 1998): 455-57.

———. Review of *Pathmarks*, by Martin Heidegger. *Review of Metaphysics* 52, no. 3 (March 1999): 684-86.

———. Review of *Ontology: Hermeneutics of Facticity*, by Martin Heidegger. *Review of Metaphysics* 54, no. 1 (September 2000): 147-49.

———. Review of *Contributions to Philosophy (From Enowning)*, by Martin Heidegger. *Review of Metaphysics* 54, no. 3 (March 2001): 656-57.

———. Review of *Elucidations of Hölderlin's Poetry*, by Martin Heidegger. *Journal of the Society for Existential Analysis* 12, no. 2 (July 2001): 351-54.

———. Review of *Introduction to Metaphysics*, by Martin Heidegger. *Review of Metaphysics* 55, no. 1 (September 2001): 138-40.

———. Review of *Zollikon Seminars*, by Martin Heidegger. *Journal of the Society for Existential Analysis* 13, no. 1 (January 2002): 164-66.

———. Review of *Towards the Definition of Philosophy*, by Martin Heidegger. *Review of Metaphysics* 56 (2003): 651-53.

———. Review of *Supplements: From the Earliest Essays to Being and Time and Beyond*, by Martin Heidegger. *Review of Metaphysics* 56 (2003): 887-88.

Harper, Ralph. "Two Existential Interpretations." *Philosophy and Phenomenological Research* 5 (1944/45): 392-97.

———. *Existentialism: A Theory of Man.* Cambridge: Harvard University Press, 1948.

———. "An Important Philosopher." *Yale Review* 39, no. 4 (June 1950): 758-60.

Harris, R. Thomas. "Is Translation Possible?" *Diogenes* 149 (1990): 110-21.

Hart, James, and John Maraldo. Translators' Preface to *The Piety of Thinking*, by Martin Heidegger, ix-x. Bloomington: Indiana University Press, 1976.

Hartt, J. N. "On the Possibility of an Existentialist Philosophy." *Review of Metaphysics* 3 (1949): 95-106.

Heim, Michael. "The Finite Framework of Language." *Philosophy Today* 31 (1987): 3-20.

Heinemann, Fritz. "What Is Alive and What Is Dead in Existentialism?" *Revue Internationale de Philosophie* 3 (1949): 306-19.

———. "Survey of Recent Philosophical and Theological Literature." *Hibbert Journal* 48 (July 1950): 395.

Heppenstall, Rayner. "Jean-Paul Sartre." *Quarterly Review of Literature* 4, no. 4 (1946): 416-27.

Herder, Johann Gottfried. "On the Origin of Language" [1772]. In *On the Origin of Language*, edited by John H. Moran and Alexander Gode, 87-166. Chicago: University of Chicago Press, 1966.

Herrmann, Friedrich-Wilhelm von. "Übersetzung als philosophisches Problem." *Zur philosophischen Aktualität Heideggers.* Vol. 3. Frankfurt: Klostermann, 1992.

Hill, E. F. F. "The Philosophy of Martin Heidegger." *World Review* 9 (November 1949): 61-67.

Hines, Thomas. *The Later Poetry of Wallace Stevens: Phenomenological Parallels with Husserl and Heidegger.* Lewisburg, Pa.: Bucknell University Press, 1976.

Hirsch, Elizabeth. "Remembrances of Martin Heidegger in Marburg." *Philosophy Today* 23 (1979): 160-69.

Hofstadter, Albert. Introduction to *Poetry, Language, Thought*, by Martin Heidegger, ix-xxii. New York: Harper and Row, 1971.

———. Translator's Preface to *The Fundamental Problems of Phenomenology*, by Martin Heidegger, xv-xxxi, 333-37. Bloomington: Indiana University Press, 1982.

Hölderlin, Friedrich. *Poems and Fragments*, translated by Michael Hamburger. Ann Arbor: University of Michigan Press, 1967.

Hopkins, Jasper. *Saint Anslem, Anselm of Canterbury*. 4 vols. New York: Edward Mellen, 1976.

Humboldt, Wilhelm von. *Linguistic Variability and Intellectual Development*. Coral Gables: University of Miami Press, 1971.

Husserl, Edmund. "Philosophie als strenge Wissenschaft." *Logos* 1 (1910): 289-314.

Ijsseling, Samuel. "Mimesis and Translation." In *Reading Heidegger: Commemorations*, edited by John Sallis, 248-351. Bloomington: Indiana University Press, 1992.

Illich, Ivan. *In the Vineyard of the Text: A Commentary to Hugh's Didascalicon*. Chicago: University of Chicago Press, 1993.

Jaeger, Werner. *Paideia*. Berlin: de Gruyter, 1934.

Jakobson, Roman. *Selected Writings*. The Hague: Mouton, 1971.

Jones, W. Tudor. *Contemporary Thought in Germany*. New York: Knopf, 1931.

Kahn, Charles H. *Anaximander and the Origins of Greek Cosmology*. New York: Columbia University Press, 1960.

―――. "The Greek Verb 'To Be' and the Concept of Being." *Foundations of Language* 2 (1966): 245-65.

―――. "The Thesis of Parmenides." *Review of Metaphysics* 22 (1969): 700-24.

―――. "More on Parmenides." *Review of Metaphysics* 23 (1969): 333-40.

―――. "On the Theory of the Verb 'To Be'." In *Logic and Ontology*, edited by Milton K. Munitz, 1-20. New York: New York University Press, 1973.

―――. *The Verb 'Be' in Ancient Greek*. Dordrecht: Reidel, 1973.

―――. *The Art and Thought of Heraclitus: An Edition of the Fragments with Translation and Commentary*. Cambridge: Cambridge University Press, 1979.

Kaufmann, Fritz W. "The Value of Heidegger's Analysis of Existence for Literary Criticism." *Modern Language Notes* 48 (1933): 487-91.

―――. "Discussion Concerning Kraft's 'Philosophy of Existence'." *Philosophy and Phenomenological Research* 1 (1940/41): 359-64.

Kaufmann, Walter, ed. *Existentialism from Dostoevsky to Sartre*. New York: New American Library, 1975.

Kean, Charles D. *The Meaning of Existence*. London: Latimer, 1947.

Kelly, Louis. *The True Interpreter: A History of Translation Theory and Practice in the West*. Oxford: Blackwell, 1979.

Kilzer, Ernest. "Existentialism and Death." *Proceedings of the American Catholic Philosophical Association* 21 (1946): 66-77.

Kirk, G. S. *Heraclitus: The Cosmic Fragments.* Cambridge: Cambridge University Press, 1962.

———., J. E. Raven, and Malcolm Schofield. *The Presocratic Philosophers.* Cambridge: Cambridge University Press, 1983.

Kirk, Robert. *Translation Determined.* Oxford: Oxford University Press, 1986.

Kisiel, Theodore. "The Language of the Event: The Event of Language." In *Heidegger and the Path of Thinking*, edited by John Sallis, 85-104. Pittsburgh: Duquesne University Press, 1970.

———. "Why the First Draft of *Being and Time* Was Never Published." *Journal of the British Society for Phenomenology* 20, no. 1 (January 1989): 3-22.

———. "Edition und Übersetzung: Unterwegs von Tatsachen zu Gedanken, von Werken zu Wegen." In *Zur philosophischen Aktualität Heideggers*, edited by Dietrich Pappenfussand Otto Pöggeler, vol. 3, 89-107. Frankfurt: Klostermann 1992.

———. "Heidegger's *Gesamtausgabe* as a Philosophical Problem: Prolegomena." In *Heidegger Conference Proceedings*, 135-48, 193-97. Stony Brook: SUNY at Stony Brook Press, 1993.

———. *The Genesis of Heidegger's* Being and Time. Berkeley: University of California Press, 1993.

———. and John van Buren, eds. *Reading Heidegger from the Start: Essays in His Earliest Thought.* Albany: SUNY Press, 1994.

———. "Heidegger's Gesamtausgabe: An International Scandal of Scholarship." *Philosophy Today* 39, no. 1 (1995): 3-15.

———. "Dis-closures of the Heidegger Archive(s): American Impressions." In *Proceedings: Heidegger Conference*, 171-211. Durham: University of New Hampshire Press, 1996.

Klein, George L., ed. *European Philosophy Today.* Chicago: Quadrangle, 1965.

Kluback, William, and Jean T. Wilde. Introduction to *What Is Philosophy?* by Martin Heidegger, 1-17. New Haven, Conn.: College and University Press, 1956.

Kockelmans, Joseph J. "Reflections on Language and Terminology." In *Martin Heidegger: A First Introduction to His Philosophy*, 130-40. Pittsburgh: Duquesne University Press, 1965.

———. *Heidegger and Language.* Evanston, Ill.: Northwestern University Press, 1972.

Kojève, Alexandre. *Introduction to the Reading of Hegel.* New York: Basic Books, 1969.
Kraft, Julius. "Philosophy of Existence." *Philosophy and Phenomenological Research* 1 (1940/41): 339-58.
——. "Reply to Kaufmann's Critical Remarks about My 'Philosophy of Existence'." *Philosophy and Phenomenological Research* 1 (1940/41): 364-65.
Krell, David. "Work Sessions with Martin Heidegger." *Philosophy Today* 26 (1982): 126-39.
Kroner, Richard. "Heidegger's Private Religion." *Union Seminary Quarterly Review* 11, no. 4 (1956): 23-37.
Kuhn, Helmut. "Existentialism and Metaphysics." *Review of Metaphysics* 1 (1947): 37-60.
——. *Encounter with Nothingness.* Chicago: Henry Regnery, 1949.
Lain Entralgo, Pedro. *The Therapy of the Word in Classical Antiquity.* New Haven, Conn.: Yale University Press, 1970.
Laird, John. "Recent Philosophy." In *Home University Library of Modern Knowledge* 181, 124-25. London: Oxford University Press, 1936.
Lefevre, André, ed. *Translation—History, Culture: A Sourcebook.* London: Routledge, 1992.
Leibniz, Gottfried Wilhelm. *Leibniz: Die philosophischen Schriften,* edited by C. I. Gerhardt. 7 vols. Berlin: Weidmann, 1875-90.
Leidecker, Kurt. Introduction to *Essays in Metaphysics: Identity and Difference,* by Martin Heidegger, 1-8. New York: Philosophical Library, 1960.
Levin, David Michael. "The Embodiment of Thinking: Heidegger's Approach to Language." In *Phenomenology: Dialogues and Bridges,* edited by Ronald Bruzinga, 61-77. Albany: SUNY Press, 1982.
Leyden, W. von. "Two Aspects of Existentialism." *Durham University Journal* 9 (1948): 84-96.
Lilly, Reginald. Translator's Introduction to *The Principle of Reason,* by Martin Heidegger, vii-xxi. Bloomington: Indiana University Press, 1991.
Lohmann, Johannes. *Philosophie und Sprachwissenschaft.* Berlin: Lohman, Duncker & Humblot, 1965.
——. "Martin Heidegger's 'Ontological Difference' and Language." In *Heidegger and Language,* edited by Joseph Kockelmans, 303-63. Evanston, Ill.: Northwestern University Press, 1972.
Lovitt, William. "A *Gespräch* with Heidegger on Technology." *Man and World* 1 (1973): 44-62.
Löwith, Karl. "M. Heidegger and F. Rosenzweig or Temporality and Eternity." *Philosophy and Phenomenological Research* 3 (1942/43): 53-77.

———. "Les Implications Politiques de la Philosophie de l'Existence chez Heidegger." *Les Temps Modernes* 2 (1946-47): 343-60.

———. "Heidegger: Problem and Background of Existentialism." *Social Research* 15 (1948): 345-69.

———. "Réponse à M. de Waehlens." *Les Temps Modernes* 4 (1948): 370-73.

———. "Background and Problem of Existentialism." In *Actas del Primer Congresso Nacional de Filosofía*, 390-99. Mendoza, Argentina: Platt, 1949.

———. "The Nature of Man and the World of Nature: For Heidegger's 80th Birthday." *Southern Journal of Philosophy* 8, no. 4 (1970): 37-46.

———. "My Last Meeting with Heidegger in Rome, 1936." In *The Heidegger Controversy: A Critical Reader*, edited by Richard Wolin, 140-43. Cambridge: MIT Press, 1991.

———. "The Political Implications of Heidegger's Existentialism." In *The Heidegger Controversy: A Critical Reader*, edited by Richard Wolin, 167-85. Cambridge: MIT Press, 1993.

———. *My Life in Germany before and after 1933: A Report*. London: Athlone, 1994.

Macann, Christopher, ed. *Heidegger: Critical Assessments*. 4 vols. London: Routledge, 1992.

MacGregor, Geddes. "What Is Existentialism?" *Modern Churchman* 35 (1947): 106-14.

MacKenna, Stephen. *Journals and Letters of Stephen MacKenna*, edited by E. R. Dodds. London: Constable, 1936.

Macmillan, J. H. "Heidegger." *Dublin Review* 224 (1950): 124-26.

Macomber, William B. *The Anatomy of Disillusion: Martin Heidegger's Notion of Truth*. Evanston, Ill.: Northwestern University Press, 1967.

Macquarrie, John. *Martin Heidegger.* Richmond: John Knox, 1968.

———. *Existentialism*. Philadelphia: Westminster, 1972.

———. *Heidegger and Christianity.* New York: Continuum, 1994.

Maiorca, Bruno. *Bibliografia degli Scritti di e su Nicola Abbagnano (1923-1973)*. Turin: Giappichelli, 1974.

Malik, Charles H. *The Metaphysics of Time in the Philosophies of A. N. Whitehead and M. Heidegger*. Dissertation, Harvard University, 1937.

Maly, Kenneth. "Language and Saying." *Philosophy Today* 30 (1986): 126-36.

———. "Reticence and Resonance in the Work of Translating." In *From Phenomenology to Thought, Errancy, and Desire: Essays in Honor of William J. Richardson, S.J.*, edited by Babette Babich, 147-60. Dordrecht: Kluwer, 1995.

Man, Paul de. "Walter Benjamin's 'The Task of the Translator.'" In *The Resistance to Theory*, 73-105. Minneapolis: University of Minnesota Press, 1986.

Marcuse, Herbert. *Reason and Revolution*. New York: Oxford University Press, 1941.

Maritain, Jacques. "From Existential Existentialism to Academic Existentialism." *Sewanee Review* 66 (1948): 210-29.

———. *Existence and the Existent*. New York: Pantheon Books, 1948.

May, Reinhard. *Heidegger's Hidden Sources: East Asian Influences on His Work*. London: Routledge, 1996.

Mayreder, Rosa Obermeyer. *Der letzte Gott*. Stuttgart: Cotta, 1933.

McCormick, Peter J. *Heidegger and the Language of the World: An Argumentative Reading of the Later Heidegger's Meditations on Language*. Ottawa: University of Ottawa Press, 1976.

McEachran, Frank. "The Existential Philosophy (Study of Kierkegaard, Heidegger, Jaspers, and Sartre)." *Hibbert Journal* 46 (1948): 232-38.

McNeill, William, and Nicholas Walker. Translators Foreword to *The Fundamental Concepts of Metaphysics: World, Finitude, Solitude*, by Martin Heidegger, xix-xxi. Bloomington: Indiana University Press, 1995.

Mehta, J. L. *Martin Heidegger: The Way and the Vision*. Honolulu: University of Hawaii Press, 1976.

Merlan, Philip. "Time Consciousness in Husserl and Heidegger." *Philosophy and Phenomenological Research* 8 (1947/48): 23-54.

Moss, B. S. "This Existentialism." *Church Quarterly Review* 3 (1948): 191-98.

Mounier, Emmanuel. *Existentialist Philosophies: An Introduction*. London: Rockliff Publishing Corporation, 1949.

Mueller, G. E. "Experiential and Existential Time." *Philosophy and Phenomenological Research* 6 (1945/46): 424-35.

Mueller-Vollmer, Kurt, ed. *The Hermeneutics Reader*. New York: Continuum Press, 1990.

Mugerauer, Robert. *Heidegger's Language and Thinking*. Atlantic Highlands, N.J.: Humanities Press, 1988.

Munier, Roger. "Visite à Heidegger." *Cahiers du Sud* 312 (1952): 292-96.

———. Introduction to *Lettre sur l'Humanisme*, by Martin Heidegger, 7-21. Paris: Aubier, 1964.

Munson, Thomas. "Heidegger's Recent Thought on Language." *Philosophy and Phenomenological Research* 21 (1961): 361-72.

Murray, Michael, ed. *Heidegger and Modern Philosophy: Critical Essays*. New Haven, Conn.: Yale University Press, 1978.

Nagley, Winfield E. "Introduction to the Symposium and Reading of a Letter from Martin Heidegger." *Philosophy East and West* 20 (1970): 221.

Neske, Günther, and Emil Kettering, eds. *Antwort: Martin Heidegger im Gespräch*. Pfullingen, Germany: Neske, 1988.

Nink, Caspar. "Grundbegriffe der Philosophie Martin Heideggers." *Philosophisches Jahrbuch des Görresgesellschaft* 45, no. 2 (1932): 129-58.

Nwodo, Christopher. "Language and Reality in Martin Heidegger." *Indian Philosophical Quarterly* 12 (1985): 23-26.

O'Connor, David D. Review of *Being and Time*, by Martin Heidegger. *Union Seminary Quarterly Review* 19 (1963): 74-77.

O'Connor, Tony. "Heidegger and the Limits of Language." *Man and World* 14 (1981): 3-14.

Opilik, Klaus. "Destruktion und Übersetzung: Zu den Aufgaben von Philosophiegeschichte nach Martin Heidegger." *Zeitschrift für Philosophische Forschung* 54 (1990): 479-84.

Ortega y Gasset, José. *The Dehumanization of Art and Other Writings on Art and Culture*. Garden City, N.J.: Doubleday, 1948.

Otto, Rudolf. *The Idea of the Holy*. New York: Oxford University Press, 1979.

Owens, Wayne. "The Way-making Movement of Thinking: Heidegger and George's 'The Word'." *Southern Journal of Philosophy* 26 (1988): 522-37.

———. "Martin Heidegger on Interpretation." *Phenomenological Inquiry* 18 (1994): 53-72.

Palmer, Richard. *Hermeneutics: Interpretation Theory in Schleiermacher, Dilthey, Heidegger, and Gadamer*. Evanston, Ill.: Northwestern University Press, 1969.

Paluch, Stanley. "Heidegger's 'What Is Metaphysics?'" *Philosophy and Phenomenological Research* 70 (1970): 603-608.

Parkes, Graham. *Heidegger and Asian Thought*. Honolulu: University of Hawaii Press, 1987.

———. "Heidegger and Japanese Thought: How Much Did He Know and When Did He Know It?" In *Heidegger: Critical Assessments*, edited by Christopher Macann, vol. 4, 377-406. London: Routledge, 1992.

Paul, Leslie A. *The Meaning of Human Existence*. London: Faber and Faber, 1949.

Pereboom, Dirk. "Heidegger-Bibliographie." *Freiburger Zeitschrift für Philosophie und Theologie* 16 (1969): 100-61.

Plato. *The Collected Dialogues of Plato*. New York: Pantheon Books, 1963.

Querido, R. M. "A Philosophy of Despair." *National Review* (London) 129 (September 1947): 237-41.

Quine, Willard van Orman. *Word and Object.* Cambridge: Cambridge University Press, 1960.

———. "Meaning and Translation." In *The Structure of Language: Readings in the Philosophy of Language*, edited by Jerry A. Fodor and Jerrold J. Katz, 460-78. Englewood Cliffs, N.J.: Prentice- Hall, 1964.

Rapaport, Herman. *Heidegger and Derrida: Reflections on Time and Language.* Lincoln: University of Nebraska Press, 1989.

Rée, Jonathan. *Heidegger.* New York: Routledge, 1999.

Reinhardt, Kurt F. "The Problem of Human Existence." *Commonweal* 49 (1949): 632-35.

———. Review of *Existence and Being*, by Martin Heidegger. *New Scholasticism* 25 (1951): 351-57.

Reiss, Katharina. *Grundlegung einer allgemeinen Translationstheorie.* Tübingen: Niemeyer, 1984.

Rener, Frederick. *Interpretatio: Language and Translation from Cicero to Tytler.* Atlanta: Rodopi, 1989.

Reulet, A. S. "Being, Value, and Existence." *Philosophy and Phenomenological Research* 9 (1948/49): 448-57.

Richards, I. A. *Mencius on the Mind: Experiments in Multiple Definition.* London: Paul, Trench, Trubner, 1932.

———. "Towards a Theory of Translating." In *Studies in Chinese Thought*, edited by Arthur F. Wright. Chicago: University of Chicago Press, 1953.

Richardson, William J. "Heidegger and the Origin of Language." *International Philosophical Quarterly* 2 (1962): 404-16.

———. *Heidegger: Through Phenomenology to Thought.* The Hague: Nijhoff, 1974 [1963].

Rohde, Erwin. *Psyche.* Tübingen: Mohr, 1910.

Rorty, Richard. *Essays on Heidegger and Others.* Cambridge: Cambridge University Press, 1991.

Rubercy, Eryck de, and Dominique le Buhan. *Douze Questions Posées à Jean Beaufret à Propos de Martin Heidegger.* Paris: Aubier Montaigne, 1983.

Ruggiero, Guido de. *Existentialism: Disintegration of Man's Soul.* London: Secker and Warburg, 1948.

Ryle, Gilbert. Review of *Sein und Zeit*, by Martin Heidegger. *Mind* 29 (1929): 355-70.

———. "Martin Heidegger: *Sein und Zeit*, Afterword." *Journal of the British Society for Phenomenology* 1, no. 3 (1969): 13-14.

Safranski, Rüdiger. *Martin Heidegger: Between Good and Evil.* Cambridge: Harvard University Press, 1998.
Sallis, John, ed. *Heidegger and the Path of Thinking.* Pittsburgh: Duquesne University Press, 1970.
———, ed. *Reading Heidegger: Commemorations.* Bloomington: Indiana University Press, 1992.
———, and Kenneth Maly, eds. *Heraclitean Fragments.* University: University of Alabama Press, 1980.
Sartre, Jean-Paul. *Existentialism and Humanism.* London: Methuen, 1947.
Sass, Hans-Martin. *Martin Heidegger: Bibliography and Glossary.* Bowling Green, Ohio: Philosophy Documentation Center, 1982.
Schalow, Frank. "Language and the Etymological Turn of Thought." *Graduate Faculty Philosophy Journal* 18, no. 1 (1995): 187-203.
Scheier, Claus-Artur. "Die Sprache spricht: Heideggers Tautologie." *Zeitschrift für philosophische Forschung* 47, no. 1 (1993): 60-74.
Schilder, Paul. *Goals and Desires of Man.* New York: Columbia University Press, 1942.
Schimanski, Stefan. Letter to *Listener* 38 (August 14, 1947): 264.
———. "On Meeting a Philosopher." *Tribune* (London) (September 19, 1947): 10-11.
———. "Martin Heidegger and Existentialism." *Listener* (London) 39 (January 29, 1948): 175-76.
Schleiermacher, F. D. E. *Hermeneutics: The Handwritten Manuscripts (1805-1833).* Atlanta: Scholars Press, 1977.
Schmidt, Dennis. "Some Reflections on Translating Philosophy." In *Translation Perspectives* I, 28-34. Binghamton: SUNY Press, 1984.
Schneider, Herbert. "Hegel, Heidegger, and 'Experience'—A Study in Translation." *Journal of the History of Philosophy* 10 (1972): 347-50.
Schöfer, Erasmus. *Die Sprache Heideggers.* Pfullingen: Neske, 1961.
Schulte, Rainer, and John Biguenet, eds. *Theories of Translation: An Anthology of Essays from Dryden to Derrida.* Chicago: University of Chicago Press, 1992.
Schuwer, André, and Richard Roicewicz. Translators' Foreword to *Parmenides*, by Martin Heidegger, xiii- xv. Bloomington: Indiana University Press, 1992.
Schweppenhauser, Hermann. *Studien über die Heideggerische Sprachtheorie.* Munich: Text Kritik, 1988.
Seidel, George. *Martin Heidegger and the Pre-Socratics: An Introduction to His Thought.* Lincoln: University of Nebraska Press, 1964.

——. "A Key to Heidegger's *Beiträge*." *Gregorianum* 76, no. 2 (1995): 365.

Serres, Michel. *La Traduction*. Paris: Minuit, 1974.

Sheehan, Thomas. *Heidegger: The Man and the Thinker*. Chicago: Precedent Publishing Company, 1981.

——. "How (Not) to Read Heidegger." *American Catholic Philosophical Quarterly* 69, no. 2 (1995): 275-94.

Shih-Yi Hsiao, Paul. "Heidegger and Our Translation of the *Tao te Ching*." In *Heidegger and Asian Thought*, edited by Graham Parkes, 93-102. Honolulu: University of Hawaii Press, 1987.

Smith, C. I. "The Single One and the Other." *Hibbert Journal* 46 (1948): 315-21.

Smith, Vincent E. "Existentialism and Existence." *Thomist* 11 (1948): 141-96, 297-329.

Spiegelberg, Herbert. *The Phenomenological Movement*. The Hague: Nijhoff, 1960.

Stace, W. T. "Metaphysics and Existence." *Philosophy and Phenomenological Research* 9 (1948/49): 458-62.

Stambaugh, Joan. Preface to *Schelling's Treatise on the Essence of Human Freedom*, by Martin Heidegger, viii. Athens: Ohio University Press, 1985.

——. Translator's Preface to *Being and Time: A Translation of Sein und Zeit*, by Martin Heidegger, xiii-xvi. Albany: SUNY Press, 1996.

Steiger, Henry W. "Heidegger and Existentialism." *Christian Science Monitor* (August 19, 1950, Magazine Section): 8.

Steiner, George. *Martin Heidegger*. New York: Viking Press, 1979.

——. *After Babel: Aspects of Language and Translation*. Oxford: Oxford University Press, 1992.

Stevens, Wallace, "The Emperor of Ice-Cream." In *The Collected Poems*, 64. New York: Vintage Books, 1982.

Stohrer, Walter. "Heidegger and Jacob Grimm: On Dwelling and the Genesis of Language." *Modern Schoolman* 62 (1984): 43-52.

Stolze, Radegundis. *Hermeneutisches Übersetzen*. Tübingen: Narr, 1992.

Sypher, Wylie. "Hamlet: The Existential Madness." *Nation* 162 (June 22, 1946): 750-51.

Taminiaux, Jacques. "'Voix' et 'Phénomene' dan l'Ontologie fondamentale de Heidegger." *Revue Philosophique Francaise* 180, no. 2 (1990): 395-408.

Thomas of Erfurt. *Grammatica Speculativa*. London: Longman, 1972.

Thompson, J. M. "Existentialism and Humanism." *Hibbert Journal* (London) 47 (1949): 170-74.

Tillich, Paul. "Existential Philosophy." *Journal of the History of Ideas* 5 (1944): 44-70.

———. *Theology of Culture*. New York: Oxford University Press, 1959.

Torrance, T. F. Review of *Being and Time*, by Martin Heidegger. *Journal of Theological Studies* 15 (1964): 471-86.

Trivers, Howard. "Heidegger's Misinterpretation of Hegel's Views on Spirit and Time." *Philosophy and Phenomenological Research* 3 (1942/43): 162-68.

Unger, Eric. "Existentialism." *Nineteenth Century and After* 142 (1947): 278-88, and 143 (1948): 28-37.

Urmson, J. O. "Gilbert Ryle." *The Encyclopedia of Philosophy*, edited by Paul Edwards, vol. 7, 271. New York: Macmillan, 1967.

Vandevelde, Pol. *Etre et Discours: La Question du Langage dans l'Itineraire de Heidegger (1927-1938)*. Brusseles: Academie Royale, 1994.

Vedder, Ben. "Schleiermacher." In *A Companion to Continental Philosophy*, edited by Simon Critchley and William R. Schroeder, 417-24. London: Blackwell, 1998.

Venuti, Lawrence. *Rethinking Translation: Discourse, Subjectivity, Ideology*. London: Routledge, 1992.

———. *The Translator's Invisibility: A History of Translation*. London: Routledge, 1995.

Vial, Fernand. "Existentialism and Humanism." *Thought* 23 (1948): 17-20.

Visscher, Luce F. de. "La Pensée du Langage chez Heidegger." *Revue Philosophique de Louvain* 64 (1966): 224-62.

Volpi, Franco. "*Being and Time*: A 'Translation' of the *Nicomachean Ethics*?" In *Reading Heidegger from the Start: Essays in His Earliest Thought*, edited by Theodore Kisiel and John van Buren, 195-211. Albany: SUNY Press, 1994.

Waelhens, Alphonse de. *La Philosophie de Martin Heidegger*. Louvain: Institut Supérieur de Philosophie, 1942.

———. "La Philosophie de Heidegger et le Nazisme." *Les Temps Modernes* 3 (1947-48): 115-27.

———. "Réponse a Cette Réponse [à Löwith]." *Les Temps Modernes* 4 (1948): 374-77.

Wahl, Jean. "Existentialism: A Preface." *New Republic* 113 (1945): 442-44.

———. "Realism, Dialectic, and the Transcendent." *Philosophy and Phenomenological Research* 8 (1947/48): 496-507.

———. "Freedom and Existence in Some Recent Philosophies." *Philosophy and Phenomenological Research* 8 (1947/48): 538-57.

———. *A Short History of Existentialism*. Translated by Forrest Williams and Stanley Maron. New York: Philosophical Library, 1949.

———. *Mots, Mythes et Réalité dans la Philosophie de Heidegger*. Paris: Centre de Documentation Universitaire, 1961.

Warnick, Barbara. "Logos in Heidegger's Philosophy of Language." *Philosophy Research Archives* 5 (1979): 660-75.

Warnock, Mary. *Existentialism*. New York: Oxford University Press, 1970.

Weil, Eric. "Le Cas Heidegger." *Les Temps Modernes* 3 (1947-48): 128-38.

Weiss, Helene. "The Greek Conceptions of Time and Being in the Light of Heidegger's Philosophy." *Philosophy and Phenomenological Research* 2 (1941/42): 173-87.

Weiss, Paul. "Existenz and Hegel." *Philosophy and Phenomenological Research* 8 (1947/48): 206-17.

Werkmeister, William H. "An Introduction to Heidegger's 'Existential Philosophy'." *Philosophy and Phenomenological Research* 2 (1941/42): 79-87.

———. Review of *Being and Time*, by Martin Heidegger. *Personalist* 44 (1963): 244.

Wild, John. "An English Version of Martin Heidegger's 'Being and Time'." *Review of Metaphysics* 16 (1962/63): 296-315.

Wisser, Richard. "La Voix qui Pense et sa Pensée." *Les Etudes Philosophiques* 13 (1959): 495-500.

Wood, David. *Heidegger and Language: A Collection of Original Papers*. Coventry, England: Parousia, 1981.

A RESEARCH BIBLIOGRAPHY OF HEIDEGGER IN ENGLISH TRANSLATION

The bibliography presents four kinds of information about books, essays, and letters that have been translated into English:

[A] Title(s) of English translation(s) (A,B,C etc.); date of first appearance of the translation (. . .); translator(s) [. . .].

[B] History of the text: occasion of composition, Heidegger's revisions.

[C] First publication in German; current German edition, or volume in the *Gesamtausgabe* [Collected Works] [=GA] edition (Frankfurt: Klostermann, 1975-).

[D] English sources corresponding to listing(s) in [A] (A, B, C etc.), including the most current edition of the source. Titles in [C] preceded by * are bilingual.

Excerpts from as yet unpublished letters by Heidegger appear in Heinrich Wiegand Petzet's *Encounters and Dialogues with Martin Heidegger, 1929-1976* (Chicago: University of Chicago Press, 1993), translated by Parvis Emad and Kenneth Maly, and in Hugo Ott's *Heidegger: A Political Life* (London: Basic Books, 1993), translated by Allan Blunden. Excerpts from other previously unpublished letters and archival material have been published for the first time in the papers of Theodore Kisiel and in his fundamental source for Heidegger scholarship, *The Genesis of Heidegger's Being and Time* (Berkeley: University of California Press, 1993), and in Thomas Sheehan's papers, especially "Heidegger's *Lehrjahre*," in *The Collegium Phaenomenologicum. The First Ten Years*, ed. John Sallis, G. Moneta, and Jacques Taminiaux (Dordrecht: Kluwer, 1988), pp. 77–137. Many passages from Heidegger's early dissertations and papers, reprinted in GA 1, are translated in John van Buren's *The Young Heidegger: Rumor of the Hidden King* (Bloomington: Indiana University Press, 1994).

References to the Heidegger *Gesamtausgabe* are based on the following list of volumes published to date. Superscript numbers immediately after the date of a volume indicate the edition number of the book.

THE HEIDEGGER *GESAMTAUSGABE*

Following is a chronological list of volumes of the GA that have been published to date (July 2003). The title of the volume and the dates of editions of the work are followed by the name(s) of the editor(s). If the text first appeared as a lecture course, the date and place of the course are given (SS = Summer Semester; WS = Winter Semester). The volumes marked ⌯ have been translated, as a whole or in part. Superscript numbers following publication dates refer to edition of the book.

1975

GA 24⌯   *Die Grundprobleme der Phänomenologie* [1975^1, 1989^2, 1997^3]

        SS 1927, University of Marburg
        (Friedrich-Wilhelm von Herrmann)

1976

GA 9⌯   *Wegmarken* [1967^1, 1978^2, 1996^3]

        (Friedrich-Wilhelm von Herrmann)

GA 21   *Logik: Die Frage nach der Wahrheit* [1976¹, 1995²]

           WS 1925/26, University of Marburg
           (Walter Biemel)

1977

GA 2✠   *Sein und Zeit* [1927¹, 1929², 1929³, 1935⁴, 1941⁵, 1949⁶, 1953⁷, 1957⁸, 1961⁹, 1963¹⁰, 1967¹¹, 1972¹², 1976¹³, 1977¹⁴, 1979¹⁵, 1986¹⁶, 1993¹⁷]

           (Friedrich-Wilhelm von Herrmann)

GA 5✠   *Holzwege* [1950¹, 1952², 1957³, 1963⁴, 1972⁵, 1980⁶, 1994⁷]

           (Friedrich-Wilhelm von Herrmann)

GA 25✠   *Phänomenologische Interpretation von Kants Kritik der reinen Vernunft* [1977¹, 1987², 1995³]

           WS 1927/28, University of Freiburg
           (Ingtraud Görland)

1978

GA 1✠   *Frühe Schriften* [1972¹]

           (Friedrich-Wilhelm von Herrmann)

GA 26✠   *Metaphysische Anfangsgründe der Logik im Ausgang der Leibniz* [1978¹, 1990²]

           SS 1928, Marburg University
           (Klaus Held)

1979

GA 20✠   *Prolegomena zur Geschichte des Zeitbegriffs* [1979¹, 1988², 1994³]

SS 1925, Freiburg University
(Petra Jaeger)

GA 55   *Heraklit: 1. Der Anfang des abendländischen Denkens. 2. Logik: Heraklits Lehre zum Logos* [1979¹, 1994³]

1. SS 1943, University of Freiburg. 2. SS 1944, University of Freiburg
(Manfred S. Frings)

1980

GA 32✠   *Hegels Phänomenologie des Geistes* [1980¹, 1988², 1997³]

WS 1930/31, University of Freiburg
(Ingtraud Görland)

GA 39   *Hölderlins Hymnen "Germanien" und "Der Rhein"* [1980¹]

WS 1934/35, University of Freiburg
(Susanne Ziegler)

1981

GA 4✠   *Erläuterungen zu Hölderlins Dichtung* [1944¹, 1951², 1963³, 1971⁴]

(Friedrich-Wilhelm von Herrmann)

GA 33✠   *Aristoteles,* Metaphysik Θ *1-3: Von Wesen und Wirklichkeit der Kraft* [1981¹, 1990²]

WS 1931, University of Freiburg
(Heinrich Hüni)

GA 51✠   *Grundbegriffe* [1981¹, 1991²]

SS 1941, University of Freiburg
(Petra Jaeger)

1982

GA 31 *Vom Wesen der menschlichen Freiheit: Einleitung in die Philosophie* [1982¹, 1994²]

SS 1930, University of Freiburg
(Hartmut Tietjen)

GA 52 *Hölderlins Hymne "Andenken"* [1982¹, 1992²]

WS 1941/42, University of Freiburg
(Curd Ochwadt)

GA 54✠ *Parmenides* [1982¹, 1992²]

WS 1942/43, University of Freiburg
(Manfred S. Frings)

1983

GA 13✠ *Aus der Erfahrung des Denkens (1910-1976)* [1954¹, 1965², 1976³]

(Friedrich-Wilhelm von Herrmann)

GA✠ 29/30 *Die Grundbegriffe der Metaphysik: Welt—Endlichkeit—Einsamkeit* [1983¹, 1992²]

WS 1929/30, University of Freiburg
(Friedrich-Wilhelm von Herrmann)

GA 40✠ *Einführung in die Metaphysik* [1953¹, 1958², 1967³, 1976⁴]

SS 1935, University of Freiburg
(Petra Jaeger)

1984

GA 41✠ *Die Frage nach dem Ding: Zu Kants Lehre von den transzendentalen Grundsätzen* [1962¹, 1975²]

WS 1935/36, University of Freiburg
(Petra Jaeger)

GA 45✠ *Grundfragen der Philosophie: Ausgewählte "Probleme" der "Logik"* [1984¹, 1992²]

WS 1937/38, University of Freiburg
(Friedrich-Wilhelm von Herrmann)

GA 53✠ *Hölderlins Hymne "Der Ister"* [1984]

SS 1942, University of Freiburg
(Walter Biemel)

1985

GA 12✠ *Unterwegs zur Sprache* [1959¹, 1960², 1971³, 1975⁵, 1979⁶, 1982⁷]
(Friedrich-Wilhelm von Herrmann)

GA 43✠ *Nietzsche: Der Wille zur Macht als Kunst* [1961¹]

WS 1936/37, University of Freiburg
(Bernd Heimbüchel)

GA 61 *Phänomenologische Interpretationen zu Aristoteles: Einführung in die phänomenologische Forschung* [1985¹, 1994²]

WS 1921/22, University of Freiburg
(Walter Bröcker and Käte Bröcker-Oltmanns)

1986

GA 15✠ *Seminare* [1970¹, 1977², 1980 (French)]

1. "Heraklit" WS 1966/67, University of Freiburg (with Eugen Fink)

2. "Vier Seminare" 1966, 1967, 1968 (Le Thor) 1973 (Zähringen)

3. "Aussprache mit Martin Heidegger" 1951, 1952 (Zürich)

(Curd Ochwadt)

GA 44✠   *Nietzsches metaphysische Grundstellung im abendländischen Denken: Die ewige Wiederkehr des Gleichen* [1961¹]

SS 1937, University of Freiburg
(Marion Heinz)

GA 48✠   *Nietzsche: Der europäische Nihilismus* [1961¹]

Second Trimester 1940, University of Freiburg
(Petra Jaeger)

1987

GA 56/57   *Zur Bestimmung der Philosophie. 1. Die Idee der Philosophie und das Weltanschauungsproblem. 2. Phänomenologie und transzendentale Wertphilosophie* [mit einer Nachschrift der Vorlesung; Über das Wesen der Universität und des akademischen Studiums"] [1987¹, 1999²]

"Kriegsnotsemester [War Emergency Semester]" 1919 and SS 1919, University of Freiburg
(Bernd Heimbüchel)

1988

GA 34   *Vom Wesen der Wahrheit: Zu Platons Höhlengleichnis und Theätet* [1988¹, 1997²]

WS 1931/32, University of Freiburg
(Hermann Mörchen)

GA 42✠   *Schelling: Vom Wesen der menschlichen Freiheit (1809)* [1971¹]

SS 1936, University of Freiburg
(Ingrid Schüßler)

GA 63✠ *Ontologie (Hermeneutik der Faktizität)* [1988¹, 1995²]

SS 1923, University of Freiburg
(Käte Bröcker-Oltmanns)

1989

GA 47✠ *Nietzsches Lehre vom Willen zur Macht als Erkenntnis* [1961¹]

SS 1939, University of Freiburg
(Eberhard Hanser)

GA 65✠ *Beiträge zur Philosophie. (Vom Ereignis)* [1989¹, 1994²]

(Friedrich-Wilhelm von Herrmann)

1990

GA 50   1. *Nietzsches Metaphysik.* 2. *Einleitung in die Philosophie: Denken und Dichten* [1991¹]

WS 1941/42 [not given] and WS 1944/45, University of Freiburg
(Petra Jaeger)

1991

GA 3✠   *Kant und das Problem der Metaphysik* [1929¹, 1951², 1965³, 1973⁴, 1998⁶; first GA 1991]

WS 1925–26, University of Marburg
(Friedrich-Wilhelm von Herrmann)

GA 49   *Die Metaphysik des deutschen Idealismus (Schelling)* [1991¹]

First Trimester 1941 and Seminar SS 1941, University of Freiburg
(Günther Seibold)

1992

GA 19✠   *Platon:* Sophistes [1992¹]

　　　　WS 1924/25, University of Marburg
　　　　(Ingeborg Schüßler)

1993

GA 58   *Grundprobleme der Phänomenologie (1919/20)* [1992¹]

　　　　WS 1919/20, University of Freiburg
　　　　(Hans-Helmuth Gander)

GA 68   *Hegel.* 1. Die Negativität. Eine Auseinandersetzung mit Hegel aus dem Ansatz in der Negativität (1938/39, 1941). 2. Erläuterung der "Einleitung" zu Hegels "Phänomenologie des Geistes" (1942) [1993¹]

　　　　(Ingrid Schüßler)

GA 59   *Phänomenologie der Anschauung und des Ausdrucks.* Theorie der philosophischen Begriffsbildung [1993¹]

　　　　SS 1920, University of Freiburg
　　　　(Claudius Strube)

GA 22   *Die Grundbegriffe der antiken Philosophie* [1993¹]

　　　　SS 1926, University of Marburg
　　　　(Franz-Karl Blust)

1994

GA 17   *Einführung in die phänomenologische Forschung* [1994¹]

　　　　WS 1923/24, University of Marburg
　　　　(Friedrich-Wilhelm von Herrmann)

GA 79⳨   *Bremer und Freiburger Vorträge* [1994¹]

        1. Einblick in das was ist (1949)
            Das Ding
            Das Ge-Stell
            Die Gefahr
            Die Kehre

        2. Grundsätze des Denkens (1957)

        (Petra Jaeger)

1995

GA 77⳨   *Feldweg-Gespräche* [1995¹]

        Erdachte Gespräche 1944/45
        (Ingrid Schüßler)

GA 60   *Phänomenologie des religiösen Lebens* [1995¹]

        1.   Einleitung in die Phänomenologie der Religion (1920/21)

        2.   Augustinus und der Neuplatonismus (1921)

        3.   Die philosophischen Grundlagen der mittelalterischen Mystik (1918/1919)

        (1. Matthias Jung and Thomas Reghely
         2. Claudius Strube
         3. Claudius Strube)

1996

GA 6.1   *Nietzsche* I [1996¹]

        (Brigitte Schillebach)

GA 27   *Einleitung in die Philosophie* [1996¹, 2001²]

            WS 1928/29, University of Freiburg
            (Otto Saame and Ina Saame-Speidel)

1997

GA 28   *Der deutsche Idealismus (Fichte, Schelling, Hegel) und die philosophische Problemlage der Gegenwart ("Einführung in das akademische Studium")* [1997¹]

            SS 1929, University of Freiburg
            (Claudius Strube)

GA 10✠   *Der Satz vom Grund* [1997¹]

            WS 1955/56, University of Freiburg
            (Petra Jaeger)

GA 6.2   *Nietzsche II* [1997¹]

            (Brigitte Schillibach)

GA 66   *Besinnung* [1997¹]

            (Friedrich Wilhelm von Herrmann)

1998

GA 69   *Die Geschichte des Seyns* [1998¹]

            1. Die Geschichte des Seyns (1938-40)

            2. KOINON: Aus der Geschichte des Seyns (1939-40)

            (Peter Trawny)

GA 38   *Logik als die Frage nach dem Wesen der Sprache* [1998¹]

SS 1934, University of Freiburg
(Günther Seubold)

1999

GA 67   *Metphysik und Nihilismus* [1999[1]]

        1. Die Überwindung der Metaphysik

        2. Das Wesen des Nihilismus

        (Hans-Joachim Friedrich)

GA 85   *Vom Wesen der Sprache: Zu Herders Abhandlung "Über den Ursprung der Sprache"* [1999[1]]

        (Ingrid Schüßler)

2000

GA 75   *Zu Hölderlin: Griechenlandreisen* [2000[1]]

        (Curt Ochwadt)

GA 7✠   *Vorträge und Aufsätze* [2000[1]]

        (Friedrich Wilhelm von Herrmann)

GA 16   *Reden und andere Zeugnisse eines Lebensweges* [2000[1]]

        (Hermann Heidegger)

2001

GA 36/37   *Sein und Wahrheit* [2001[1]]

        (Hartmut Tietjen)

2002

GA 18   *Grundbegriffe der aristotelischen Philosophie* [2002¹]

         (Mark Michalski)

GA 8   *Was heibt Denken?* [2002]

         WS 1951-52 and SS 1952, University of Freiburg
         Paola-Ludovika Coriando

2003

GA 46   *Zur Auslegung von Nietzsches II. Unzeitgemäßer Betrachtung
         "Vom Nutzen und Nachteil der Historie für das Leben"* [2003]

         (Hans-Joachim Friedrich)

BIBLIOGRAPHY ENTRIES

1.   [A]   "Acknowledgment on the Conferment of the National Hebel Memorial Prize" (1997) [Miles Groth].
     [B]   "Dank bei der Verleihung des staatlichen Hebelgedenkenpreises": Address given May 10, 1960, on the occasion of the 200th anniversary of the birth of Johann Peter Hebel.
     [C]   *Hebel-Feier: Reden zum 200: Geburtstag des Dichters* (1960) Karlsruhe: C. F. Müller, pp. 27-29. Reprinted in *Reden und andere Zeugnisse eines Lebensweges*. GA 16 (2000), pp. 565-67.
     [D]   "Acknowledgement on the Conferment of the National Hebel Memorial Prize," *Delos* 19/20, April 1997 (summer-winter 1994): 30-34.

2.   [A]   "Adalbert Stifter's 'Ice Tale'" (1993) [Miles Groth].
     [B]   "Adalbert Stifters 'Eisgeschichte'": Lecture broadcast on Radio Zürich, January 26, 1964.
     [C]   Daniel Bodmer, ed., *Wirkendes Wort* (1964) Zürich: Schweizerische Bibliophilen-Gesellschaft, pp. 23-38. Reprinted in *Aus der Erfahrung des Denkens [From the Experience of Thinking]*: GA 13 (1983), pp. 185-98.

>
> Volume 13 takes its title from a privately printed volume (1954) of a series of reflections written in 1947.
>
> [D] *Adalbert Stifter's "Ice Tale" by Martin Heidegger* (1993) New York: Nino Press. Published in part in Robert Crease, ed., *Proceedings: 27th Annual Heidegger Conference* (1993) Stony Brook: SUNY at Stony Brook Press, pp. 21-23 and Appendix A.

3. [A] (A) "The Age of the World View" (1951) [Marjorie Grene].
   (B) "The Age of the World Picture" (1977) [William Lovitt].
   (C) "The Age of the World Picture" (2002) [Julian Young].

   [B] "Die Begründung des neuzeitlichen Weltbildes durch die Metaphysik [The Founding of the Modern World View by Metaphysics]": Lecture given June 9, 1938, Freiburg. Revised title (1950): "Die Zeit des Weltbildes."

   [C] *Holzwege* (1950): GA 5 (1977), pp. 75-113.

   [D] (A) *Measure* (Chicago) 2, 1951, pp. 269-84. Reprinted in *Boundary 2* (Binghamton) 4, no. 2, 1976, pp. 1-15, and William V. Spanos, ed., *Martin Heidegger and the Question of Literature: Toward a Postmodern Literary Hermeneutics* (1979) Bloomington: Indiana University Press, pp. 1-15 (a reissue of the journal).
   (B) *The Question Concerning Technology and Other Essays* (1977) New York: Garland, 1982, pp. 115-54.
   (C) *Off the Beaten Track* (2002) Cambridge: Cambridge University Press, pp. 57-85.

4. [A] "Alētheia (Heraclitus, Fragment B 16)" (1975) [Frank Capuzzi].

   [B] "Heraklit": Text written in 1954 for a *Festschrift* based on material from the lecture course "Der Anfang des abendländischen Denkens [The Beginning of Western Thinking]," prepared for the Summer Semester 1943, University of Freiburg. (Cf. *Heraklit*: GA 55 (1979), pp. 1-181.) Revised title (1954): "Alētheia (Heraklit, Fragment 16)."

| | [C] | *Festschrift zur Feier des 350jährigen Bestehens des Heinrich-Suso-Gymnasiums in Konstanz* (1954) Konstanz: Heinrich-Suso-Gymnasium, pp. 60-76. Reprinted in *Vorträge und Aufsätze* III (1954) Pfullingen: Neske, 1978, pp. 53-78. |
| | [D] | *Early Greek Thinking* (1975) New York: Harper and Row, 1985, pp. 102-23. |

5. [A] (A) "The Anaximander Fragment" (1975) [David Farrell Krell].
   (B) "Anaximander's Saying" (2002) [Julian Young].
   [B] "Der Spruch des Anaximander": Essay written in 1946, Todtnauberg.
   [C] *Holzwege* (1950): GA 5 (1977), pp. 321-73.
   [D] (A) *Arion* (Boston) 4, 1974, pp. 576-626. Reprinted in *Early Greek Thinking* (1975) New York: Harper and Row, 1985, pp. 13-58.
   (B) *Off the Beaten Track* (2002) Cambridge: Cambridge University Press, pp. 242-81.

6. [A] *Aristotle's* Metaphysics Θ *1-3: On the Essence and Actuality of Force* (1995) [Walter Brogan and Peter Warnek].
   [B] "Interpretationen zur antiken Philosophie/Aristoteles, *Metaphysik* Θ": Lecture course given Summer Semester 1931, University of Freiburg.
   [C] *Aristoteles*, Metaphysik Θ *1-3: Vom Wesen und Wirklichkeit der Kraft*: GA 33 (1981).
   [D] *Aristotle's* Metaphysics Θ *1-3. On the Essence and Actuality of Force* (1995) Bloomington: Indiana University Press.

7. [A] "Art and Space" (1973) [Charles Seibert].
   [B] "Raum, Mensch und Sprache": Revised version of a lecture given October 3, 1964, at the Galerie im Erker, St. Gallen, Switzerland.
   [C] *Die Kunst und der Raum* (1969) St. Gallen: Erker-Verlag. Appears with a French translation. Heidegger reads the text on a recording (1969) St. Gallen: Erker. Reprinted in the GA edition of *Aus der Erfahrung des Denkens* [*From the Experience of Thinking*]: GA 13 (1983), pp. 203-10.

Volume 13 takes its title from a privately printed volume (1954) of a series of reflections written in 1947.
[D] *Man and World* (Dordrecht) 6, 1973, pp. 3-8.

8. [A] "Art and Thinking" (1963) [Hannah Arendt].
   [B] "Die Kunst und das Denken [Art and Thinking]": Colloquy with Hoseki Shin'ichi Hisamatsu on May 18, 1958, University of Freiburg, transcribed by Alfredo Guzzoni.
   [C] Alfred L. Copley, *Heidegger und Hisamatsu und ein Zuhörender* [*Heidegger and Hisamatsu and a Listener*] (1963) Kyoto: Bokubi Press, pp. 43-80. Includes Japanese text of the colloquy. Reprinted in *Reden und andere Zeugnisse eines Lebensweges* (2000): GA 16 (2000), pp. 552-57.
   [D] Alfred L. Copley, *Listening to Heidegger and Hisamatsu* (1963) Kyoto: Bokubi Press, pp. 48-78.

9. [A] "As When on a Holiday ..." (2000) [Keith Hoeller].
   [B] "Wie wenn am Feiertage ...": Lecture presented often in 1939-40.
   [C] Hölderlins Hymne 'Wie wenn am Feiertasge ... (1941) Halle: Niemeyer. Reprinted in GA 4 (1981): pp. 47-77.
   [D] "As When on a Holiday," in *Elucidations of Hölderlin's Poetry* (2000) Amherst, N.Y.: Humanity Books, pp. 67-99.

10. [A] "Author's Book Notice" (2002) [John van Buren]
    [B] "Selbstanzeige. *Die Kategorien- und Bedeutungslehre des Duns Scotus*: Journal book notice from 1917 of the author's postdoctoral dissertation.
    [C] *Kant-Studien* 21, 1917, pp. 467-68.
    [D] *Supplements. From the Earliest Essays to* Being and Time *and Beyond* (John van Buren, ed.) (2002) Albany: SUNY Press, pp. 61-62.

11. [A] *Basic Concepts* (1993) [Gary E. Aylesworth].
    [B] "Grundbegriffe": Lecture course given during the Winter Semester 1941, University of Freiburg.
    [C] *Grundbegriffe*: GA 51 (1981).
    [D] *Basic Concepts* (1993) Bloomington: Indiana University Press.

12.	[A]	*The Basic Problems of Phenomenology* (1982) [Albert Hofstadter].
	[B]	"Die Grundprobleme der Phänomenologie": Lecture course given during the Spring Semester 1927, University of Marburg.
	[C]	*Die Grundprobleme der Phänomenologie* (1975): GA 24 (1989).
	[D]	*The Basic Problems of Phenomenology* (1982) Bloomington: Indiana University Press; rev. ed., 1988.
13.	[A]	"The Basic Question of Being as Such" (1986) [Parvis Emad and Kenneth Maly].
	[B]	Text dictated to Jean Beaufret in September 1946.
	[C]	A French translation is included in [D].
	[D]	*Heidegger Studies* (Berlin) 2, 1986, pp. 4-5.
14.	[A]	*Basic Questions of Philosophy* (1994) [Richard Rojcewicz and André Schuwer].
	[B]	"Grundfragen der Philosophie: Ausgewählte 'Probleme' der 'Logik'": Lecture course given during the Winter Semester 1937/38, University of Freiburg.
	[C]	*Grundfragen der Philosophie. Ausgewählte "Probleme" der "Logik"*: GA 45 (1984).
	[D]	*Basic Questions of Philosophy: Selected "Problems" of "Logic"* (1994) Bloomington: Indiana University Press.
15.	[A]	(A) *[Being and Time]. Sein und Zeit. An Informal Paraphrase of Sections 1-53, with Certain Omissions as Noted* (1955) [Robert J. Trahern, John Wild, Hubert Dreyfus, and Cornelis de Deugd].
		(B) *Being and Time* (1962) [John Macquarrie and Edward Robinson].
		(C) "Being and Time: Introduction" (1977) [Joan Stambaugh, in collaboration with J. Glenn Gray and David Farrell Krell].
		(D) *Being and Time* (1996) [Joan Stambaugh].
	[B]	*Sein und Zeit* (Erste Hälfte [First Half]): Text dedicated April 8, 1926, Todtnauberg.
	[C]	*Jahrbuch für Phänomenologie und phänomenologische*

Forschung [*Annual of Phenomenology and Phenomenological Research*] (Halle) 8, 1927, pp. 1-438. First brought out as a separate volume in 1929. *Sein und Zeit* (1927): GA 2 (1977).

- [D]
  - (A) *Sein und Zeit: An Informal Paraphrase of Sections 1-53* (1955) Cambridge: Harvard Divinity School.
  - (B) *Being and Time* (1962) New York: Student Christian Movement Press. §§ 31-34 reprinted in Kurt Mueller-Vollmer, ed., *The Hermeneutics Reader* (1990) New York: Continuum, pp. 214-40. §§ 2-7 and an excerpt from § 40 reprinted in Richard Kearney and Mara Rainwater, eds., *The Contemporary Philosophy Reader* (1996) New York: Routledge, pp. 27-52.
  - (C) *Basic Writings* (1977) San Francisco: HarperSanFrancisco, (rev. ed., 1993), pp. 37-87.
  - (D) *Being and Time: A Translation of* Sein und Zeit (1996) Albany: SUNY Press.

16. [A] "Building Dwelling Thinking" (1971) [Albert Hofstadter].
    [B] "Bauen Wohnen Denken": Lecture given August 5, 1951, Darmstadt.
    [C] *Darmstädter Gespräch* II ["Mensch und Raum"] (1952) Darmstadt: Neue Darmstädter Verlagsanstalt, pp. 72-84. Reprinted in *Vorträge und Aufsätze* II (1954) Pfullingen: Neske, 1978, pp. 19-36, and in GA 7 (2000), pp. 145-64.
    [D] *Poetry, Language, Thought* (1971) New York: Harper and Row, 1975, pp. 145-61. Reprinted in *Basic Writings* (1977) San Francisco: HarperSanFrancisco, (rev. ed., 1993), pp. 343-63.

17. [A]
    - (A) "A Cassirer-Heidegger Seminar" (1964) [Carl H. Hamburg].
    - (B) "A Discussion between Ernst Cassirer and Martin Heidegger" (1971) [Francis Slade].
    - (C) "Davos Disputation between Ernst Cassirer and Martin Heidegger" (1990) [Richard Taft].
    [B] "Davoser Disputation zwischen Ernst Cassirer und Martin Heidegger [Protokoll der 'Arbeitsgemeinschaft Cassirer-Hei-

degger']": Summary of seminar discussions held March 17-April 4, 1929, Davos Academy, prepared by Otto Bollnow and Joachim Ritter.

[C] Guido Schneeberger, *Ergänzungen zu einer Heidegger-Bibliographie* (1960) Bern: [n.d.], pp. 17-27. Reprinted in *Kant und das Problem der Metaphysik* (1929): GA 3 (1991), pp. 274-96.

[D] (A) *Philosophy and Phenomenological Research* (Providence) 25, 1964-65, pp. 208-22.

(B) Nino Langiulli, ed., *The Existentialist Tradition: Selected Writings* (1971) Garden City: Doubleday, 1981, pp. 192-203. Reprinted in Nino Langiulli, ed., *European Existentialism* (1997) New Brunswick, N.J.:Transaction Publishers, pp. 192-203.

(C) *Kant and the Problem of Metaphysics* (1990) Bloomington: Indiana University Press, pp. 171-85.

18. [A] "Comments on Karl Jaspers's *Psychology of Worldviews* (1998) [John van Buren].

[B] "Anmerkungen zu Karl Jaspers *Psychologie der Weltanschauungen*": Review article, 1920.

[C] Hans Saner, ed., *Karl Jaspers in der Diskussion* (Munich: Pieper (1973), pp. 70-100. Reprinted in *Wegmarken* (1967): GA 9 (1976), pp. 1-44.

[D] *Pathmarks* (1998) Cambridge: Cambridge University Press, pp. 1-38. Revised version published in *Supplements: From the Earliest Essays to* Being and Time *and Beyond* (John van Buren, ed.) (2002) Albany: SUNY Press, pp. 71-103.

19. [A] "The Concept of Time" (1992) [William McNeill].

[B] "Der Begriff der Zeit": Lecture delivered to the Marburg Theological Society on July 25, 1924.

[C] *Der Begriff der Zeit: Vortrag vor der Marburger Theologenschaft Juli 1924* (1989) Tübingen: Niemeyer.

[D] * *The Concept of Time* (1992) London: Blackwell.

20. [A] (A) "The Concept of Time in the Science of History" (1978) [Harry S. Taylor and Hans W. Uffelmann].

(B) "The Concept of Time in the Science of History"

(2002) [Harry S. Taylor, Hans W. Uffelmann, and John van Buren].

[B] "Der Zeitbegriff in der Geschichtswissenschaft": Trial lecture [*Probevorlesung*] for the *venia legendi* [right to lecture] at the University of Freiburg im Breisgau, presented to the philosophy faculty on July 27, 1915.

[C] *Zeitschrift für Philosophie und philosophische Kritik* (Leipzig) 161, 1916, pp. 173-88. Reprinted in *Frühe Schriften* (1972): GA 1 (1978), pp. 413-33.

[D] (A) *Journal of the British Society for Phenomenology* (Manchester) 9, no. 1, January 1978, pp. 3-10.

 (B) *Supplements: From the Earliest Essays to* Being and Time *and Beyond* (John van Buren, ed.) (2002) Albany: SUNY Press, pp. 49-60.

21. [A] "Consolation" (1993) [Allan Blunden].
 [B] "Trost": Poem written in early 1915.
 [C] *Heliand* (Berlin) March 1915. Reprinted in Hugo Ott, *Martin Heidegger: Unterwegs zu seiner Biographie* (1988) Frankfurt: Campus, p. 89, and in *Reden und andere Zeugnisse eines Lebensweges* (2000): GA 16 (2000), p. 36.
 [D] Hugo Ott, *Martin Heidegger: A Political Life* (1993) London: Basic Books, pp. 88-89.

22. [A] *Contribtutions to Philosophy: From Enowning* (1999) [Parvis Emad and Kenneth Maly]
 [B] Texts from 1936-1938.
 [C] *Beiträge zur Philosophie (Vom Ereignis)* (1989): GA 65 (1989).
 [D] *Contributions to Philosophy: From Enowning* (1999) Bloomington: Indiana University Press.

23. [A] "Conversation with Martin Heidegger" (1976) [James G. Hart and John C. Maraldo].
 [B] "Gespräch mit Martin Heidegger": Protocol of informal discussions at the Protestant Academy of Hofgeismar, held in early December 1953, recorded by Hermann Noack, corrected and completed by Heidegger in 1973.
 [C] *Anstösse: Berichte aus der Arbeit der Evangelischen*

		Akademie Hofgeismar [*Initiatives: Reports of the Proceedings of the Hofgeismar Protestant Academy*] (Hofgeismar) 1, 1954, pp. 31-37.

[D] *The Piety of Thinking* (1976) Bloomington: Indiana University Press, pp. 59-71.

24. [A] "Conversation on a Country Path about Thinking" (1966) [John M. Anderson and E. Hans Freund].

    [B] "Zur Erörterung der Gelassenheit: Aus einem Feldweggespräch über das Denken [On the Discussion of Releasement: From a Conversation on a Country Path about Thinking]":Text from the years 1944-45.

    [C] *Gelassenheit* (1959 [Japanese, 1958]) Pfullingen: Neske (8th ed., 1985), pp. 27-71. Reprinted in the GA edition of *Aus der Erfahrung des Denkens* [*From the Experience of Thinking*]: GA 13 (1983), pp. 37-74. Volume 13 takes its title from a privately printed volume (1954) of a series of reflections written in 1947.

    [D] *Discourse on Thinking* (1966) New York: Harper and Row, 1970, pp. 58-90.

25. [A] "Cüppers, Ad. Jos. *Sealed Lips: The Story of the Irish Folk Life in the 19th Century*" (1991) [Protevi].

    [B] "Cüppers, Ad. Jos. *Versiegelte Lippen: Erzählung aus den irishcen Volkleben des 19. Jahrhunderts*" Book review from December 1910.

    [C] *Der Akademiker* 3, no. 2, December 1910, p. 29. Reprinted in *Reden und andere Zeugnisse eines Lebenswege 1910-1976* (2000): GA 16 (2000), p. 9.

    [D] *Graduate Faculty Philosophy Journal* (New York) 14-15, 1991, p. 495.

26. [A] (A) "*Curriculum vitae*" (1965) [Therese Schrynemakers].
        (B) "Curriculum vitae 1913" (1988) [Thomas Sheehan].

    [B] "Lebenslauf":Text appended to Heidegger's doctoral dissertation (1914), University of Freiburg.

	[C]	*Die Lehre vom Urteil im Psychologismus: Ein kritisch-positiver Beitrag zur Logik* (1914) Leipzig: Barth, p. 111.
	[D]	(A) Joseph J. Kockelmans, *Martin Heidegger: A First Introduction to His Philosophy* (1965) Pittsburgh: Duquesne University Press, pp. 1-2. Reprinted in *Listening* (Dubuque) 12, no. 3, 1977, p. 110.
		(B) Thomas Sheehan, "Heidegger's *Lehrjahre*," in John Sallis, Giuseppina Moneta and Jacques Taminiaux, eds., *The Collegium Phaenomenologicum: The First Ten Years* [*Phaenomenologica* 105] (1988) Dordrecht: Kluwer, p. 106. This is, in fact, an earlier version, somewhat different from the published curriculum vitae.
27.	[A]	(A) "Curriculum vitae 1915" (1988) [Thomas Sheehan].
		(B) "Résumé" (1993) [Allan Blunden].
	[B]	*Curriculum vitae*: Document written to accompany his qualifying dissertation, *Die Kategorien- und Bedeutungslehre des Duns Scotus* (1915). Reprinted in *Reden und andere Zeugnisse eines Lebensweges* (2000): GA 16 (2000), pp. 37-39.
	[C]	Hugo Ott, "Der junge Martin Heidegger: Gymnasial-Konviktszeit und Studium," *Freiburger Diözesan-Archiv* (Freiburg) 104, 1984, pp. 315-25. Reprinted in *Martin Heidegger. Unterwegs zu seiner Biographie* (1988) Frankfurt: Campus, pp. 85-87.
	[D]	(A) Thomas Sheehan, "Heidegger's *Lehrjahre*," in *The Collegium Phaenomenologicum: The First Ten Years* [*Phaenomenologica* 105] ed. John Sallis, G. Moneta, and Jacques Taminiaux (1988) Dordrecht: Kluwer, pp. 78-80 (German text pp. 116-17).
		(B) Hugo Ott, *Martin Heidegger: A Political Life* (1993) London: Basic Books, pp. 84-86.
28.	[A]	"A Dialogue on Language" (1971) [Peter D. Hertz].
	[B]	"Aus einem Gespräch von der Sprache: Zwischen einem Japaner und einem Fragenden [From a Conversation on

Language: Between a Japanese and a Questioner]": Dialogue from the years 1953-54.
- [C] *Unterwegs zur Sprache* (1959): GA 12 (1985), pp. 79-146.
- [D] *On the Way to Language* (1971) New York: Harper and Row, 1982, pp. 1-54.

29. [A]   (A)   *Duns Scotus' Theory of the Categories and of Meaning* (1978) [Harold J. Robbins].
      (B)   "Signification and Radical Subjectivity in Heidegger's Habilitationsschrift" (1979) [Roderick M. Stewart].
- [B] *Die Kategorien- und Bedeutungslehre des Duns Scotus: Habilitationsschrift* [Faculty Thesis], University of Freiburg (1915).
- [C] *Die Kategorien- und Bedeutungslehre des Duns Scotus* (1916) Tübingen: Mohr. Reprinted in *Frühe Schriften* (1972): GA 1 (1978), pp. 189-411.
- [D]   (A)   *Duns Scotus' Theory of the Categories and of Meaning* (1978) Ann Arbor: University Microfilms International. Dissertation reprint (DePaul University, 1978).
      (B)   Roderick M. Stewart, "Signification and Radical Subjectivity in Heidegger's Habilitationsschrift," *Man and World* (Dordrecht) 12, 1979, pp. 378-86 [= pp. 242-57 and lvi-lviii in (A)].

30. [A]   "Editor's Foreword" to Edmund Husserl, *The Phenomenology of Inner Time-Consciousness [1905]*" (1964) [James D. Churchill].
- [B] "Vorbemerkungen des Herausgebers ("Einleitung")": Introduction to Heidegger's edition of Husserl's lectures, written in 1928.
- [C] *Jahrbuch für Phänomenologie und phänomenologische Forschung* (Halle) 9, 1928, pp. 367-68. Reprinted in Edmund Husserl, *Zur Phänomenologie des inneren Zeitbewusstseins (1893-1917)* [Husserliana 9, Rudolf Boehm, ed.] (1966) The Hague: Martinus Nijhoff, pp. xxiv-xxv.
- [D] Edmund Husserl, *The Phenomenology of Inner Time-Consciousness* (1964) Bloomington: Indiana University Press, 1966, pp. 15-16.

31. [A] (A) "The End of Philosophy and the Task of Thinking" (1972) [Joan Stambaugh].
(B) "The End of Philosophy and the Task of Thinking" (1977) [David Farrell Krell].
[B] "Das Ende der Philosophie und die Aufgabe des Denkens": Lecture given during a colloquium on Kierkegaard in Paris, April 21-23, 1964.
[C] Jean Beaufret and François Fédier, eds., *Kierkegaard vivant* (1966) Paris: Gallimard, pp. 165-204. This French translation was followed by the first German edition in *Zur Sache des Denkens* [*The Matter of Thought*] (1969) Tübingen: Niemeyer, pp. 61-80.
[D] (A) *On Time and Being* (1972) New York: Harper and Row, 1978, pp. 55-73.
(B) *Basic Writings* (1977) San Francisco: HarperSanFrancisco, (rev. ed., 1993), pp. 427-49. Modified version of (A).

32. [A] *The Essence of Human Freedom: An Introduction to Philosophy* (2002) [Ted Sadler].
[B] "Vom Wesen der menschlichen Freiheit: Einleitung in die Philosophie": Lecture course given during the Summer Semester of 1930, University of Freiburg.
[C] *Vom Wesen der menschlichen Freiheit: Einleitung in die Philosophie.* GA 31 (1982; 2nd ed., 1994).
[D] *The Essence of Human Freedom. An Introduction to Philosophy* (2002) New York: Continuum.

33. [A] "The Eternal Recurrence of the Same" (1984) [David Farrell Krell].
[B] "Nietzsches metaphysische Grundstellung im abendländischen Denken: Die ewige Wiederkehr des Gleichen": Heidegger's second lecture course on Nietzsche, given during the Summer Semester 1937, University of Freiburg.
[C] *Nietzsche* I (1961) Pfullingen: Neske, pp. 255-472 [part 2]. Heidegger's substantially revised text of the lectures appears as *Nietzsches metaphysische Grundstellung im abendländischen Denken: Die ewige Wiederkehr des Gle-*

ichen: GA 44 (1986). *Nietzsche* I/II (1961) will be reprinted as GA 6.1-6.2. Volume 6.1 appeared in 1996 and 6.2 in 1997.

[D] *Nietzsche*, volume 2: *The Eternal Recurrence of the Same* (1984) New York: Harper and Row, pp. 3-208 [part 1]. The HarperCollins paperback reprint (1991) of all four volumes of *Nietzsche* combines volumes I and II. Excerpts of an earlier version of the translation were published in *Boundary 2* (Binghamton) 9, no. 3-10, no. 1, 1981, pp. 25-39, under the title "Tragedy, Satyr-Play, and Telling Silence in Nietzsche's Thought of Eternal Recurrence." These include the epigraph to the lecture series, Section 4 ("*Incipit tragoedia*'"), all but the last four paragraphs of Section 8 ("The Convalescent"), and the last two paragraphs of the concluding section ("Nietzsche's Fundamental Metaphysical Position") [= *Nietzsche* I (1961) pp. 255, 278-83, 302-16, 471-72].

34. [A] "The Eternal Recurrence of the Same and the Will to Power" (1987) [David Farrell Krell].

[B] "Die ewige Wiederkehr des Gleichen und der Wille zur Macht": A two-lecture conclusion to the first three courses on Nietzsche given at the University of Freiburg. These lectures, written in 1939, were never presented.

[C] *Nietzsche* II (1961) Pfullingen: Neske, pp. 7-29 [Part IV]. This appears as part 3 of *Nietzsches Lehre vom Willen zur Macht als Erkenntnis*: GA 47 (1989), pp. 275-95. *Nietzsche* I/II (1961) will be reprinted as GA 6.1-6.2. Volume 6.1 appeared in 1996 and 6.2 in 1997.

[D] *Nietzsche*, volume 3: *The Will to Power as Knowledge and as Metaphysics* (1987) New York: Harper and Row, pp. 159-83 [part 2]. The HarperCollins paperback reprint (1991) of all four volumes of *Nietzsche* combines volumes 3 and 4.

35. [A] "European Nihilism" (1982) [Frank A. Capuzzi].

[B] "Nietzsche: Der europäische Nihilismus": Heidegger's fourth and last course on Nietzsche, given during the second trimester of 1940 at the University of Freiburg.

[C] *Nietzsche* II (1961) Pfullingen: Neske, pp. 31-256 [part 5]. A substantially revised text of this lecture course has been published as *Nietzsche: Der europäische Nihilismus*: GA

48 (1986). *Nietzsche* I/II (1961) will be reprinted as GA 6.1-6.2. Volume 6.1 appeared in 1996 and 6.2 in 1997.

[D]   *Nietzsche*, volume 4: *Nihilism* (1982) New York: Harper and Row, pp. 3-196 [part 1]. The HarperCollins paperback reprint (1991) of all four volumes of *Nietzsche* combines volumes 3 and 4.

36. [A] (A) "Eventide on Reichenau" (1963) [William J. Richardson].
        (B) "Evening on the Reichenau" (1970) [John Peck].
        (C) "Evening Walk on Reichenau" (1998) [Ewald Osers].

[B]   "Abendgang auf der Reichenau [An Evening Walk on Reichenau]": Poem written in 1916.

[C]   *Das Bodenseebuch* (Konstanz) 4, 1917, p. 152. Reprinted in the GA edition of *Aus der Erfahrung des Denkens* [*From the Experience of Thinking*]: GA 13 (1983), p. 7. Volume 13 takes its title from a privately printed volume (1954) of a series of reflections written in 1947.

[D] (A) *William J. Richardson, *Heidegger: Through Phenomenology to Thought* [Phaenomenologica 13] (1963) The Hague: Martinus Nijhoff, 1974, p. 1.
        (B) **Delos* (College Park) 3, 1970, pp. 60-61.
        (C) Rüdiger Safranski, *Martin Heidegger: Between Good and Evil* (1998) Cambridge: Harvard University Press, p. 69.

37. [A] "For Edmund Husserl on His Seventieth Birthday" (1997) [Thomas Sheehan].

[B]   "Edmund Husserl zum 70. Geburtstag": Speech given on April 8, 1929, on the occasion of the presentation to Husserl of a *Festschrift* in his honor.

[C]   *Akademische Mitteilungen* (Freiburg), May 14, 1929, pp. 46-47.

[D]   Thomas Sheehan and Richard E. Palmer, eds., *Psychological and Transcendental Phenomenology and the Confrontation with Heidegger (1927-1931)* (Dordrecht: Kluwer, 1997), pp. 475-77.

38. [A] "Förster, Fr. W. *Authority and Freedom: Observations on the Cultural Problem of the Church*" (1991) [John Protevi]
    [B] "Förster, Fr. W. *Autorität und Freiheit. Betrachtungen zum Kulturproblem der Kirche*": Book review from May 1910.
    [C] *Der Akademiker* (Munich) 2, May 1910, pp. 109-110. Reprinted in *Reden und andere Zeugnisse eines Lebensweges* (2000): GA 16 (2000), pp. 7-8.
    [D] *Graduate Faculty Philosophy Journal* (New York) 14-15, 1991, pp. 491-93.

39. [A] (A) "From the Last Marburg Lecture Course" (1971) [John Macquarrie].
        (B) "From the Last Marburg Lecture Course" (1998) [William McNeill and Michael Heim].
    [B] "Aus der letzten Marburger Vorlesung": Text based on §5 of the lecture course "Logik," given during the Summer Semester 1928 at the University of Marburg, published as *Metaphysische Anfangsgründe der Logik im Ausgang von Leibniz*: GA 26 (1978).
    [C] Erich Dinkler and Hartwig Thyen, eds., *Zeit und Geschichte. Dankesgabe an Rudolf Bultmann zum 80. Geburtstag im Auftrag der Alten Marburger* (1964) Tübingen: Mohr, pp. 491-507. Reprinted in *Wegmarken* (1967): GA 9 (1976), pp. 79-101.
    [D] (A) Edward Robinson, ed., *The Future of Our Religious Past: Essays in Honor of Rudolf Bultmann* (1971) London: Student Christian Movement Press, pp. 312-32.
        (B) *Pathmarks* (1998) Cambridge: Cambridge University Press, pp. 63-81. Cf. §5 of *The Metaphysical Foundations of Logic* (1984) Bloomington: Indiana University Press, pp. 82-99.

40. [A] *The Fundamental Concepts of Metaphysics: World, Finitude, Solitude* (1995) [William McNeill and Nicholas Walker].
    [B] "Die Grundbegriffe der Metaphysik: Welt, Endlichkiet, Einsamkeit": Lecture course given during the Winter Semester 1929-30, University of Freiburg.

| | [C] | *Der Grundbegriffe der Metaphysik: Welt-Endlichkeit-Einsamkeit*: GA 29/30 (1983; 2nd ed., 1992). |
| | [D] | *The Fundamental Concepts of Metaphysics: World, Finitude, Solitude* (1995) Bloomington: Indiana University Press. |

41.   [A]   (A)   "Gethsemane Hours" (1993) [Allan Blunden].
                     (B)   "Gethsemane Hours" (1998) [Ewald Osers].
        [B]   "Oelbergstunden": Poem written in early 1911.
        [C]   *Allgemeine Rundschau* (Munich) April 8, 1911. Reprinted in Hugo Ott, *Martin Heidegger: Unterwegs zu seiner Biographie* (1988) Frankfurt: Campus, p. 71.
        [D]   (A)   Hugo Ott, *Martin Heidegger: A Political Life* (1993) London: Basic Books, p. 68.
                     (B)   Rüdiger Safranski, *Martin Heidegger: Between Good and Evil* (1998) Cambridge: Harvard University Press, p. 41.

42.   [A]   "A Glimpse into Heidegger's Study" (2000) [Keith Hoeller].
        [B]   "Ein Blick in die Werkstatt": Facsimile of Heidegger's marginal notes to the texts of the second and third versions of Hölderlin's "Griechenland" in the *Grosse Stuttgarter Ausgabe* of Hölderlin's works, edited by Friedrich Beissner (Volume 2, pp. 257-58).
        [C]   *Erläuterungen zu Hölderlins Dichtung*, GA 4 (1981): pp. 199-202.
        [D]   *Elucidations of Hölderlin's Poetry* (2000) Amherst, N.Y.: Humanity Books, pp. 227-30.

43.   [A]   "Gredt, Jos. O. S. B. *Elements of Aristotelian-Thomistic Philosophy*, vol. 1: *Logic*, Philos. Nat. Edit. II" (1991) [John Protevi].
        [B]   "Gredt, Jos. O. S. B. *Elementa Philosophiae Aristotelico-Thomisticae: Logica, Philos. Nat. Edit. II.*": Book review from 1912.
        [C]   *Der Akademiker* 4, no. 5, March 1912, pp. 76-77. Reprinted in *Reden und andere Zeugnisse eines Lebenswege 1910-1976* (2000): GA 16 (2000), p. 29-30.
        [D]   *Graduate Faculty Philosophy Journal* 14-15, 1991, pp. 517-19.

44. [A] "A Greeting to the Symposium in Beirut in November 1974" (1990) [Lisa Harries].
    [B] "Ein Grußwort für das Symposion in Beirut November 1974": Note written in 1974 to participants in a conference at the Goethe Institute in Beirut, Lebanon.
    [C] *Ekstasis* (Beirut) 8, 1981, pp. 1-2. Reprinted in Günther Neske and Emil Kettering, eds., *Antwort: Heidegger im Gespräch* (1988) Pfullingen: Neske, pp. 275-76.
    [D] Günther Neske and Emil Kettering, eds., *Martin Heidegger and National Socialism* (1990) New York: Paragon House, pp. 253-54.

45. [A] "Hebel—Friend of the House" (1983) [Bruce V. Foltz and Michael Heim].
    [B] *Hebel—der Hausfreund*: Expanded version of "Gespräch mit Hebel beim 'Schatz-kästlein' zum Hebeltag 1956 [Conversation with Hebel on the *Little Treasury* on Hebel Day, 1956]."
    [C] *Hebel—der Hausfreund* (1957) Pfullingen: Neske (5th ed., 1985). Reprinted in the GA edition of *Aus der Erfahrung des Denkens* [*From the Experience of Thinking*]: GA 13 (1983), pp. 133-50. Volume 13 takes its title from a privately printed volume (1954) of a series of reflections written in 1947.
    [D] Darrel E. Christensen et al., eds., *Contemporary German Philosophy*, vol. 3 (1983) University Park: Pennsylvania State University Press, pp. 89-101.

46. [A] "Hegel and the Greeks" (1998) [Robert Metcalf, John Sallis, and William McNeill].
    [B] "Hegel und die Griechen": Lecture given at the Heidelberg Academy of Sciences, July 26, 1958. An earlier version (Aix-en-Provence, March 20, 1958) was published in a French translation, by Jean Beaufret and Pierre-Paul Sagave, in *Cahiers du Sud* (Paris) 47, no. 349, January 1959, pp. 355-68.
    [C] *Holzwege* (1950): GA 5 (1977), pp. 427-44.
    [D] *Pathmarks* (1998) Cambridge: Cambridge University Press, pp. 323-36.

47. [A] (A) *Hegel's Concept of Experience* (1970) [J. Glenn Gray and Fred D. Wieck].
         (B) "Hegel's Concept of Experience" (2002) [Kenneth Haynes].
     [B] "Hegels Begriff der Erfahrung": Text written in 1942-43, based on a series of seminars devoted to Hegel's *Phänomenologie des Geistes* given at the University of Freiburg.
     [C] *Holzwege* (1950): GA 5 (1977), pp. 115-208.
     [D] (A) *Hegel's Concept of Experience* (1970) New York: Harper and Row, 1989.
         (B) *Off the Beaten Track* (2002) Cambridge: Cambridge University Press, pp. 86-156.

48. [A] *Hegel's Phenomenology of Spirit* (1988) [Parvis Emad and Kenneth Maly].
     [B] "Hegels Phänomenologie des Geistes": Lecture course given during the Winter Semester 1930-31, University of Freiburg.
     [C] *Hegels Phänomenologie des Geistes*: GA 32 (1980).
     [D] *Hegel's Phenomenology of Spirit* (1988) Bloomington: Indiana University Press.

49. [A] *The Heidegger-Jaspers Correspondence (1920-1963)* (2003) [Gary E. Aylesworth].
     [B] Letters between Heidegger and Karl Jaspers: 1920-1963. Edited by Walter Biemel and Hans Saner.
     [C] *Martin Heidegger/Karl Jaspers Briefwechsel: 1920-1963* (1990) Frankfurt: Klostermann.
     [D] *The Heidegger-Jaspers Correspondence (1920-1963)* (2003) Amherst, N.Y.: Humanity Books, 2003.

50. [A] "A Heidegger Seminar on Hegel's *Differenzschrift*" (1980) [William Lovitt].
     [B] "Seminar in Le Thor 1968": Record of the eight sessions of the second "Seminar in Le Thor," held August 30-September 8, 1968, Provence. A French translation appeared in 1976.
     [C] *Vier Seminare* (1977) Frankfurt: Klostermann, pp. 24-63. Reprinted in *Seminare*: GA 15 (1986), pp. 286-325.
     [D] *Southwestern Journal of Philosophy* (Norman) 11, no. 3, 1980, pp. 9-45.

51. [A] "Heidegger's Letter to the Boss's Daughter" (1988) [Russell A. Berman and Paul Piccone].
    [B] "Brief Martin Heideggers an Elisabeth Husserl": Letter of April 24, 1919, to Elli Husserl.
    [C] "Brief Martin Heideggers an Elisabeth Husserl," in *Aut-Aut* (Scandicci) January-April, 1988, pp. 6-14.
    [D] *Telos* (New York) 77, fall 1988, pp. 125-27.

52. [A] *Heraclitus Seminar 1966/67* (1979) [Charles H. Seibert].
    [B] *Heraklit: Martin Heidegger-Eugen Fink: Seminar 1966/67*: Seminar on Heraclitus, with Eugen Fink, given during the Winter Semester 1966-67, University of Freiburg.
    [C] *Heraklit: Martin Heidegger-Eugen Fink: Seminar 1966/67* (1970) Frankfurt: Klostermann. Reprinted in *Seminare*: GA 15 (1986), pp. 9-263.
    [D] *Heraclitus Seminar 1966/67* (1979) University: Alabama University Press, 1979.

53 [A] *History of the Concept of Time* (1985) [Theodore Kisiel].
   [B] "Prolegomena zur Geschichte des Zeitbegriffs": Lecture course given during the Summer Semester 1925, University of Marburg.
   [C] *Prolegomena zur Geschichte des Zeitbegriffs* (1979): GA 20 (1988).
   [D] *History of the Concept of Time: Prolegomena* (1985) Bloomington: Indiana University Press.

54. [A] (A) "Hölderlin and the Essence of Poetry" (1949) [Douglas Scott].
        (B) "Hölderlin and the Essence of Poetry" (1959) [Paul de Man].
        (C) "Hölderlin and the Essence of Poetry" (2000) [Keith Hoeller].
    [B] "Hölderlin und das Wesen der Dichtung": Lecture given April 2, 1936, Rome.
    [C] *Das innere Reich* (Munich) 3, 1936, pp. 1065-78. Reprinted in *Erläuterungen zu Hölderlins Dichtung* [*Elucidations of Hölderlin's Poetry*] (1944): GA 4 (1981), pp. 33-48.

[D] (A) *Existence and Being* (1949) Washington, D.C.: Regnery Gateway, 1988, pp. 270-91.
    (B) *Quarterly Review of Literature* (Chapel Hill) 10, 1959, pp. 79-94.
    (C) *Elucidations of Hölderlin's Poetry* (2000) Amherst, N.Y.: Humanity Books, pp. 51-65.

55. [A] *Hölderlin's Hymn "The Ister"* (1996) [William McNeill and Julia Davis].
    [B] "Hölderlins Hymnen": Lecture course given during the Summer Semester 1942, University of Freiburg.
    [C] *Hölderlins Hymne "Der Ister"* (1983): GA 53 (1984).
    [D] *Hölderlin's Hymn "The Ister"* (1996) Bloomington: Indiana University Press.

56. [A] "Hölderlin's Heaven and Earth" (2000) [Keith Hoeller].
    [B] "Hölderlins Erde und Himmel": Lecture given June 6, 1959, for the Munich Hölderlin Society.
    [C] *Hölderlin-Jahrbuch* 11 (1958-60), pp. 17-39. Heidegger reads the lecture on a recording (1960) Pfullingen: Neske.
    [D] *Elucidations of Hölderlin's Poetry* (2000) Amherst, N.Y.: Humanity Books, pp. 175-207.

57. [A] (A) "Homeland: Festival Address at a Centennial Celebration" (1971) [Thomas F. O'Meara].
        (B) "Messkirch's Seventh Centennial" (1973) [Thomas J. Sheehan].
    [B] "Ansprache zum Heimatabend [Address to a Homeland Gathering]": Speech given July 22, 1961, Messkirch.
    [C] *700 Jahre Stadt Messkirch* (1962) Messkirch: Aker, pp. 7-16.
    [D] (A) *Listening* (Dubuque) 6, 1971, pp. 231-38.
        (B) * *Listening* (Dubuque) 8, 1973, pp. 41-57.

58. [A] (A) "The Idea of Phenomenology" (1970) [John N. Deely and Joseph A. Novak].
        (B) "The Idea of Phenomenology" (1977) [Thomas Sheehan].
        (C) "'Phenomenology': The *Encyclopaedia Britan-*

nica Article. Draft B ('Attempt at a Second Draft')" (1997) [Thomas Sheehan].

[B] "Versuch einer zweiten Bearbeitung: Einleitung: Die Idee der Phänomenologie und der Rückgang auf das Bewusstsein [Attempt at a Second Version: Introduction: The Idea of Phenomenology and Getting Back to Consciousness]": Article written in 1927 for the Fourteenth Edition of the *Encyclopædia Britannica*.

[C] Edmund Husserl, *Phänomenologische Psychologie* [Husserliana 9] (Walter Biemel, ed.) (1962) The Hague: Martinus Nijhoff, 1968, pp. 256-63.

[D] (A) *New Scholasticism* (Washington, D.C.) 44, 1970, pp. 325-44.

(B) *Listening* (Dubuque) 12, no. 3, 1977, pp. 111-17. Includes a letter of October 10, 1927, to Edmund Husserl.

(C) Thomas Sheehan and Richard E. Palmer, eds., *Psychological and Transcendental Phenomenology and the Confrontation with Heidegger (1927-1931)* (Dordrecht: Kluwer, 1997), pp. 107-16. This volume contains fragments from previously untranslated letters to Karl Löwith, Karl Jaspers, Georg Misch, and Elisabeth Blochmann (pp. 17, 25, 140-42).

59. [A] (A) "In Memory of Max Scheler" (1981) [Thomas Sheehan].

(B) "Max Scheler: In Memoriam" (1984) [Michael Heim].

[B] "In memoriam Max Scheler": Eulogy on the death of Max Scheler, given on May 21, during the Summer Semester 1928, University of Marburg.

[C] Paul Good, ed., *Max Scheler im Gegenwartsgeschehen der Philosophie* (1975) Bern: Francke, pp. 9-10. Reprinted in *Metaphysische Anfangsgründe der Logik im Ausgang der Leibniz*: GA 26 (1978), pp. 62-64.

[D] (A) Thomas Sheehan, ed., *Heidegger. The Man and the Thinker* (1981) Chicago: Precedent Publishing, pp. 159-60.

		(B)	*The Metaphysical Foundations of Logic* (1984) Bloomington: Indiana University Press, pp. 50-52.
60.	[A]	(A)	*An Introduction to Metaphysics* (1959) [Ralph Manheim].
		(B)	*Introduction to Metaphysics* (2000) [Gregory Fried and Richard Polt]
	[B]		"Einführung in die Metaphysik": Lecture course given during the Summer Semester 1935, University of Freiburg.
	[C]		*Einführung in die Metaphysik* (1953): GA 40 (1983).
	[D]	(A)	*An Introduction to Metaphysics* (1959) New Haven, Conn.: Yale University Press, 1974. Chapter 1, "The Fundamental Question of Metaphysics," was reprinted in William Barrett and Henry D. Aiken, eds., *Philosophy in the Twentieth Century: An Anthology*, vol. 3 (1962) New York: Random House, 1982, pp. 219-50.
		(B)	*Introduction to Metaphysics* (2000) New Haven, Conn.: Yale University Press.
61.	[A]		"Jörgensen, Joh. *Travelogue: Light and Dark Nature and Spirit* (1991) [John Protevi].
	[B]		"Jörgensen, Joh. *Das Reisebuch. Licht und dunke Natur und Geist*": Book review from July 1911.
	[C]		*Der Akademiker* 3, no. 3, January 1911, p. 45. Reprinted in *Reden und andere Zeugnisse eines Lebenswege 1910-1976* (2000): GA 16 (2000), p. 10.
	[D]		*Graduate Faculty Philosophy Journal* (New York) 14-15, 1991, pp. 495.
62.	[A]		"July Night" (1993) [Allan Blunden].
	[B]		"Julinacht": Poem written during the summer of 1911.
	[C]		Hugo Ott, *Martin Heidegger: Unterwegs zu seiner Biographie* (1988) Frankfurt: Campus, p. 72. "Private bequest" to the author.
	[D]		Hugo Ott, *Martin Heidegger: A Political Life* (1993) London: Basic Books, p. 69.
63.	[A]	(A)	*Kant and the Problem of Metaphysics* (1962) [James S. Churchill].

| | | | (B) | *Kant and the Problem of Metaphysics* (1991) [Richard Taft]. |

- [B] "Kant und das Problem der Metaphysik": Lecture course given during the Winter Semester 1925-26, University of Marburg.
- [C] *Kant und das Problem der Metaphysik* (1929) Frankfurt: Klostermann (4th ed., 1973): GA 3 (1991). The 4th edition also includes (a) "Davoser Vorträge: Kants *Kritik der reinen Vernunft* und die Aufgabe einer Grundlegung der Metaphysik" (1929), Heidegger's summary of three lectures given in March 1929 at the Davos Academy; (b) "Davoser Disputation zwischen Ernst Cassirer und Martin Heidegger" (1929), the transcript of a discussion between Heidegger and Cassirer at the Davos Academy; (c) "Ernst Cassirer, *Philosophie der symbolischen Formen* [Philosophy of Symbolic Forms]. 2. Teil: *Das mythische Denken* [*Mythical Thought*], a review of Cassirer's book published in 1928; and (d) three other related texts.
- [D] (A) *Kant and the Problem of Metaphysics* (1962) Bloomington: Indiana University Press. Does not contain any of the supplementary texts. Doctoral dissertation (Indiana University, 1960).
  - (B) *Kant and the Problem of Metaphysics* (1991) Bloomington: Indiana University Press. Contains [C]:(a-c).

64. [A] "Kant's *Critique of Pure Reason* and the Task of a Laying of the Ground of Metaphysics" (1991) [Richard Taft].
    [B] "Davoser Vorträge: Kants *Kritik der reinen Vernunft* und die Aufgabe einer Grundlegung der Metaphysik": Summary of three lectures given in March 1929, at the Davos Academy.
    [C] *Davoser Revue* (Davos) 4, no. 7, 1929, pp. 194-96. Reprinted in *Kant und das Problem der Metaphysik* (4th ed., 1973): GA (1991), pp. 271-73.
    [D] *Kant and the Problem of Metaphysics* (1991) Bloomington: Indiana University Press, pp. 169-71.

65. [A] (A) "Kant's Thesis about Being" (1973) [Ted E. Klein Jr. and William E. Pohl].

(B) "Kant's Thesis about Being" (1998) [William McNeill, Ted E. Klein Jr., and William E. Pohl].

[B] "Kants These über das Sein": Lecture given May 17, 1961, Kiel.

[C] Thomas Würtenberger et al., eds., *Existenz und Ordnung [Existence and Order]: Festschrift für Erik Wolf zum 60. Geburtstag* (1962) Frankfurt: Klostermann, pp. 217-45. Reprinted in *Wegmarken* (1967): GA 9 (1978), pp. 445-80.

[D] (A) *Southwestern Journal of Philosophy* (Norman) 4, 1973, pp. 7-33. Reprinted in Robert W. Shahan and J. N. Mohanty, eds., *Thinking about Being* (1984) Norman: University of Oklahoma Press, pp. 7-33.

(B) *Pathmarks* (1998) Cambridge: Cambridge University Press, pp. 337-63.

66. [A] "Language" (1971) [Albert Hofstadter].
    [B] "Die Sprache": Lecture given October 7, 1950, Bühlerhöhe.
    [C] *Unterwegs zur Sprache* (1959): GA 12 (1985), pp. 7-30.
    [D] *Poetry, Language, Thought* (1971) New York: Harper and Row, 1975, pp. 189-210.

67. [A] "Language" (1976) [Thomas Sheehan].
    [B] "Sprache": Poem written in 1972 sent to Raymond Panikkar, University of California, Santa Barbara, in March 1976.
    [C] *Argile* (Paris) I, winter 1973, pp. 4-5, 158 (with French translation by Roger Munier). Reprinted in the GA edition of *Aus der Erfahrung des Denkens* [*From the Experience of Thinking*]: GA 13 (1983), p. 229. Volume 13 takes its title from a privately printed volume (1954) of a series of reflections written in 1947.
    [D] * *Philosophy Today* (Celina) 20, no. 4, 1976, p. 291.

68. [A] "Language in the Poem: A Discussion on Georg Trakl's Poetic Work" (1971) [Peter D. Hertz].
    [B] "Die Sprache im Gedicht: Eine Erörterung von Georg Trakls Gedicht [Language in the Poem: A Discussion of Georg Trakl's Poetry]" (1959): Revised version of "Georg Trakl: Eine Erörterung seines Gedichtes [Georg Trakl: A Discussion of His Poetry]," essay written in 1953.

	[C]		*Merkur* (Munich) 61, 1953, pp. 226-58. Revised title in *Unterwegs zur Sprache* (1959): GA 12 (1985), pp. 31-78.
	[D]		*On the Way to Language* (1971) New York: Harper and Row, 1982, pp. 159-98.
69.	[A]	(A)	["Letter on Humanism":] "The Meaning of 'Humanism'" (1949) [no translator named].
		(B)	"Letter on Humanism" (1962) [Edgar Lohner].
		(C)	"Letter on Humanism" (1977) [Frank A. Capuzzi and J. Glenn Gray].
		(D)	"Letter on 'Humanism'" (1998) [William McNeill, David Farrell Krell].
	[B]		"Brief über den Humanismus":Text based on a letter to Jean Beaufret written in 1946.
	[C]		*Platons Lehre von der Wahrheit: Mit einem Brief über den Humanismus* (1947) Bern: Francke, pp. 53-119. Reprinted in *Wegmarken* (1967): GA 9 (1976), pp. 313-64.
	[D]	(A)	*World Review* (London) 2 [New Series], April 1949, pp. 29-33. This appears to be the first translation into English of something by Heidegger.
		(B)	William Barrett and Henry D. Aiken, eds., *Philosophy in the Twentieth Century: An Anthology*, Vol. 3 (1962) New York: Random House, 1982, pp. 270-302. Reprinted in Nino Langiulli, ed., *The Existentialist Tradition* (1971) Garden City: Doubleday, 1981, pp. 204-45; and Nino Langiulli, ed., *European Existentialism* (1997) New Brunswick, N.J.:Transaction Publishers, pp. 204-45.
		(C)	*Basic Writings* (1977) San Francisco: HarperSanFrancisco, (rev. ed., 1993), pp. 213-65.
		(D)	*Pathmarks* (1998) Cambridge: Cambridge University Press, pp. 239-76.
70.	[A]		"A Letter from Heidegger" (1968) [William J. Richardson].
	[B]		"Brief an Manfred S. Frings": Letter written October 20, 1966.
	[C]		Manfred S. Frings, ed., *Heidegger and the Quest for Truth* (1968) Chicago: Quadrangle Books, pp. 19-21. Reprinted in *Reden und andere Zeugnisse eines Lebensweges* (2000): GA 16 (2000), pp. 684-86.

[D]   * Ibid., pp. 17-19.

71. [A]   "A Letter from Martin Heidegger" (1970) [Arthur H. Schrynemakers].
    [B]   "Brief an Arthur H. Schrynemakers": Letter written September 20, 1966, for the American Heidegger Conference, Duquesne University, Pittsburgh.
    [C]   John Sallis, ed., *Heidegger and the Path of Thinking* (1970) Pittsburgh: Duquesne University Press, pp. 9-10. Reprinted in *Reden und andere Zeugnisse eines Lebensweges* (2000): GA 16 (2000), pp. 650-51.
    [D]   * Ibid., pp. 10-11.

72. [A]   Letter from Martin Heidegger (1970) [Albert Borgmann].
    [B]   "Brief an Albert Borgmann": Letter written in 1969 to participants in the conference on "Heidegger and Eastern Thought," University of Honolulu, Hawaii, November 17-21, 1969.
    [C]   *Reden und andere Zeugnisse eines Lebensweges* (2000): GA 16 (2000), pp. 721-22.
    [D]   Winfield E. Nagley, "Introduction to the Symposium and Reading of a Letter from Martin Heidegger," *Philosophy East and West* (Honolulu) 20, 1970, p. 221.

73. [A]   "Letter to A. L. Copley" (1963) [William Barrett].
    [B]   "Brief an Alfred L. Copley": Letter 1959.
    [C]   Alfred L. Copley, *Heidegger und Hisamatsu und ein Zuhörender [Heidegger and Hisamatsu and a Listener]* (1963) Kyoto: Bokubi Verlag, pp. 34-35, 84. Contains a transcript of a dialogue between Heidegger and Hisamatsu Hoseki, by Copley. Reprinted in *Reden und andere Zeugnisse eines Lebensweges* (2000): GA 16 (2000), p. 562.
    [D]   * Ibid., p. 37.

74. [A]   Letter to Carl Schmitt (1987) [no translator given].
    [B]   Letter, dated August 22, 1933, Freiburg im Bresigau.
    [C]   *Telos* 72, summer 1987, p. 132 (n. *). Reprinted in *Reden und andere Zeugnisse eines Lebensweges* (2000): GA 16 (2000), p. 156.
    [D]   *Telos* 72, summer 1987, p. 132.

A Research Bibliography of Heidegger in English Translation   261

75. [A] Letter to David L. Edwards (1965) [John Macquarrie]
    [B] "Brief an David L. Edwards": Letter written to the director of S[tudent] C[hristian] M[ovement] Press, London, January 28, 1965.
    [C] John Macquarrie, *Heidegger and Christianity* (1994) London: SCM Press, pp. 111-12.
    [D] * Ibid., p. 111.

76. [A] (A) " ... a Letter to Edmund Husserl" (1977) [Thomas Sheehan].
        (B) "Heidegger's Letter and Appendices [to Draft B of the *Encyclopaedia Britannica* article 'Phenomenology']" (1997) [Thomas Sheehan].
    [B] "Brief an Edmund Husserl": Letter written October 22, 1927, to accompany "The Idea of Phenomenology."
    [C] Edmund Husserl, *Phänomenologische Psychologie* [Husserliana 9] (1962) The Hague: Martinus Nijhoff, 1968, pp. 600-601.
    [D] (A) *Listening* (Dubuque) 12, no. 3, 1977, pp. 118-19.
        (B) Thomas Sheehan and Richard E. Palmer, eds., *Psychological and Transcendental Phenomenology and the Confrontation with Heidegger (1927-1931)* (Dordrecht: Kluwer, 1997), pp. 136-37. This volume contains excerpts from previously untranslated letters to Karl Löwith, Karl Jaspers, and Elisabeth Blochmann (pp. 17, 25, 140-42).

77. [A] (A) Letter to Father Engelbert Krebs (1988) [Thomas Sheehan]
        (B) Letter to Father Englesbert Krebs (1988) [Allan Blunden].
    [B] Letter of July 19, 1914.
    [C] Hugo Ott, *Martin Heidegger. Unterwegs zur seiner Biographie* (1988) Frankfurt: Campus, p. 83.
    [D] (A) Thomas Sheehan, "Heidegger's *Lehrjahre*," in *The Collegium Phaenomenologicum: The First Ten Years* [Phaenomenologica 105], ed. John Sallis, G. Moneta and Jacques Taminiaux (1988) Dordrecht: Kluwer, p. 113.

		(B)	Hugo Ott, *Martin Heidegger: A Political Life* (1993) New York: Basic Books, p. 81.
78.	[A]	(A)	Letter to Father Engelbert Krebs (1988) [John van Buren].
		(B)	Letter to Engelbert Krebs (1993) [Allan Blunden].
	[B]		"Brief an Engelbert Krebs": Letter written January 9, 1919.
	[C]		Bernhard Casper, "Martin Heidegger und die Theologische Fakultät Freiburg 1909-1923," *Freiburger Diözesan-Archiv* (Freiburg) 100, 1980, pp. 534-41. Reprinted in Hugo Ott, *Martin Heidegger: Unterwegs zu seiner Biographie* (1988) Frankfurt: Campus, pp. 106-107.
	[D]	(A)	John van Buren, "The Young Heidegger" (1989) McMaster University, pp. 573-74.
		(B)	Hugo Ott, *Martin Heidegger: A Political Life* (1993) London: Basic Books, pp. 81-83.
79.	[A]		Letter to Herbert Marcuse (1991) [Richard Wolin].
	[B]		"Brief an Herbert Marcuse": Letter written January 20, 1948.
	[C]		*Reden und andere Zeugnisse eines Lebensweges* (2000): GA 16 (2000), p. 430-31.
	[D]		"Herbert Marcuse and Martin Heidegger: An Exchange of Letters," *New German Critique* (Ithaca) 53, 1991, pp. 30-31. Reprinted in Richard Wolin, ed., *The Heidegger Controversy: A Critical Reader* (1991) Cambridge: MIT Press, 1993, pp. 163-64.
80.	[A]		Letter to J. Glenn Gray and Joan Stambaugh [excerpts] (1973) [Joan Stambaugh].
	[B]		"Brief an J. Glenn Gray and Joan Stambaugh": Responses written in the summer of 1970 to questions posed by the co-editors of the projected English *Works* of Martin Heidegger.
	[C]		German text unpublished.
	[D]		*The End of Philosophy* (1973) New York: Harper and Row, pp. xi-xiv.
81.	[A]		"Letter to Jean Beaufret" (1988) [Steven Davis].
	[B]		"Brief an Jean Beaufret:" Letter written February 22, 1975,

Freiburg. A French translation by Jean Beaufret, "La Question Portant Fondamentalment sur l' tre-même," follows the letter.

[C] *Heidegger Studies* (Berlin) 3/4, 1987-88, pp. 3-4.
[D] * Ibid., pp. 5-6.

82. [A] Letter to Manfred Frings (1964) [Thomas Sheehan].
[B] "Brief an Manfred Frings": Letter written August 6, 1964.
[C] German text unpublished.
[D] Translator's introductory note to Max Scheler, "Reality and Resistance: On *Being and Time*, Section 43," *Listening* (Dubuque) 12, no. 3, 1977, p. 61. Reprinted in Thomas Sheehan, ed., *Heidegger: The Man and the Thinker* (1981) Chicago: Precedent Publishing, p. 133.

83. [A] Letter to William J. Richardson (1963) [William J. Richardson].
[B] "Brief an William J. Richardson:" Letter written in early April, 1962, Freiburg.
[C] William J. Richardson, *Heidegger: Through Phenomenology to Thought* [Phaenomenologica 13] (1963) The Hague: Martinus Nijhoff, 1974, pp. ix-xxiii.
[D] * Ibid., pp. viii-xxii.

84. [A] (A) "Letters to Elisabeth Blochmann" (1991) [Frank W. H. Edler].
(B) Excerpt of a letter written September 12, 1929 (1993) [Allan Blunden].
[B] "Briefe an Elisabeth Blochmann": Letters from the Heidegger-Blochmann correspondence, 1929-1933.
[C] Martin Heidegger—Elisabeth Blochmann, *Briefwechsel 1918-1969* (Joachim W. Storck, ed.) (1989) Marbach: Deutsche Schillergesellschaft, pp. 31-33 (letter #22), pp. 36-39 (letter #25), pp. 45-46 (letter #32), pp. 49-50 (letter #35), pp. 52-53 (letter #37), pp. 55-58 (letters #40 and #42), pp. 60-63 (letters #46 and #47), pp. 69-70 (letter #57), pp. 73-74 (letter #61), pp. 76-77 (letter #64).
[D] (A) *Graduate Faculty Philosophy Journal* (New York) 14, no. 2-15, no. 1, 1991, pp. 563-77. Excerpts from letters in [C]: #25 (September 20, 1930, Freiburg),

#32 (December 20, 1931, Freiburg), #35 (May 25, 1932, Freiburg), #37 (June 22, 1932, Freiburg), #40 (December 19, 1932, Freiburg), #42 (January 19, 1933, Freiburg), #46 (March 30, 1933, Freiburg), #47 (April 12, 1933, Freiburg), #57 (August 30, 1933, the hut [Todtnauberg]), #61 (September 19, 1933, Messkirch), and #64 (October 16, 1933, Freiburg).

(B) Hugo Ott, *Martin Heidegger: A Political Life* (1993) London: Basic Books, pp. 377-78. Only the letter of September 12, 1929 (letter #22 in [C]).

85. [A] Letter to Medard Boss [excerpt] (1963) [Ludwig B. Lefebre].

[B] Excerpt from a letter, no date.

[C] Medard Boss, *Psychoanalyse und Daseinsanalytik* (1957) Bern: Huber.

[D] Medard Boss, *Psychoanalysis and Daseinsanalysis* (1963) New York: Basic Books, p. 36, n. 4.

86. [A] (A) Letters to Emil Staiger (1981) [Arthur A. Grugan].

(B) "An Exchange of Letters between Emil Staiger and Martin Heidegger" (1990) [Berel Lang and Christine Ebel].

[B] "Briefe an Emil Staiger": Letters written in the autumn of 1950 and December 28, 1950, to Emil Staiger about a poem by Eduard Mörike, "Auf eine Lampe [On a Lamp]."

[C] In Emil Staiger, "Zu einem Vers von Mörike: Ein Briefwechsel mit Heidegger [On a Poem by Mörike: Correspondence with Martin Heidegger]," *Trivium* (Zürich) 9, no. 1, 1951, pp. 1-16. Reprinted in Staiger's *Die Kunst der Interpretation* (1963) Zürich:Atlantis Verlag, pp. 34-49, and in the GA edition of *Aus der Erfahrung des Denkens* [*From the Experience of Thinking*]: GA 13 (1983), pp. 93-109.

[D] (A) Emil Staiger, "The Staiger-Heidegger Correspondence," *Man and World* (Dordrecht) 14, 1981, pp. 291-307.

(B) Part of "A 1951 Dialogue on Interpretation: Emil

Staiger, Martin Heidegger, Leo Spitzer," *Publications of the Modern Language Association* 105, no. 3, 1990, pp. 420-27.

87. [A] Letters to Karl Löwith.
- (A) (1970) [R. Philip O'Hara].
- (B) (a) (1988) [Richard Wolin and Melissa J. Fox].
  - (b) (1994) [Elizabeth King].
- (C) (1995) [Gary Steiner].

[B] (A) "Auszüge aus Briefen Heideggers an Karl Löwith [Excerpts of Letters of Martin Heidegger to Karl Löwith] 1921-29": Letters written August 19, 1921; March 26, 1924; August 21, 1924; June 30, 1925; August 20, 1927; February 3, 1929; and September 3, 1929.

(B) Five brief excerpts from (A).

[C] (A) Hans-Georg Gadamer, ed., *Die Frage Martin Heideggers* (1969) Heidelberg: Winter, pp. 36-39. Reprinted in Karl Löwith, *Aufsätze und Vorträge 1930-1970* (1971) Stuttgart: W. Kohlhammer, pp. 189-203.

(B) Karl Löwith, "Les Implications Politiques de la Philosophie de l'Existence chez Heidegger," *Les Temps Modernes* (Paris) 14, 1946, pp. 343-60. This is a French translation by Joseph Rovan of an edited version of Löwith's essay, which was written in 1939 and first published in German in *Heidegger Denker in dürftiger Zeit: zur Stellung der Philosophie im 20. Jahrhundert* (1984) Stuttgart: J.B. Metzler, pp. 61-68. The complete text of the essay appeared as "Martin Heideggers Philosophie der Zeit (1919-1936)," in *Mein Leben in Deutschland vor und nach 1933: Ein Bericht* (1986) Stuttgart: J.B. Metzler, pp. 27-42.

(C) Dietrich Papenfuss and Otto Pöggeler, eds., *Zur philosophischen Aktualität Heideggers*, vol. 2: *Im Gespräch der Zeit* (1990) Frankfurt: Klostermann, pp. 235-39.

[D] (A) Karl Löwith, "The Nature of Man and the World of

Nature: For Heidegger's 80th Birthday," *Southern Journal of Philosophy* (Memphis) 8, no. 4, 1970, pp. 309-18. Reprinted in Edward G. Ballard and Charles Scott, eds., *Martin Heidegger: In Europe and America* (1973) The Hague: Martinus Nijhoff, pp. 37-46.

(B)   (a)   Karl Löwith, "The Political Implications of Heidegger's Philosophy," *New German Critique* (Ithaca) 45, fall 1988, pp. 117-34. Reprinted in Richard Wolin, ed., *The Heidegger Controversy: A Critical Reader* (1991) New York: Columbia University Press, pp. 167-85.

     (b)   Karl Löwith, "Martin Heidegger's Philosophy of Time (1919-1936), in *My Life in Germany before and after 1933: A Report* (1992) Urbana: University of Illinois Press, pp. 27-33.

(C)   Gary Steiner and Richard Wolin, eds., *Martin Heidegger and European Nihilism* (1995) New York: Columbia University Press, pp. 235-39.

88.   [A]   Letter to Medard Boss [excerpt] (1963) [Ludwig B. Lefebre].

     [B]   Excerpt from a letter, no date.

     [C]   Medard Boss, *Psychoanalyse und Daseinsanalytik* (1957) Bern: Huber.

     [D]   Medard Boss, *Psychoanalysis and Daseinsanalysis* (1963) New York: Basic Books, p. 36, n. 4.

89.   [A]   Letter to Carl Schmitt (1987) [NN].

     [B]   Letter, dated August 22, 1933, Freiburg im Bresigau.

     [C]   *Telos* 72, summer 1987, p. 132 (n. *). Reprinted in *Reden und andere Zeugnisse eines Lebensweges* (2000): GA 16 (2000), p. 156.

     [D]   *Telos* 72, summer 1987, p. 132.

90.   [A]   "*Library of Valuable Novellas and Stories,* vol. 9, O. Hellinghaus, ed." (1991) [John Protevi].

[B]   *"Bibliothek vertvoller Novellen und Erzählungen*: Herausgegeben von Prof. Dr. O. Hellinghaus: Bd. IX": Book review from 1913.

[C]   *Der Akademiker* 4, no. 3, January 1913, p. 45. Reprinted in *Reden und andere Zeugnisse eines Lebenswege 1910-1976* (2000): GA 16 (2000), p. 31.

[D]   *Graduate Faculty Philosophy Journal* 14-15, 1991, p. 519.

91. [A] "Logos (Heraclitus, Fragment B 50)" (1975) [David Farrell Krell and Frank Capuzzi].

[B]   "Logos (Heraklit, Fragment 50)": Essay written in 1944, based on the lecture course "Logik: Heraklits Lehre vom Logos [Heraclitus's Teaching on Logos]," given during the Summer Semester 1944, University of Freiburg. Cf. GA 55 (1979), pp. 185-387.

[C]   Kurt Bauch, ed., *Festschrift für Hans Jantzen* (1951) Berlin: Mann, pp. 7-18. Reprinted in *Vorträge und Aufsätze* III (1954) Pfullingen: Neske, 1978, pp. 3-25.

[D]   *Early Greek Thinking* (1975) New York: Harper and Row, 1985, pp. 59-78.

92. [A] (A)   "Martin Heidegger: An Interview" (1971) [Vincent Gualiardo and Robert Pambrun].

        (B)   "Martin Heidegger in Conversation" (1977) [B. Srinirasa Murthy].

        (C)   "Martin Heidegger in Conversation with Richard Wisser" (1990) [Lisa Harries].

[B]   "Martin Heidegger im Gespräch:" Transcript of a conversation on September 17, 1969, between Martin Heidegger and Richard Wisser, filmed for broadcast on television [ZDF].

[C]   Richard Wisser, ed., *Martin Heidegger im Gespräch* (1970) Freiburg: K. Alber, pp. 67-77. Reprinted in Günther Neske and Emil Kettering, eds., *Antwort: Martin Heidegger im Gespräch* (1988) Pfullingen: Neske, pp. 21-28.

[D]   (A)   *Listening* (Dubuque) 6, 1971, pp. 34-40.

        (B)   Richard Wisser, ed., *Martin Heidegger in Conversation* (1977) New Delhi: Arnold-Heinemann/Rakesh Press, pp. 38-47.

		(C)	Günther Neske and Emil Kettering, eds., *Martin Heidegger and National Socialism* (1990) New York: Paragon House, pp. 81-87.
93.	[A]	(A)	"Martin Heidegger's Zollikon Seminars" (1978) [Brian Kenny].
		(B)	"On Adequate Understanding of Daseinsanalysis" and "Marginalia on Phenomenology, Transcendence and Care" (1988) [Michael Eldred].
	[B]	(A)	Excerpts from the protocol of Heidegger's seminar on January 26, 1961, for medical students and psychiatric residents from the Zurich Psychiatric University Clinic, given with Medard Boss in Zollikon (Zürich), Switzerland. Includes marginalia to the manuscript for *Grundriß der Medizin: Ansätze zu einer phänomenologischen Physiologie, Psychologie, Therapie und zu einer daseinsgemäßen Präventiv-Medizin in der modernen Industriegesellschaft*, by Medard Boss. The work was published in 1971 (Bern: Huber) and translated as *Existential Foundations of Medicine and Psychology* (1979) New York: Aronson.
		(B)	"Protokollen—Gespräche": Excerpts from protocols of conversations with Medard Boss, seminar transcripts and ancillary texts prepared for meetings with Boss and his students in Zollikon (Zürich) on the meaning of Heidegger's work for psychiatry and psychotherapy: March 8, 1965; November 23, 1965; November 28-30, 1965; and July 14, 1969.
	[C]		*Zollikoner Seminare: Protokolle—Gespräche—Briefe* (1987) Frankfurt: Klostermann. (A) The quoted protocol is summarized on pp. 8-9. (B) pp. 150-52, 157, 236-38, 238-42, 253, 254-56, 259, 286-87.
	[D]	(A)	*Review of Existential Psychology and Psychiatry* (Pittsburgh) 16, no. 1-3, 1978-79, pp. 7-20. Reprinted in Keith Hoeller, ed., *Heidegger and Psychology* (1988) Seattle: Review of Existential Psychology and Psychiatry.

| | (B) | *Humanistic Psychologist* (Carrollton) 16, no. 1, 1988, pp. 75-98 and 218-23. |

94. [A] "Memorial Address" (1966) [John M. Anderson and E. Hans Freund]
    [B] "Gelassenheit: Bodenständigkeit im Atomzeitalter [Releasement: Stability in the Atomic Age]": Address given October 30, 1955, on the 175th anniversary of the birth of the composer Conradin Kreuzer, Messkirch.
    [C] *Gelassenheit* (1959 [Japanese edition, 1958]) Pfullingen: Neske (8th ed., 1985), pp. 9-28.
    [D] *Discourse on Thinking* (1966) New York: Harper and Row, 1970, pp. 43-57.

95. [A] *The Metaphysical Foundations of Logic* (1984) [Michael Heim].
    [B] "Metaphysische Anfangsgründe der Logik im Ausgang von Leibniz": Lecture course given during the Spring Semester 1928, University of Marburg.
    [C] *Metaphysische Anfangsgründe der Logik im Ausgang von Leibniz*: GA 26 (1978).
    [D] *The Metaphysical Foundations of Logic* (1984) Bloomington: Indiana University Press.

96. [A] "Metaphysics as History of Being" (1973) [Joan Stambaugh].
    [B] "Die Metaphysik als Geschichte des Seins": Essay written in 1941, Freiburg.
    [C] *Nietzsche* II (1961) Pfullingen: Neske, pp. 399-457 [part 8].
    [D] *The End of Philosophy* (1973) New York: Harper and Row, pp. 1-54.

97. [A] "Modern Natural Science and Technology" (1977) [John Sallis].
    [B] "Neuzeitliche Naturwissenschaft und moderne Technik": Letter written April 11, 1976, to the participants of 10th American Heidegger Conference, held May 14-16, 1976, DePaul University, Chicago, Illinois.
    [C] *Research in Phenomenology* (Pittsburgh) 7, 1977, pp. 1-2

		(reprinted as John Sallis, ed., *Radical Phenomenology* [1978] Englewood Cliffs, N.J.: Humanities Press). Reprinted in *Reden und andere Zeugnisse eines Lebensweges* (2000): GA 16 (2000), pp.747-48.
	[D]	* Ibid., pp. 3-4.
98.	[A]	"Moira (Parmenides VIII, 34-41)" (1975) [Frank Capuzzi].
	[B]	"Moira (Parmenides VIII, 34-41)": Undelivered portion of the lecture course "Was heißt Denken?" given during Winter Semester 1951-52 and Summer Semester 1952, University of Freiburg. It is a supplement to *What Is Called Thinking?* (1968) New York: Harper and Row, 1976, p. 240 ff. [part 2, lecture 11].
	[C]	*Vorträge und Aufsätze* III (1954) Pfullingen: Neske, 1978, pp. 27-52.
	[D]	*Early Greek Thinking* (1975) New York: Harper and Row, 1985, pp. 79-101.
99.	[A]	"My Way to Phenomenology" (1972) [Joan Stambaugh].
	[B]	"Mein Weg in die Phänomenologie": Essay written in 1963 in honor of the publisher Hermann Niemeyer. Supplement added in 1969.
	[C]	*Hermann Niemeyer zum 80: Geburtstag am 16. April 1963* (1963) Privately published. Reprinted in *Zur Sache des Denkens* [*The Matter of Thought*] (1969) Tübingen: Niemeyer, pp. 81-90.
	[D]	*On Time and Being* (1972) New York: Harper and Row, 1978, pp. 74-82. Reprinted in Walter Kaufmann, ed., *Existentialism from Dostoevsky to Sartre* (rev. ed., 1975 [1956]) New York: New American Library, 1984, pp. 234-41.
100.	[A]	"The Nature of Language" (1971) [Peter D. Hertz].
	[B]	"Das Wesen der Sprache": Text from a lecture series given December 4 and 18, 1957, and February 5, 1958, University of Freiburg.
	[C]	*Unterwegs zur Sprache* (1959): GA 12 (1985), pp. 147-204.
	[D]	*On the Way to Language* (1971) New York: Harper and

Row, 1982, pp. 57-108. Translated as "The Essence of Language" (1964), master's dissertation, Columbia University.

101. [A] *Nietzsche* (1979-1987) [Frank A. Capuzzi, David Farrell Krell, Joan Stambaugh].
- (1) Volume 1: *The Will to Power as Art* (1979). See "The Will to Power as Art" for details.
- (2) Volume 2: *The Eternal Recurrence of the Same* (1984). See "The Eternal Recurrence of the Same" and "Who Is Nietzsche's Zarathustra?" for details.
- (3) Volume 3: *The Will to Power as Knowledge and as Metaphysics* (1987). See "The Will to Power as Knowledge," "The Eternal Recurrence of the Same," and "Nietzsche's Metaphysics" for details.
- (4) Volume 4: *Nihilism* (1982). See "European Nihilism" and "Nihilism as Determined by the History of Being" for details. All four volumes were reprinted in the two-volume paperback edition *Nietzsche* (1991) San Francisco: HarperCollins, which combines volumes 1 and 2, 3 and 4, respectively. Three parts of the original two-volume *Nietzsche*, published in 1961 (Pfullingen: Neske), were not included in this translation. They had been previously translated by Joan Stambaugh and published in *The End of Philosophy* (1973) New York: Harper and Row, pp. 1-83. See "Metaphysics as History of Being," "Sketches for a History of Being as Metaphysics," and "Recollection in Metaphysics" for details.

102. [A] "Nietzsche's Metaphysics" (1987) [Frank A. Capuzzi].
- [B] "Nietzsches Metaphysik": Lecture course prepared in 1940 for the Winter Semester of 1941-42 at the University of Freiburg but not given.
- [C] *Nietzsche* II (1961) Pfullingen: Neske, pp. 257-333 [part 6]. A substantially revised text has been published in *Nietzsches Metaphysik*: GA 50 (1990), pp. 1-87. *Nietzsche* I/II (1961) will be reprinted as GA 6.1-6.2. Volume 6.1 appeared in 1996.

	[D]	*Nietzsche*, volume 3: *The Will to Power as Knowledge and as Metaphysics* (1987) New York: Harper and Row, pp. 185-251 [part 3]. The translation has been somewhat modified by the editor of *Nietzsche*. The HarperCollins paperback reprint (1991) of all four volumes of *Nietzsche* combines Volumes 3 and 4.
103.	[A]	"Nihilism as Determined by the History of Being" (1982) [Frank A. Capuzzi].
	[B]	"Die seinsgeschichtliche Bestimmung des Nihilismus": Essay written during the years 1944-46 in conjunction with the author's study of Nietzsche.
	[C]	*Nietzsche* II (1961) Pfullingen: Neske, pp. 335-98 [part 7]. *Nietzsche* I/II (1961) will be reprinted as GA 6.1-6.2. Volume 6.1 appeared in 1996 and 6.2 in 1997.
	[D]	*Nietzsche*, volume 4: *Nihilism* (1982) New York: Harper and Row, pp. 197-250 [part 2]. The HarperCollins paperback reprint (1991) of all four volumes of *Nietzsche* combines volumes 3 and 4.
104.	[A]	"On Adequate Understanding of Daseinsanalysis" and "Marginalia on Phenomenology, Transcendence, and Care" (1988) [Michael Eldred].
	[B]	Excerpts from protocols of conversations with Medard Boss, and seminar transcripts and ancillary texts prepared for meetings with Boss and his students in Zollikon (Zürich) on the general topic of the meaning of Heidegger's work for psychiatry and psychotherapy: March 8, 1965; November 23, 1965; November 28-30, 1965; and July 14, 1969.
	[C]	Medard Boss, ed., *Zollikoner Seminare* (1987) Frankfurt: Klostermann, 150-52, 157, 236-38, 238-42, 253, 254-56, 259, 286-87.
	[D]	*Humanistic Psychologist* (Carrollton) 16, no. 1, 1988, 75-98 and 218-23.
105.	[A]	"On a Philosophical Orientation for Academics" (1991) [John Protevi].
	[B]	"Zur philosophischen Orientierung für Akademiker": Essay written in 1911.

[C] Der Akademiker 3, no. 5, March 1911, pp. 66-67. Reprinted in *Reden und andere Zeugnisse eines Lebenswege 1910-1976* (2000): GA 16 (2000), pp. 11-14.
[D] *Graduate Faculty Philosophy Journal* (New York) 14-15, 1991, pp. 497-501.

106. [A] "On Still Paths" (1993) [Allan Blunden].
[B] "Auf stillen Pfaden": Poem written in early 1911.
[C] *Der Akademiker* (Munich), July 1911. Reprinted in Hugo Ott, *Martin Heidegger: Unterwegs zu seiner Biographie* (1988) Frankfurt: Campus, p. 71, and in *Reden und andere Zeugnisse eines Lebensweges* (2000): GA 16 (2000), p. 16.
[D] Hugo Ott, *Martin Heidegger: A Political Life* (1993) London: Basic Books, p. 68.

107. [A] (A) "On the Being and Concept of Φύσις in Aristotle's *Physics* B, 1" (1976) [Thomas Sheehan].
       (B) "On the Essence and Concept of Φύσις in Aristotle's *Physics* B, 1" (1998) [Thomas Sheehan and William McNeill].
[B] "Vom Wesen und Begriff der Φύσις: Aristoteles *Physik* B,1": Essay written in 1939 for a seminar entitled "Über die Φύσις bei Aristoteles [On Φύσις According to Aristotle]," given the First Trimester 1940, University of Freiburg.
[C] *Il Pensiero* (Milan) 3, no. 2/3, 1958, pp. 131-56, 265-90. Reprinted in *Wegmarken* (1967): GA 9 (1976), pp. 239-301.
[D] (A) *Man and World* (Dordrecht) 9, 1976, pp. 219-70.
       (B) *Pathmarks* (1998) Cambridge: Cambridge University Press, pp. 183-230.

108. [A] (A) "On the Essence of the Ground" (1962) [Jean T. Wilde and William Kimmel].
       (B) *The Essence of Reasons* (1969) [Terrence Malick].
       (C) "On the Essence of Ground" (1998) [William McNeill].
[B] "Vom Wesen des Grundes": Essay for a Festschrift celebrating the 70th birthday of Edmund Husserl. The third edition (1949) of the book was supplemented with a "Vorwort [Preface]."
[C] *Festschrift: Edmund Husserl zum 70. Geburtstag.*

Ergänzungsband zum Jahrbuch für Philosophie und phänomenologische Forschung [*Supplemental Volume to the Yearbook for Philosophy and Phenomenological Research*] (1929) Halle: Niemeyer, pp. 71-100. Reprinted with "Vorwort" in *Vom Wesen des Grundes* (1949) Frankfurt: Klostermann. Reprinted in *Wegmarken* (1967): GA 9 (1976), pp. 123-75.

[D] (A) Jean T. Wilde and William Kimmel, eds., *The Search for Being* (1962) New York: Twayne, pp. 507-20. Includes the "Preface" (1949) and the text of the essay through the end of part 1 ["The Problem of the Ground"].

  (B) * *The Essence of Reasons* (1969) Evanston: Northwestern University Press.

  (C) *Pathmarks* (1998) Cambridge: Cambridge University Press, pp. 97-135.

109. [A] (A) "On the Essence of Truth" (1949) [R. F. C. Hull and Alan Crick].

  (B) "On the Essence of Truth" (1977) [John Sallis].

  (C) "On the Essence of Truth" (1998) [John Sallis and William McNeill].

[B] "Vom Wesen der Wahrheit": Lecture written in 1930.

[C] *Vom Wesen der Wahrheit* (1943) Frankfurt: Klostermann. A concluding note (§ 9) was added for the second edition (1949). Reprinted in *Wegmarken* (1967): GA 9 (1976), pp. 177-202.

[D] (A) *Existence and Being* (1949) Washington, D.C.: Regnery Gateway, 1988, pp. 292-324.

  (B) *Basic Writings* (1977) San Francisco: HarperSanFrancisco, (rev. ed., 1993), pp. 111-38.

  (C) *Pathmarks* (1998) Cambridge: Cambridge University Press, pp. 136-54.

110. [A] "On the Way to Being: Reflecting on Conversations with Martin Heidegger" (1970) [Zygmunt Adamczewski].

[B] Record of Heidegger's conversations with Zygmunt Adamczewski in Freiburg and Todtnauberg, October 1968.

[C] German text unpublished.

	[D]		John Sallis, ed., *Heidegger and the Path of Thinking* (1970) Pittsburgh: Duquesne University Press, pp. 12-36.
111.	[A]	(A)	"Only a God Can Save Us: *Der Spiegel's* Interview with Martin Heidegger" (1976) [Maria P. Alter and John D. Caputo].
		(B)	"Only a God Can Save Us Now" (1977) [David Schendler].
		(C)	"'Only a God Can Save Us': The *Spiegel* Interview with Martin Heidegger" (1981) [William J. Richardson].
		(D)	"*Der Spiegel* Interview with Martin Heidegger" (1990) [Lisa Harries].
	[B]		"Nur noch ein Gott kann uns retten": Transcript of an audiotaped interview with Heidegger on September 23, 1966. Reprinted in Günther Neske and Emil Kettering, eds., *Antwort: Martin Heidegger im Gespräch* (1988) Pfullingen: Neske, pp. 81-114.
	[C]		*Der Spiegel* (Hamburg) May 31, 1976, pp. 193-219. Reprinted in *Reden und andere Zeugnisse eines Lebensweges* (2000): GA 16 (2000), pp. 652-83.
	[D]	(A)	*Philosophy Today* (Celina) 20, no. 4, 1976, pp. 267-84. Reprinted in Richard Wolin, ed., *The Heidegger Controversy: A Critical Reader* (1991) Cambridge: MIT Press, 1993, pp. 91-116.
		(B)	*Graduate Faculty Philosophy Journal* (New York) 6, no. 1, 1977, pp. 5-27.
		(C)	Thomas Sheehan, ed., *Heidegger: The Man and the Thinker* (1981) Chicago: Precedent Publishing Company, pp. 45-67.
		(D)	Günther Neske and Emil Kettering, eds., *Martin Heidegger and National Socialism* (1990) New York: Paragon House, pp. 41-66.
112.	[A]		*Ontology—The Hermeneutics of Facticity* (1999) [John van Buren].
	[B]		"Ontologie (Hermeneutik der Faktizität)": Lecture course given during the Summer Semester of 1923, University of Freiburg.

| | [C] | *Ontologie (Hermeneutik der Faktizität)*: GA 63 (1988). |
| | [D] | *Ontology—The Hermeneutics of Facticity* (Bloomington: Indiana University Press, 1999). |

113. [A] (A) "The Onto-theo-logical Nature of Metaphysics" (1960) [Kurt F. Leidecker].
      (B) "The Onto-theo-logical Constitution of Metaphysics" (1969) [Joan Stambaugh].
   [B] "Die onto-theo-logische Verfassung der Metaphysik": Concluding lecture for a seminar during the Winter Semester 1956-57 on Hegel's *Science of Logic*, given on February 24, 1957, in Todtnauberg.
   [C] *Identität und Differenz* (1957) Pfullingen: Neske, pp. 35-73.
   [D] (A) *Essays in Metaphysics: Identity and Difference* (1960) New York: Philosophical Library, pp. 33-67.
       (B) * *Identity and Difference* (1969) New York: Harper and Row, pp. 42-74.

114. [A] (A) "The Origin of the Work of Art" (1965) [Albert Hofstadter].
      (B) "The Origin of the Work of Art" (2002) [Julian Young].
   [B] "Der Ursprung des Kunstwerkes": Lecture given November 13, 1935, in Freiburg. Expanded to a series of three lectures given November 17 and 24, 1936, and December 1, 1936, in Frankfurt. An "Zusatz [Addendum]" was added in 1956.
   [C] *Holzwege* (1950): GA 5 (1977), pp. 1-74.
   [D] (A) Albert Hofstadter, ed., *Philosophies of Art and Beauty* (1965) New York: Random House, pp. 647-701 [without addendum]. Reprinted in *Poetry, Language, Thought* (1971) New York: Harper and Row, 1975, pp. 17-87, with addendum. Complete version reprinted in revised edition of *Basic Writings* (1993 [1977]) San Francisco: HarperSanFrancisco, pp. 139-212.
       (B) *Off the Beaten Track* (2002) Cambridge: Cambridge University Press, pp. 1-56.

115. [A]   "Overcoming Metaphysics" (1973) [Joan Stambaugh].
     [B]   "Seinsverlassenheit und Irrnis": Notes on Nietzsche from the years 1936-46.
     [C]   "Seinsverlassenheit und Irrnis [Forgottenness of Being and Error]" (1951), in *Ernst Barlach: Dramatiker, Bildhauer, Zeichner* (1951) Darmstadt: Kulturverwaltung der Stadt Darmstadt, pp. 5-12 [section 26]. "Anmerkungen über die Metaphysik [Notes on Metaphysics]," in F. Hollwich, ed., *Im Umkreis der Kunst* [*In the Ambit of Art*]. Festschrift für Emil Preetorius (1954) Wiesbaden: Insel-Verlag, pp. 117-36 [sections 1-25 and 27-28]. The complete text appears as "Überwindung der Metaphysik" in *Vorträge und Aufsätze* I (1954) Pfullingen: Neske, 1978, pp. 63-91.
     [D]   *The End of Philosophy* (1973) New York: Harper and Row, pp. 84-110. Reprinted in Richard Wolin, ed., *The Heidegger Controversy: A Critical Reader* (1991) Cambridge: MIT Press, 1993, pp. 67-90.

116. [A]   *Parmenides* (1992) [André Schuwer and Richard Rojcewicz].
     [B]   "Parmenides": Lecture course given during the Winter Semester 1942-43, University of Freiburg.
     [C]   *Parmenides*: GA 54 (1982).
     [D]   *Parmenides* (1992) Bloomington: Indiana University Press.

117. [A]   (A)   ["The Pathway":] "The Field Path: A Meditation" (1950) [no translator given].
             (B)   "The Pathway" (1967) [Thomas F. O'Meara].
             (C)   "The Pathway" (1973) [Thomas Sheehan].
             (D)   "The Fieldpath" (1986) [Berit Mexia].
     [B]   "Zur Zuspruch des Feldweges [The Consolation of the Country Path]": Essay written in 1949. Revised title: "Der Feldweg" (1950).
     [C]   *Hamburg Sontagsblatt* (Hamburg) 2, no. 43, October 23, 1949, 5-23, and earlier in the year in several privately published editions. Published under the revised title in *Wort und Wahrheit* (Vienna) 5, 1950, pp. 267-69. Reprinted in the GA edition of *Aus der Erfahrung des Denkens* [*From the Experience of Thinking*]: GA 13 (1983), pp. 87-90. Volume 13 takes its title from a privately printed volume

(1954) of a series of reflections written in 1947.

[D]   (A)   *World Review* (London) 11 [New Series], January 1950, pp. 5-6.
       (B)   *Listening* (Dubuque) 2, 1967, pp. 88-91.
       (C)   * *Listening* (Dubuque) 8, 1973, pp. 32-39. Reprinted in Thomas Sheehan, ed., *Heidegger: The Man and the Thinker* (1981) Chicago: Precedent Publishing Company, pp. 69-72, and in Thomas Frick, ed., *The Sacred Theory of the Earth* (1986) Berkeley: North Atlantic Books, pp. 45-48 (English only).
       (D)   *Journal of Chinese Philosophy* (Dordrecht) 13, 1986, pp. 455-57.

118.   [A]   (A)   *"Per mortem ad vitam* (Thoughts on Johannes Jörgensen's *Lies of Life and Truth of Life*)" (1991) [John Protevi].
               (B)   *"Per mortem ad vitam* (Thoughts on Johannes Jörgensen's *Lies of Life and Truth of Life*)" (1991) [John Protevi and John van Buren].
       [B]   "Per mortem ad vitam (Gedanken über Jörgensens *Lebenslüge und Lebenswahrheit*)": Book review essay written in March 1910.
       [C]   *Der Akademiker* 2, no. 5, March 1910, pp. 72-73. Reprinted in *Reden und andere Zeugnisse eines Lebenswege 1910-1976* (2000): GA 16 (2000), pp. 3-6.
       [D]   (A)   *Graduate Faculty Philosophy Journal* (New York) 14-15, 1991, pp. 487-91.
               (B)   *Supplements: From the Earliest Essays to* Being and Time *and Beyond* (John van Buren, ed.) (2002) Albany: SUNY Press, pp. 35-37.

119.   [A]   *Phenomenological Interpretation of Kant's* Critique of Pure Reason (1997) [Parvis Emad and Kenneth Maly].
       [B]   "Phänomenologische Interpretation von Kants Kritik der reinen Vernunft": Lecture course given during the Winter Semester 1927-28, Marburg University.
       [C]   *Phänomenologische Interpretation von Kants Kritik der reinen Vernunft*: GA 25 (1977).

[D]   *Phenomenological Interpretation of Kant's* Critique of Pure Reason (1997) Bloomington: Indiana University Press.

120. [A]   *Phenomenological Interpretations of Aristotle: Initiation into Phenomenological Research* (2001) [Richard Rojcewicz]
[B]   *Phänomenologische Interpretationen zu Aristoteles. Einführung in die phänomenologische Forschung*: Lecture course given during the Winter Semester 1921-22, Freiburg University.
[C]   *Phänomenologische Interpretationen zu Aristoteles. Einführung in die phänomenologische Forschung*: GA 61 (1985).
[D]   *Phenomenological Interpretations of Aristotle: Initiation into Phenomenological Research* (2001) Bloomington: Indiana University Press, 2001.

121. [A]   (A)   "Phenomenological Interpretations with Respect to Aristotle: Indication of the Hermeneutical Situation" (1992) [Michael Baur].
            (B)   "Phenomenological Interpretations in Connection with Aristotle: An Indication of the Hermeneutical Situation" (2002) [John van Burne].
[B]   "Phänomenologische Interpretationen zu Aristoteles (Anzeige der hermeneutischen Situation)": Text written in the fall of 1922 outlining current and future research, submitted as part Heidegger's application for a full-time teaching position.
[C]   *Dilthey-Jahrbuch für Philosophie und Geschichte der Gesisteswissenschaften* (Göttingen) 6, 1989, pp. 235-69. Text edited by Hans-Ulrich Lessing.
[D]   (A)   *Man and World* 25, no. 3/4, 1992, pp. 355-93.
            (B)   *Supplements: From the Earliest Essays to* Being and Time *and Beyond* (John van Buren, ed.) (2002) Albany: SUNY Press, pp. 111-45.

122. [A]   (A)   "Phenomenology and Theology" (1976) [James G. Hart and John C. Maraldo].
            (B)   "Phenomenology and Theology" (1998) [William McNeill, James G. Hart, and John C. Maraldo].

	[B]	"Phänomenologie und Theologie": Lecture given March 9, 1927, in Tübingen. A preface ["Vorwort"] was added in 1970 for the first German publication of the lecture.
	[C]	*Archives de Philosophie* (Paris) 32, 1969, pp. 356-95. First German edition: *Phänomenologie und Theologie: Rudolf Bultmann gewidmet in freundschaftlichem Gedenken an die Marburger Jahre 1923 bis 1928* (1970) Frankfurt: Klostermann, pp. 9-10, 13-33. Reprinted in *Wegmarken* (1967): GA 9 (1976), pp. 45-67.
	[D]	(A) *The Piety of Thinking* (1976) Bloomington: Indiana University Press, pp. 3-21.
		(B) *Pathmarks* (1998) Cambridge: Cambridge University Press, pp. 39-54.

123. [A] (A) "Plato's Doctrine of Truth" (1962) [John Barlow].
     (B) "Plato's Doctrine of Truth" (1998) [William McNeill and Thomas Sheehan].
[B] "Platons Lehre von der Wahrheit": Essay written in 1940 for a private lecture, related to the lecture course "Vom Wesen der Wahrheit" given during the Winter Semester 1930-31, University of Freiburg.
[C] *Geistige Überlieferung* [*Spiritual Tradition*] (Berlin) 2, 1942, pp. 96-124. Printed as a separate work *Platons Lehre von der Wahrheit: Mit einem Brief über den Humanismus* [*Plato's Teaching on Truth: With a Letter on Humanism*] (1947) Bern: Francke, pp. 5-52. Reprinted in *Wegmarken* (1967): GA 9 (1976), pp. 203-38. Cf. *Vom Wesen der Wahrheit: Zu Platons Höhlengleichnis und Theätet:* GA 34 (1988).
[D] (A) William Barrett and Henry D. Aiken, eds., *Philosophy in the Twentieth Century: An Anthology*, vol. 3 (1962) New York: Random House, 1982, pp. 251-70.
    (B) *Pathmarks* (1998) Cambridge: Cambridge University Press, pp. 155-82.

124. [A] *Plato's* Sophist (1997) [Richard Rojcewicz and André Schuwer].
[B] "*Sophistes*": Lecture course given during the Winter Semester 1924-25, Marburg University.

[C]   *Platon: Sophistes:* GA 19 (1992).
[D]   *Plato's* Sophist (1997) Bloomington: Indiana University Press.

125. [A]   "The Poem" (2000) [Keith Hoeller].
[B]   "Das Gedicht": Revised version of a lecture given on August 25, 1968, in honor of Friedrich Ernst Jünger's 70th birthday.
[C]   *Erläuterungen zu Hölderlins Dichtung* [4th ed.] (1971) Frankfurt: Klostermann, pp. 182-92.
[D]   *Elucidations of Hölderlin's Poetry* (2000) Amherst, N.Y.: Humanity Books, pp. 209-19.

126. [A]   " ... Poetically Man Dwells ..." (1971) [Albert Hofstadter].
[B]   " ... dichterisch wohnet der Mensch ...": Lecture given on October 6, 1951, Bühlerhöhe.
[C]   *Akzente: Zeitschrift für Dichtung* (Munich) 1, 1954, pp. 57-71. Reprinted in *Vorträge und Aufsätze* II (1954) Pfullingen: Neske, 1978, pp. 61-78, and in GA 7 (2000), pp. 189-208.
[D]   *Poetry, Language, Thought* (1971) New York: Harper and Row, 1975, pp. 213-29.

127. [A]   (A)   "Postscript" to "What Is Metaphysics?" (1949) [R. F. C. Hull and Alan Crick].
         (B)   "Postscript" to "What Is Metaphysics?" (1998) [William McNeill].
[B]   "Nachwort [1943] zu 'Was ist Metaphysik?'": Postscript to the inaugural address, added in 1943 for the 4th edition of the lecture. Revised in 1949 for the 5th edition.
[C]   *Was ist Metaphysik?* (1929) Frankfurt: Klostermann, 1981 (12th ed.), pp. 43-52. Reprinted in *Wegmarken* (1967): GA 9 (1976), pp. 303-12.
[D]   (A)   *Existence and Being* (1949) Washington: Regnery Gateway, 1988, pp. 349-61 (revised version). Reprinted in Walter Kaufmann, ed., *Existentialism from Dostoevsky to Sartre* (rev. ed., 1975 [1956]) New York: New American Library, 1984, pp. 257-64 (revised version).
         (B)   *Pathmarks* (1998) Cambridge: Cambridge University Press, pp. 231-38.

128. [A] "Preface" to *Pathmarks* (1998) [William McNeill].
     [B] "Vorbemerkung": Prefatory note to the first edition of *Wegmarken*, Freiburg im Breisgau, early summer 1967.
     [C] *Wegmarken* (1967): GA 9 (1976), pp.ix-x.
     [D] *Pathmarks* (1998) Cambridge: Cambridge University Press, p. xiii.

129. [A] (A) "Preface to a Reading of Hölderlin's Poems" (2000) [Keith Hoeller].
         (B) "A Word on Hölderlin's Poetry" (2001) [Franz Mayr and Richard Askay].
     [B] "Vorwort zur Lesung von Hölderlins Gedichten": Text of introductory comments on the recording *Martin Heidegger liefßt Hölderlin* (1963) Pfullingen: Neske.
     [C] *Erläuterungen zu Hölderlins Dichtung*, GA 4 (1981): pp. 195-97.
     [D] (A) *Elucidations of Hölderlin's Poetry* (2000) Amherst, N.Y.: Humanity Books, pp. 224-26.
         (B) *Zollikon Seminars. Protocols-Conversations-Letters* (2001) Evanston: Northwestern University Press, pp. 265-67.

130. [A] "Prefaces to *Elucidations of Hölderlin's Poetry* (2000) [Keith Hoeller].
     [B] "Vorwort": Preface to 2nd Edition (1951) and 4th Edition (1971) of *Erläuterungen zu Hölderlins Dichtung*. The 1971 preface is an abbreviated version of the 1st Edition introductory note. The 1951 preface includes the concluding part of the "Preface to the Repetition of the Address 'Homecoming'," of June 21, 1943.
     [C] *Erläuterungen zu Hölderlins Dichtung*, GA 4 (1981): pp. 7-8.
     [D] *Elucidations of Hölderlin's Poetry* (2000) Amherst: Humanity Books, pp. 21-22.

131. [A] (A) "Prefatory Remark to a Repetition of the Address" (1949) [Douglas Scott].
         (B) "Preface to a Repetition of the Address 'Homecoming'" (2000) [Keith Hoeller].

	[B]	"Vorbemerkung zur Wiederholung der Rede": Introductory remark to the lecture given on June 21, 1943, University of Freiburg im Breisgau. The text consists of two paragraphs followed by what was published as the Preface to the 1st Edition (1944) of *Erläuterungen zu Hölderlins Dichtung*. It appeared following the text of the address "Heimkunft/ An die Verwandten."
	[C]	*Erläuterungen zu Hölderlins Dichtung* (1944) Frankfurt: Klostermann, pp. 31-32. The text was not included in the 2nd Edition (1951), but was restored in the 4th edition (1971). GA 4 (1981), pp. 193-94.
	[D]	(A) *Existence and Being* (1949) Washington: Regnery Gateway, 1988, pp. 233-35.
		(B) *Elucidations of Hölderlin's Poetry* (2000) Amherst, N.Y.: Humanity Books, pp. 221-23.
132.	[A]	(A) "The Principle of Ground" (1974) [Keith Hoeller].
		(B) "The Principle of Reason" (1991) [Reginald Lilly].
	[B]	"Der Satz vom Grund": Lecture given May 25, 1956, at the Bremen Club and October 24, 1956, at the University of Vienna. Included with the publication of Heidegger's course of the same name given during the Winter Semester 1955-56, University of Freiburg.
	[C]	*Wissenschaft und Wahrheit* (Vienna) 9, 1956, pp. 241-50. Reprinted in *Der Satz vom Grund* (1957) Pfullingen: Neske, 1986, pp. 191-211.
	[D]	(A) *Man and World* (Dordrecht) 7, 1974, pp. 207-22.
		(B) *The Principle of Reason* (1991) Bloomington: Indiana University Press, pp. 117-29.
133.	[A]	(A) "The Principle of Identity" (1960) [Kurt F. Leidecker].
		(B) "The Principle of Identity" (1969) [Joan Stambaugh].
	[B]	"Der Satz der Identität": Lecture given June 27, 1957, at the University of Freiburg, on the occasion of the 500th anniversary of the founding of the university.
	[C]	*Die Albert-Ludwigs-Universität Freiburg 1457-1957. Die Festvorträge bei der Jubiläumsfeier* (1957) Freiburg: F. K. Schulz, pp. 69-79. Reprinted in *Identität und Differenz* (1957) Pfullingen: Neske, pp. 11-34. Heidegger reads the

			lecture on a recording (1957) Pfullingen: Neske. Reprinted in GA 79, *Bremer und Freiburger Vorträge*, pp. 115-29.

      [D]   (A)   *Essays in Metaphysics: Identity and Difference* (1960) New York: Philosophical Library, pp. 13-32.

              (B)   * *Identity and Difference* (1969) New York: Harper and Row, pp. 23-41.

134. [A] *The Principle of Reason* (1991) [Reginald Lilly].
     [B] "Der Satz vom Grund": Lecture course given during the Winter Semester 1955-56, University of Freiburg.
     [C] *Der Satz vom Grund* (1957) Pfullingen: Neske, pp. 13-188.
     [D] *The Principle of Reason* (1991) Bloomington: Indiana University Press, pp. 3-113.

135. [A] "Principles of Thinking" (1976) [James G. Hart and John C. Maraldo].
     [B] "Grundsätze des Denkens": Essay written in 1958 as a contribution in honor of the 75th birthday of Viktor Emil von Gebsattel.
     [C] *Jahrbuch für Psychologie und Psychotherapie* (Freiburg) 6, 1958, pp. 33-41. Reprinted in GA 79, *Bremer und Freiburger Vorträge*, pp. 81-96.
     [D] *The Piety of Thinking* (1976) Bloomington: Indiana University Press, pp. 46-58.

136. [A] (A) "The Problem of the Categories" (1979) [Roderick M. Stewart].
          (B) "Conclusion: The Problem of Categories" (2002) [Roderick M. Stewart and John van Buren].
     [B] "Schluss: Das Kategorienproblem": Conclusion to *Die Kategorien- und Bedeutungslehre des Duns Scotus* (1916).
     [C] *Die Kategorien- und Bedeutungslehre des Duns Scotus* (1916) Tübingen: Mohr, pp. 341-53. Reprinted in *Frühe Schriften* (1972): GA 1 (1978), pp. 399-411.
     [D] (A) "The Problem of Categories," *Man and World* (Dordrecht) 12, 1979, pp. 378-86.
          (B) *Supplements: From the Earliest Essays to* Being

and Time *and Beyond* (John van Buren, ed.) (2002) Albany: SUNY Press, pp. 62-68.

137. [A] (A) "The Problem of a Non-objectifying Thinking and Speaking in Contemporary Theology" (1968) [Jerry Gill].
(B) "The Theological Discussion of 'The Problem of a Non-objectifying Thinking and Speaking in Contemporary Theology'—Some Pointers to Its Major Aspects" (1976) [James G. Hart and John C. Maraldo].
(C) "The Theological Discussion of 'The Problem of a Non-objectifying Thinking and Speaking in Contemporary Theology'—Some Pointers to Its Major Aspects" (1998) [William McNeill, James G. Hart, and John C. Maraldo].

[B] "Einige Hinweise auf Hauptgesichtspunkte für das theologische Gespräch über 'Das Problem eines nichtobjectivierenden Denkens und Sprechens in der heutigen Theologie'": Letter written March 11, 1964 to participants of a conference held April 9-11, 1964, at Drew University.

[C] *Archives de Philosophie* (Paris) 32, 1969, pp. 396-415. Appears in *Phänomenologie und Theologie: Rudolf Bultmann gewidmet in freundschaftlichem Gedenken an die Marburger Jahre 1923 bis 1928* (1970) Frankfurt: Klostermann, pp. 37-46. Reprinted in *Wegmarken* (1967): GA 9 (1976), pp. 68-77.

[D] (A) Jerry Gill, ed., *Philosophy and Religion. Some Contemporary Perspectives* (1968) Minneapolis: Burgess, pp. 59-65.
(B) *The Piety of Thinking* (1976) Bloomington: Indiana University Press, pp. 22-31.
(C) *Pathmarks* (1998) Cambridge: Cambridge University Press, pp. 54-62.

138. [A] (A) "The Problem of Reality in Modern Philosophy" (1973) [Phillip J. Bossert].
(B) "The Problem of Reality in Modern Philosophy" (2002) [Phillip J. Bossert and John van Buren].

[B] "Das Realitätsproblem in der modernen Philosophie": Heidegger's first published paper (1912).

[C] *Philosophisches Jahrbuch der Görresgesellschaft* [*Philosophical Yearbook of the Görres Society*] (Fulda) 25, 1912, pp. 353-63. Reprinted in GA edition of Frühe Schriften (1972): GA 1 (1978), pp. 1-15.

[D] (A) *Journal of the British Society for Phenomenology* (Manchester) 4, 1973, pp. 64-71.

(B) *Supplements: From the Earliest Essays to* Being and Time *and Beyond* (John van Buren, ed.) (2002) Albany: SUNY Press, pp. 39-48.

139. [A] "The Problem of Sin in Luther" (2002) [John van Buren]

[B] "Das Problem der Sünde bei Luther": Student transcript of a two-part talk given in Rudolf Bultmann's seminar on "The Ethics of St. Paul" on February 14 and 21, 1924.

[C] Bernd Jaspert, ed., *Sachgemäße Exegese: Die Protokolle aus Rudolf Bultmanns Neutestamentlichen Seminaren 1921-1951* (1996) Marburg: Elwert, pp. 28-33.

[D] *Supplements: From the Earliest Essays to* Being and Time *and Beyond* (John van Buren, ed.) (2002) Albany: SUNY Press, pp. 105-10.

140. [A] "Psychology of Religion and the Subconscious" (1991) [John Protevi].

[B] "Religionspsychologie und Unterbewusstsein": Essay from 1912.

[C] *Der Akademiker* 4, no. 5, March 1912, pp. 66-68. Reprinted in *Reden und andere Zeugnisse eines Lebensweges* (2000): GA 16 (2000), pp. 18-28.

[D] *Graduate Faculty Philosophy Journal* (New York) 14-15, 1991, pp. 503-17.

141. [A] (A) *The Question of Being* (1958) [William Kluback and Jean T. Wilde].

(B) "On the Question of Being" (1998) [William McNeill].

[B] *Zur Seinsfrage*: Essay, original title "Über 'die Linie' [Concerning 'The Line']," a contribution written in 1955 for a volume dedicated to Ernst Jünger. Jünger's paper had been printed in a *Festschrift* for Heidegger, *Anteile: Martin Heidegger zum 60. Geburtstag* (1950) Frankfurt: Klostermann, pp. 245-84.

[C] *Freundschaftliche Begegnungen: Festschrift für Ernst Jünger zum 60. Geburtstag* (1955) Frankfurt: Klostermann, pp. 9-45. Printed as a separate volume with the title *Zur Seinsfrage* (1956) Frankfurt: Klostermann. Reprinted in *Wegmarken* (1967): GA 9 (1976), pp. 385-426.

[D] (A) * *The Question of Being* (1958) New York: Twayne.
 (B) *Pathmarks* (1998) Cambridge: Cambridge University Press, pp. 291-322.

142. [A] (A) "Martin Heidegger's *The Question about Technic*: A Translation and Commentary" (1973) [Edwin Michael Alexander].
 (B) "The Question Concerning Technology" (1977) [William Lovitt].

[B] "Das Gestell [The Setting]": The second of four lectures first presented in the series "Einblick in das was ist [Glance into That Which Is]," given December 1, 1949, at the Bremen Club. A revised and expanded version with the title "Die Frage nach der Technik" was given on November 18, 1953, at the Bavarian Academy of Fine Arts, Munich.

[C] *Gestalt und Gedanke* [*Form and Thought*] (Munich) 3, 1954, pp. 70-108 (revised version). Reprinted in *Vorträge und Aufsätze* I (1954) Pfullingen: Neske, 1978, pp. 5-36, and as "Das Ge-Stell" in GA 79, *Bremer und Freiburger Vorträge*, pp. 24-45. The revised version appears in *Vorträge und Aufsätze* (2000): GA 7, pp. 5-36.

[D] (A) *Martin Heidegger's* The Question about Technic: *A Translation and Commentary* (1973) Ann Arbor: University Microfilms. Dissertation, McMaster University, 1973.
 (B) *The Question Concerning Technology and Other Essays* (1977) New York: Harper and Row, 1982, pp. 3-35. Reprinted in *Basic Writings* (1977) San Francisco: HarperSanFrancisco, (rev. ed., 1993), pp. 311-41.

143. [A] "A Recollection" (1970) [Hans Seigfried].
    [B] "Antrittsrede": Lecture at the Heidelberg Academy of Sciences, fall 1957, on being admitted to the Academy.
    [C] *Jahresheft der Heidelberger Akademie der Wissenschaften* (Heidelberg) 48, 1957/58, pp. 20-21. Reprinted in the "Vorwort [Foreword]" to the first edition of *Frühe Schriften* (1972): GA 1 (1978), pp. 55-57.
    [D] *Man and World* (Dordrecht) 3, no. 1, 1970, pp. 3-4. Reprinted in Thomas Sheehan, ed., *Heidegger: The Man and the Thinker* (1981) Chicago: Precedent Publishing, pp. 21-22.

144. [A] "Recollection in Metaphysics" (1973) [Joan Stambaugh].
    [B] "Die Erinnerung in die Metaphysik": Essay written in 1941.
    [C] *Nietzsche* II (1961) Pfullingen: Neske, pp. 481-490 [part 10].
    [D] *The End of Philosophy* (1973) New York: Harper and Row, pp. 75-83.

145. [A] "Remembrance" (2000) [Keith Hoeller].
    [B] "Andenken": Contribution to a Hölderlin 100th anniversary memorial volume.
    [C] Paul Kluckhohn, ed., *Hölderlin: Gedenkschriften zu seinem 100. Todestag* (1943) Tübingen: J. B. C. Mohr, pp. 267-324. Reprinted in GA 4 (1981): pp. 79-15.
    [D] *Elucidations of Hölderlin's Poetry* (2000) Amherst, N.Y.: Humanity Books, pp. 101-73.

146. [A] (A) "Remembrance of the Poet" (1949) [Douglas Scott].
        (B) "Homecoming/To Kindred Ones" (2000) [Keith Hoeller].
    [B] "Heimkunft/An die Verwandten [Homecoming/To His Relatives]": Lecture given at the University of Freiburg on June 6, 1943, on the 100th anniversary of the death of Friedrich Hölderlin.
    [C] *Erläuterungen zu Hölderlins Dichtung* [*Elucidations of Hölderlin's Poetry*] (1944): GA 4 (1981), pp. 9-31.
    [D] (A) *Existence and Being* (1949) Washington, D.C.: Regnery Gateway, 1988, pp. 232-69.

(B) *Elucidations of Hölderlin's Poetry* (2000) Amherst, N.Y.: Humanity Books, pp. 23-49.

147. [A] "Review of Ernst Cassirer's *Mythical Thought*" (1976) [James G. Hart and John C. Maraldo].
[B] "Besprechung: Ernst Cassirers *Philosophie der symbolischen Formen*. 2.Teil: *Das mythische Denken* [1925]": Book review published in 1928.
[C] *Deutsche Literaturzeitung* (Berlin) 21, 1928, pp. 1000-12. Reprinted in *Kant und das Problem der Metaphysik* (4th ed., 1973): GA 3 (1991), pp. 255-70.
[D] *The Piety of Thinking* (1976) Bloomington: Indiana University Press, pp. 32-45.

148. [A] *Schelling's Treatise on the Essence of Human Freedom* (1985) [Joan Stambaugh].
[B] "Schellings Abhandlung über das Wesen der menschlichen Freiheit": Lecture course given during the Summer Semester 1936, University of Freiburg, with excerpts from the manuscripts of an advanced seminar on Schelling (Summer Semester 1941) and selected seminar notes on Schelling from the years 1941 to 1943.
[C] *Schellings Abhandlung über das Wesen der menschlichen Freiheit* (1971) Tübingen: Niemeyer. Reprinted as *Schelling: Vom Wesen der menschlichen Freiheit (1809)*: GA 42 (1988).
[D] *Schelling's Treatise on the Essence of Human Freedom* (1985) Athens: Ohio University Press.

149. [A] "Science and Reflection" (1977) [William Lovitt].
[B] "Wissenschaft und Besinnung": Lecture first given May 15, 1953, at a conference held by the Arbeitsgemeinschaft wissenschaftlicher Sortimenter [Science Book Dealers Study Group] near Freiburg. Revised for presentation on August 4, 1953, to a small group.
[C] *Börsenblatt für den Deutschen Buchhandel* (Frankfurt) 10, no. 29, 1954, pp. 321-30 (original version). Reprinted in *Vorträge und Aufsätze* I (1954) Pfullingen: Neske, 1978, pp. 37-62 (revised version). Reprinted in *Vorträge und Aufsätze* (2000): GA 7, pp. 37-65.

[D] *The Question Concerning Technology and Other Essays* (1977) New York: Harper and Row, 1982, pp. 155-82.

150. [A] "Sketches for a History of Being as Metaphysics" (1973) [Joan Stambaugh].
[B] "Entwürfe zur Geschichte des Seins als Metaphysik": Notes on Nietzsche written in 1941.
[C] *Nietzsche* II (1961) Pfullingen: Neske, pp. 458-80 [part 9].
[D] *The End of Philosophy* (1973) New York: Harper and Row, pp. 55-74.

151. [A] "Summary of a Seminar on the Lecture 'Time and Being'" (1972) [Joan Stambaugh].
[B] "Seminar Protokoll zu Heideggers Vorlesung 'Zeit und Sein'": Transcript of a six-session seminar given September 11-13, 1962, in Todtnauberg, prepared by Alfredo Guzzoni and edited by Heidegger.
[C] *Zur Sache des Denkens* [*The Matter of Thought*] (1969) Tübingen: Niemeyer, pp. 27-58.
[D] *On Time and Being* (1972) New York: Harper and Row, 1978, pp. 25-54.

152. [A] "The Thing" (1971) [Albert Hofstadter].
[B] "Das Ding [Things]": First of four lectures in the series "Einblick in das was ist [Glance into That Which Is]," originally given December 1, 1949, Bremen Club.
[C] *Gestalt und Gedanke* [*Form and Thought*] (Munich) 1, 1951, pp. 128-48. Reprinted with an epilogue written June 18, 1950, "A Letter to a Young Student [Hartmut Buchner]," in *Vorträge und Aufsätze* II (1954) Pfullingen: Neske, 1978, pp. 37-59. Reprinted in *Vorträge und Aufsätze* GA 7 (2000), pp. 165-87. The lecture and several notes appear in, GA 79, *Bremer und Freiburger Vorträge*, pp. 5-23.
[D] *Poetry, Language, Thought* (1971) New York: Harper and Row, 1975, pp. 165-86.

153. [A] "The Thinker as Poet" (1971) [Albert Hofstadter].
[B] "Aus der Erfahrung des Denkens": Text written during 1947.

[C] Privately printed on the occasion of the 25th anniversary of the Todtnauberg hut, the text was published as *Aus der Erfahrung des Denkens* [*From the Experience of Thinking*] (1954) Pfullingen: Neske. Reprinted in the GA edition in a volume of the same title: GA 13 (1983), pp. 75-86.

[D] *Poetry, Language, Thought* (1971) New York: Harper and Row, 1975, pp. 1-14.

154. [A] "Thoughts" (1976) [Keith Hoeller].

[B] "Gedachtes. Für René Char in freundschaftlichen Gedenken [For René Char, in Friendly Remembrance]": Poems written in 1970:"Zeit [Time],""Wege [Paths],""Winke [Hints]," "Ortschaft [Locale]," "Cézanne," "Vorspiel [Prelude],""Dank [Thanks]."

[C] Dominique Fourcade, ed., *Hommage à René Char* (1971) Paris: Edition de L'Herne, pp. 169-87. Reprinted in the GA edition of *Aus der Erfahrung des Denkens* [*From the Experience of Thinking*]: GA 13 (1983), pp. 221-24. Volume 13 takes its title from a privately printed volume (1954) of a series of reflections written in 1947.

[D] * *Philosophy Today* (Celina) 20, no. 4, 1976, pp. 286-90.

155. [A] "Time and Being" (1972) [Joan Stambaugh].

[B] "Zeit und Sein": Lecture given January 31, 1962 at the University of Freiburg.

[C] *L'Endurance de la Pensée* [*The Staying Power of Thinking*]: *Festschrift für Jean Beaufret* (1968) Paris: Plon, pp. 12-71. Reprinted in *Zur Sache des Denkens* [*The Matter of Thought*] (1969) Tübingen: Niemeyer, pp. 1-25.

[D] *On Time and Being* (1972) New York: Harper and Row, 1978, pp. 1-24.

156. [A] *Towards the Definition of Philosophy* (2000) [Ted Sadler]

[B] "Die Idee der Philosophie und das Weltanschauungsproblem": Lecture course given during the Wartime Semester 1919, University of Freiburg; "Phänomenologie und tranzendentale Wertphilosophie": Lecture course given during the Summer Semester 1919, University of

Freiburg; Über das Wesen der Universität und das akademischen Studiums": Lecture course given during the Summer Semester 1919, University of Freiburg.
- [C] *Zur Bestimmung der Philosophie:* GA 56/57 (1987).
- [D] *Towards the Definition of Philosophy* (2000) New Brunswick: Athlone.

157.
- [A] "Traditional Language and Technological Language" (1998) [Wanda Torres Gregory]
- [B] "Überlieferte Sprache und Technische Sprache": Lecture given July 18, 1962, Comburg (Schwäbische Hall).
- [C] *Überlieferte Sprache und Technische Sprache* (1989) St. Gallen: Erker Verlag.
- [D] "Traditional Language and Technological Language," in *Journal of Philosophical Research* 23, 1998, pp. 129-45.

158.
- [A]
  - (A) "The Turning" (1971) [Kenneth R. Maly].
  - (B) "The Turning" (1977) [William Lovitt].
- [B] "Die Kehre [The Turn]": The last of four lectures in the series "Einblick in das was ist [Glance into That Which Is]," originally given December 1, 1949, at the Bremen Club.
- [C] *Die Technik und die Kehre* (1962) Pfullingen: Neske, pp. 37-47. Reprinted in GA 79, *Bremer und Freiburger Vorträge*, pp. 68-77.
- [D]
  - (A) *Research in Phenomenology* (Pittsburgh) 1, 1971, pp. 3-16.
  - (B) *The Question Concerning Technology and Other Essays* (1977) New York: Harper and Row, 1982, pp. 36-49.

159.
- [A] "The Understanding of Time in Phenomenology and in the Thinking of the Being-Question" (1979) [Thomas Sheehan and Frederick Elliston].
- [B] "Über das Zeitverständnis in der Phänomenologie und im Denken der Seinsfrage": Essay written in 1969 in commemoration of the 30th anniversary of the death of Edmund Husserl.
- [C] Helmut Gehrig, ed., *Phänomenologie—lebendig oder tot?* (1969) Karlsruhe: Badenia, p. 47.

| | [D] | *Southwestern Journal of Philosophy* (Norman) 10, no. 2, 1979, pp. 199-201. |

160. [A] "The Want of Holy Names" (1985) [Bernhard Radloff].

[B] "Der Fehl heiliger Namen": Essay written in 1974, dedicated to Hugo Friedrich.

[C] *Contre Toute Attente* (Sens) 2/3, 1981, pp. 40-55. Published with a French translation by Roger Munier and Philippe Lacoue-Labarthe. Reprinted in the GA edition of *Aus der Erfahrung des Denkens* [*From the Experience of Thinking*]: GA 13 (1983) 231-35. Volume 13 takes its title from a privately printed volume (1954) of a series of reflections written in 1947.

[D] *Man and World* (Dordrecht) 18, 1985, pp. 261-67.

161. [A] (A) "The Way Back into the Ground of Metaphysics": Introduction [1949] to "What Is Metaphysics?" (1956) [Walter Kaufmann].

(B) "Introduction to 'What Is Metaphysics?'" (1998) [William McNeill].

[B] "Einleitung zu 'Was ist Metaphysik?': Der Rückgang in den Grund der Metaphysik [Introduction to 'What Is Metaphysics?': Getting to the Bottom of Metaphysics]": Introductory essay to the inaugural lecture, written for the 5th edition of the lecture (1949).

[C] *Was ist Metaphysik?* (1929) Frankfurt: Klostermann, 1981 (12th ed.), pp. 7-23 (rev. ed., 1975). Reprinted in *Wegmarken* (1967): GA 9 (1976), pp. 365-83.

[D] (A) Walter Kaufmann, ed., *Existentialism from Dostoevsky to Sartre* (1956) New York: New American Library, 1984, pp. 265-79. Reprinted in William Barrett and Henry D. Aiken, eds., *Philosophy in the Twentieth Century: An Anthology*, vol. 3 (1962) New York: Random House, 1982, pp. 206-18.

(B) *Pathmarks* (1998) Cambridge: Cambridge University Press, pp. 277-90.

162. [A] (A) "The Way to Language" (1971) [Peter D. Hertz].

		(B)	"The Way to Language" (1993) [David Farrell Krell].
	[B]		"Der Weg zur Sprache": Essay, original title "Die Sprache," a lecture first given in January 1959.
	[C]		*Gestalt und Gedanke* [*Form and Thought*] (Munich) 4, 1959, pp. 137-70. Reprinted with a few changes in *Unterwegs zur Sprache* (1959): GA 12 (1985), pp. 227-57.
	[D]	(A)	*On the Way to Language* (1971) New York: Harper and Row, 1982, pp. 111-36.
		(B)	*Basic Writings* (1977) San Francisco: HarperSanFrancisco, (rev. ed., 1993), pp. 397-426.

163. [A] (A) "What Are Poets For?" (1971) [Albert Hofstadter].
     (B) "Why Poets?" (2002) [Kenneth Haynes].
[B] "Wozu Dichter?": Lecture given December 29, 1946, in remembrance of the 20th anniversary of the death of Rainer Maria Rilke.
[C] *Holzwege* (1950): GA 5 (1977), pp. 269-320.
[D] (A) *Poetry, Language, Thought* (1971) New York: Harper and Row, 1975, pp. 91-142.
    (B) *Off the Beaten Track* (2002) Cambridge: Cambridge University Press, pp. 200-41.

164. [A] *What Is Called Thinking?* (1968) [Fred D. Wieck and J. Glenn Gray].
[B] "Was heißt Denken [What Does It Mean to Think]?": Lecture course given during the Winter Semester 1951-52 and Summer Semester 1952, University of Freiburg.
[C] *Was heißt Denken?* (1954) Tübingen: Niemeyer (4th ed., 1984). In May 1952, Bavarian Radio broadcast Heidegger's reading of an address entitled "Was heißt Denken?" which served as the basis of the opening lectures of the course. The address appeared in *Merkur* (Berlin) 6, 1952, pp. 601-11. Reprinted in *Vorträge und Aufsätze* (2000): GA 7, pp. 127-43. Full text: GA 8 (2002).
[D] *What Is Called Thinking?* (1968) New York: Harper and Row, 1976. Excerpts reprinted in Richard Zaner et al., eds., *Phenomenology and Existentialism* (1977) New York: G.P. Putnam, pp. 326-32 [part 2, lecture 5] and *Basic Writings*

(1977) San Francisco: HarperSanFrancisco, (rev. ed., 1993), pp. 369-91 [part 1, lecture 1; part 2, lecture 2, excluding the "Summary and Transition," under the title "What Calls for Thinking?"].

165.   [A]   (A)   "What Is Metaphysics?" (1949) [R. F. C. Hull and Alan Crick].

            (B)   "What Is Metaphysics?" (1977) [David Farrell Krell].

            (C)   "What Is Metaphysics?" (1998) [William McNeill and David Farrell Krell].

    [B]   "Was ist Metaphysik?": Heidegger's inaugural lecture to the faculties of the University of Freiburg, given on July 24, 1929. The text was expanded for the 4th edition (1943) of the work with the addition of a "Nachwort [Postscript]." The "Nachwort" was revised and an introduction ("Einleitung: Der Rückgang in der Grund der Metaphysik [Introduction: The Way Back into the Ground of Metaphysics]" was added for the 5th Edition (1949).

    [C]   *Was ist Metaphysik?* (1929) Frankfurt: Klostermann (12th ed., 1981). Reprinted in *Wegmarken* (1967): GA 9 (1976), pp. 103-22.

    [D]   (A)   *Existence and Being* (1949) Washington: Regnery Gateway, 1988, pp. 325-49. Reprinted in J. L. Jarrett et al., eds., *Contemporary Philosophy* (1954) New York: Holt, Rinehart and Winston, pp. 448-58. Reprinted in Walter Kaufmann, ed., *Existentialism from Dostoevsky to Sartre* (rev. ed., 1975 [1956]) New York: New American Library, 1984, pp. 242-64 (revised edition). Reprinted in *Twentieth Century Philosophy and Religion* (2nd ed.) [Great Books of the Western World, vol. 55, ed. Mortimer Adler] (1990) Chicago: Encyclopedia Britannica, pp. 296-310. Reprinted with "footnotes deleted and postscript omitted" in Diane Barsoum Raymond, ed., *Existentialism and the Philosophical Tradition* (1991) Englewood Cliffs, N.J.: Prentice-Hall, pp. 251-64.

            (B)   *Basic Writings* (1977) San Francisco: HarperSanFrancisco, (rev. ed., 1993), pp. 93-110.

		(C)	*Pathmarks* (1998) Cambridge: Cambridge University Press, pp. 82–96.
166.	[A]	(A)	*What Is Philosophy?* (1958) [William Kluback and Jean T. Wilde].
		(B)	"Philosophy—What Is It?" (1962) [Jean T. Wilde and William Kimmel].
		(C)	*What Is That—Philosophy?* (1991) [Eva T. H. Brann].
	[B]	"Was ist das—die Philosophie?": Lecture given in Cérisy-la-Salle in August 1955.
	[C]	*Was ist das—die Philosophie?* (1956) Pfullingen: Neske.
	[D]	(A)	* *What Is Philosophy?* (1958) New York: Twayne, 1989.
		(B)	Jean T. Wilde and William Kimmel, eds., *The Search for Being* (1962) New York: Twayne, pp. 493–507. Revised excerpt (pp. 41–97) of (A).
		(C)	*What Is That—Philosophy?* (1991) Annapolis: St. John's College.
167.	[A]	*What Is a Thing?* (1967) [W. B. Barton Jr. and Vera Deutsch].
	[B]	"Grundfragen der Metaphysik [Basic Questions of Metaphysics]": Lecture course given during the Winter Semester 1935–36 at the University of Freiburg.
	[C]	*Die Frage nach dem Ding: Zu Kants Lehre von der transzendentalen Grundsätzen* [*The Question of the Thing: On Kant's Doctrine of the Transcendental Basic Principles*] (1962) Tübingen: Niemeyer. Reprinted in GA 41 (1984).
	[D]	*What Is a Thing?* (1967) Washington, D.C.: Regnery Gateway, 1985. A slightly modified translation of Section B 5 (a–f3) [pp. 66–108], "The Characteristics of Modern Science in Contrast to Ancient and Medieval Science," is reprinted in *Basic Writings* (1977) San Francisco: HarperSanFrancisco, (rev. ed., 1993), pp. 271–305, under the title "Modern Science, Metaphysics, and Mathematics."
168.	[A]	(A)	"Who Is Nietzsche's Zarathustra?" (1967) [Bernd Magnus].

		(B)	"Who Is Nietzsche's Zarathustra?" (1984) [David Farrell Krell].
	[B]		"Wer ist Nietzsches Zarathustra?": Lecture given May 8, 1953, at the Bremen Club.
	[C]		*Vorträge und Aufsätze* I (1954) Pfullingen: Neske, 1978, pp. 93-118. Reprinted in *Vorträge und Aufsätze* (2000): GA 7, pp. 99-124.
	[D]	(A)	*Review of Metaphysics* (Washington) 20, 1967, pp. 411-31. Reprinted in David B. Allison, ed., *The New Nietzsche: Contemporary Styles of Interpretation* (1977) New York: Dell Publishing Company, 1985, pp. 64-79.
		(B)	*Nietzsche*, volume 2: *The Eternal Recurrence of the Same* (1984) New York: Harper and Row, pp. 211-33 [part 2]. The HarperCollins paperback reprint (1991) of all four volumes of *Nietzsche* combines volumes 1 and 2.

169 [A] "Why Do I Stay in the Provinces?" (1977) [Thomas Sheehan].

[B] "Schöpferische Landschaft: Warum bleiben wir in der Provinz [Creative Landscape: Why Do I Live in the Country]?": Essay written in the fall of 1933.

[C] *Der Alemanne* (Freiburg), March 7, 1934, p. 1. Reprinted in the GA edition of *Aus der Erfahrung des Denkens* [*From the Experience of Thinking*]: GA 13 (1983), pp. 9-13. Volume 13 takes its title from a privately printed volume (1954) of a series of reflections written in 1947.

[D] *Listening* (Dubuque) 12, no. 3, 1977, pp. 122-24. Reprinted in Thomas Sheehan, ed., *Heidegger: The Man and the Thinker* (1981) Chicago: Precedent Publishing Company, pp. 27-30.

170. [A] "Wilhelm Dilthey's Research and the Struggle for a Historical Worldview" (2002) [Charles Bambach].

[B] "Wilhelm Diltheys Forschungsarbeit und der Kampf um eine historische Weltanschauung": Walter Bröcker's transcript of a lecture series given April 16-21, 1925, in Kassel.

[C] Frithjof Rodi, "Wilhelm Diltheys Forschungsarbeit und der

Kampf um eine historische Weltanschauung," *Dilthey-Jahrbuch* 8, 1992-93, pp. 123-30, 143-80.

[D] *Supplements: From the Earliest Essays to* Being and Time *and Beyond* (John van Buren, ed.) (2002) Albany: SUNY Press, pp. 147-76.

171. [A] (A) "The Will to Power as Art": First Section: "Nietzsche as Metaphysical Thinker" (1973) [Joan Stambaugh].

(B) "The Will to Power as Art" (1979) [David Farrell Krell].

[B] "Nietzsche: Der Wille zur Macht als Kunst [Nietzsche: The Will to Power as Art]": Heidegger's first lecture course on Nietzsche, given during the Winter Semester 1936-37, University of Freiburg. First Section: "Nietzsche als metaphysicher Denker."

[C] *Nietzsche* I (1961) Pfullingen: Neske, pp. 11-254 [part 1]. First Section, pp. 11-15. A substantially revised version of the text has been published as *Nietzsche: Der Wille zur Macht als Kunst*: GA 43 (1985). *Nietzsche* I/II (1961) will be reprinted as GA 6.1-6.2. Volume 6.1 appeared in 1996 and 6.2 in 1997.

[D] (A) Robert C. Solomon, ed., *Nietzsche: A Collection of Critical Essays* (1973) New York: Doubleday, pp. 105-108.

(B) *Nietzsche*, volume 1: *The Will to Power as Art* (1979) New York: Harper and Row. The HarperCollins paperback reprint (1991) of all four volumes of *Nietzsche* combines volumes 1 and 2. Section 15 was reprinted in Peter Sedgwick, ed., *Nietzsche: A Critical Reader* (1995) Oxford: Blackwell, pp. 104-10, as "Kant's Doctrine of the Beautiful: Its Misinterpretation by Schopenhauer and Nietzsche."

172. [A] "The Will to Power as Knowledge" (1987) [Joan Stambaugh].

[B] "Nietzsches Lehre vom Willen zur Macht als Erkenntnis": Heidegger's third lecture course on Nietzsche, given during the Summer Semester 1939 at the University of Freiburg.

[C]   *Nietzsche* I (1961) Pfullingen: Neske, pp. 473-658 [part 3]. A substantially revised version of the text has been published as *Nietzsches Lehre vom Willen zur Macht als Erkenntnis*: GA 47 (1989). *Nietzsche* (1961) will be reprinted as GA 6.1-6.2. Volume 6.1 appeared in 1996 and 6.2 in 1997.

[D]   *Nietzsche*, volume 3: *The Will to Power as Knowledge and as Metaphysics* (1987) New York: Harper and Row, pp. 1-158 [part 1]. The translation has been somewhat modified by the editor of *Nietzsche*. The HarperCollins paperback reprint (1991) of all four volumes of *Nietzsche* combines volumes 3 and 4. The first section of this text, "Nietzsche als Denker der Vollendung der Metaphysik [Nietzsche as Thinker of the Completion of Metaphysics]" (*Nietzsche* I [1961], pp. 473-81), was published in a translation by Joan Stambaugh, in 1973, under the title "Nietzsche as Metaphysician," in Robert C. Solomon, ed., Nietzsche (1973) New York: Doubleday, pp. 108-13.

173. [A]   (A)   "The Word of Nietzsche: 'God Is Dead'" (1977) [William Lovitt].
            (B)   "Nietzsche's Word: 'God Is Dead'" (2002) [Kenneth Haynes].
      [B]   "Nietzsches Wort 'Gott ist tot' [Nietzsche's Utterance 'God Is Dead']": Lecture written in 1943, based on the Nietzsche courses (1936-40) at the University of Freiburg.
      [C]   *Holzwege* (1950): GA 5 (1977), pp. 209-67.
      [D]   (A)   *The Question Concerning Technology and Other Essays* (1977) New York: Harper and Row, 1982, pp. 53-112.
            (B)   *Off the Beaten Track* (2002) Cambridge: Cambridge University Press, pp. 157-99.

174. [A]   "Words" (1971) [Peter D. Hertz].
      [B]   "Dichten und Denken: Zu Stefan Georges Gedicht 'Das Wort' [Writing and Thinking: On Stefan Georg's Poem 'The Word']": Lecture given May 11, 1958, in Vienna. Revised title: "Das Wort."
      [C]   *Unterwegs zur Sprache* (1959): GA 12 (1985), pp. 205-25.

[D]   *On the Way to Language* (1971) New York: Harper and Row, 1982, pp. 139-56.

175.   [A]   *Zollikon Seminars: Protocols, Seminars, Letters* (2001) [Franz Mayr and Richard Askay].

        [B]   *Zollikoner Seminare: Protokolle—Zwiegespräche—Briefe*: Texts from 1947-1971, edited by Medard Boss, including records of seminars, conversations and letters.

        [C]   *Zollikoner Seminare: Protokolle—Zwiegespräche—Briefe* (1987) Frankfurt: Klostermann, 1994.

        [D]   *Zollikon Seminars: Protocols, Seminars, Letters* (2001) Evanston: Northwestern University Press, 2001. Brief excerpts were published as "Martin Heidegger's Zollikon Seminars" (1978) [Brian Kenny] and "On Adequate Understanding of Daseinsanalysis" and "Marginalia on Phenomenology, Transcendence, and Care" (1988) [Michael Eldred].

SUPPLEMENTAL BIBLIOGRAPHY: HEIDEGGER AND POLITICS

176.   [A]   (A)   "Documents from the Denazification Proceedings Concerning Martin Heidegger" (1991) [Jason M. Wirth].

                (B)   "Letter to the Rector of Freiburg University, November 4, 1945" (1991) [Richard Wolin].

                (C)   "Report of the Denazification Commission, September 1945" (1993) [Allan Blunden].

        [B]   "Briefe": Letters, written November 4, 1945, and December 15, 1945, following Heidegger's appearance before the denazification committee. Report by the committee (University of Freiburg, September 1945).

        [C]   Letter of November 4, 1945: Karl Augustus Moehling, *Martin Heidegger and the Nazi Party: An Examination* (Ph.D. dissertation, Northern Illinois University, 1972), Appendix B, pp. 264-68; letter of December 15, 1945: Archiv für Christlich-Demokratische Politik (St. Augustin); committee report: Hugo Ott, *Martin Heidegger: Unterwegs zur seiner Biographie* (1988) Frankfurt: Campus, pp.

305-307. Reprinted in *Reden und andere Zeugnisse eines Lebensweges* (2000): GA 16 (2000), pp. 397-404.

[D]   (A)   * *Graduate Faculty Philosophy Journal* (New York) 14, no. 2-15, no. 1, 1991, pp. 528-56.

(B)   Richard Wolin, ed., *The Heidegger Controversy* (1991) Cambridge: MIT Press, 1993, pp. 61-66.

(C)   Hugo Ott, *Martin Heidegger: A Political Life* (1993) London: Basic Books, pp. 324-27.

177. [A]   (A)   "The Rectorate 1933/34: Facts and Thoughts" (1985) [Karsten Harries].

(B)   "The Rectorate 1933/34: Facts and Thoughts" (1990) [Lisa Harries].

[B]   "Das Rektorat 1933/34: Tatsachen und Gedanken": Essay written in 1945.

[C]   Hermann Heidegger, ed., *Die Selbstbehauptung der deutschen Universität/Das Rektorat 1933/34: Tatsachen und Gedanken* (1983) Frankfurt: Klostermann, pp. 21-43.

[D]   (A)   *Review of Metaphysics* (Washington, D.C.) 38, 1985, pp. 481-502.

(B)   Günther Neske and Emil Kettering, eds., *Martin Heidegger and National Socialism* (1990) New York: Paragon House, pp. 15-32.

178. [A]   (A)   "The Self-Assertion of the German University: Address, Delivered on the Solemn Assumption of the Rectorate of the University [of] Freiburg" (1985) [Karsten Harries].

(B)   "The Self-Assertion of the German University" (1990) [Lisa Harries].

(C)   "The Self-Assertion of the German University" (1991) [William S. Lewis].

[B]   "Die Selbstbehauptung der deutschen Universität": Heidegger's rectorial address, given May 27, 1933.

[C]   "Die Selbstbehauptung der deutschen Universität." Rede, gehalten bei der feierlichen Übernahme des Rektorats der Universität Freiburg i. Br. am 27.5.1933 (1933) Breslau: Korn. Reprinted in Hermann Heidegger, ed., *Die Selbstbehauptung der deutschen Universität/Das Rektorat*

1933/34: Tatsachen und Gedanken (1983) Frankfurt: Klostermann, pp. 9-19.

[D] (A) *Review of Metaphysics* (Washington, D.C.) 38, 1985, pp. 470-80.

(B) Günther Neske and Emil Kettering, eds., *Martin Heidegger and National Socialism* (1990) New York: Paragon House, pp. 5-13.

(C) Richard Wolin, ed., *The Heidegger Controversy: A Critical Reader* (1991) Cambridge: MIT Press, 1993, pp. 29-39. NOTE: A newspaper article (*Freiburger Zeitung* [Freiburg], May 29, 1933, p. 1) reporting on the address was translated in Dagobert Runes, ed., *German Existentialism* (1965) New York: Philosophical Library, pp. 148-50 (translation by the editor).

179. [A/B] Speeches and newspaper articles from the period May 27, 1933 and February 1, 1934.

(A) Dagobert Runes (1965).

(B) William S. Lewis (1988).

[C] (1) "Schlageterfeier der Freiburger Universität [University of Freiburg's Schlageter Celebration]," speech [May 26, 1933], published in *Der Alemanne* (Freiburg), May 27, 1933, p. 6; (2) "Arbeitsdienst und Universität [Labor Service and the University]," newspaper article, published in the *Freiburger Studentenzeitung*, June 20, 1933, p. 1; (3) "Die Universität im Neuen Reich [The University in the New State]," speech [June 30, 1933], published in the *Heidelberger Neueste Nachrichten*, July 1, 1933, p. 4; (4) "Deutschen Studenten [German Students]," newspaper article, published in the *Freiburger Studentenzeitung*, November 3, 1933, p. 1; (5) "Deutsche Männer und Frauen! [German Men and Women!]," newspaper article, published in the *Freiburger Studentenzeitung*, November 10, 1933, p. 1; (6) speech [November 11, 1933], published in *Bekenntnis der Professoren an den deutschen Universitäten und Hochschulen zu Adolf Hitler und dem nationalsozialistischen Staat: Überreicht vom Nationalsozialistischen Lehrerbund* [*Pledge of German University Profes-*

A Research Bibliography of Heidegger in English Translation 303

sors and High School Teachers to Adolf Hitler and the National Socialist State: Given by the National Socialist Teachers' Association] (Dresden), November 11, 1933, pp. 13-14; (7) "Das Geleitwort der Universität [Prefatory Word from the University]," newspaper article, published in *150 Jahre Freiburger Zeitung*, January 6, 1934, p. 10; (8) "Der Ruf zum Arbeitsdienst [Call to Labor Service]," newspaper article, published in the *Freiburger Studentenzeitung*, January 23, 1934, p. 1; (9) "Nationalsozialistische Wissensschulung [National Socialist Education]," speech [January 22, 1934], published in *Der Alemanne* (Freiburg), February 1, 1934, p. 9. All reprinted in Guido Schneeberger, ed., *Nachlese zu Heidegger: Dokumente zu seinem Leben und Denken, mit zwei Bildtafeln* (1962) Bern: Suhr, (1) pp. 47-49, (2) pp. 63-64, (3) pp. 73-75, (4) pp. 135-36, (5) pp. 144-46, (6) pp. 148-50, (7) p. 171, (8) pp. 180-81, and (9) pp. 198-202. Schneeberger's volume runs to 288 pages. See also "Why Do We Live in the Provinces?" which is from this period.

[D]   (A)   *German Existentialism* (1965) New York: Philosophical Library, pp. 21-42. Includes excerpts of six of the texts in [C]: (2)-(4), (6), and (8)-(9); and extracts from twelve newspaper articles reporting on Heidegger. No (9) is titled "Follow the Führer." Rune's brief selection does not present complete texts and does not always clearly distinguish Heidegger's texts from journalists' reports.

     (B)   *New German Critique* (Ithaca) 45, fall 1988, pp. 96-114. Reprinted in Richard Wolin, ed., *The Heidegger Controversy: A Critical Reader* (1991) Cambridge: MIT Press, 1993, pp. 40-60.

180.   [A]   "On My Relation to National Socialism" (1982) [Frank Meklenberg].

     [B]   "Brief an *Münchner Süddeutschen Zeitung*: Letter in response to "Hanfstaengel contra Heidegger," printed in the *Münchner Süddeutschen Zeitung* (Munich), June 14, 1950.

     [C]   *Münchner Süddeutschen Zeitung* (Munich), June 24, 1950.

Reprinted in *Reden und andere Zeugnisse eines Lebensweges* (2000): GA 16 (2000), pp. 452-53.
[D] *Semiotext(e)* (New York) 4, no. 2, 1982, pp. 253-54.

UNPUBLISHED TRANSLATION

[A] "Heidegger's Last Seminar" (1995) [Iain Thompson]
[B] "Die Herkunft des Denkens" [*Nachtrag*]. Postscript to Heidegger's 1973 seminar in Zähringen including a reflection on Parmenides' Fragment 1. Those in attendance, whose notes were the basis for the published texts of the seminars, were Jean Beaufret, François Fédier, François Vezin, Henri-Xavier Mongis, and Jacques Taminiaux. The notes were in French and the seminar was first published in French in 1976. The German text, which is the basis of the translation, is by Curt Ochwadt.
[C] *Seminare* (1986): GA 15 (1986), pp. 401-407.
[D] http://orpheus.ucsd.edu/eands/page1.html

INDEX OF PROPER NAMES

Note: Entries are referenced and consulted sources for the main text but do not include individuals named in the **Bibliography of Heidegger Translations.**

Abbagnano, Nicola, 65, 203
Adorno, Theodore, 203
Agee, James, 90, 203
Allen, E. L., 203
Allen, Robert van Roden, 153, 203
Allers, Rudolf, 209
Allison, David B., 162, 203
Anaximander, 129, 130, 138-40
Anders, Günther (Stern), 60-64, 203
Aquinas, Thomas, 19
Arendt, Hannah, 50-52, 88, 204
Aristotle, 18, 19, 26, 80, 120, 124-25, 129, 134, 140, 142, 148, 150, 160-61, 166, 180-81, 183-84, 187, 192, 204
Ashton, E. B., 204
Augustine, 31
Aylesworth, Gary, 203, 204

Babich, Babette, 204, 205, 215
Ballard, Edward, 204
Ballard, Michel, 204
Barnstone, Willis, 204
Barrett, William, 50, 72-74, 87, 92, 204
Barzun, Jacques, 204
Baumgardt, David, 53-55, 61, 204
Beaufret, Jean, 111, 196
Beck, Maximilian, 204
Bekker, Immanuel, 120
Benjamin, Andrew, 27, 205
Benjamin, Walter, 205, 216
Berdayev, Nikolai, 77
Bernasconi, Robert, 26, 205, 207
Biemel, Walter, 205
Biguenet, John, 219
Binswanger, Ludwig, 107

Bixler, Julius, 36-38, 205
Blanchot, Maurice, 205
Bleicher, Josef, 116-17, 205
Bobbio, Noberto, 205
Bock, Irmgard, 153, 205
Borgmann, Albert, 148
Boss, Medard, 25
Braig, Carl, 205
Brentano, Franz, 205
Brock, Werner, 29, 48, 71-72, 87, 98-101, 106, 108-10, 205
Brower, Reuben, 205
Bruns, Gerald L., 156, 205
Buber, Martin, 105, 109
Buren, John van, 85, 205, 210, 213, 224
Burnet, John, 120

Carnap, Rudolf, 34
Catlin, George, 205
Celan, Paul, 18
Cerf, Walter, 38-39, 206
Cézanne, Paul, 18
Chiereghin, Franco, 27, 206
Chillida, Eduardo, 18
Cicero, 19
Cocks, E. M., 74-75
Collins, James, 45-46, 51, 86, 206
Cometti, Jean-Pierre, 153, 206
Copleston, Frederick, 66, 95-96, 108, 111, 112, 206
Copley, Alfred L., 162, 206
Corbin, Henry, 79, 93, 98, 102, 107, 206
Crick, Alan, 96, 98, 101-103, 109, 110
Cristin, Renato, 112, 162, 206
Cruz, I. Fernando, 91
Cumming, Robert, 106-108, 206

Dastur, Francoişe, 153, 206
Davidson, Donald, 206
Delp, Alfred, 33-34, 45, 206
Derrida, Jacques, 27, 118, 154, 162, 191, 206-207
Descartes, René, 19, 63, 142, 161
Deurzen-Smith, Emmy van, 25
Diels, Hermann, 120, 155, 158, 168, 207
Dilthey, Wilhelm, 10, 48, 59, 89, 116-17, 152
Downing, A. B., 81, 207
Dreyfus, Hubert, 151, 207
Duns Scotus, John, 122, 156
du Plock, Simon, 25
Dyroff, Adolf, 45, 86, 207

Edler, Frank, 160, 207
Emad, Parvis, 20-21, 27, 154, 207
Erickson, Stephen, 26, 208
Ertel, Christof, 45, 86, 208
Escoubas, Elaine, 21, 27-28, 208
Etinger, Elzbieta, 88, 208
Evans, Oliver, 208

Farber, Marvin, 111, 208
Ferrata Mora, José, 208
Farrère, Claude, 81, 208
Fichte, J. G., 31, 66
Fink, Eugen, 156, 159, 189, 191
Fóti, Véronique, 154, 208
Foulquié, Paul, 208
Frawley, William, 208
Freehof, S. B., 208
Freeman, Kathleen, 120, 155, 190, 208
Frege, F. L. G., 192, 193, 208
Freund, Ernst Hans, 47, 86, 208
Frings, Manfred, 158, 208

Index of Proper Names

Gadamer, Hans-Georg, 27, 118, 154, 209
Gandillac, Maurice de, 77
Gebsattel, Viktor von, 109
Geiger, Moritz, 209
Genzler, Edwin, 209
George, Stefan, 18, 98, 143, 166
Georgiades, Niki, 209
Gibson, A. Boyce, 209
Gilson, Étienne, 209
Glicksman (Grene), Marjorie. *See* Grene, Marjorie.
Grabmann, Martin, 156
Gray, J. Glenn, 110, 141, 191, 209
Grene, Marjorie, 34-36, 52, 82, 209
Grimm, Jacob, 127, 157, 209
Groddeck, Georg, 209
Groth, Miles, 154, 158, 209-11
Gurvitch, Georges, 77

Hanselmann, Johannes, 85
Harper, Ralph, 49, 75-76, 110, 211
Harris, R. Thomas, 162, 211
Hart, James, 211
Hartt, J. N., 211
Hebel, Johann Peter, 158, 166, 189
Hegel, G. W. F., 18, 19, 31, 87, 132, 142, 155, 161, 166, 189
Heim, Michael, 153, 211
Heinemann, Fritz, 110, 211
Heppenstall, Rayner, 74-75, 211
Heraclitus, 19, 26, 137-38, 155, 156, 159, 189, 191
Herder, J. G., 127, 157, 211
Herrigel, Eugen, 109
Herrmann, Friedrich-Wilhelm von, 211
Hicks, G. Daws, 81
Hill, E. F. F., 105, 110, 111, 211
Hines, Thomas, 211

Hirsch, Elizabeth, 211
Hisamatsu, Shin'ichi, 146, 162
Hoeller, Keith, 198
Hofstadter, Albert, 88, 211
Hölderlin, Friedrich, 18, 26, 98, 107, 112, 130, 132, 143, 155, 158-59, 162, 166-67, 170, 189, 191, 198, 212
Homer, 140-41
Hopkins, Jasper, 93, 212
Hull, R. F. C., 96, 98, 101-103, 109, 110
Hulton, Edward, 111
Humboldt, Wilhelm von, 127, 212
Husserl, Edmund, 18, 31-32, 41, 55, 61, 66, 80, 81, 148, 155, 212

Ijsseling, Samuel, 21, 212
Illich, Ivan, 155, 212

Jaeger, Werner, 160, 212
Jakobson, Roman, 212
James, William, 31
Jansen, Bernhard, 45
Jaspers, Karl, 30, 51-52, 55, 65-66, 74-75, 81, 83, 91, 100, 102
Jones, William Tudor, 69-71, 212
Jung, Carl, 109

Kahn, Charles, 155, 158, 212
Kant, Immanuel, 18, 31, 45, 105, 132, 142, 161
Kaufmann, Fritz, 39-40, 212
Kaufmann, Walter, 212
Kean, Charles D., 212
Kelly, Louis, 212
Kettering, Emil, 163, 217
Kierkegaard, Søren, 33, 37, 45-46, 49, 52, 66-67, 72, 74, 83, 94, 100, 155

Kilzer, Ernest, 213
Kirk, G. S., 120, 155, 158, 190, 213
Kirk, Robert, 213
Kisiel, Theodore, 152, 153, 155, 213
Klein, George, 213
Kluback, William, 213
Kockelmans, Joseph J., 118, 153, 213
Kojève, Alexandre, 214
Koyré, Alexandre, 77-79, 94, 98, 112, 158
Kraft, Julius, 39-40, 214
Kranz, Walther, 120, 155, 158, 168, 207
Krell, David, 214
Kroner, Richard, 214
Kuhn, Helmut, 214

Lain Entralgo, Pedro, 214
Laird, John, 214
Le Buhan, Dominiqe, 196, 218
Lefevre, André, 214
Leibniz, G. W., 18, 53, 108, 112, 142-43, 147-48, 161-62, 191, 214
Leidecker, Kurt, 214
Levin, David Michael, 153, 214
Levinas, Emmanuel, 8, 77, 79-81, 94
Leyden, W. von, 214
Lilly, Reginald, 214
Lohmann, Johannes, 118, 214
Lovitt, William, 214
Löwith, Karl, 43-45, 47, 67-68, 85, 86, 214-15
Luther, Martin, 45

Macann, Christopher, 154, 190, 215
MacGregor, Geddes, 215
MacKenna, Stephen, 215
Macmillan, J. H., 106, 215

Macomber, William B., 19, 215
Macquarrie, John, 21-22, 28, 84-85, 215
Maiorca, Bruno, 91, 215
Malik, Charles, 81, 215
Maly, Kenneth, 153, 159, 191, 207, 215
Man, Felix, 105
Man, Paul de, 216
Maraldo, John, 211
Marcel, Gabriel, 69, 77, 79, 83
Marcuse, Herbert, 48, 87, 216
Marcuse, Ludwig, 110, 216
Maritain, Jacques, 216
Marvell, Andrew, 82
May, Reinhard, 25, 83, 190, 216
Mayreder, Rosa Obereyer, 34, 216
Mays, Wolfe, 81
McCarthy, Mary, 87
McCormick, Peter J., 153, 216
McEachran, Frank, 66-67, 216
McNeill, William, 216
Mehta, J. L., 117-18, 216
Merlan, Philip, 55-57, 216
Misch, Georg, 109
Moneta, Giuseppina, 224
Moran, Stanley, 77
Moss, B. S., 216
Mounier, Emmanuel, 216
Mueller, G. E., 216
Mueller-Vollmer, Kurt, 116, 152, 216
Mugerauer, Robert, 153, 216
Munier, Roger, 216
Munson, Thomas, 153, 216

Murray, Michael, 153, 216
Nagley, Winfield E., 217
Neske, Günther, 217
Nietzsche, Friedrich, 18, 80, 129, 130, 142, 158, 161

Index of Proper Names

Nink, Caspar, 45, 217
Nwodo, Christopher, 153, 217

O'Connor, David, 217
O'Connor, Tony, 153, 217
Opilik, Klaus, 162, 217
Ortega y Gasset, José, 92, 217
Ott, Hugo, 223
Otto, Rudolf, 217
Owens, Wayne, 151, 217

Palmer, Richard, 116, 152, 217
Paluch, Stanley, 217
Parkes, Graham, 25, 83, 190, 217
Parmenides, 19, 21, 61, 133-37, 141-44, 146, 148, 165-88, 191, 191, 195-96
Paul, Leslie, 217
Pereboom, Dirk, 217
Petzet, Heinrich Wiegand, 223
Pindar, 170
Plato, 18, 19, 42, 61, 85, 116, 118, 120, 123, 125-26, 135, 140, 142, 148, 150, 160-61, 163, 178, 180-81, 183-85, 187, 192-93, 217
Polt, Richard, 198
Protagoras, 130, 158

Querido, R. M., 218
Quine, Willard van Orman, 218

Rahner, Karl, 86
Rapaport, Herman, 154, 218
Raven, J. E., 120, 158, 190, 213
Rée, Jonathan, 89, 218
Reinhardt, Kurt F., 106, 110, 218
Reiss, Katharina, 218
Rener, Frederick, 218
Reulet, A. S., 218

Richards, I.A., 218
Richardson, William J., 148, 153, 162-63, 218
Rilke, Rainer Maria, 18, 20, 98, 166
Rohde, Erwin, 218
Roicewicz, Richard, 219
Rorty, Richard, 25, 218
Rosenzweig, Franz, 43
Rousselot, Pierre, 49
Rovan, Joseph, 111
Rubercy, Eryck de, 196, 218
Ruggiero, Guido de, 74-75, 218
Ryle, Gilbert, 18, 24, 29-33, 58, 71, 81-82, 218, 221

Safranski, Rüdiger, 88, 219
Sallis, John, 20, 153-54, 159, 191, 219, 224
Sartre, Jean-Paul, 75, 83, 89, 91, 96, 219
Sass, Hans-Martin, 219
Schalow, Frank, 28, 219
Scheier, Claus-Artur, 152, 219
Schelling, F. W. J. von, 18, 50, 87, 142, 161
Schilder, Paul, 219
Schimanski, Stefan, 58, 60, 95-98, 109, 219
Schleiermacher, F. D. E., 116, 125, 143, 151, 219
Schmidt, Dennis, 219
Schneider, Herbert, 189, 219
Schöfer, Erasmus, 219
Schofield, Malcolm, 120, 158, 190, 213
Schulte, Rainer, 219
Schuwer, André, 219
Schweppenhauser, Hermann, 153, 219

Scott, Charles E., 204
Scott, Douglas, 96, 101, 109
Seidel, George, 26, 91, 160, 193, 219-20
Serres. Michel, 220
Sextus Empiricus, 19
Sheehan, Thomas, 220, 224
Shih-Yi Hsiao, Paul, 25, 190, 220
Smart, Lester, 47, 86
Smith, C. I., 220
Smith, Vincent Edward, 68-69, 220
Spiegelberg, Herbert, 220
Spinelli, Ernesto, 25
Stace, W. T., 220
Staiger, Emil, 107
Stambaugh, Joan, 110, 198, 220
Steiger, Henry W., 110, 220
Stein, Edith, 86
Steiner, George, 20, 167, 190, 220
Stevens, Wallace, 162, 220
Stohrer, Walter, 156, 220
Stolze, Ragemundis, 220
Sypher, Wylie, 220
Szilazi, Wilhelm, 107

Taft, Richard, 198
Taminiaux, Jacques, 153, 220, 224
Thomas of Erfurt, 155, 220
Thompson, J. M., 220
Tillich, Paul, 47-49, 87, 221
Torrance, T. E., 221
Trakl, Georg, 18, 166
Trivers, Howard, 221

Unger, Eric, 57-60, 221
Urmson, J. O., 81, 221

Vandevelde, Pol, 154, 221
Vedder, Ben, 151, 221

Venuti, Lawrence, 221
Vial, Fernand, 221
Visscher, Luce D. de, 153, 221
Volpi, Franco, 155, 221

Waelhens, Alphonse de, 69, 92, 221
Wahl, Jean, 77-81, 221-22
Walker, Nicholas, 216
Warnick, Barbara, 153, 222
Warnock, Mary, 222
Weil, Eric, 222
Weiss, Helene, 42-43, 222
Weiss, Paul, 22
Weizäcker, Carl-Friedrich von, 107
Werkmeister, William, 40-42, 222
Whitehead, Alfred North, 72
Wild, John, 222
Wilde, Jean T., 213
William of Moerbecke, 19
Williams, Forest, 77
Wisser, Richard, 222
Wittgenstein, Ludwig, 18
Wood, David, 153, 222

Yorck von Wartenburg, Paul, Count, 117, 152

GENERAL INDEX

Note: A word or phrase is bolded when the German word it renders is also given. Alternate translations of the German are indicated. Taken together the bolded entries should not be construed as a glossary.

art, 18
authenticity, 18
   and translation, 196

be[-ing] (*Sein*), 8-9, 10-11, 21, 23-24, 41, 43, 48, 53-54, 61, 76, 81, 92, 94, 116-18, 121, 162, 168, 170, 179-87, 192-93
be-ing (*Seiende*), 8-10, 24, 32, 35, 39, 43-44, 52, 55-56, 61, 64, 71, 76, 78, 124, 145, 178-88, 190
   grammar of, 8-9, 56, 125, 134, 140-43, 150, 163, 180, 185
being in a world (*In-der-Welt-sein*), 34, 62, 94
beingness (or **be-ingness**) (*Seiendheit*), 8, 39, 41, 43

care (*Sorge* also = **sorrow**), 54, 61, 74, 90, 136
Catholicism, 46, 66
coming about (*Wesen* also = **essence** and **nature**), 187-88
coming to pass (*Anwesen* also = **apprésenting**), 139, 187-88
conversation (*Gespräch* also = **dialogue**), 166, 193. See also **dialogue**

dialogue (*Gespräch* also = **conversation**), 116, 135, 141, 196. See also **conversation**
difference
   ontological, 9, 24, 31-32, 39, 47, 51-52, 62, 64, 76, 181-82, 184

essence (*Wesen*), 50, 60, 76, 99
  of language, 132, 142
  of thinking, 135, 171
  of translation, 130-35
  of the word, 131
essence-like (*wesenshaft*), 40
existence (*Dasein* and *Da-sein*), 8-9, 17, 18, 24, 28, 32, 36, 39, 43-44, 47-49, 51-52, 54-55, 57, 59-63, 68, 71, 74, 76, 82, 92, 97, 102-103, 110, 117, 122
existentialism, 48-49, 57-60, 65, 66-67, 72-81

German
  language, 19, 38, 41, 73, 107, 133
God, 9, 48-49, 97, 129
grammar, 56, 122, 140, 142-43, 150, 160, 163, 192
  infinitive, 81, 183-84
  middle voice, 9
  participle, 179, 180, 183-84, 192
  root (*Grundwort*), 18, 25, 169, 178
Greek
  grammar, 180, 185
  language, 19, 38, 121, 127, 133, 140, 144, 150, 155-56, 171, 183, 185

hermeneutics, 115-22, 125, 135, 144-45, 167
human being (*Mensch*), 8, 32, 38, 42, 44, 46, 62-63, 79, 102, 118, 124, 170, 179

interpretatio (*Interpretation*), 123-27, 150, 157, 173
interpretation (*Auslegung*), 20, 116, 117, 123-28, 130-34, 141, 145, 147, 149-50, 166, 170-71, 191

language (*Sprache*), 9, 17, 27-28, 43, 76, 117-18, 127, 135, 146, 173, 175-76, 179, 186
  difficulty of Heidegger's texts, 21-22, 36, 40-41, 54, 56-58, 63, 69, 72-73, 84-85, 97-98, 103-104, 106, 107, 121-23, 139, 140, 152-53
  and fundamental ontology, 80
  and hermeneutics, 117, 159
  and saying, 144
  and single words, 20, 26, 118, 131, 133, 136, 141, 167
  and speaking, 117, 144, 159
  spirit of (*Sprachgeist*), 127, 131, 146-47, 149
  and thinking, 108, 117, 121-22, 154, 193
  and translating, 144, 147, 149
  and utterance, 144, 175
Latin, 150
  translation of Greek words, 19-21, 26, 122, 124, 126, 148, 172, 176
legend (*Sage*), 144
life (*Leben* also = **everyday life, living**), 10, 117
linguistics, 120, 167
logic, 163, 176
  of the word, 191

matter (*Sache* also = **what matters**), 19, 121, 128, 141, 173, 175
  of thinking, 148
meaning (*Bedeutung* and *Meinen*), 123, 131-32, 157, 169, 193
  and signification or sense (*Sinn*), 193
  See also ***interpretatio*** (*Interpretation*)

General Index

metaphor (*Metapher*), 158
metaphysics, 43, 46, 85-86, 90, 180-85, 193
modernity, 18
monologue (*Selbstgespräch*), 21, 135

nature (*Wesen*), 117, 133, 135, 138, 152
neoscholasticism, 19, 33-34, 45-46, 68, 106
nothing (or **no-thing**) (*Nichts*), 10, 34, 36, 53-55, 64, 75, 82, 83, 90-91, 111-12

ontology, 21, 71, 117
  fundamental, 46, 64, 80, 90, 122
  phenomenological, 123

paraphrase (*Umschreibung*), 27, 118, 135, 157
philology, 120-21, 160
philosophy, 18-20, 43
  Christian, 49, 192-93
  of existence (*Existenzphilosophie*), 39-40, 50-52
  existential, 39-40, 78, 96
  history of, 7, 18, 19
  Japanese, 18, 25, 83, 162
  of life (*Lebensphilosophie*), 10, 48, 50, 59
poetry (*Dichtung*), 107, 132, 138-39, 145, 147-48, 166, 190
pre-Socratics, 18-19, 120, 130, 140, 142, 148, 150, 165, 189
psychology
  clinical, 17, 25, 61

reading (*Lesen*), 116, 121, 130, 136, 138, 149, 152, 155-56, 177

authentic, 132
reinterpretation (*Umdeutung*), 27, 154, 157
revival (*Wiederholung*), 56
  of thinking, 140, 196
risk (*Gefahr*), 151

saying (*Spruch*), 130, 138-39, 166, 178. *See also* **utterance** (*Sagen*)
sense (*Sinn*), 53, 123, 125, 193
sorrow (*Sorge*). *See* **care**
speaking (*Sprechen*), 134-35, 144, 193
spirituality, 18
structure (*Struktur* and *Gefüge*), 54, 61, 75-76, 79, 90, 100, 141, 178
syntax, 119, 141, 143, 150, 163, 165, 168, 191

temporality, 8, 10, 53, 55-57
terms (*Wörte*), 119, 122, 128, 137, 147, 185, 189, 193
theology, 33-34, 36-37, 46, 47-49, 66
thinking (*Denken*), 18, 19, 20-24, 26, 34, 53, 76, 116-18, 121-26, 130-39, 148, 149, 156, 159, 168-69, 173, 175, 185, 193, 195
  grammatical, 43
  Greek, 19, 21, 23, 121, 130, 148
  way of, 36, 108, 119, 124-28, 134-37, 149-51, 186, 195-97
  and writing (*see* **translating** and **writing**)
transition (*Versetzung* and *Sprung*), 27, 126, 135, 145-46, 186, 196

translation (*Übersetzung*), 19-22, 25-26, 122
  access to thinking and, 7-8, 22-24, 28, 108, 119, 124, 128, 129, 141, 143, 149, 150, 160, 167, 195
  authentic (*echt*), 26, 120, 133, 141, 149, 150, 196
  faithful (*wortgetreu* = **thoughtful**), 119, 120, 122, 130, 131, 137, 140, 144, 147, 149, 150, 154, 171, 181
  in hearing, 134
  intralingual, 131, 154, 159
  legitimate (*rechtgemäßig*), 149
  literal (*wörtlich*), 118, 134, 136-37, 148, 154
  and music, 10-11, 129, 149, 158, 191, 193
  paratactic (*parataktisch*), 142-43, 147, 160, 163, 163, 168-88
  as rewriting, 130
  and single words, 20, 26, 118, 131-33, 136, 141, 167
  in speaking, 134
  thoughtful (*wortgetreu* = **faithful** or *denkende*), 23, 120, 122, 127, 131-32, 134, 136-37, 139, 142-43, 145, 149-50, 159, 160, 169-70, 186
  as **transformation** (also *Sprung*), 125, 128, 129, 145, 149, 150, 186
  as **transition** (*Versetzung*), 27, 126, 135-36, 145-46, 186, 196
  as **transposition** (*Versetzung*), 129, 193
    and voice, 146
  and writing, 23, 117, 130, 138, 144, 159, 175
transcription (*Übertragung*), 27, 129, 134, 154, 157, 158
  as *Metapher,* 158

utterance (*Sagen*), 10-11, 20, 23, 123, 130, 135, 137-38, 143-51, 159, 171-75, 179, 186-87, 193, 195-96
  as silences between words, 142, 167
  See also **saying** (*Spruch*)

voice, 9, 146, 175

way of life (*Existenz* and *Ek-sistenz*), 9-10, 19, 24, 28, 32, 51, 55, 89, 102-103, 110, 117
what matters (*Sache* = **matter**), 121, 128, 141, 171, 173, 175-76
words (*Worte*), 137, 193
  fundamental words (*Grundworte*), 7, 18-19, 23, 190
  logic of, 191
  of thinking, 21
  as traces of thinking, 99, 124, 136, 149, 150, 156, 167, 195
world (*Welt*), 34, 60, 62-63, 80, 82-83, 89, 128, 139, 154
writing, 23, 116-17, 130, 136, 138, 139, 144, 159, 174-75

New Studies in Phenomenology and Hermeneutics

General Editor: Kenneth Maly

Gail Stenstad, *Transformations: Thinking after Heidegger*

Parvis Emad, *On the Way to Heidegger's* Contributions to Philosophy

Bernhard Radloff, *Heidegger and the Question of National Socialism: Disclosure and Gestalt*

Kenneth Maly, *Heidegger's Possibility: Language, Emergence – Saying Be-ing*

Robert Mugerauer, *Heidegger and Homecoming: The Leitmotif in the Later Writings*

Graeme Nicholson, *Justifying Our Existence: An Essay in Applied Phenomenology*

Ladelle McWhorter and Gail Stenstad, eds., *Heidegger and the Earth: Essays in Environmental Philosophy*, Second, Expanded Edition

Richard Capobianco, *Engaging Heidegger*

Peter R. Costello, *Layers in Husserl's Phenomenology: On Meaning and Intersubjectivity*

Friedrich-Wilhelm von Herrmann, *Hermeneutics and Reflection: Heidegger and Husserl on the Concept of Phenomenology.* Translated by Kenneth Maly. Published in German as *Hermeneutik und Reflexion. Der Begriff der Phänomenologie bei Heidegger und Husserl*

Richard Capobianco, *Heidegger's Way of Being*

Janet Donohoe, *Husserl on Ethics and Intersubjectivity: From Static to Genetic Phenomenology*

Miles Groth, *Translating Heidegger*

www.ingramcontent.com/pod-product-compliance
Lightning Source LLC
Chambersburg PA
CBHW030305080526
44584CB00012B/448